Word
2000

GW00360881

Word

2000

simple to understand

easy to use

informative

First published in Great Britain in 2000 by
Michael O'Mara Books Limited
9 Lion Yard
Tremadoc Road
London SW4 7NQ

First published in Germany by Mixing, 74172
Neckarsulm

Copyright © 1999

All rights reserved. No part of this publication may be reproduced, stored in a
retrieval system, or transmitted by any means, without the prior permission in
writing of the publisher, nor be otherwise circulated in any form of binding or cover
other than that in which it is published and without a similar condition including this
condition being imposed on the subsequent purchaser.

Windows™ is a registered trademark of the Microsoft Corporation Inc. The other
products mentioned in this publication, as well as hardware and software, are all
protected by the Patents Act and these products are included for information only.
This book is not an authorised product of the Microsoft Corporation.

At the time of printing, all information contained within this publication is deemed to
be correct, however, the publishers cannot accept responsibility for any errors.
A CIP catalogue record for this book is available from the British Library

13579108642

Printed in Germany

Contents

Chapter 1:
Basics

Chapter 2:
Views and Screen Settings

Chapter 3:
File Administration and File Protection

Chapter 4:
Formatting

Chapter 5:
Setting up Pages and Sections

Chapter 6:
Printing, Faxing and Sending

Chapter 7:
Tables

Chapter 8:
Styles and Templates

Chapter 9:
Automatic Functions

Chapter 10:
Special Effects for Online Documents

Chapter 11:
Letters, Mail Merge, Fields

Chapter 12:
Data Exchange

Chapter 13:
Search and Replace

Chapter 14:
Help

Chapter 15:
Customizing and Installation

Glossary

1. Basics

Word 2000 is a program that provides you with a comprehensive set of tools for modern word processing. In addition to a daily organizer and a scheduler, it allows you to format special documents and tables, create form letters and graphical presentations, and to exchange data with other applications, along with options which enable you to access the Internet and to organize Web sites.

Apart from learning how to use the above commands, you will learn the basic set of commands essential for quickly entering and managing most text documents. In this chapter you will become acquainted with the most important steps necessary to work with the mouse or the keyboard in order to start or end *Word*, to enter, reorganize, and correct texts.

Starting and Ending Word

Before you can use your PC for text editing, the operating system has to be loaded. Then you can choose between several ways to proceed.

Starting Windows 98 for Word

Windows 98 is a 32-bit system which can operate independently of the MS-DOS (Microsoft Disk Operation System) which was previously in vogue. For this reason no specific command is required to launch the graphic interface of *Windows 98*.

Windows 98

All you have to do to start *Windows 98* is to turn on your computer. After turning on your PC it will automatically perform a self-test. The BIOS (Basic Input Output System) will ensure that the computer will recognize and can work with all available components: hard disk, diskette and CD-ROM drive or memory and graphic card. On most computers you will be able to visually follow these messages on the screen. You do not have to be concerned about this. As soon as the system diagnostics are completed, the starting graphics with the *Windows 98* logo floating in a background of clouds will be displayed. At the bottom of this screen you will see an animated bar indicating the loading process of all necessary files for *Windows 98*. When you see this you know that your hard disk is doing a heavy-duty job of loading hundreds of system files, fonts and drivers, as well as starting the first programs.

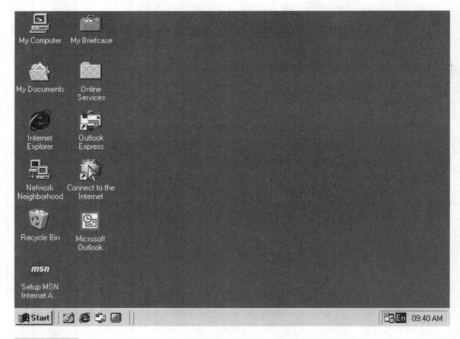

Fig. 1.1:   Windows 98 desktop after turning on the computer

After the loading process the Windows desktop will appear on a stand-alone workstation on which the *Welcome* screen has been opened as shown in Figure 1.3.

If this *Welcome* screen is not displayed on your desktop, your dealer has already turned off this dialog box (see tip further down). In a *Windows 98* network, the *Enter Network Password* dialog will appear. (Figure 1.2)

Insert your name in the *User name* box and the password which has been given to you by the administrator in the *Password* box. Then press the ⏎ key or click the *OK* button.

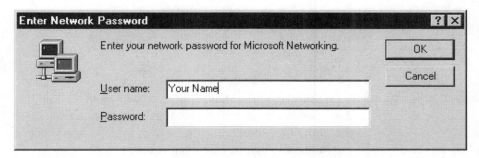

Fig. 1.2: This dialog box is for logging on to Windows 98 networks.

When the *Welcome* screen appears, press the ⏎ key or click on the *Close* button. Then the *Windows* desktop shown in Figure 1.1 is displayed.

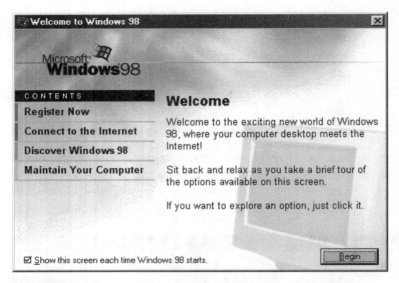

Fig. 1.3:   The *Welcome* screen is a part of the Windows Help.

Closing the start screen

To ensure that the *Welcome to Windows 98* dialog box does not reappear when you start Windows again, clear the *Show this screen each time Windows 98 starts* check box in the dialog box and click *Close*.

Discover Windows 98

Via the *Welcome* screen you have access to other *Windows Help* functions which are specifically designed for people who are new to the program or who have previously been working with a different operating system.

The *Discover Windows 98* link gives you a multimedia tour of Microsoft's products if you insert the setup CD-ROM. If you have a modem installed, the *Register Now* link will enable you to register the product via the telephone line.

Connect to the Internet

The *Connect to the Internet* link will call up the *Internet Connection Wizard* dialog box. You can use this wizard to set up a new or existing Internet account.

Maintain Your Computer makes your programs run faster and optimizes the performance of your hard disk. Close the dialog box by clicking on the *Close* button. Now everything is ready to start the word processing program *Word*.

Starting Word

Before you can use *Microsoft Word* to manage your texts, you first have to start the program. For this, open the *Start* menu with a click on the *Start* button on the taskbar. Select *Programs* and click on the *Microsoft Word* item in the submenu.

The application window of *Word* is displayed on the screen. After closing the *Office Assistant* the cursor will blink in the upper left-hand corner.

In order to display the entries of the *Start* menu as program groups, right-click the *Start* menu and choose *Open* from the shortcut menu which appears on the screen. Then double-click on the *Programs* command in order to open the corresponding folder. From here start *Microsoft Word* by clicking the *Microsoft Word* icon.

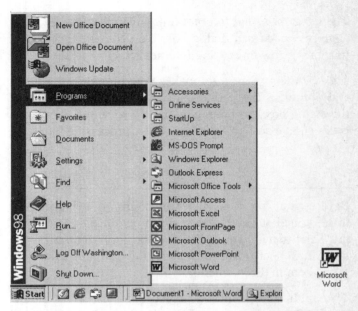

Office Assistant

After starting *Word 2000* the small *Office Assistant* window appears at the lower right-hand side of the screen. To help you with your daily work with *Word 97*, tips and tricks relevant to your current operation are given in a 'bubble' and, if necessary, give you access to more help on the topic. When you start *Word 97* for the first time, click on the *Use Microsoft Word* option in the *Office Assistant* bubble in order to activate the *Word 97* application window. Click the *Close* button ⊠ in the title bar of the *Office Assistant* to close it. If you need assistance again, you can restore this window by clicking on the *Office Assistant* button ⅌.

Quitting Word

After working with *Word* you have to close the program and *Windows 98* correctly. You should never simply switch off your PC without having closed *Word* properly.

Close ☒

To close *Word* you usually activate the *Exit* command in the *File* menu. However, to close *Word* you can also use key combinations or double-clicks. You can close *Word* instantly with a click on the *Close* button ☒ in the title bar of the program window.

Double-clicking on the system menu icon

Alternatively, *Word* can also be closed by double-clicking on the *System* menu icon of the *Word* application window. To do this, quickly double-click on the *Word* icon at the far left of the title bar.

Fig. 1.5:   The title bar of Word with the *System* menu icon

You can also open the *System* menu with a single click on the *System* menu icon and then on the *Exit* command. Another way to quit *Word* is to use the key combination Alt + F4.

If any document has been altered after saving, or has not previously been saved at all, you will now be reminded to do so.

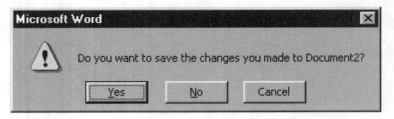

Fig. 1.6:   Save confirmation dialog while ending Word

Saving changes

Click on *Yes* if you want to save any changes you have made to the document. If the document has not been saved hitherto, the *Save As* dialog box will be displayed. If the document has already been saved previously, alterations will be saved in that file.

In case you do not want to save the alterations, select *No*. *Word* will close without saving.

If you have selected the *Exit* command by mistake and want to return to *Word*, click *Cancel*.

Shutting down Windows 98 after Working with Word

After you have completed all your work with the computer and with *Word*, you will inevitably reach the point of having to turn off your computer. At this point you should strictly observe the following routine.

During the startup of Windows hundreds of files are being loaded. And while you are working with *Word*, the computer is constantly storing certain information on the hard disk and in the memory without you noticing it.

These data have to be correctly saved or deleted before turning off the PC. Therefore, never simply turn off your computer at the power switch. The consequences could be loss of data and system errors.

To exit *Windows 98* you have to return to the beginning. Since the *Start* button represents the control centre of the graphic operation system, you will have to go back to the *Start* menu in order to close *Windows 98*. Click the *Start* button and in the *Start* menu choose the *Shut down* command.

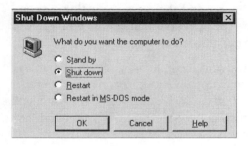

Fig. 1.7: *Shut down Windows* dialog box

What happens now depends on whether or not you have already saved all the documents opened in *Word*. If this is the case, the desktop appears shaded and the *Shut down Windows* dialog box as shown in Figure 1.7 will be displayed. Select the *Shut down* option and press ⏎ or click *OK*.

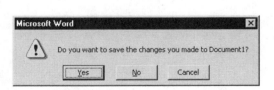

Fig. 1.8: Enquiry dialog, which appears if Word documents have not been saved

If there are documents still open in *Word* that you did not save before you selected the *Exit* command, the message shown in Figure 1.6 will appear giving you the option to save your text. If you do not want to save it, click the *No* button.

Save As

If you want to save any alterations you made to the text, click on the *Yes* button and the *Save As* dialog box appears. Then change to the drive and folder you want to save the file in, select a file name and click *Save*.

If you have several unsaved documents, this message will appear for each document. If there are any other open applications with unsaved files, each program will display similar messages. See, nothing untoward can happen ...

Windows 98 now automatically closes the *Word* program as well as all other open applications and the computer shuts down. The message 'Windows 98 is shutting down ...' appears on the graphic cloud screen. The screen then turns black and in the middle of it the message 'It is now safe to turn off your computer' appears. Now you can safely turn off the power switch of your computer. Computer models of the last generation turn off automatically and you do not need to carry out any further operation.

A Quick Mouse Tutorial for Windows 98

If you have never worked with a graphic operating system and with programs such as *Word*, you will no doubt be somewhat nervous about your first contact with a computer mouse.

Particularly those who are new to the system often have the impression that the mouse pointer on the screen, rather than adhering to the user's intentions, has a life of its own!

Using the mouse

However, the first difficulties will soon be overcome. You will quickly discover that you have fallen in love with your mouse and that soon you will not want to be without your mouse any more. Apart from a few basic tips about how to use the mouse and how to move it, you should also know the most important mouse commands. In this book we will show you many ways of using the mouse.

This precisely is the enormous advantage of a graphical interface. Nearly every operation in *Word* and Windows can be completed by using the mouse. Now put your hand on the mouse so that the palm of your hand touches the mouse pad.

Your index finger should touch the left mouse button when you do this, but not press it. In order to talk about (and do) the same thing all the time in the future we definitely require clear commands for the most important mouse actions.

Mouse pointer

After starting Windows a small arrow like this one ⌇ appears on the screen. This is the mouse pointer, also known as a *cursor* or *pointer*. If at this moment you cannot see the mouse pointer on your screen, just move the mouse a little bit to and fro on your mouse pad. See, the mouse pointer of this rodent is a highly affectionate being.

When you move the mouse, the cursor on the screen always follows your exact movements. This means that when you move the mouse upwards, the little arrow ⌇ also moves upwards; if you move the mouse to the left, the cursor also moves to the left.

Pointing

The faster you move the mouse, the faster it moves across the screen. If you move the mouse very slowly, the pointer follows you very obediently and moves just a little bit. This ballistic rendering is very important. This is because before you issue a command with the mouse, you should first move your mouse pointer to a particular position. This procedure is called *pointing*. Move your mouse now until the mouse pointer is on the *Recycle Bin* icon on the desktop.

  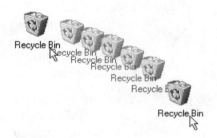

Fig. 1.9:   Mouse actions: Pointing, clicking and dragging

Clicking

Just pointing your mouse is not enough to make your computer react. For this, you have to quickly press one of the mouse buttons either once or several times, depending on the operation you want to carry out. If you now quickly press the left mouse button once, the *Recycle Bin* icon will be highlighted. This brief touch on the mouse button is called *clicking*. For most operations, you will require the left mouse button.

Shortcut menu

A click on the right mouse button (also known as right-clicking) always brings up the so-called shortcut menu, a command menu that corresponds to the current work situation. Unless the right mouse button is specifically referred to, mouse clicks refer to the left mouse button.

Drag-and-drop

Now move the mouse pointer to the highlighted *Recycle Bin*, press the left mouse button and hold it down. Move the mouse slightly to the right. This operation is called *dragging*. As you can observe, the *Recycle Bin* icon literally 'sticks' to the mouse pointer (see Figure 1.9, on the right-hand side). Release the mouse button to place the icon at this position. This combination is called *drag-and-drop*.

It is also necessary to drag the mouse in text areas of dialog boxes or during word processing. By *dragging* you highlight text or text ranges that you want to format, overwrite, copy or delete.

Copy and move

To do this, put the cursor in front of the first character that you want to highlight and, with the mouse button pressed, move the mouse cursor until you come to the end of the text you want to select. You can now use the drag-and-drop technique in *Word* to copy and reposition this highlighted text range with the mouse.

Now move the cursor onto the *Recycle Bin* icon again. If you are new to this system, you will now have to concentrate:

Double-click

Press the mouse button twice in quick succession. This is called *double-clicking* and it highlights words in *Word*, opens documents and executes commands more quickly. If the window shown in Figure 1.10 appears in front of you, you have done everything correctly.

If nothing happens, you most probably paused for too long in between the clicks. In that case simply try again. You will see that with a little practice, double-clicking works just fine.

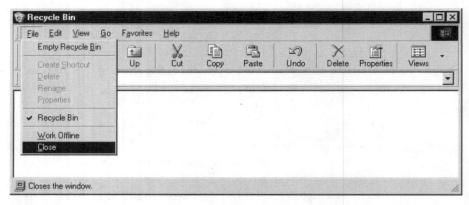

Fig. 1.10: Opening the menu, pointing to commands and executing them with a click

Finally, let's practice the most important mouse applications on the *Recycle Bin* once more: Point to the *File* menu and click it once to open it. Put the pointer on the *Close* command – it is highlighted – and click it to close the window. Drag the icon and put it in its former position. You should be now familiar with using the mouse.

Activating Commands and Buttons with the Mouse

Word commands are displayed in menus. For this, the *Word* application window has a menu bar with menu items. Every menu contains a list of *commands* grouped according to topic. Using these, certain operations can be performed. One of the special menus, which contains commands to change the size and position of screens, is the *System* menu. *Word* displays this menu when you click the *System* menu icon in the shape of the *Word* application icon ▣ in the upper left-hand corner of the title bar.

Activating Menu Commands

Menu commands

The number and significance of menu commands available in the menus is dependent on the nature of the highlighted text objects and the current operation. The *Word* menu bar contains menus specific to the program with commands corresponding to the application, and are different from the menus of the *Explorer* screen in *Windows 98*, for example.

Independent of the nature of the menus or their commands, the controls will, however, always operate in the same way. This also applies to the commands selected.

Fig. 1.11: Menu bar and title bar (above) in Word

To open a menu using the mouse, move the mouse pointer to the menu name and click. The menu will drop down and display a list of several items. Once one menu is open, all you have to do to open an adjacent menu is to point to the other menu name.

Perhaps you will not see all of the commands of the current menu. If after opening a menu you see a double arrow at the end of it, it means that you are currently seeing only the last used commands. To see the remaining commands, set the mouse pointer on the double arrow and after a short delay all menu commands will appear. You can deactivate this function by choosing the *Customize* command in the *Tools* menu and by clearing the *Menus show recently used commands first* check box in the *Options* tab page.

If a menu command has submenu items, it is sufficient to position the cursor over the corresponding item to open the overlapping menu. Submenus appear whenever a small black triangle ▶ is displayed on the right-hand side of the menu item, e.g. *View/Toolbars*.

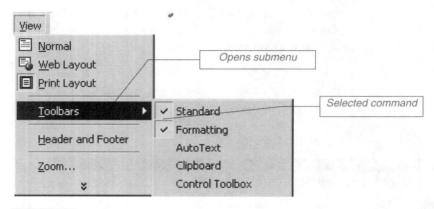

Fig. 1.12:   Menu items

To select a command listed in a menu, simply click on the desired item. Whether or not a command can be executed directly or whether *Word* needs to open further controls in order to activate the command can be determined by menu conventions.

Selected
Command

A small tick in front of a menu item indicates, for example, that a command is active, that a window is currently being displayed, or that an attribute is activated. Such ticks are used in cases when several commands can be accessed simultaneously, e.g. the *Ruler* command in the *View* menu. However, if only one of several options can be chosen, the icon in front of the corresponding item appears raised.

An example of this can be seen in Figure 1.13 in the *View* menu, as the active *Print Layout* item is raised.

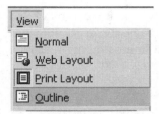

Fig 1.13: Raised command

If you see an ellipsis (...) after a menu item, the command calls up a dialog box in which you have to provide further information in order to execute the command (e.g. *File/Print*). Independent of the menu conventions, the quickest way to choose a menu command is by clicking the mouse. By merely pointing on a menu command it becomes highlighted with a coloured bar.

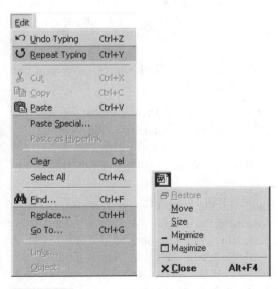

Fig. 1.14: A menu (left) and the *System* menu of a document window

A menu that has been opened accidentally can be closed
again by clicking on the menu name again. Commands
given accidentally are reversible in most cases – but not
always – with *Edit/Undo*.

Selecting Commands and Buttons with the Keyboard

In *Word*, the mouse is not the only way to select menus
and commands, although this is the preferred method for
most people. This is simply due to the principle of
Word's graphic user interface. You can also access commands via the keyboard, which is always advantageous
since you already have your hands on the keyboard while
typing your text.

**Activating the
menu bar**

When using the keyboard, activate the menu bar by pressing [Alt] or [F10]. An activated menu appears raised.
Immediately after activating the menu bar the *File* menu
appears raised. Now press the [→] key, in order to move
to the next menu on the right. With the [←] key you can
jump back to the menu on the left.

Opening a menu

In order to open an activated menu, press [↵] or [↓]
Then move to the desired menu item with [↓] and [↑]
and press the [↵] key. If overlapping menus are available, press [→] and [←] to move into the submenu or to
return to the parent menu.

**Menu shortcut
keys**

Underlined letters in the menu name refer to the key
combinations opening the menu. To open a menu using
this method, press the [Alt] key and hold it down. Then
type the underlined letter in the menu name. To open the
Edit menu, for example, press the key combination
[Alt]+[E]. To open another menu, press the [Alt] key and
then the underlined letter in the other menu name.

Closing a menu

When a menu is open, you can also change to the desired menu name with ⟨←⟩ or ⟨→⟩. In order to close a menu using the keyboard, press either ⟨Alt⟩ or ⟨F10⟩ again. Alternatively you can also use ⟨Esc⟩ to close the menu; however, the menu bar remains active and you can now select another menu. The menu last chosen in the menu bar is displayed raised.

Shortcuts inside the menus

You can work even faster by using key combinations accessing commands without even having to open a menu. The available key combinations appear to the right of the commands in the menus.

Using Controls in Dialog Boxes

Windows 98 differentiates several types of windows. Programs such as *Word* run in application windows or are presented in document windows containing text. Folders are also document windows.

Application Window

The dialog box window-type however serves to specify a command that has been issued in *Word*. For this, uniform controls are used in dialog boxes which we will introduce you to in this section.

Dialog boxes

Dialog boxes are always displayed without a menu bar. Furthermore, the toolbar is not available and there is no status bar either. A dialog box's size is fixed and cannot be changed although it can be moved or closed. All commands in *Word* that require more user input to be completed automatically activate a dialog box. You can recognize this in menus by an ellipsis (...) at the right of a menu item (Example: the *Print...* command in the *File* menu).

Print ? X

Fig. 1.15: Title bar of a dialog box

If a command offers many settings, the various options will be sorted on different tab pages, grouped by topic. A tab page is activated and brought to the front by clicking on the tab label which appears at the top of the tab page. On these pages various controls are used to represent the different settings for a command.

Rectangular boxes with a label in the center are called *command buttons*. The name on a command button always describes its function. The most important command buttons are labeled OK and Cancel. By clicking *OK* you confirm all changes made to a dialog box and execute the selected command using the settings you specified. Clicking on *Cancel* will close a dialog box without saving any changes made to it. To activate the default button press ↵.

Command buttons

A default button is displayed with a thick border. Press Esc to close a dialog box without executing any instructions.

Options...

If there is an ellipsis after the label of a command button, clicking it will display another dialog box.

Insert

If the label on a command button appears in light grey the corresponding command is not available at the moment, the button is disabled and cannot be selected. The underlined letter in a button label represents the key that has to be pressed in conjunction with the Alt key in order to execute the command via the keyboard.

Radio buttons

Radio buttons are available if only a single option can be selected from a list of options presented in a dialog box. Deselected radio buttons appear with an empty circle. A selected radio button is shown with a black dot in it. Underlined letters in the radio button's name identify the key that has to be pressed while holding down the $\boxed{\text{Alt}}$ key in order to select the option via the keyboard.

Check box

If several options can be selected within an option group, *Word* uses the so-called check box in dialog boxes. These are small square boxes in front of each option. Selected check boxes contain a tick. To select one or more check boxes, simply click on the box itself or on its label.

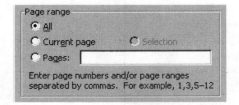

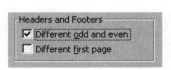

Fig. 1.16: Check box (left) and radio button

Spin box

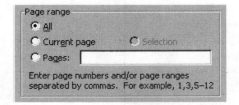

You can insert alphanumerical values into dialog boxes via the keyboard. These can be file names as well as numerical information, e.g., for setting a margin. The text cursor is displayed as a blinking vertical line which marks the insertion position in text boxes. With the $\boxed{\leftarrow}$ key you can delete the character to the left of the cursor, while with the $\boxed{\text{Del}}$ key you can delete one character right of the cursor. If a text box contains default values, sometimes spin buttons appear behind them with which the default values can be increased or decreased step-by-step.

Drop-down button

Open a so-called drop-down box with a click on the little arrow called button. Then select an item with a mouse click. The drop-down list closes again and the item you selected appears in the drop-down box. If you have long lists, use the scroll bar which will automatically be displayed. A control in a dialog containing several list items is called a list box or simply list. An item can be chosen with a mouse click and in most cases it will appear in a text box above the list. The scroll bar appears automatically if there are many items in the list.

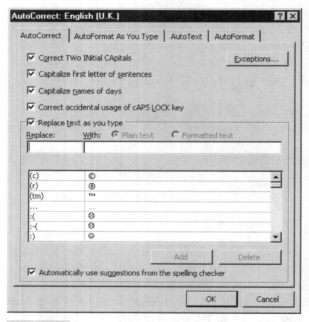

Fig. 1.17:   A scroll bar in a list box

Scroll box

Scroll arrows

A scroll bar contains a scroll box and scroll arrows. In the list of items you can scroll from one line to another or from one column to another with the scroll arrows. If you click in the free space above or below the scroll box, the screen will scroll a page at a time. The scroll box can also be moved by holding down the mouse button above it. The size of the scroll box indicates the ratio between the text displayed on the screen and the total text contained in the document.

Buttons in the *Standard* Toolbar

Word displays the *Format* toolbar and the *Standard* toolbar under the *Menu* bar by default. With a mouse click on the buttons of these two toolbars you access the most important program commands. These toolbars share the same row in the document window, but you can change their position by dragging the vertical grey bar in front of the *Font Size* drop-down box.

You will find buttons for the most important *Word* functions on the *Standard* toolbar.

Fig. 1.18:   The *Standard* toolbar

ScreenTip

The names of the individual buttons on the *Standard* toolbar are displayed approximately one second after you point the mouse on a button. *Word* then displays what is known as a *ScreenTip*. If this *ScreenTip* does not appear on your screen, select the *Toolbars* item from the *View* menu and select the *Customize* command from the submenu. Click on the *Options* tab, select the *Show Screen-Tips on toolbars* check box and click on the *Close* button.

In the following summary you will find all of the *Standard* toolbar control elements, along with their *ScreenTip* names and their significance:

	Name	Description
⬜	*New*	Creates a new document
📂	*Open*	Loads a saved document

	Name	Description
	Save	Saves a document
	E-mail	Sends the document via E-mail
	Print	Prints a document
	Print Preview	Switches to *Print Preview* view
	Spelling and Grammar	Starts Spelling and Grammar Check
	Cut	Deletes the selected text in a document and stores it in the Windows clipboard
	Copy	Copies the selected text of a document into the Windows clipboard
	Paste	Inserts the contents from the clipboard into the document at the position of the cursor
	Format Painter	Copies formatting information
	Undo	Cancels the last command
	Redo	Cancels the *Undo* command
	Insert Hyperlink	Inserts a hyperlink (shortcut) into another document
	Web Toolbar	Turns the *Web* toolbar on and off
	Tables and Borders	Turns the *Tables and Borders* toolbar on and off
	Insert Table	Inserts a table
	Insert Microsoft Excel Worksheet	Inserts an *Excel* worksheet
	Columns	Creates columns
	Drawing	Displays the *Drawing* toolbar
	Document Map	Displays the document map

	Name	Description
¶	*Show/Hide*	Shows or hides all nonprinting characters
58%	*Zoom*	Maximizes and minimizes the display
?	*Microsoft Word Help*	Displays the *Office-Assistant*

The buttons that have drop-down buttons can be used in two ways. You can either click on the button and activate the standard command or you can open the list by clicking on the spin box.

Information in the Status Bar

The *Word* status bar is at the bottom of the *Word* application window. Its main purpose is to give you information. You can, however, access some *Word* commands faster via the status bar than via a menu, which would be the more useful way to proceed.

Status bar sections

The status bar is divided into sections indicated by certain abbreviations. The current text page is indicated at the far left, for example: *Page 1*. This value always refers to the current page, i.e., the page where the cursor is presently located. Furthermore, if any page numbers have been inserted, this page number takes that into account.

Page number
Page 1

Section
Sec 1

The number of the current section is indicated right next to it, for example, *Sec 1*. A *Word* document can consist of several sections to which the individual page, paper or header and footer formats can be allotted.

| Page 1 | Sec 1 | 1/1 | At 4.4cm | Ln 5 | Col 1 | REC | TRK | EXT | OVR | English (U.K | |

Fig. 1.20: The status bar in Word

37

Total Number of Pages 5/12

The figures which follow indicate the current position of the insertion cursor vis a vis the total number of pages in the document. For example, *5/12* means that the document has a total of 12 pages and the text cursor is presently on the fifth page. In contrast to the text page indicated at the far left, the actual page numbers are indicated here. The first text page of a document beginning with the inserted page number 124 is displayed at the left as '124', although '1/X' will appear under the document pages section.

At: 12,4 cm
Ln 15

The next section of the status bar indicates the position of the text cursor on the current page. The vertical position is displayed first using the current measurement unit (e.g., centimeters) and then by line count (e.g., Ln 15).

Col

The *Col* abbreviation indicates columns as well as the number of characters in the actual line up to the text cursor. If you double-click on one of the two sections on the left of the status bar the *Find and Replace* dialog box will appear. We will introduce this to you later on in this chapter.

Status functions

On the right part of this section there are five small boxes, each of which contains an abbreviation. The abbreviation is greyed as long as the function is inactive. *REC* stands for *Record Macro*. A double-click on *REC* activates the *Record Macro* dialog box .

Toggling TRK

The *TRK* shortcut stands for *Track Changes* and indicates whether the so-called *Track Changing* mode is active. *EXT* is the abbreviation for *Extend Selection*. You can activate *Extend Selection* with the F8 key or with a double-click on *EXT*.

OVR
Overtype

The *OVR* shortcut next to it indicates whether the *Overtype* mode is activated. If the *Overtype* mode is activated in *Word*, every character that you type in overwrites every other character to the right of the text cursor. With a double-click on *OVR* or by pressing the ⌈Ins⌋ key you can switch between the *Overtype* and the *Insertion* mode.

Language English (U.K.) is the language set for the document. By double clicking this box the *Language* dialog box will appear allowing you to change the language settings.

Fig. 1.21:   Icons for spelling and grammar checkers

The icon of the small book symbolizes that the *Spelling and Grammar Checker* is active. In this case *Word* checks for spelling errors in your text as you are typing, and underlines them, if any, with a wavy red line. Grammar mistakes are underlined with a wavy green line.

Documents with or without errors Different animations of the book icon in the status bar demonstrate this. A tick indicates that no errors have been found, a cross indicates that there are errors, and the pen signals that the check is still going on. A double-click on the icon displays the context menu of a word highlighted by the spell-check.

Additional icons When *Word* is accessing commands involving a lengthy process, the status bar displays additional icons. The process of saving is indicated in the status bar by a progress bar, when saving in the background a blinking diskette icon appears and during printing jobs a small animated printer icon appears that gleefully shoots out the printed pages.

Accessing a Shortcut Menu

If you have already worked with an older version of *Windows 98* or if you have worked with one of the first

Word for Windows versions, you may have asked yourself what the second mouse button on the right was for. This button seemed, with a few exceptions, to be completely unnecessary, because there was nothing you could do with it. This has changed completely since *Word 95*.

Using the right
mouse button

In *Windows 98* and programs such as *Word*, this second mouse button has now been given a very useful function. With the right mouse button you can access the so-called shortcut menus for almost all elements or sections of a screen and their components. These little menus at the mouse pointer are also called context menus because they contain information which is useful in the context of the mouse pointer's current position.

Why not try out some of the context-dependent menus right now? If you right-click anywhere within a *Word* document, a shortcut menu appears with the *Font* and *Paragraph* items. These are precisely the commands that you will use most often in connection with text formatting. More commands are available if text ranges are selected. In that case the shortcut menu also displays the *Cut* and *Copy* commands with which a highlighted text can be copied to the clipboard. At the new insertion position you will find the *Paste* item in the shortcut menu. This takes a copy of the copied text out of the clipboard and pastes it at the current position.

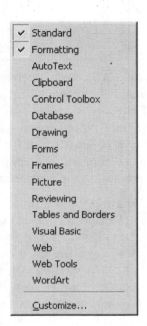

Fig. 1.22:   Different shortcut menus

A left mouse click on an item accesses the selected command. A click on an empty space or Esc closes the context menu again. You can call up more context menus, e.g., for the *Word* toolbars.

If you are left-handed and have changed the mouse button function from the standard *Right-handed* to the *Left-handed* setting, the mouse buttons are reversed. In other words, you have to click on the left mouse button for the shortcut menu.

Inserting Text in Word

Don't expect a basic typewriting course at this stage. Unfortunately we cannot help you to hit the right keys. In the following paragraph we mention a few things that you should definitely take into consideration while inserting text into a word processing program such as *Word*. In this way the most common mistakes people who are new to the program often make can be avoided.

Text cursor

After starting *Word* a blinking text cursor appears in the upper left-hand corner of your document. If you are inserting text in *Word*, you should definitely keep your fingers away from the good old 'carriage return' you used on your old typewriter. On a computer keyboard this is equivalent to the ⏎ key. Unlike what you're used to with a typewriter, you should not press carriage return at the end of a line while working in *Word*.

Automatic line-wrap

Word processing programs such as *Word* use an automatic *Line Wrap*. Every time you have completed a line *Word* automatically brings the text that does not fit on that line to the next line. This procedure enables you to write your whole letter without having to press the ⏎ key even once.

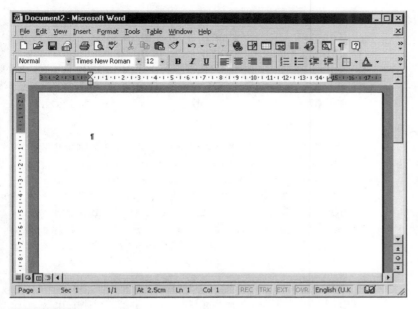

Fig. 1.23: The text cursor blinking at the top left

⏎ only at the end of a paragraph

Press the ⏎ key only at the end of a paragraph. This is necessary because *Word* manages text separately, paragraph by paragraph. These paragraphs can be aligned or indented independently of each other. Furthermore, the spaces before and after the paragraph can be fixed. Therefore you should insert the text that belongs in one paragraph all at once. You will quickly discover the advantages of entering text in this mode.

On the one hand you needn't worry about reaching the end of the line and, on the other hand, the paragraph management renders word processing much more flexible. Here's an example: If you're writing a new letter and press the ⏎ key at the end of each line, and then later on decide to increase the character size from 10 point to 14 point, it's more than likely that in the end your text will look completely fragmented. The same thing applies to font or margin changes. Due to the fixed paragraphs settings, *Word* is unable to join the lines automatically any more. But on the other hand, if you don't press the ⏎ key in your text, *Word* can automatically activate a new line wrap for any subsequent changes and adapt the text accordingly.

Proportional characters

Another important issue to keep in mind when inserting text is the characters used in *Word*. These are what is known as proportional characters as opposed to the non-proportional characters that most typewriters use. A non-proportional or monospaced character requires the same space for each letter (example: wwwiii). That is how it is possible to determine that 70 characters, for example, will exactly fit into one line while using an ordinary typewriter.

Each letter in the computer fonts has a different width, which depends on the one hand on the specific letter, and on the other on the font you are using. In a proportional font individual letters vary in width depending upon their appearance.

Enter a Date in a Document

Anyone who uses the word processing program *Word* to do the day-to-day correspondence on the computer usually needs to use the current date in a document several times a day. Of course you can just type in the date using the keyboard.

Why date and time formats?

But why not use the assistance that your computer and the word processing program *Word* offers for this job instead? This has two advantages. First, you can select the most suitable format from the various date formats on offer and second, you will always have the current date in your letter. In this way the margin for human error is reduced right from the beginning.

System date

A prerequisite for having the correct date in *Word* documents is of course having the correct system date in *Windows 98*.

To enter the date into a *Word* document, position the text cursor at the insertion point. Then choose the *Date and Time* command on the *Insert* menu. In the *Date and Time* dialog box, select one of the available formats in the *Available formats* list.

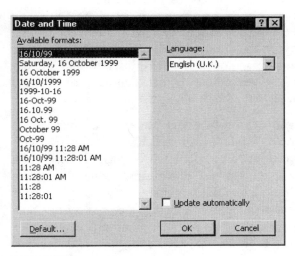

Fig. 1.24:   Entering date and time in Word

Update automatically

The significance of the *Update automatically* check box will be explained to you in the next section. For now, in order to insert the current date or the current time into the document, clear the check box. The selected date format appears in the document if you click on the *OK* button or on ⏎.

You can work more quickly if the *Date* 📅 or *Time* ⊙ buttons are integrated into the corresponding toolbar. These icons can be incorporated into any toolbar with a click on the *Customize* command in the shortcut menu of a toolbar, followed by a click on *Insert*. The *Date* 📅 or *Time* ⊙ buttons write the current date or the time directly in the selected default format.

Inserting a New Date into the Document

If you write your daily correspondence on the computer using the word processing program *Word*, no doubt you will need to use the current date in a document several times a day. In the previous section we showed you how the current date and/or time can be inserted into a document. You can choose between several date formats and with a mouse click, the actual date appears in the letter.

Date and time as a field

Now we will explain how you can enter the date or the time as a field. A field is a special *Word* feature that automatically reads certain variables or displays the result of a query. In our present case this means reading the system clock and the system date. A prerequisite for the correct date in *Word* documents is naturally a correct system date in *Windows 98*. If you insert a date into a document as a field, the date is always updated during saving, opening or printing operations.

Take this example: you are writing a letter on the 15th of May, 1999 and you insert an automatic date. When you open this letter on the 12th of July, 1999 the entry 12th July, 1999 will appear in the place where you had earlier inserted the date. This date mode is unsuitable for archival purposes, because you won't know when the letter was written originally. Therefore, when you are preparing important documents such as invoices or time freight, it is essential to avoid the update feature.

In order to enter an automatic date in a *Word* document, move your text cursor to the insertion point. Then select the *Date and Time* command on the *Insert* menu to bring up the *Date and Time* dialog box. Select one of the available formats in the *Available formats* list box.

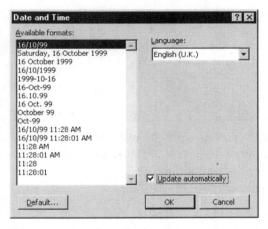

Fig. 1.25:   Entering automatic date and time in Word

Then check *Update automatically*. With a click on the *OK* button or on ⏎, the selected date format appears in the document. If you click on the date itself, a light grey highlight appears which shows you the inserted field. The field feature appears when you press on `Alt`+`F9` and disappears when you press the same combination again.

Automatic dates in document templates

Automatic dates or times are suitable for document templates. If you write a letter using such a template, the current date will appear automatically. By the way, with the `⇧`+`Ctrl`+`F9` key combination a field can be converted to text. This way an automatic date changes into the pure date text.

Changing a Default Date Format

In the *Date and Time* dialog box a highlighted date format can be stored as the new default date and time settings with a click on the *Default* button. Confirm this with *Yes* and close the dialog box by clicking on *OK*.

This alteration influences the date and time buttons inserting the date or time in the selected default format.

Use the ⌐Alt⌐+⌐⇧⌐+⌐d⌐ key combination to insert the automatic date and the ⌐Alt⌐+⌐⇧⌐+⌐t⌐ keystroke combination to insert the time more quickly.

Inserting Special Characters into the Text

Not all the characters you might want to insert into a document when creating a text are available on the keyboard. In the following section we will explain how to access special characters in *Word 2000*.

What are special characters?

If you sometimes need special characters like ☎, ✂, ■ or ➜, 💾 or ✉ in your *Word* documents, this section will be of special interest to you. Such characters can quickly and easily be inserted into any text.

To insert a special character, just move your text cursor to the desired place and select the *Symbol* command on the *Insert* menu. The *Symbol* dialog box appears and presents the 256 available characters of the font, shown in the *Font* drop-down list box.

Open the list and select the character set that contains the character you want. Two fonts particularly suitable for symbols are *Symbol* or *Wingdings*. These fonts are actually *TrueType* fonts, containing symbols instead of letters.

Symbol dialog box | If you click on one of the special characters, an enlarged preview will appear. Transfer the character into the document with a click on the *Insert* button. The *Symbol* dialog box remains open and you can now insert additional characters.

If you want to change the insertion position beforehand, then simply click on your document and reposition the text cursor. Click on *Cancel* or the *Close* button to close the dialog box.

Inserting special characters automatically | The great advantage of *Insert/Symbol* is that the characters do not deviate from the font used in the text. This way, the inserted characters remain unchanged, even if a font is changed. If you are using one of the characters very often, try activating the *AutoCorrect* or *Shortcut Key*.

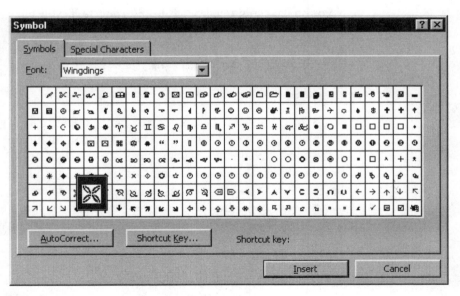

Fig. 1.26: Inserting special characters

Special characters
via shortcut keys

Click on the *Shortcut Key* button in the *Symbol* dialog box. Using this, you can assign a key combination to a character. If you click on the *Special Characters* tab, special characters are displayed for selection. If you click on the *Shortcut Key* button you are given key combinations enabling you to transfer the character directly into the text without the *Symbol* dialog box.

Correcting Text

You will probably make some typing errors when working in *Word*, especially in the beginning. Here, the advantages of a computer become obvious, with the correction of mistakes, for example. The following section will tell you all the ways it can be done.

If you make typing errors while inserting text, you have many different ways to correct them. We will now look at the most important methods. Afterwards you can always use the method, which suits you best.

Deleting Characters Left or Right of the Text Cursor

Errors to the left of the text cursor can be deleted character by character with the `←` key. You can then type in the correct characters. Typing errors to the right of the text cursor can be deleted character by character using the `Del` key. You can then insert new text. To delete the entire word on the left of the text cursor, press `Ctrl`+`←`. To delete the whole word which appears on the right of the text cursor press `Ctrl`+`Del`.

Activating the Overtype or Insert Functions

If you want to replace a long character sequence which is located to the right of the text cursor, press the `Ins` key.

With this you switch from the default *Insert* mode into the *Overtype* mode. When you enter the text now, every new character that you type in replaces the character that was formerly visible to the right of the text cursor. Press [Ins] again to return to the *Insert* mode.

Deleting and Overtyping Selections

You can also highlight typing errors and delete the selected text with the [Del] key, and then reinsert the text again. However, you can also directly overtype the highlighted area by simply typing in the new text. Alternatively, you can also delete a selection via the *Edit/Clear* command.

Copy, Cut and Paste

To move, cut or copy long passages of text use the Windows clipboard and the *Copy*, *Cut* and *Paste* commands in the *Edit* menu. Read the instructions on how to do this further down in this chapter

Managing the Text Cursor in Word

Text cursor I

In text boxes and in word processing programs such as *Word* the shape of the mouse pointer changes every time it is moved above the text. The mouse pointer has the shape of a vertical line when it appears above the text. This is also called the *Text Select Cursor*.

While inserting text in *Word*, another element moves along with your insertion, the *Insertion Point*. It shows the current insertion position in the text and corresponds to the spot where you are currently writing text. The mouse pointer may be in a totally different place at this moment.

The position of *Insertion Point* in *Word* is mainly of importance when you are inserting text or when you are altering the text later on, and doesn't depend on the location of the mouse pointer. The position of the *Insertion Cursor* can be set in several ways.

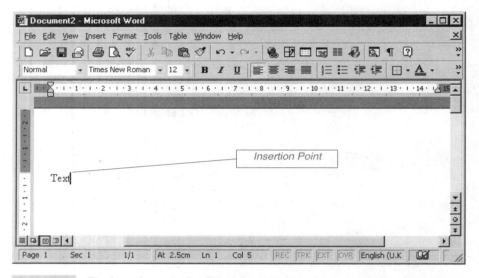

Fig. 1.27: The insertion point in a Word document

Positioning the insertion point

The most comfortable way to position your insertion point is by clicking the mouse. To do this, simply point the mouse on the place in the text you want to position your insertion cursor at and click the mouse button. The *Insertion Point* will be visible as a blinking vertical line in this position.

Scroll bar

To jump to an undisplayed text range use the scroll bar(s) or the `PgUp` and `PgDn` keys. Once you have found the part you're looking for, simply click with the mouse button to position the *Insertion Point* there. Now you can alter the text there or start entering new text.

Since you already have your hands on the keyboard when working with a word processing program, it is often better to use this method to change the position of the insertion point. Especially people who are new to the program often find it easier to position the text or insertion cursor more precisely when using the keyboard rather than the mouse. This method also has the advantage that you don't have to keep shifting between the keyboard and the mouse. For the most important movements of the insertion point *Word* offers special key combinations:

Keystroke	Description
← →	Jump one character to the left or to the right
↑ ↓	Jump one character above or below
Home	Position the insertion cursor at the beginning of a line
End	Position the insertion cursor at the end of a line
Ctrl + Home	Jump to the beginning of a document
Ctrl + End	Position the insertion cursor at the end of a document
Ctrl + →	Jump to the beginning of the next word
Ctrl + ←	Jump to the beginning of the previous word
Ctrl + ↑	Move insertion cursor back to the beginning of a paragraph
Ctrl + ↓	Move insertion cursor to the beginning of the next paragraph
Ctrl + PgUp	Jump to the first line in a window
Ctrl + PgDn	Jump to the last line in a window

Memorize these key combinations well, as they can facili-tate your work in *Word* enormously. By the way, most key shortcuts also apply to the text boxes in dialog boxes.

Moving to Invisible Document Parts

The position of the insertion cursor is decisive for most *Word* functions. The text you type is inserted at the posi-tion of the insertion cursor. The position of the mouse pointer has no bearing on this.

Point and click

Use the mouse pointer to position the insertion cursor at a particular place in the text. To do this, point the mouse to the place in the document where you want to position the insertion cursor, and click once with the left mouse but-ton. This method only works, if the desired position in the document is visible on the screen. If this is not the case, then first move through your document until the part of the document you want is displayed on the screen. The scroll bars and the mouse will help you to move between the pages.

Scrolling text

You might picture a long *Word* document as a thick roll of paper. The text on the screen is the window through which you can see only a small section of the whole roll. The paper roll can be scrolled up or down by means of the scroll bars, thus shifting new text into the part of the window which you can see.

Scroll bars

If you click on the scroll arrow that points upwards ▲ in the vertical scroll bar, the content of the window is scrolled up one line at a time. This will enable you to see the text written at the beginning of your document in the document window. However, if you click on the scroll arrow that points down ▼, you scroll the text down line by line towards the end of your document. If your text is several pages long, the pages will be scrolled automatically to the next or the previous page with the scroll bar arrows. This can easily be observed in the *Print Layout* view as the margins are visible here.

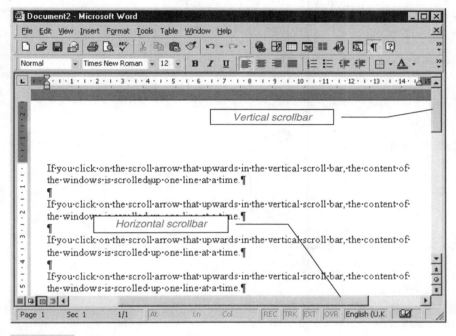

Fig. 1.28: The scroll bars in Word

Scrolling pagewise

In the *Normal* view a dotted line denotes the end of the page. With the ▲ or ▼ buttons you scroll one page backward or one page forward in your document.

Scroll bar box

If you are working with lengthy documents this method is fairly time-consuming. If you want to scroll to the end of a text several pages long, click and hold down the mouse button over the square box in the scroll bar. The scroll bar box ■ indicates where you are in terms of the whole text and, carrying the analogy of the paper roll further, the section of it which would be visible to you if you were to view it in the window. Here, the actual scroll bar represents the total length of the text. If you click in the scroll bar above or below the scroll bar box, the section will scroll screen by screen.

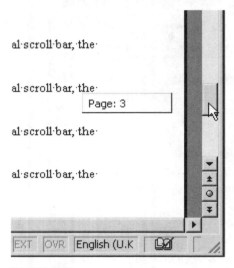

Proportions of the scroll bar box

By the size of the scroll bar box you can estimate the ratio of the text section displayed on the screen to the length of the entire text. A narrow scroll box means that only a small part of the entire text is displayed, a long scroll box that there is already a lot of text visible on the screen.

ScreenTip indicates where you are

If you drag the scroll bar box up or down while keeping the mouse button held down, a hint appears containing the current page number. Release the mouse button to find yourself on the page indicated. Within a single page, drag the scroll bar box to the desired position by visual estimation.

Repeating Commands, Undoing and Redoing

Whoever uses word processing wants to work as efficiently as possible. In order to work easily and effectively it is essential to have the possibility of repeatedly accessing commands frequently required, as well as those difficult to access, such as the formatting command, for which a dialog box has to be opened. To repeat a command in *Word*, all you have to do is pressing a key or accessing a menu command.

Almost more important than being able to repeat a command quickly is the option to undo an erroneous command. In *Word* you can undo not only one command, but as many as you like. This fact should give you enough courage – even if you are new to the program – to try out a few things, especially since after undoing a command it can be redone, i.e., almost every work situation can be reestablished.

Some commands such as the saving operation cannot be undone. But this fact will be indicated next to the command.

Undoing Commands

If you are working in *Word* for the first time you will encounter certain difficulties from time to time. What we are trying to say is that in the beginning, you might put your mouse on the wrong button in a toolbar or dialog box and initiate a command that you didn't want. This way things you did not intend to do or have not (yet) understood will probably happen to your text. If, for example, you press the Del key by mistake when formatting selected text ranges, your whole text will disappear, it will be deleted!

Stay calm. Such mistakes can easily be undone, because *Word* contains a function enabling you to undo the last operations again.

Undoing the last command

To undo only the last erroneous command, carry out any one of the following steps:

- Click on the ⟲⟲ button

- Select the *Undo* command in the *Edit* menu.

- Press the ⌈Ctrl⌉+⌈Z⌉ key combination

The last alteration is instantly undone. The command label indicates which operations you can undo. Certain commands, such as *Save* or *Print*, cannot be undone!

Undo up to 100 operations

However, *Word* can do even better than that. Suppose you discover you've made a mistake, but only after you've already performed many further operations. A button offers you the possibility to undo all the last steps you have taken. The list you can access by pressing the drop-down list button next to the *Undo* button ⟲⟲ in the *Standard* toolbar facilitates this. If you click on the curved arrow to the left, the last thing you did will be undone. Of course this is nothing new. However, if you click on the drop-down list button to the right of the *Undo* button ⟲⟲, a list box will appear containing a summary of the most recent actions.

Fig. 1.30: The list box of the *Undo* button

Select all the actions that you want to undo in the list box with the mouse button pressed. If you go all the way to the bottom of the list box *Word* automatically scrolls down. You can also go on clicking the *Undo* ⟲▾ button to undo actions one by one.

Repeating Commands

Certain operations in *Word* are accessible only via several dialog boxes. This detour can be very annoying if you want to apply a certain formatting or to perform actions repeatedly, in different parts of the document. Naturally there is a simpler solution for this, otherwise this chapter wouldn't make any sense. Every time you have to repeat certain commands, insertions or operations, *Word* supports you with the *Repeat* command.

Edit/Repeat

It only makes sense to repeat actions, if you want to use identical commands for sections of the document nowhere near each other or in case you cannot, or do not want to, highlight the corresponding text ranges independently of each other. To repeat the last action open the *Edit* menu and click on the *Repeat* command. The key combination for this is Ctrl+Y. The last action is repeated and affects the cursor position or the selection. The command label indicates which actions can be repeated. Certain commands such as *Save* or *Print* cannot be repeated in this manner!

Redo Commands

You have to take care not to mistake the *Repeat* function for the *Redo* button ⟳▾ in the *Standard* toolbar. With this button you can only redo actions you have undone.

Fig. 1.31: To redo is not the same as repeating

If you have undone one or several operations too many by mistake with the *Undo* button ⟳▾, you can redo them with the *Redo* button ⟳▾. The button and the list box that you can access with it function in the same way as the *Undo* button introduced before.

In *Word 2000* you theoretically can *Redo*, not *Repeat*, any number of actions. We have already tested this with more than 10,000 actions – and it worked. The only limitations here are the memory and hard disk space available.

Selecting with the Mouse and the Keyboard

Prior to accessing any commands in a word processing program such as *Word*, you have to highlight the corresponding text range.

Paragraph formatting

The insertion cursor blinking within a paragraph is only sufficient, if you want to format that special paragraph. If several paragraphs are to receive the same formatting, they should be highlighted beforehand.

In order to format a document already available, you have to inform *Word* by selecting which parts you want to format in which way. There are several possibilities to highlight text parts.

Selecting with the Mouse

To select a range of text with the mouse, place the mouse pointer in front of the first character you want to select. Now hold the mouse button down, and move the cursor to the right of the last character you want to select. The selection appears as a black bar. *Word* selects the whole word automatically if you position the cursor in any part of a word and then move the cursor to the right or to the left.

If you want to select single characters in a word simply switch off the automatic select feature or use the keyboard. The automatic select feature works both forwards and backwards!

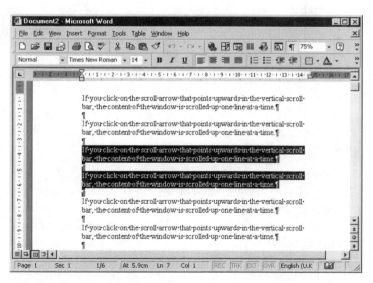

Fig. 1.32: Selecting text in Word

**Select single
characters**

In order to temporarily turn off the automatic select feature press the `Ctrl`+`⇧` key combination and keep it pressed down. Now drag the mouse character by character. Then release the mouse button and the `Ctrl`+`⇧` key combination.

You can also select entire lines, paragraphs or pages using the mouse without any problem. When the cursor reaches the top or bottom of the *Word* document window while you are selecting, the visible section of the document will automatically move and be scrolled line by line over the screen.

Selecting with the Mouse and the Keyboard

When selecting using keyboard and mouse simultaneously, click in front of the first character to be selected. Then hold the `⇧` key down, and click on the space behind the last character in the text to be selected. Now release the `⇧` key, too. Highlighting using mouse and keyboard also works with more than one page. To achieve this, the scroll bar has to be used in between.

Selecting Words, Lines and Paragraphs

There is a quicker way to select a text section recognizable to *Word*, e.g., a word or a paragraph, than by simple dragging.

If you want to select a word, simply double-click on the word. If you want to select an entire line, position the mouse pointer on the left of the line in the (invisible) selection bar (see Figure 1.33). Now click with the mouse pointer inclined to the right ↗. This enables you to select several lines by keeping the mouse button pressed. A double-click in the selection bar selects an entire paragraph.

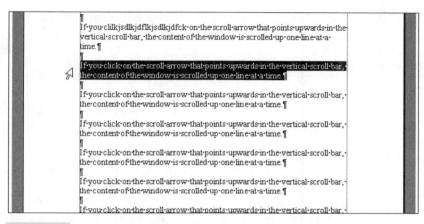

Fig. 1.33: The mouse pointer in the selection bar

Extend the selection

If you want to extend the selection press the ⬛ key and move the mouse up or down with the button pressed. For a sentence, keep the ⬛Ctrl⬛ key pressed and click on any character within the sentence for it to be selected.

Selecting sentences

To select several sentences keep the ⬛Ctrl⬛ key pressed and click on any character within the first sentence. Hold the left mouse button down and drag the mouse cursor over the last sentence that is to be selected. Then release ⬛Ctrl⬛ as well as the mouse button.

Selecting paragraphs

Select a paragraph by double-clicking the selection bar in front of the paragraph or by triple-clicking any character within the paragraph. Select several paragraphs by double-clicking the selection bar. Start before the first paragraph and keep the left mouse button pressed down. Move the mouse in the selection bar up or down until the corresponding paragraphs are marked. Then release the mouse button. Or quickly triple-click any character within the paragraph and keep the left mouse button pressed down. Then drag the selection up or down until the corresponding paragraphs are selected, and release the mouse button.

Selecting with Menu Commands

If you want to apply a command to the entire document, e.g., change the font for the whole document, you have to select the entire content of the document beforehand.

Edit/Select All

In *Word,* if you press the ⎡Ctrl⎤+⎡A⎤ keyboard combination corresponding to the *Edit/Select All* command, the whole document will be selected. To select everything, you can also use the combination ⎡Ctrl⎤+⎡5⎤. Here the ⎡5⎤ key refers to the numeric keypad. Likewise you can select the whole document with the ⎡Ctrl⎤ key and a click into the selection bar, or with a triple-click into the selection bar.

Selecting with Shortcuts

Sometimes it is preferable to use shortcuts for selecting in a word processing program, as your hands are already on the keyboard anyway. Often the insertion cursor can be positioned more precisely using the keyboard than using the mouse. The most important key combinations for selecting using the keyboard have been summarized as follows:

Shortcut	**Description**
⎡⇧⎤+⎡←⎤⎡→⎤	Select character by character, to the left or to the right
⎡⇧⎤+⎡↑⎤⎡↓⎤	Select line by line, up or down
⎡⇧⎤+⎡Home⎤	Select from cursor to beginning of line
⎡⇧⎤+⎡End⎤	Select from cursor to end of line

Shortcut	Description
⬆ + Ctrl + Home	Select from cursor to beginning of document
⬆ + Ctrl + End	Select from cursor to end of document
⬆ + Ctrl + →	Extend selection to the next word
⬆ + Ctrl + ←	Extend selection to the previous word
⬆ + Ctrl + PgUp	Extend selection from cursor to the first line in the window
⬆ + Strg + PgDn	Extend selection from cursor to the last line in the window
Ctrl + A	Select whole document

Memorize these shortcuts, too, since they can be of great help to you while working in *Word*. Most of the shortcuts also function in the text boxes of dialog boxes or in the *Notepad* Windows editor.

EXT

An alternative to the key combinations summarized above is to work with the so-called *Extend Selection* mode on the keyboard. Select a word by clicking on the word and press F8 to activate the *Extend Selection* mode. Then press F8 once more in order to select the current word. Press Esc to end the extend mode.

Switch off extend selection

Select a sentence by clicking into the sentence. Press F8 to activate the extend selection mode. Afterwards press F8 again twice to select the current sentence. Switch off the *Extend Selection* mode with the Esc key. For a paragraph, position the insertion cursor inside the paragraph and press the F8 key to activate the *Extend Selection* mode. Then press F8 again three times to select the current paragraph. Deactivate the *Extend Selection* mode with [Esc]. For several paragraphs, position the insertion cursor in the first paragraph and press the [F8] key. Then press [F8] three more times to select the first paragraph.

Selecting Vertical Text Sections

Word makes the selection of text sections easy for you by automatically extending the selection bar to the end of the line as soon as you move the mouse or cursor to any position in the following line while you are selecting.

This automatic extension is, however, undesirable in certain situations. If you want to select only one column, for instance, the *Amount* column, in your invoice – which you have created with tabs –, you should select this one column only and not entire lines. In this case use *Column Selection*.

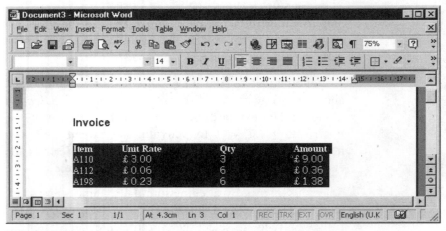

Fig. 1.34: Extend selection extends to the end of the line

Click in front of the first character and drag the mouse, while pressing down the ⟨Alt⟩ key, to the space behind the last character of the desired section, or position the cursor in front of the first character, press ⟨Alt⟩+⟨⇧⟩+⟨F8⟩ and move the cursor with the arrow keys to the space behind the last character of the section.

As long as the vertical block selection is activated, the abbreviation *COL* for *Column Selection* is displayed in the status bar instead of *EXT* for *Extend Selection*. The *Column Selection* can be turned off with ⟨Esc⟩ or with a double-click on *COL* in the status bar.

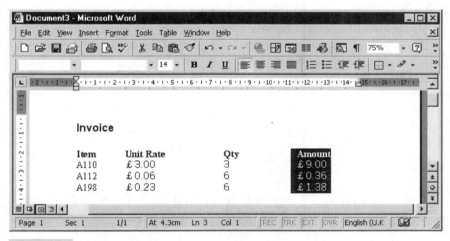

Fig. 1.35:   Column selection

Automatic Word Selection

If you select text ranges in *Word* using the mouse, *Word* extends the selection to an entire word, independent of the cursor's position. This is a really practical feature for a couple of reasons; one, because the automatic selection of entire words works forwards and backwards and, secondly, because you do not have to position the cursor directly in front of the word and then drag it to the space behind the word.

But this extend selection might not be suitable for everyone, because, after all it makes it nearly impossible to select parts of a word. Luckily, however, *Word* is very flexible. In order to turn off the extend selection choose the *Options* command in the *Tools* menu.

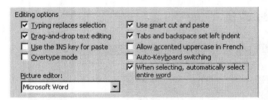

Fig. 1.36x: The last check box is responsible for word selection

Clear the *When selecting, automatically select entire word* check box in *Editing options* and confirm with *OK*. From now on you can select character by character using the mouse.

 You can also turn off the *Extend Selection* by pressing the ⟨⇧⟩+⟨Strg⟩ keys while selecting using the mouse.

If you now want to select an entire word, point to the exact beginning of the word and press the mouse button, thus extending the selection to the space behind the last character to be selected.

Copy and Move Text in Word with the Mouse/Keyboard

We have already explained how you can correct errors quickly and easily while entering text in *Word*. At this point we will now explain the more sophisticated methods of moving text or copying text ranges that are required over and over again. *Word* gives you a choice between using either only the mouse or the keyboard, or a combination of the two.

No matter which method you select, you will normally proceed as follows:

- Select the text part that you want to rearrange or copy.

- Copy or cut text to the clipboard.

- Select the new insertion point.

- Insert the text into one or several insertion points by pasting.

Using the Clipboard

To move portions of text in *Word*, you can use the clipboard in *Windows 98*. This is the operating system's invisible memory buffer, into which you can copy text (and other objects) and insert them into other places in the document (or any other application). To do this, select the desired part of your document. There are several ways to activate the clipboard commands: through key combinations, buttons or commands.

Office 2000, to which Word 2000 also belongs, has a new function based on the well known operating system's clipboard. It is the *Clipboard* toolbar which allows you to store up to twelve different content items and to paste them in another position irrespective of the order in which you copied or cut them. The clipboard of the operating system on the contrary was able to store only one content item each time. Using the right mouse button click on one of the displayed toolbars and choose the *Clipboard* toolbar in order to display it.

Copy

Copy 📇

Choose *Edit/Copy* to copy selected text to the clipboard without deleting the text from its original position. You can also click the *Copy* button 📇 on the *Standard* toolbar or press ⌈Ctrl⌋+⌈C⌋. If you now display the *Clipboard* toolbar you will see a corresponding symbol in the first compartment.

Cut

Cut ✂

If you select the *Edit/Cut* command, however, the selected text will be deleted from the screen and moved to the clipboard. You can also click the Cut button ✂ in the *Standard*-toolbar or press ⌈Ctrl⌋+⌈X⌋ to do this.

Paste Cut or Copied Objects

The contents of the clipboard can now be inserted into other parts of the *Word* document (or any other application). To do this, position the insertion cursor at the point where the text is to be inserted and choose the *Paste* command in the *Edit* menu.

Paste 📋

Alternatively, you can click the *Paste* button 📋 on the *Standard* toolbar or press ⌈Ctrl⌋+⌈V⌋. You can repeat this procedure at other points in the text or in completely different documents as often as you like. Text copied or cut to the clipboard can only be overwritten by copying new text and will be deleted when the computer is shut down.

Tip! If you apply one of the last described procedures, you will insert the last selected content item in the document. If you want to insert a previously selected item instead, click on the corresponding compartment in the *Clipboard* toolbar. If you set the mouse pointer on one of the compartments, a ScreenTip shows the content item stored in it.

Copy and Move with Drag-and-Drop

Now we will deal with copying and moving parts of text using the mouse. The so-called drag-and-drop technique makes this very simple. You can also use this method to copy or rearrange text from one document into another. First you have to select the passage. Now point the mouse on the selected part of the text. Press the left mouse button and hold it down. If you move the mouse now, you will see a small square attached to the bottom of the mouse pointer. This square represents the text.

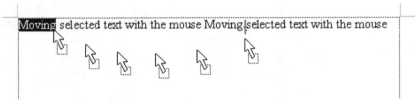

Fig. 1.37:   Moving selected text with the mouse

While holding down the mouse button, move the mouse to the point where you want to insert the text that is being moved. A horizontal dotted line appears at the insertion point in *Word*. The whereabouts of the mouse pointer with its little box need not concern you, the dotted line is all that matters! Release the mouse button at the final insertion point. The text stands deleted from its original position and is now inserted in the new position.

Copy

For copying using the mouse, there is only one small but very important difference. Select the text you want to copy and press the ⌈Ctrl⌉ key. In addition to the pressed down ⌈Ctrl⌉ key, press the mouse button, hold it down, and move the mouse: At the end of the mouse pointer a little '+'-sign appears in the small square, informing you that you are in the copy mode.

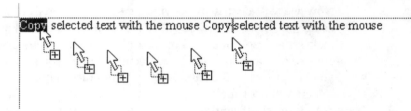

Fig. 1.38: Copy text with the mouse and ⌈Ctrl⌉

Move the mouse to the insertion point. *Word* shows you a horizontal dotted line. Once again, don't worry about where the mouse pointer is right now, what matters most is the insertion selection. Release the mouse button at the final insertion point. A copy of the text is inserted in the intended position, while the original remains where it was.

The *drag-and-drop* technique has one disadvantage: Both the original position and the insertion point have to be visible in the text. However, it is possible to move or copy a text beyond the section of the document which is visible. First select the text range that you want to move. Then scroll to the end position with the help of the scroll bars. Point to the insertion point with the mouse. <u>Do not click!</u> Now press the ⌈Ctrl⌉ button and hold it down. Now click the right mouse button to move the text.

To copy a passage using the right mouse button, press the ⟨⇧⟩ key along with the ⟨Ctrl⟩ key to copy the selected text beyond the text part visible on the screen.

Manual and Automatic Hyphenation

Word hyphenates a word at the right margin if it does not entirely fit onto a line. If the word is particularly long, this can result in ugly gaps in the *Justify* mode or in a very ragged *Left-aligned* mode. In Chapter 9 you will be told how to apply automatic hyphenation in *Word*.

Manual hyphenation

In this chapter, we will explain to you how you can hyphenate words at the end of a line, manually or according to suggestions given by *Word*. For manual hyphenation use *Word's* special character. Just typing an ordinary hyphen into a word at the end of the line doesn't work. Why? Simply because *Word* cannot automatically join hyphenated words again if changes to the font or the font size are made which alter the end of the line. The same applies to manually inserted paragraph breaks. The hyphen remains in the place in which you 'in-ser-ted' it.

It is too much of a bother to remove the hyphens which have been typed in this way one after the other. *Word* can do this much more efficiently. However, you have to use a special character for this. You can insert a hyphen which will be printed only in case the word is hyphenated at that point. Such a hyphen is called an 'optional hyphen' and it is inserted with ⟨Ctrl⟩+⟨-⟩. Henceforth *Word* will hyphenate with the optional hyphen. If the line break changes, *Word* can automatically rejoin these words again.

Special characters for hyphens

If the nonprinting characters are switched on, don't get confused by the character for the optional hyphen, which looks like this ⌐, becoming visible. This symbol can only be seen on the screen and will not be printed out.

Controlled Hyphenation

Semi-automatic hyphenation

Let's start with the semi-automatic hyphenation mode. For this you apply a function of the automatic hyphenation mode. Ask *Word* for hyphenating suggestions which you can accept, correct or reject. This procedure takes much longer than fully automatic hyphenation, but it allows you to keep a tighter control on the text. Create your document for the semi-automatic hyphenation, then select the *Language* command on the *Tools* menu and choose *Hyphenation* on the submenu.

Make sure that the *Automatically hyphenate document* check box is cleared in the *Hyphenation* dialog box and click on the *Manual* button

Word displays all the possible ways in which the word can be hyphenated, including the current hyphenation proposal, shown by a blinking black bar. If you confirm the proposal with *Yes* in the dialog box, *Word* hyphenates the word at the marked point. If you want to choose another hyphenation option, simply click the hyphen at the point in the word where you want the hyphen and confirm with *Yes*.

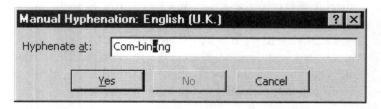

Fig. 1.39:   The *Manual Hyphenation* dialog box

If you want to reject all the possibilities offered for hyphenation, click on the *No* button. *Word* will then indicate the next word that can be hyphenated. If you want to discontinue the semi-automatic hyphenation click on the *Cancel* button.

2. Views and Screen Settings

Word can display a document in different ways. Each display mode is called a *View*. You can use different views for various applications and operation areas of your document. Each display mode has its advantages and disadvantages, and some display modes make sense only for certain very special operations, whereas others are adaptable as all-purpose modes.

What are views able to do?

Some views can display texts very quickly when formatting is not called into question, while others display the document exactly as it will be printed, and still other views are useful for certain special operations only, e.g. in order to display an overview of the headings or to merge several documents in a file.

Showing Document Contents in Different Views

Word shows documents in different ways. The view chosen does not alter the contents of a document, but only the way the document is displayed.

Which view?

The *View* you choose depends upon:

- the size of your document. What matters is not the number of pages but the size of the memory;

- which operation you want to perform;

- which kind of document you want to create, e.g. an online document or a document meant for printing;

- how powerful your computer is.

For most documents not exceeding a certain size it is up to you to choose which view you prefer to work in and which screen elements you want to display in your text.

Using *Normal* View

Select the *Normal* command on the *View* menu to change to normal view, or click on the *Normal View* button ▤ to the left of the horizontal scroll bar above the status bar.

Normal View displays your documents with all the paragraph and character formatting in place, but it does not display elaborate graphic formatting.

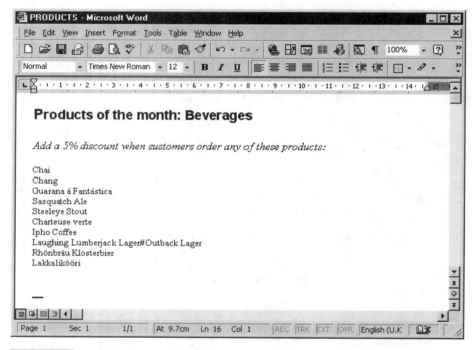

Fig. 2.1: The *Normal View* of Word

Furthermore, *Word* does not display paper margins or headers and footers in the *Normal View*.

Tabs, inserted graphics and paragraph formatting, such as indentations or line spacing, etc. are displayed more or less as

Invisible headers they will eventually appear when printed. Particular elements of a document, like footnotes, endnotes, headers, footers or position frames are, however, not displayed. Nevertheless, they can be made visible in an extra window section.

You cannot use the *Normal View* to position graphics and frames. The *Header and Footer* command on the *View* menu, e.g. divides the *Word* document window into two sections:

The document text is displayed at the top, while the text for headers and footers can be clearly inserted at the bottom. The same applies to foot and endnotes.

High display speed This display is suitable for long documents that are going to be formatted at the end. The display speed in the *Normal* view is very fast.

Quick Display in *Normal* View

This feature is the reason why the *Normal* view is suited best for any computer slower than a Pentium. To configure elements displayed in the *Normal* view, choose the *Options* command on the *Tools* menu. Formatting can be further reduced and the display of graphics turned off via the *View* tab page. Check the *Picture placeholders* check box of the *Show* option group. In the *Outline and Normal options* option group you can also choose to select the *Draft font* check box.

Wrap to window If you want a lot of text to be displayed on the screen, check the *Wrap to window* check box. However, what is then displayed will no longer correspond to the rough print picture. Click *OK* to confirm the *Options* dialog box.

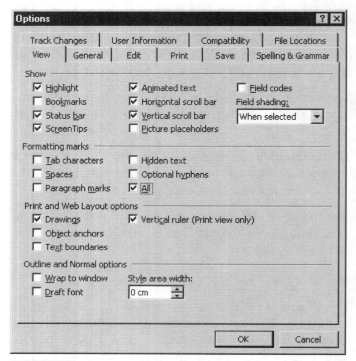

Fig. 2.2:   Quick display in *View*

Many users prefer the *Normal* view to enter or check headers and footers or footnotes and endnotes, etc.

If you are still practicing with *Word*, enter and format separately, as it simplifies the learning process and error correction. Use the *Normal* view to enter your documents.

Print Layout View

In *Word* the *Print Layout* view corresponds more or less to the standard view. To change to the print layout view select the *Print Layout* command from the *View* menu, or click on the *Print Layout View* button ▦ in the horizontal scroll bar.

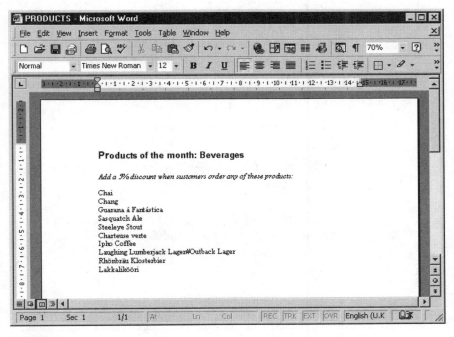

Fig. 2.3:   *Print Layout* View – it shows documents as they will be printed

The *Print Layout* view displays your document on the screen as it will look later on when printed. All the elements of the document, like footnotes, endnotes, headers and footers, paper borders and margins, text boxes, etc. are displayed in their actual position and include all formatting.

Visible headers and footers

You can easily recognise the *Print Layout view* by the page borders, which are displayed against a grey background. Elements in the margins, such as headers and footers, are also visible.

This view, corresponding exactly to the printout, will of course somewhat slow down the display speed. But nowadays, with the advent of Pentium computers, this is no longer a problem.

Therefore, we recommend using the *Print Layout* view while formatting all *Word* documents, except for extremely long ones. That way you can avoid unnecessary printouts and constant corrections. What you see on the screen is what you'll actually get. This is what is meant by the acronym *WYSIWYG* (*What You See Is What You Get*).

Use the *Print Layout* view to format and create documents that are meant for printing.

You can also switch between different views using key combinations. Switch back and forth from *Normal* view to *Print Layout* view with Alt+Ctrl+N and Alt+Ctrl+P.

Web Layout

The *Web Layout* view optimizes document layouts meant to be read on the screen. You can either select the *Web Layout* view or click on the *Web Layout View* ▣ button to change to this view.

The *Web Layout* view is not the same as the *Print Preview*. Online implies being connected to a data provider. However, with the *Web Layout* view this is not necessary. Nevertheless, this layout is of great help when you are creating HTML documents for the Internet. Furthermore, several formatting commands can be used in this display, such as text effects displaying animated or blinking text, for example. These effects only appear on-screen and cannot be printed.

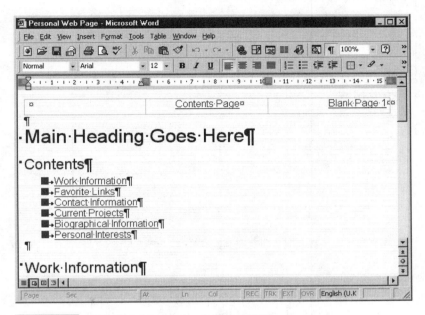

You can also add background colors and structures to your documents in the *Web Layout* view. These will appear only in this view and not in the *Print Layout* view or in the *Normal* view, and they cannot be printed out.

If you open a document in HTML format or if you create a new Web site on the basis of a Web site template, *Word* automatically switches to the *Web Layout* view.

Outline View

Select the *Outline* command on the *View* menu to change to *Outline* view or click the *Outline View* button ▦.

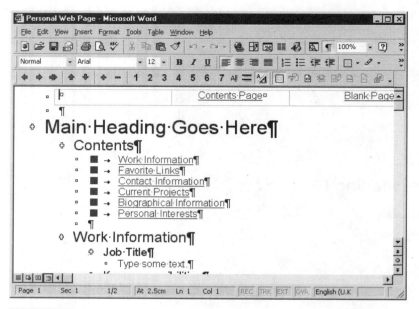

Fig. 2.5: A document in the *Outline* view in *Word*

The *Outline* view displays different levels of the document structure. However, this only works if the document is outlined using the *Heading 1* to *Heading 9* format templates, since *Word* evaluates the heading formats in the *Outline* view:

The outline levels displayed can be expanded or reduced using buttons. A long document can be displayed very clearly in this view and text can also be easily rearranged.

In the *Outline* view, it is possible to create an outline document which is interesting as for corrections or changes to be made in very long paragraphs. Select this view to work on documents whose content has been divided among different files or to create a content list for the whole document.

Print Preview

The *Print Preview* is actually no *Word* view. That is why you will not find this command on the *View* menu. It is called *Print Preview* because it displays the text exactly as it will appear when printed.

Print Preview

To switch to the *Print Preview*, select the *Print Preview* command in the *File* menu or click on the *Print Preview* button in the *Standard* toolbar. The *Print Preview* shows on-screen one or more pages in a reduced format.

Editing text in
Print Preview

You can also edit text in *Print Preview* mode. Click on the *Magnifier* button to activate this edit mode.

The *Print Preview* is an on-screen version of a printout showing exactly how the text will look on paper. Your default printer driver is used for this view.

That is why the *Print Preview* is a true *WYSIWYG*, what you see in front of you corresponds 100 per cent to the paper printout.

Therefore you can check all texts in the *Print Preview* prior to giving the print command. The *Print Preview* in *Word* also allows you to make changes on the margins and to manipulate the page breaks.

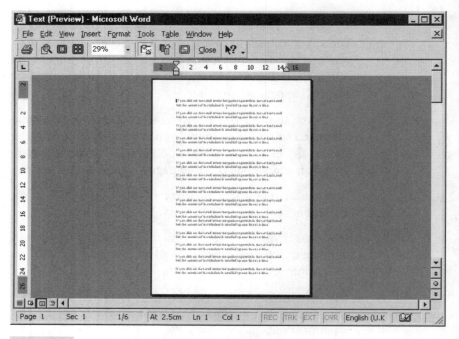

Printout on the screen: the *Print Preview*

Full Screen View

The two principal reasons for using the *Full Screen* view are:

Reason 1: You have a relatively small 14- or 15-inch monitor, and need to switch constantly between different zoom levels in order to insert text and modify the layout.

Reason 2: The document is all that you can see on your screen, no control elements or portions of the *Word* program window are visible, and you don't know how this happened.

Documents can be displayed with all window elements in *Word* switched off and the text covering the entire screen. This display facilitates checking for errors without distraction.

Full Screen view

If you want to fill the whole screen with your document, first maximise the document window. Then apply a suitable magnification scale for your editing with the *Zoom* feature. Now select the *Full Screen* command from the *View* menu.

The application window of *Word* will disappear and nothing will be visible on the screen apart from the text. The advantage deriving from this is that you use all monitor space available, and most of your document can be displayed at the same time.

The disadvantage is that you need to be acquainted with the *Word* key combinations since the usual control elements, such as the toolbar buttons for example, are not available.

Fig. 2.7:   With this toolbar you can return to the *Standard* view

If you have activated the *Full Screen* view by mistake, there is a simple way to return the usual *Word* display on your screen. There is a small *Full Screen* toolbar on the screen with only one button.

Close Full Screen

Click on the *Close Full Screen* command button or press the [Esc] key to display the missing screen elements once again.

If you activate the ruler before you change to *Full Screen* view, it will appear on the screen. If you want even more free space, select *Ruler* on the *View* menu to hide it before switching views.

Calling-up Document Map

In *Word 2000* there is yet another feature, besides the already introduced *Web Layout* view, which is linked to the Internet. This feature isn't novel in its own right, but because it calls up another frame. This frame displays the document map, which contains the hierarchy of headings in the document.

Document Map 🔲   Call-up the document map by selecting the *Document Map* command on the *View* menu or by clicking on the *Document Map* button 🔲. This document map can be activated to get an overview of the entire document even while you are editing a particular portion of the text. The *Document Map* is also useful when you want to move quickly between sections within the document.

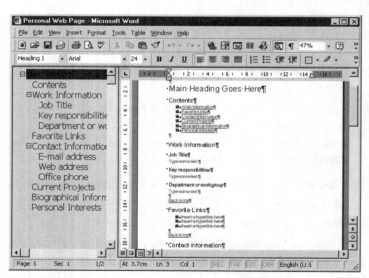

Fig. 2.8:   *Print Layout* view with *Document Map*

Simply click on the heading in the *Document Map* you want to move to. Next to the headings there are buttons with a plus or minus sign. Click on this sign to expand or collapse the sub-headings. The *Document Map* can be called-up in all views.

Calling-up Screen Elements

There are a number of elements in the *Word* application window to help you create and check documents. They include:

- Toolbars
- Rulers
- Status bar
- Scroll bars

The more elements are visible on the screen, the less space remains to display the document content. Some of these elements can therefore be switched on or off through the *View* command, depending on whether you are using them for your current editing work.

Select for example *Ruler* on the *View* menu to display the horizontal ruler in the *Normal* view and the horizontal and vertical rulers in the *Print Layout* view.

Displaying Paragraph Marks and Other Special Characters

Word works with document texts paragraph by paragraph. Each paragraph has a joined range of text that can later be uniformly formatted without any gaps occurring in the text. Press the return ↵ key to create a paragraph in *Word*. Even empty lines are made of paragraphs.

Nonprinting special characters

Other special characters are displayed for tabs, spaces, optional hyphens and nonbreaking spacings. By default, *Word* does not display the control buttons for paragraphs and other nonprinting characters. The disadvantage is that superfluous paragraph marks, spaces or tabs can only be discerned with difficulty, not to mention that they cannot be manually deleted or changed to a manual line break.

Calling-up special characters

However, *Word* provides a solution. Paragraph marks and other nonprinting characters can be made visible by clicking on the *Show/Hide ¶* button ¶ on the *Standard* toolbar.

Fig. 2.9: Calling-up nonprinting special characters

Press the `Ctrl`+`⇧`+`*` key combination to switch the paragraph marks on and off. *Word* will now indicate with `↵` created paragraphs by the paragraph mark ¶.

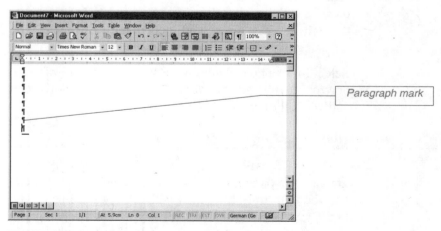

Fig. 2.10: Displaying paragraph marks

Deleting a paragraph mark

To delete a paragraph mark select the ¶ character and press `Del`. If your insertion cursor is at the beginning of the next line you can also press the `←` key to delete unnecessary paragraphs. To change a paragraph to a manual line break, delete the ¶ mark and then press the `⇧`+`↵` key combination.

If you want to hide the paragraph marks for better layout control, click on the *Show/Hide* ¶ button ¶ or press `Ctrl`+`⇧`+`*` again.

Displaying Toolbars

By default *Word* starts with the two toolbars, the *Standard* and the *Formatting* toolbar, both of which are anchored underneath the menu bar. Other toolbars will appear only when particular actions or operations have to be performed. And still others can be shown or hidden by clicking buttons on either the *Standard* or the *Formatting* toolbar.

Drawing toolbar, Tables and Borders toolbar

The *Drawing* button ✐ on the *Standard* toolbar is one case in point, and clicking on it shows or hides the *Drawing* toolbar, placed above the status bar, which allows you create drawings in *Word* documents.

Similarly, if you click on the *Tables and Borders* button ▦ on the *Standard* toolbar, another toolbar with buttons for formatting paragraphs as well as tables with borders and frames will be displayed.

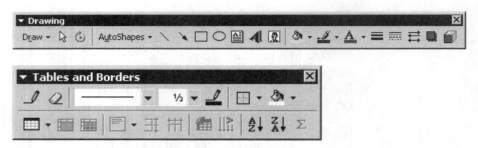

Fig. 2.11:   Calling-up additional toolbars

However, *Word* contains more toolbars that can be switched on or off by using one of two methods. Either select the *Toolbars* command on the *View* menu or point to a toolbar and right-click the mouse. The available toolbars are listed in the *Toolbars* submenu and in the shortcut menu. To display additional toolbars simply click on the name of the toolbar.

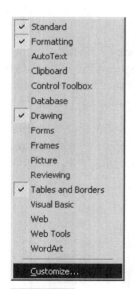

Fig. 2.12:   Toolbar menu

Some button submenus or selection menus can be shifted like toolbars. Whenever you see a grey line at the top of a selection (e.g. in the command submenu *Insert/Autotext*), you can set on it with your mouse and drag it with the mouse button pressed. The selection then appears in another toolbar and remains open on screen until you close it by clicking on the *Close* button.

Toolbars can either be docked along the border of the *Word* window or displayed as floating toolbars. Floating toolbars can be moved and positioned freely anywhere on the screen, even outside the *Word* window. To do this, click the toolbar's title bar and drag the floating toolbar with the mouse button pressed.

Dock toolbars

To display a docked toolbar as a floating toolbar, click the toolbar's move handle and drag the toolbar, mouse button pressed, into the space you are working on.

To dock a toolbar, drag the toolbar to one edge of the *Word* program window. A frame automatically indicates the new position of the toolbar on the border. Release the mouse button when you have placed it where you wish.

Hiding toolbars

To hide a toolbar, either click on the name of the toolbar in the shortcut menu of a docked toolbar to deactivate it, or select *Toolbars* on the *View* menu and choose the toolbar to clear the check mark. To hide floating toolbars click on the *Close* button ☒ on its title bar.

Zoom

Word can display documents not only in different views but also in different display sizes or scales. With the views you change the display of document elements. For example, the *Print Layout* view displays the paper borders and all the formatting in the way it will later be printed.

The *Normal* view does not have this *WYSIWYG* display. But in addition to the view, the contents of each document window in *Word* can be displayed in different scales.

Zoom

If you use the *Zoom* feature in *Word*, you can adapt the size of the document to your current work area. You can 'zoom in' the document to get a close-up view of it, for example, or to enter text.

Zoom out

To work on the text flow of a one-page letter, however, you could 'zoom out' to be able to see more of the page in a reduced size. This can all be done through the *Zoom* feature (both to "zoom in" and "zoom out").

Zoom-in

If you 'zoom in' on the document in order to let it appear larger than its original size, for instance, this implies zoom settings of more than 100 %. If you want to enlarge the text by 1.5 times, for example, this corresponds to a zoom setting of 150%. The maximum zoom setting is 500%. A one-to-one-appearance corresponds to a zoom setting of 100%. Of course you should consider all zoom settings in relation to the original size.

'Zooming out' is expressed in zoom settings less than 100%. If you 'zoom out' a document to half of its original size, this corresponds to a zoom setting of 50%. You can edit a document at any zoom setting. In addition, each document window can have its own zoom setting.

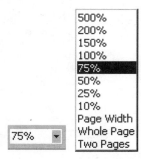

The *Zoom* list box in the *Standard* toolbar

To change the zoom setting of your document, use the *Zoom* 75% drop-down list box on the *Standard*-toolbar. To select a preset value, click on the drop-down button to display the available list box entries.

You can also click on the *Zoom* text box and overtype the current setting with the precise zoom setting you want, e.g. 93%. It is not necessary to type the percentage sign. Once you have typed in your setting, press ↵.

Whole page

Click in the list box to select either a percentage value or one of the following items: *Page Width*, *Whole Page* or *Two Pages*. The *Page Width* item sets the zoom at a setting with the full line of text visible in the window.

Two pages

The *Whole Page* item automatically sets the zoom value at a setting with the whole page being displayed on the screen. The *Two Pages* item displays two pages next to each other in the document window.

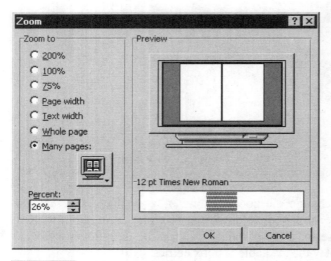

Fig. 2.14: Setting the *Zoom* via a dialog box

Another way to proceed is to modify the setting in the *Zoom* dialog box which appears when you select *Zoom* on the *View* menu. In the *Preview* box you can see how much of a document is displayed using different settings. By default the value set is equal to 10 points. Click *OK* to confirm your choice.

Please note that the *Whole Page* and *Two Pages* zoom items appear only on the *Zoom* list in the *Print Layout* view.

Controlling Windows

It is very useful to work with several documents in *Word* if you want to copy or move text ranges between different texts. When you open a new Word document, a new program application is applied. This means that each file is shown in its own Word window with all menubars and toolbars available. In the left-hand corner of the title bar you will see the name of the open file and in the upper right-hand corner of each Word window you will find three buttons with which you can resize the window. If only one file is open on-screen, you will find a *Close* button, which refers to the file, to the right of the menu bar. Where several files are open, the button is not visible and the file can be closed by selecting the *Close* button in Word.

Document Window

Maximize

If one of several windows in *Word* is maximized with the *Maximize* button ▣, then this document is the only one visible on the screen. The other open documents will be hidden. Contrary to all previous Word releases, it is not possible to modify the size of a document in a Word window.

Restore

Maximized windows can be restored to their original size with the *Restore* button ▣. This will also make the other open window visible once again.

Minimize

Use the *Minimize* button ▬ to reduce a window that you do not currently need to its smallest size. It will appear as a button in the taskbar only. To bring the window back to its original size, click on the taskbar button.

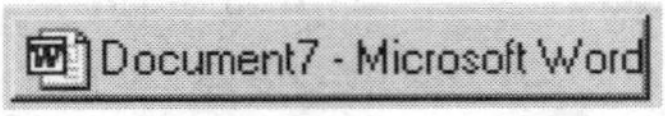

Ⓦ Document7 - Microsoft Word

Fig. 2.15:   Minimized *Word* document window

Even though each document is displayed in separate Word applications, you can move from one document to another with the *Window* menu. There you will see a list of open documents, with the active document window tagged with a check mark.

To switch to another open document simply click on the corresponding item in the *Window* menu.

The list on the *Window* menu shows the documents currently open, while the list on the *File* menu only shows the most recently saved documents.

Fig. 2.16: Moving to other documents with the *Window* menu

Arranging all Windows

Using the items on the *Window* menu, you can display only one maximized document at a time. If you want to have several documents displayed simultaneously, select the *Arrange All* command on the *Window* menu. The *Word* application windows are arranged and they can then be moved, maximized or minimized independently. This is a bit confusing since for each window the menu bar and toolbar are also shown. Close some elements to create more space on the screen. Even with several arranged windows open, only one document can be active. All commands or entries refer only to the active document. You can activate a document by clicking on the corresponding window or on its title bar. The title bar of the application window is then highlighted in the active window color.

Maximizing or Minimizing Word Windows

Document and application window

A document is always displayed in its maximum size within its *Word* application window and, together with it, can be moved, maximized and minimized.

To change the window size of an application window, there are many options available. First make the window active. Generally, in Windows only one application window can be active at any given time, i.e. all entries and commands will affect only this one window. To activate the *Word* application window click anywhere within the window itself. The title bar is then highlighted in the active window color. If the title bar is not visible, click on the button representing the window in the taskbar.

Moving Windows

To move a window, point on its title bar, press and hold down the mouse button and drag the window to its new position.

Fig. 2.17: Mouse pointer on window borders

If the Word window is not maximized, it is surrounded by an edge. The point of intersection of the horizontal and vertical window borders is called the window corner. You can change the width and height of a window with these window elements using the mouse. If you move the mouse pointer to the vertical edge of the window, the mouse pointer changes into a *Double-headed arrow* ←→ .

99

Dragging to resize windows

You can 'grab' the edge of the window with this arrow. To change the width of the window, hold the mouse button down and move the mouse either to the right or the left. As you are doing this, the new size of the window will be visible on the screen as a dotted frame. Simply release the mouse button to set the new size.

To change the window height, move the mouse pointer to a horizontal edge. The shape of the mouse pointer will change to a vertical *Double-headed arrow* ↕. 'Grab' the edge by clicking and drag the mouse until the window height has been changed to your satisfaction.

Fig. 2.18:   Mouse pointer in the window corner

Changing height and width simultaneously

To change the height and width of a window simultaneously use any window corner. The mouse pointer changes to a diagonal double-headed arrow like this ↖ or ↗ . Now you can change the height and width of a window simultaneously by holding down the mouse.

A dotted frame indicates the future shape of the window. If you release the mouse button, the window will be resized. *Word* document windows cannot be enlarged further than the size of the *Word* application window.

You cannot resize maximized windows in this manner. To do that, first reduce the maximized window by clicking the *Restore* button 🗗.

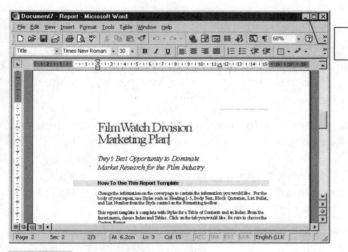

Buttons of the application window

Fig. 2.19: *Maximize/Minimize* buttons

To close a document, click on the *Close* button ☒. The document will be taken out of the main memory. If you have not saved the document, you will be prompted to do so before closing it.

If only a Word document is open on the screen, a second *Close* button appears in the menu bar. Click on the *Close* button in the title bar to close both the Word program and the document – they are both taken out of the main memory. Click on the *Close* button in the menu bar to close only the document - an empty application window is then available. You can now load a file with the *File/Open* command or create a new one with the *File/New* command.

Splitting Windows

In long texts, like contracts or client and product lists, it is often necessary to display text portions at the same time although they are far apart.

It is stressful to have to change each time from one document part to another with the scroll bar or with the [PgUp] or [PgDn] keys, all the more so if, by the time you have scrolled back to the current insertion position, you have forgotten the content of a text or a list that you scrolled to in the beginning.

Split

To view two parts of a document simultaneously *Word* offers the possibility of splitting a document window into two panes. You may have searched in vain for the *Split* command in the *View* menu. Select the *Split* command on the *Window* menu instead.

The mouse pointer changes to a double-headed arrow, the split pointer, and moves together with the split bar. Drag the split bar up and down with the mouse to the position you want. Then click once to split the window.

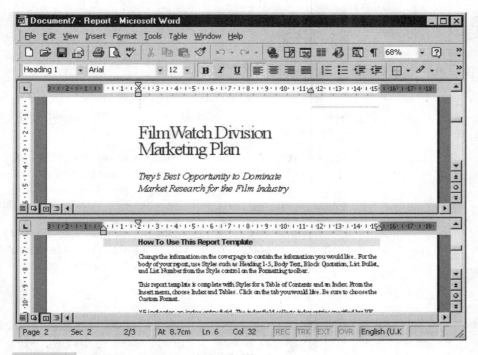

Fig. 2.20:   Splitting document window in Word

Word splits the document window into two panes. Each pane has its own scroll bar to move through the document. First activate the pane you want to work in by clicking into the text area. You can now for example display a list of headings in the top pane while you write your text in the bottom pane.

It is possible, however, to insert text into either pane. To return to a single window, click *Remove Split* on the *Window* menu.

Split box ▦ You can also split a document window by using the mouse. To do this, point at the *Split* box ▦ at the top of the vertical scroll bar just above the scroll arrow and split the window by clicking the mouse button and dragging the split bar.

Displaying Headers and Footers

Headers and footers at the top and bottom of page borders are displayed in light grey in the *Print Layout* view. In the *Normal* view they are not displayed at all.

You can display headers and footers in order to check or edit them by selecting *Header and Footer* from the *View* menu. While the headers and footers are displayed on the screen, the normal text appears greyed.

The *Header and Footer* toolbar appears as soon as the headers and footers are shown. Click the *Close* button on this toolbar to hide the headers and footers once again.

In the *Print Layout* view, you can also double-click in the header area to activate headers and footers for editing. Instead of clicking the *Close* button on the *Header and Footer* toolbar, you can also double-click outside of the header and footer area to hide the header and footer again.

Fixing Standard Settings for Display

Click on the *View* menu to show or hide the ruler and the toolbars. From there you can also determine which other screen elements you want to be displayed.

Select the *Tools/Options* command. In *View* tab page you can determine by acting on the buttons which window elements you want to display or to hide. Some options refer only to some views, while others apply to all of them. Options are divided into groups.

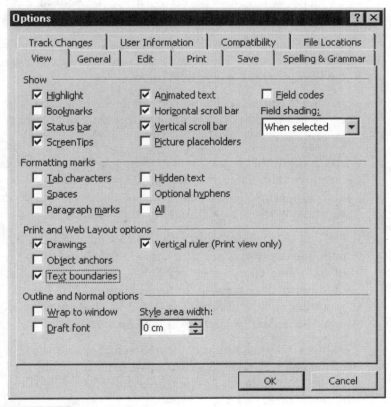

Fig. 2.21:   The *View* tab page

In the *View* options group you can check or uncheck elements using a lot of memory capacity, such as drawings, graphics, animated text, or display them by dummy placeholders.

In addition, you can display the actual *Field codes* instead of the field results (which are usually displayed) and determine whether or not and when these are to be displayed with shaded background.

Moreover, it is possible to display or hide supplementary elements which may be of assistance to you such as status bars, ScreenTip or scroll bars.

If you want to have more screen space or if you edit documents mainly by using the keyboard, you can hide the scroll bars and the vertical ruler.

In the *Nonprinting characters* options group you can check or uncheck single special characters (we discussed this earlier in this chapter).

All special characters for which you check the check boxes in this dialog box remain displayed even if you hide all special characters by clicking on the button ¶ or by pressing the Ctrl + ⬆ + * key combination.

Draft font

Only in the *Normal* and *Outline* views do you have the option to show text in a *Draft font* which is independent of the actual font formatting. This accelerates the speed of the display. Moreover, it is possible to modify the text according to the present width of the window (previously described). All this happens in *Web Layout* view.

Style area width

In this view, you also have the option to display the name of the selected style. Select a value between 0 and 8.86 cm in the *Width of Selected Style* box. Selecting 0 cm turns off the styles display.

Vertical ruler

You can either display or hide the vertical ruler in the *Print* and *Web Layout* views. This option is active only together with the *View/Ruler* command and the ruler can be displayed only when the command is active.

Drawings

Drawings are not displayed in the *Normal* and *Outline* views, while this is an option in the *Print* and *Web Layout* ones. If drawings are not displayed, display on the screen is much faster.

Docking objects

Both drawings and photos, which can be moved within your document, shall be always docked to a paragraph. It does not necessarily have to be close to the drawing but it does influence the object itself. In fact, if the paragraph moves to a new page, the drawing will be moved to the new page as well. A small anchor indicates the paragraph the object is docked to. If you do not want it displayed, you can choose to hide the view in the options menu.

3. File Administration and File Protection

A modern program such as *Word 2000* for Windows relieves you of many tedious tasks. But there are still some you have to do by yourself. One of these tasks is the administration of documents created with *Word*. Here is a list of administration tasks:

- creating new files
- creating folders
- saving files
- searching for files to re-edit
- deleting unused *Word* documents

Creating a New Word Document

After starting *Word* a new blank document in which you can enter text is automatically displayed. But how do you create a new document after entering the text, saving it and closing a file?

There are various ways available. The quickest and easiest way is by clicking a button or pressing a key combination to create a new default document.

You can also call-up a dialog box in case you do not want to create a default document, but rather a new document based on a certain template instead. Furthermore, you will learn the commands for creating new *Word* documents outside *Word* in the Windows environment.

Creating a Blank Document in Word

Of course *Word* is equipped with a facility for easily creating new blank documents. Theoretically, you can open any number of document windows in *Word* and you can enter or edit text independently in each. The number of simultaneously opened documents is only limited by your PC's hard disk.

New ☐

The quickest way to create a new document is by clicking on the *New* button ☐ in the *Standard* toolbar. The blank document is always based on the *Blank Document (Normal.dot)* template.

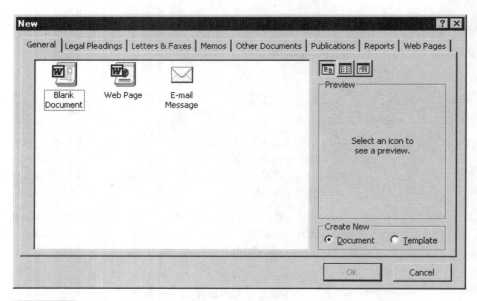

Fig. 3.1:   The *New* dialog box

This is a *Word* default template based on an A-4 page size in portrait format with specific margins, and *Times New Roman* font with 10 point font size and some other settings as well. This new document has exactly the same characteristics as the one displayed on your screen after starting *Word*.

Dialog box

Alternatively, you can also create a new document by clicking the *New* command on the *File* menu. If necessary, activate the *General* tab in the *New* dialog box and select the *Blank Document* template.

Choose the *Document* button in the *Create New* option group and confirm the dialog box with *OK* or ⏎. Immediately a new document based on the *Blank Document (Normal.dot)* template appears.

Creating a New Blank Word Document in Windows 98

In *Word* you generally save a document from the *Word* processing program. The *Windows 98* graphic operation system, however, also offers you the possibility of doing it the other way around.

First create a new blank document with a *Word* option in Windows, name it and then open the application linked to the file type, in this case *Word*. What may appear very complicated now will prove to be simple in your day-to-day practice.

New document with Explorer

You can create the new document at its final file location. In this case, start *Explorer* or open the *My Computer* folder and change to the folder or subfolder in which the document is to be saved. In *My Computer* select the *New* command on the *File* menu in the target folder window.

In *Explorer* the target folder for the file should be open. To accomplish this, click the folder on the folder structure in the left pane of *Explorer*.

Shortcut menu

Alternatively, you can activate the *New* command in the shortcut menu. For this, it is essential not to have any object selected in either *My Computer* or in *Explorer*. The mouse pointer should be in the right part of the folder window in *Explorer*.

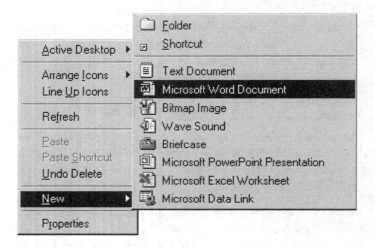

Fig. 3.2: New Microsoft Word document

All the file types available on your system appear in the lower command group. The number and type of documents you can create with this depends on the Windows 98 applications installed on your PC. For a *Word* document click on the *Microsoft Word Document* item.

DOC suffix

A new document icon labelled *New Microsoft Word Document* is created in the current folder, and the name is selected for editing. Now overtype it with your own name. If the file extension is shown, the DOC suffix should definitely be retained. Confirm with ⏎, and double-click to open the blank document. After you have finished your changes, select *File/Save*. It is not necessary to select the target location or to give the file name here.

Opening Documents

If you want to print or edit a particular document, open it first. If you cannot remember for sure which document contains the text you are searching for or if you just want to view the content, but not edit it, you can preview the content of a file with the help of *Quick View*. In order to view the contents of a *Word* document, you normally open the file in the *Word* application. However, it will be faster, if you double-click the document icon in *Explorer*. *Windows 98* offers you yet another method.

Document Preview with or without Word Using Quick View

Supplied is a file viewer able to read the file formats of the most important applications. For this reason it can display the file contents very quickly. There is not much else that you can do with *Quick View*.

Quick View

Now as before, it is still the responsibility of *Word* when it comes to making changes in the displayed document. If you only want to display the preview of a document, change to the folder that contains the document icon in *My Computer* or in *Explorer*. Select the document that you want to view. Then open the *File* menu or the short-cut menu and choose the *Quick View* command.

If the *Quick View* command is not available in the *File* menu, then *Quick View* has not been installed in your system. If this is the case, read how to install *Quick View* in the next section.

If the *Quick View* command is available, the preview of the document appears in the program window of the file viewer.

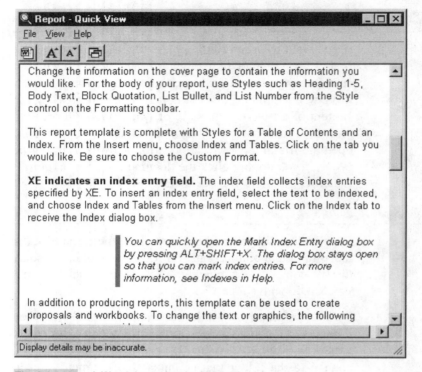

Fig. 3.3:   A Word document in Quick View

In *Quick View* you can change the display mode of certain files by clicking either the *Landscape* or the *Rotate* command on the *View* menu, although this is not the case with *Word* documents. You can edit the document by clicking on the *Open File for Editing* command on the *File* menu or by clicking the 📄 button featuring the *Word* document icon.

When a *Quick View* window is open, a different document can be previewed by dragging its icon into the *Quick View* window.

File viewer

Quick View is a file viewer used for checking unknown file contents quickly and easily without having to start the source program. *Quick View* can be used for other file types too, such as bitmaps.

Installing Quick View

Unfortunately, *Quick View* cannot not be installed by default with *Windows 98*. Therefore, here is how to install it. If the *Quick View* command is not available, do the following: choose the *Settings* command in the *Start* menu and click *Control Panel* in the submenu.

Control Panel/Software/ Setup

In the *Control Panel* folder double-click on the *Add/Remove Programs* icon. In the *Add/Remove Programs Properties* dialog box change to the *Windows-Setup* tab. With the help of the scroll bar in the *Components* list, click the *Accessories* item and then click the *Details* button.

Scroll through the *Components* list with the scroll bar. Check the *Quick View* check box. Then insert your *Windows 98* setup CD-ROM into the CD drive, and confirm twice with *OK*. All files will be copied. Close the *Control Panel*. Now the file viewer to preview *Word* documents is available on your computer.

Preview picture

If you have saved a *Word* document after having selected the *Save preview picture* check box in the *Document Properties* dialog box, a preview of the unopened file will appear after clicking the *Preview* button in the *Open* dialog box.

Starting Word or Word Documents Together with Windows 98

In case you always work with just one program in Windows 98, for example with the word processing program *Word*, it would be very convenient to start automatically the program at the same time you start up Windows.

This also applies to *Word* documents you will be working on over a longer period, such as a thesis. In the latter case opening the document automatically would save you two steps: first, accessing *Word* and second, opening the document in the program.

Exactly for these cases Windows 98 has provided a special folder in which all the objects you want to work with immediately after starting Windows can be saved.

StartUp

This folder is named *StartUp* and it resides on the *Programs* submenu of the *Start* menu. After installing *Microsoft Office Suite*, there are already some program icons available in the *StartUp* folder that automatically load the *Microsoft Office Shortcut Bar* or the *Microsoft Office Startup* program after starting Windows.

Programs/StartUp

Open the *Start* menu and point to *Programs/StartUp*. If the folder does not contain any objects, the submenu will only display the deactivated *(Empty)* item. But if you have installed the *Microsoft Office Suite*, the program icons shown in Figure 3.4 will be displayed in the *StartUp* folder. Further program and/or document icons can be copied into the *StartUp* folder any time you want.

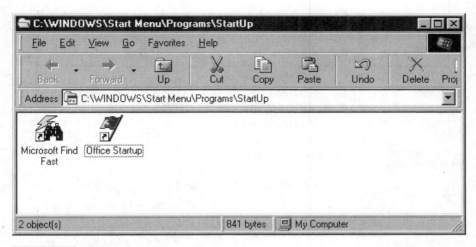

The *StartUp* folder with program icons

If, for example, you want to start *Word* automatically with each Windows start, copy the *Microsoft Word* shortcut into the *StartUp* folder. There are several methods for doing this. First of all, we will introduce you to the method of adding items to the *Start* menu via the *Taskbar Properties* window.

Create shortcut in StartUp

Click on the *Start* button and then point to *Settings*. Next click on the *Taskbar* item and activate the *Start Menu Programs* tab page.

Next click the *Add* button and then the *Browse* button in the *Create Shortcut* dialog box. Now you should know where the required *Word* program file or its shortcut has been saved.

Fig. 3.5: Localize the program file path in *Word*

Create Shortcut

The *C:\Program\Microsoft Office\Microsoft* folder contains the *Word* shortcut by default unless you have specified another path during installation. Select the *Microsoft Word* shortcut and click on the *Open* button. In the *Create Shortcut* dialog box, click *Next* and then double-click the *StartUp* folder in the list of folders.

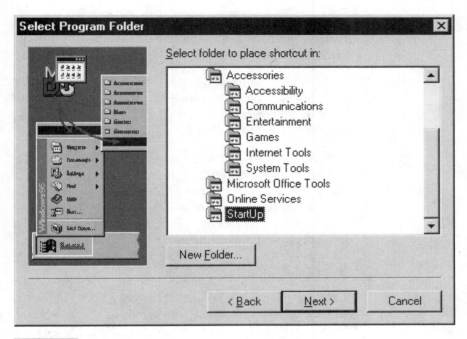

Fig. 3.6: Select the *StartUp* program group

Finish

You can now enter a name that is to be displayed on the *StartUp* menu into the text box or use the default text *Microsoft Word*. Click on *Finish*. Close the *Taskbar Properties* window with *OK*, and check the contents of the *StartUp* program group in the *Start* menu.

Word documents in StartUp

The changes only become effective with your next system start. Then the *Word* program will start simultaneously with Windows 98 and display a blank document.

You should add only the most important applications to the *StartUp* folder as this will otherwise delay the system start unnecessarily and overload the physical memory.

Instead of *Word* you can also add *Word* documents to the *StartUp* folder at any time. In this case *Word* will start automatically and the document will be opened thereafter. However, delete the superfluous shortcut to *Word* before doing this.

Copy shortcut

It is easier to copy existing shortcuts into the *StartUp* folder via the folder window.Open the shortcut menu of the *Start* button and click on *Open*. Double-click on the *Programs* icon in the *Start Menu* folder.

Here you will find the *Microsoft Word* shortcut icon. Repeat the same procedure and double-click on the *StartUp* folder in the folder window. Move the folder in such a way that the folder with the *Microsoft Word* shortcut icon is also visible. Drag a copy of the *Microsoft Word* icon to the *StartUp* folder while pressing the Ctrl key.

Opening Documents with Windows 98 *Start* Menu

Word documents can be loaded not only with *File/Open*, but they can be opened with the Windows 98 *Start* menu, if they have been previously saved as *Word* files. In the *Documents* menu Windows 98 always shows you the last 15 documents used, regardless of the related application.

The only prerequisite is that programs possess file extensions registered in Windows 98 which, of course, is the case with *Word*. Besides, the Word document has to be saved.

Open with the
Documents menu

To call-up one of the 15 last-used documents click the *Start* button on the taskbar. Point to the *Documents* item to open the submenu. The program icon is shown next to the file name of the document.

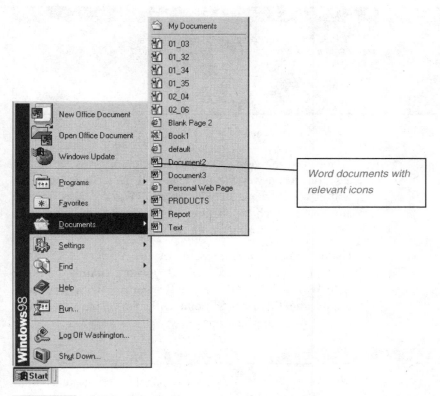

Word documents with relevant icons

Fig. 3.7: Display of the 15 documents last used

To open a *Word* document, click on the desired file name (it has the 📄 document icon in front of it) in the sub-menu. *Word* will start then, if it is not already running, and automatically open the selected document.

Should you have moved a file listed in the *Documents* menu to another folder, *Windows 98* automatically searches your hard disk for the file name. If the file is found, a message similar to the one shown in Figure 3.8 will appear. Confirm the message with *Yes* to open the document in *Word*.

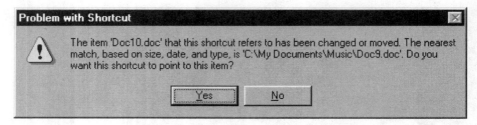

Problem with Shortcut ☒

⚠ The item 'Doc10.doc' that this shortcut refers to has been changed or moved. The nearest match, based on size, date, and type, is 'C:\My Documents\Music\Doc9.doc'. Do you want this shortcut to point to this item?

[Yes]   [No]

Fig. 3.8:   Search for similar file names

If you have already deleted the document, it is absolutely essential to answer the message with *No*, otherwise a file with a similar name may be opened. You can also stop the automatic search by clicking on the *Browse* button and, in this case, by choosing the file yourself.

Using the *Documents* menu of the Windows 98 *Start* menu is recommended only if you are mainly working with *Word*. If you are frequently working with other programs, the *Documents* menu will also display the saved files of these applications.

Opening Word Documents with My Computer or Explorer

My Computer and *Windows Explorer* offer more alternatives. Switch to the folder and simply double-click on a Word document icon 📄 in the Windows applications. You can do this without even starting *Word*. The *Microsoft Office Shortcut Bar* offers another possibility with which all office documents can be loaded for editing.

Opening Documents in Word

Word documents that have been saved can be opened again for editing in several different ways. To open a document you should remember the file location. Let us begin with the quickest method to open files.

Opening Recently Used Files

There is one very quick method of opening recently used files for editing. In *Word*, select the *File* menu on the Menu bar. The names of the four most recently used *Word* documents are listed at the bottom of the menu.

There is a number in front of each name. To open one of the documents either click on the file name or type the relevant number.

Show more than 4 files

You can extend this list if four files is not enough for you. To do so, click *Options* on the *Tools* menu, select the *General* tab page and increase the value in the *Recently used file list* spin box.

Fig. 3.9: The four recently used Word documents

It is possible to show up to nine recently used files. If you want to open a still older file, click the *History* button in the dialog window of the *File/Open* command. All the files opened the previous week will appear there. The list is ordered by file name by default. Click one of the grey buttons at the top of the File list window to order the files by a different means.

Opening a Single Document in Word

Select the *Open* command on the *File* menu or click on the *Open* button 🖼 in the *Standard* toolbar. The *Open* dialog box now shows the contents of the standard document folder. If the file that you want to use happens to be there, select it and click the *Open* button.

Instead of selecting the file name and then clicking the *Open* button, you can open files more quickly by double-clicking directly on the file name. This closes the dialog box at the same time.

Searching for and Opening Files

If you cannot find the file you are searching for in the standard document folder, you can resort to the integrated search feature to look for it. In the *Open* dialog box use the *Look in* drop-down list box to change to the drive or folder that contains the documents you want to open. The subfolders of the drive/folder shown in the drop-down box appear in the large list box. Double-click on a folder to open it. *Word* documents saved here are shown with the *Word* document icon 📝 followed by their file name. To move up one level in the folder hierarchy, click the *Up One Level* button 🔼.

Use the *Views* button in the *Open* dialog box to change the way documents are displayed in the list box. Click the arrow directed downwards and belonging to the icon to choose from the following items:

- *List*
  Lists all folder and document names together with their icon in columns.

- *Details*
  Lists all folder and document names with their icon along with file size, file type and date modified in columns.

- *Properties*
  Lists all folders and documents with their name and icon and shows, provided that the document is selected, the file properties of the *Contents* and *Statistics* tab pages.

- *Preview*
  Lists all folders and documents with icon and name and shows, provided that a document is selected, a preview of the file contents.

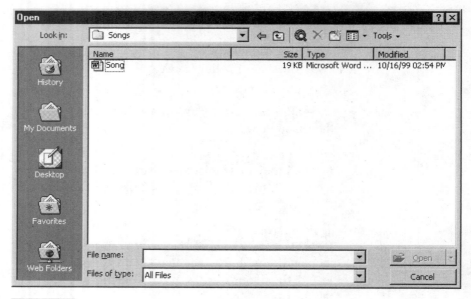

Fig. 3.10: The *Open* dialog box

Select the document you want to open using the mouse, and click on *Open*. *Word* loads the file and displays the contents in a new Word window. The file name appears in the title bar of the Word window after the application name *Microsoft Word – [document name]*.

A selected document can also be opened by pressing the ⏎ key. In the next section you will learn all about opening several documents simultaneously for editing in *Word*.

New Search

If you do not remember where you have saved your files, you can look for them. Click on the *Tools* icon and choose from the *Look in* menu. In the *Look in* dialog box you can enter more precise search criteria with AND or OR.

Property

You can access all file properties that you want to apply as search criteria in the *Property* drop-down list. In the *Condition* and *Value* boxes you can set the condition for the text property you are searching for. Click the *Add to list* button to use the selected criteria while looking for files.

Search subfolders

Check the *Search subfolders* check box if all folders contained in the folder displayed in the *Look in* drop-down box are to be included in the search.

Click on the *Find Now* button to start the search using the search criteria you have entered.

Save Search

If the search criteria you have entered are to be used for further search runs, click the *Save Search* button and give the search criteria a name.

Open Search

If, at a later stage, you want to run a new search with the search criteria you have saved earlier, you can go back to it by clicking the *Open Search* button.

Opening Several Word Files Simultaneously

You can open documents in *Word* for editing in several ways. In your daily routine it will happen quite often that several documents are required simultaneously in *Word*, for example to compare the contents of certain letters or contracts with other texts, or to exchange data among several documents.

In this section we will introduce you to some convenient methods by which you can open several files you need in one go. To do this, however, all files that you want to open should be saved in the same folder.

Open 📄

Select the *Open* command in the *File* menu or click on the *Open* button 📄. In the *Open* dialog box change to the drive and folder that contains the files you want to open.

Depending on the selected list box display mode, you can now use various methods to select all required documents. If the file names are listed one beneath the other in the list, then click on the first file name, hold down the ⌂ key and click on the last file name. Thus, all the file names in between are also selected.

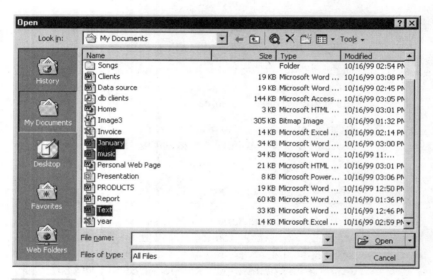

Fig. 3.11:   Opening selected files simultaneously

Select individual
file names

Alternatively, you can select documents by dragging the mouse. To do this, drag a selection rectangle with the mouse pointer. When the rectangle comes in contact with a file icon or a file name, it selects it. If you want to select the file names regardless of their sequence in the list, then start by clicking on the first file name. Hold down the Ctrl key and click on the second file name in order to select that as well. Repeat this procedure for all the documents required.

To open the selected document click on the *Open* button or press ⏎. *Word* opens the files in the sequence of the file names and displays the contents of each file in a separate Word window.

Saving Documents

If you want to use *Word* to create text documents on your PC, you will certainly want to save your correspondence in order to be able to access the documents again later. Only texts which have been saved can be loaded again, printed or used for other documents with slight modifications. In this section you will learn about how texts can be saved and re-opened in *Word* and what you have to pay attention to in the process.

Rule for File Names

When saving a *Word* document for the first time, select a folder and specify a file name. There are still certain rules for entering a file name:

- Length not to exceed 255 characters

- Spaces and diaeresis are allowed

- Special characters are allowed, excluding the following characters: / \ | > < ? *

You don't have to be concerned with the suffix, i.e. the file extension. *Word* will automatically attach the ending DOC to the name. If possible, select a file name long enough to give a precise description of the contents but still short enough to be comfortably displayed in the dialog boxes.

Saving Documents for the First Time

If you want to save a *Word* document on the hard disk, select the *Save* command in the *File* menu or the *File/Save As* command. A quicker way is to click the *Save* button ▣ on the *Standard* toolbar. If you are saving your text for the first time, which will be clear from the text: *Microsoft Word – Document [X]* in the title bar, the *Save As* dialog box will be displayed automatically.

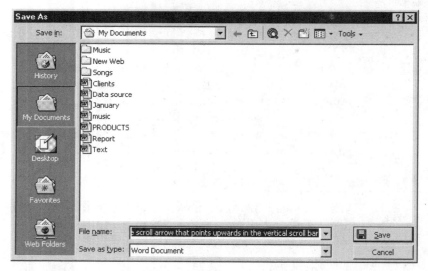

Fig. 3.12: The *Save As* dialog box

The name given in the *File name* text box consists of the first sentence of your document and is already selected. You can use this name or overwrite it with your own file name. When you are giving a file name, observe the rules for file names in *Windows 98* mentioned above.

Select a folder   Switch to the folder in which you want to save your file. When you open the dialog box first, *Word* displays the standard document folder, but the next time you save, the most recently used folder will be displayed. The Windows folder system is hierarchically arranged.

Up One Level

Using the *Up One Level* button 🔼 you can move from the current folder to the folder just above it. The currently active folder is displayed in the *Save in* box.

Create New Folder

You can create and name a new folder with the *Create New Folder* button 🗂. Click the *Save* button to save the text on the hard disk or on another storage media.

File format

By default *Word* uses the file format of the *Word for Windows 2000* processing program. The files receive the *DOC* file extension. In the *Save as type* box in the *Save As* dialog box, this appears as *Word Document (*.doc)*. Please note that this file format is not backward compatible with older *Word* versions. However, you have the possibility to save your *Word* documents in other text formats.

Save and Save As

What is the difference between the *Save* and *Save As* commands? As long as a file has not been saved either of these commands calls up the *Save As* dialog box. If you have already saved a file by a name, you can update the existing version by selecting *Save* in the *File* menu or by clicking on the *Save* button 💾 on the *Standard*-toolbar.

Save As for other save options

The *Save As* command in the *File* menu, however, calls up the *Save As* dialog box again. Choose this command to save changes under a different name or to store the file in another location, for example on a diskette, or in a different file format.

File Format

Microsoft Word 2000 works with a file format different from earlier *Word* versions. In *Word 2000* you can directly open files created in *Word 97*, *Word 95* or *Word 6.x*. All files and formatting that you created in the previous Word versions are supported by *Word 2000*. But, to be able to read *Word 2000* documents in *Word 95* you have to save a document created in *Word 2000* in *Word 95/Word 6.x* format. To do this, select the item *Word 6.0/95* in the *Save as type* drop-down list box.

If you have to change quite often from a *Word 2000* to a *Word 97* format, maybe because you have the former at home and the latter in the office, you can set in *Options* that all new *Word 2000* features are removed and replaced with features that are supported by Word 97 and then save your document. Select the *Options* command in the *Tools* menu and activate the *Save* tab page. Select the *Disable features not supported by Word 97*. You can call up the tab page directly when saving by clicking the *Tools* button in the *Save as* dialog box and choose it in *the General Options* menu.

Since not all *Word 2000* properties are supported in older *Word* versions, certain data or formatting information may be lost. Although documents stored in a previous Word version file format will also have the *DOC* ending, *Word 2000* will save them as *RTF* files.

If you open such a document, it is possible in certain cases that the *File conversion* dialog box opens and important formatting is missing.

Setting File Folders for Documents in Word

My Documents

When calling up the *Save As* command in the *File* menu the *My Documents* folder is, by default, always displayed in the *Save in* drop-down box in the *Save As* dialog box.

If you now type in a name for the file and click on *Save,* all documents that you create in *Word* are stored in this folder which is in the root directory of the hard disk *(C:\)*.

Custom folders

If you regularly use *Word* for your correspondence, you will certainly desire to organize your own folder structure so as to store your documents according to topic or task. This can be a rather laborious task, if you have to switch to your own folder every time you call-up the *Save As* command in the *File* menu.

Change default folder

However, you can tell *Word* which folder the program should propose for text storage when saving. To do this, select the *Options* command in the *Tools* menu and activate the *File Locations* tab page. Under *File types* highlight the *Documents* item and click on the *Modify* button.

To set the new standard folder open the *Look in* dropdown list in the *Modify Location* dialog box. If, for example, you are storing your files in subfolders of a folder named 'Songs', select this folder. To select the file location for a document later on, all you have to do is to double-click on a subfolder (e.g. *Jazzy*) in the list box in the *Save As* dialog box. Confirm your folder name changes by clicking on *OK* twice.

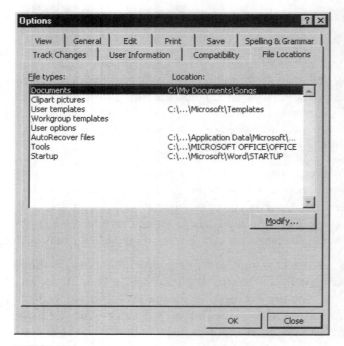

Fig. 3.13:   Setting folder for single documents

Calling-up Properties Automatically when Saving

To search for *Word* documents, click the *Tools* icon and select the *Find* option in the *Open* dialog box. Type in your search criteria and click the *Find Now* button – the search in the folder selected starts.

For this search feature, however, *Word* requires additional file information such as the *Title*, *Subject, Category* or *Keywords*.

This information can be entered prior to saving a document by selecting *Properties* on the *File* menu and activating the *Summary* tab page.

Automatic display
of properties

It is indeed easy to forget to call-up the *Summary* tab page, but we can make it simple for you: Activate the *Options* command in the *Tools* menu, select the *Save* tab page, check the *Prompt for document properties* check box and confirm with *OK*.

When you initially call-up *File/Save* or *File/Save As*, Word then automatically displays the *[Name of the Document].doc Properties* dialog box with the *Summary* tab page.

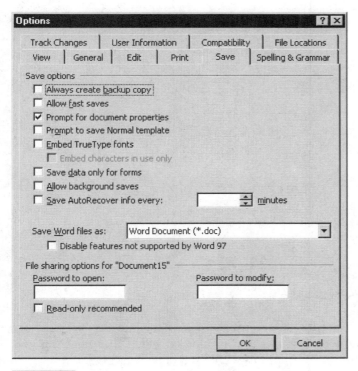

Fig. 3.14:   Activating automatic prompt for file properties

You can now enter further document information in the text boxes of this tab page that can be used by the search feature and by other *Word* features as well (e.g. *Revision*). Type in the title you want to use for the file search in the *Title* text box. The title you selected may be different from the file name.

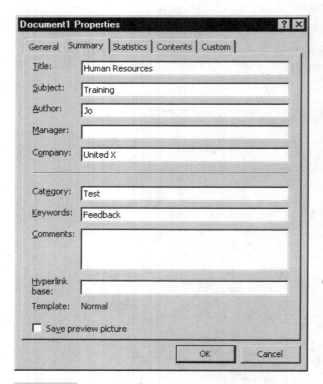

Fig. 3.15: The file information is asked for while saving

Enter the subject of the document into the *Subject* box. Use this property to group connected files enabling you to search for all files with the same subject.

Use *Category* to group related files enabling you to search for all files of the same category.

In the *Keywords* box enter one or more words you want to use when searching for this file.

In the *Comments* box write remarks that may help you locate the file when searching with the *Comments* criteria. Click *OK* to save the document. The file properties can be changed afterwards by choosing *File/Properties*.

Statistics tab page

The *Statistics* tab page contains information about the number of words, lines and letters. On the *Custom* tab page you can specify your own file properties.

Save preview
picture

If you check the *Save preview picture* check box on the *Summary* tab page, a miniature picture of the file contents is saved. In this case you can get a preview display of the graphically saved first page in other programs besides *Word*.

Accelerating the Saving Process

Should you save your files using the *Word* default settings, a so-called *full save* will always be performed. If you are editing long documents, it is highly advisable to save every once in a while at regular intervals, as this will protect your documents in the event of system errors or power cuts. In this instance, however, the occasionally very long storage times are a distinct disadvantage.

Such long storage times occur predominantly for documents in which you have inserted many graphics, since these can quickly increase the file size to values of approximately 10 MB. However, *Word* offers you a saving option allowing documents saved once to be saved quickly while you are working with them.

Fast saves

To activate the *Allow fast saves* feature, first select the *Options* command in the *Tools* menu and then select the *Save* tab page. Next check the *Allow fast saves* check box in the *Save options* group and confirm the *Options* dialog box by clicking *OK*.

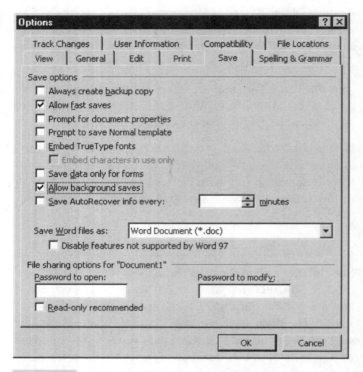

Fig. 3.16: Activating *Allow fast saves* of documents

Word is now able to accelerate the saving procedure. However, the document should have been saved completely once before this. Only then this in-between saving feature saves the changes made in the document at the end of the file.

Should you have completed editing a long document, uncheck the *Allow fast saves* feature again in order to save the entire document. A complete save reduces the file size of the document as the changes that have been saved with the *Allow fast saves* feature are added at the end of the document.

Backup copy

As soon as you check the *Always create backup copy* check box, the *Allow fast saves* check box is automatically unchecked and vice versa, as only one saving option can be operational at a time.

Closing Documents

After creating a document with *Word*, you should save your work, allowing you to come back to this information later. Now the question arises what you can do with the saved or printed letter on the screen. Firstly, it is possible to open several documents in *Word* at the same time.

Open - Close

However, this does not answer our question. If you do not need a document any more, you may remove it from the *Word* memory. This procedure is called 'Close'. This feature is, so to speak, the opposite of the *Open* command by which you load a saved document in the memory.

File/Close

You have many ways of closing a document. For example, select the *Close* command on the *File* menu. If you have not made any changes in your document since you last saved it, the document will close without further prompts.

If, on the other hand, you have made changes since you last saved it, then a message will appear asking you whether you want to save the changes you have made and giving you the option to either accept, reject or cancel them.

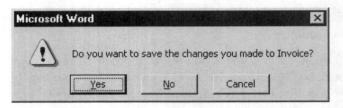

Fig. 3.17:   Prompt before closing

Confirm this prompt with *Yes* if you want to save the changes before closing the document.

Click on *No* if you do not want to save the document. In this case, any changes that you have made will be lost in the process.

If you have called up the *Close* command by mistake, click on *Cancel*. You will then return to your document.

Close ☒

You can close a *Word* window and all files within it very quickly by clicking on the *Close* button ☒ in the title bar of the program window. If only a Word window is open, there is a separate *Close* button ☒ to close the document at the end of the menu.

System menu box

It is also possible to close a document by double-clicking the *System Menu* box. Double-click the 🖺 Word icon in the title bar. The close command is in the System menu.

Preventing Data Loss

Word provides different safety measures to prevent your data from being lost due to unintentional deletion or sudden power cuts. Firstly, it can keep a *backup copy*, which is a duplicate of the saved file. Secondly, *Word* automatically saves your documents at a predefined time interval so that it can recover them if, for example, a power cut occurs.

Creating an Automatic Backup Copy of the Document

If you want *Word* to create a backup copy of each document it saves, select the *Options* command in the *Tools* menu and activate the *Save* tab page. Check the *Always create backup copy* check box under *Save options* and confirm by clicking *OK*.

Thereafter, *Word* will create a backup copy of the previous version of a document whenever it saves. A new backup copy always replaces the existing one.

Word saves the backup copy in the same folder as the original document with the file extension WBK *(Word BacKup)* and indicates the document as *backup copy of [document name]*.

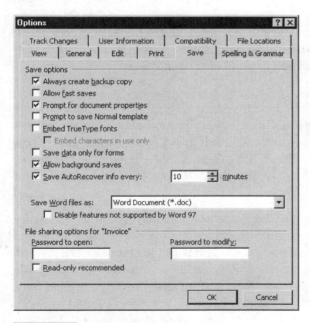

Fig. 3.18:   Setting save options

Always create
backup copy
not available

If you activate the *Always create backup copy* check box, the *Allow fast saves* check box will be cleared automatically as *Word* can only create a backup copy when it performs a full save.

Opening Backup Copies

If you have unintentionally deleted an original document and have also emptied the *Recycle bin*, you can open the saved backup copy of a document, provided *Always create backup copy* has been selected in the check box on the *Save* tab in the *Options* dialog box.

To open a backup, select *File/Open*. Select *All Files* in the *File type* box and click the name of the folder that contained the document. Click the *Details* button ▦ in the *Views* menu to display the contents of this folder. The backup copy will be saved under *Backup of [document name]* and its file type is *.wbk*. Click the name of the desired backup copy and then click *Open*.

Recovering Documents after a Power Cut

If a *Word* document is not properly closed, you may not be able to open and edit it any more in certain cases. This may occur due to a power cut or a power fluctuation, or when you have switched off your PC without shutting it down properly.

Automatic saving
all ...

Should you want to protect yourself from data losses by saving an opened file at regular intervals, then activate the automatic saving feature. Select the *Options* command on the *Tools* menu and activate the *Save* tab page. Decide how often your files must be saved by selecting the *Save AutoRecover info every* check box. Don't forget to check whether the option is on (a tick is shown).

Automatically saved documents are stored in a particular format and in a special folder until the actual saving procedure takes place. When restarting *Word* after a power cut or some other problem that occurred before you had the chance to save your document, *Word* opens all automatically saved documents which can then be saved correctly.

Location for backup copies

You decide where to locate your backup copies. Click the *Options* command in the *Tools* menu and then *File location*. Activate the *Save AutoRecover file* icon in the *File type* box. Confirm by pressing the *Modify* button and then confirm with *OK*.

[Name of Document] Recovered

Usually, after a power cut all you have to do is restart *Word*. Then all the documents that were open when the problem occurred will be displayed again. *[Name of Document] Recovered* will appear in the title bar. Now save the files in a folder by clicking *Save As* in the *File* menu. If a message appears asking you whether or not you want to replace the existing document, click on *Yes*.

With this method you lose only the changes that you made after the last automatic saving procedure. Repeat these steps for each recovered document. All recovered unsaved documents are deleted in case you close *Word* with *File/Exit*.

ASD

In case the recovered document cannot be saved or opened by *Word* after a power cut, proceed as follows:

Restart *Word* and select *File/Open*. Open the *Temp* folder which is generally found in the *Windows* folder. If you have assigned a different folder for temporary files in your *AUTOEXEC.BAT* start file, open this folder instead. Click on the *All Files* item in the *File type* box. All recovered documents will appear with the *ASD* (*AutoSave Document*) extension.

Open the restored document and save it as described above. In case a message appears enquiring whether or not you want replace the existing document, click on *Yes*.

Searching

Autosave

documents

You can find automatically saved documents more quickly by selecting the *Open* command in the *File* menu and typing **.asd* with *Tools/Find* and for the file name property. Then click the *Find now* button.

Protect Files from Unauthorized Access and Modification

Important documents have to be managed in a particular way. You should prevent such documents from being unintentionally modified or deleted.

To avoid file data loss or undesired file modifications you can create backup copies and set a password.

Confidential documents should be inaccessible or unreadable for unauthorized persons within or outside *Word*.

To prevent any unauthorized persons from accessing and reading *Word* documents, you can assign a password. These measures of protection are effective by setting a password given only to those persons whom you want to allow access to the document.

Thanks to these mechanisms it is made clear, even in a team, who can open or modify a file.

With *Password to Open*, it is possible to open and modify a file only if the password is known. If you insert a password in the *Password to Modify* box, it is possible to open the file even without knowing the password, but the file cannot be saved with the same name anymore.

Insert the password in the *Save* tab page of the *Tools/Options* command. It is also possible to enter the tab page via the *Save* dialog box.

Passwords

A password gives you efficient protection. Only people who know the password are able to remove the protection.

Setting a password in *Word* is mainly a matter of a saving procedure. Valid passwords abide by the following rules:

- A maximum of 15 characters in length

- Case-sensitive

- Combination of letters, numbers and symbols

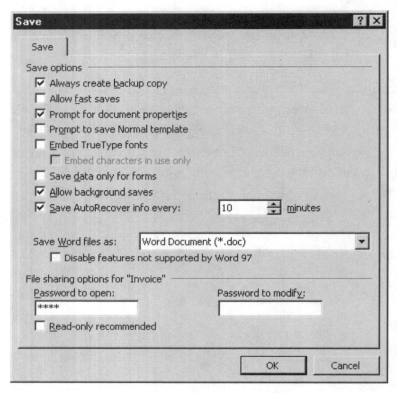

Entering a Password to modify

The password entry is displayed with '*' and, to ensure that there are no typing errors, it has to be re-entered and confirmed by clicking *OK*.

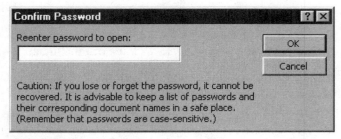

Fig. 3.20:   Confirming a password

Next start saving by clicking on the *Save* button in the *Save as* dialog box.

Protection Options

Word offers you many methods of protecting your documents from unauthorized persons. Such methods of protection are of importance for content-sensitive documents, such as client files, income tax declarations or even very private texts. Naturally you should protect the files from unauthorized access especially in situations with other users working on your computer or having access to it in any way.

This happens frequently and sooner than it might initially appear. Good examples of this are company PCs, computers in networks but also Internet or online access. Unauthorized persons have, in all of the above cases, access to these computers.

Word offers you three steps enabling you to protect your files:

Step 1

Step 1 – *Read only recommended* – this message appears when a file is opened.

Step 2

Step 2 – *Password to Modify* – this enables only those persons who know the password to open the files in such a way that they can be saved again with the original name.

Step 3

Step 3 – *Password to Open* – this offers the maximum protection: Unless you know the password, you cannot access it at all.

Setting a Password

To save a document that contains very important personal or secret information with password protection, select *File/Save As*. In the *Save As* dialog box enter a file name in the *File name* box. Then click on the *Tools* button and select the *General Options* command to display the following dialog box:

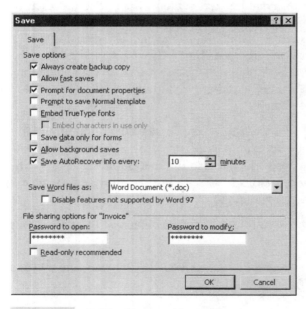

Fig. 3.21:   Setting Password to modify

Now enter a password in the *Password to Open* text box to allow only authorized users to open and edit the document, or to cancel the protection of the document. Your password will only be displayed as '*' so that those who may be present while you are entering it cannot read it.

A good password contains more than four characters and is not identical with your name or your wife's/husband's one. Number combinations such as dates of birthdays or the like are also risky.

Such passwords can frequently be guessed too easily. When you are setting the password, observe any capitalization of letters. Confirm your password by clicking the *OK* button.

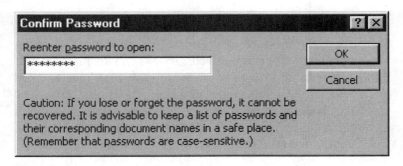

Fig. 3.22:   Confirm your password

For safety reasons *Word* will display a new dialog box in which you have to re-enter a second time the same password. Again confirm by clicking the *OK* button. If the passwords are not identical, an error message will appear and you will have to enter your password again. Then click *Save* in the *Save As* dialog box to finally save the file.

Close the file and try to open the document again, for example by clicking the entry on the *Recently Used File List* on the *File* menu. The *Password* dialog box will appear and you will be expected to type in the correct password. Enter the password and confirm by clicking *OK*. *Word* will then open the document.

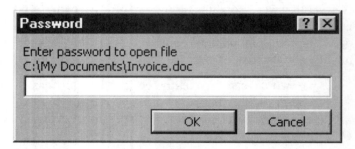

Fig. 3.23: Password prompt when opening a file

An error message will appear if you enter the wrong password. If this does occur, try again with *File/Open*. If you want to change a password, you first have to open your file with the correct password. Then access the *Save As* dialog box and click *Options*, or the *Save* tab page in the dialog box of the *Tools/Options* command. Delete or change the present password and confirm by clicking the *OK* button.

Opening a File with Temporary Protection

If you want to open a file and still be sure that you will not be able to accidentally overwrite the original version while you are working in it, it is not worthwhile to set a password.

Commands and settings

In this case you can choose the *Read-Only* option when you're opening the file. To do this, click *File/Open*, select the file name in the *Name* list and click the triangle next to *Open*.

Open

Open
Open Read-Only
Open as Copy
Open in Browser

Fig. 3.24:   Opening a document as read only

Click the *Open Read Only* command on the popup menu. The protection is lost after closing the file.

Protecting Documents with Read Only Recommended

Word offers different modes for protecting your documents from access by unauthorized persons or from accidental overwriting. If you are the only one working on your PC, the protection given by Step 1 – *Read only recommended* – is generally sufficient. It can be accepted or rejected every time you open the document.

Options

To prevent data that you want to protect from being overwritten, select *Save As* on the *File* menu. Select the file location in the *Save As* dialog box and enter the file name. Then click the *Tools* button and select in the *General Options* menu to display the following dialog box:

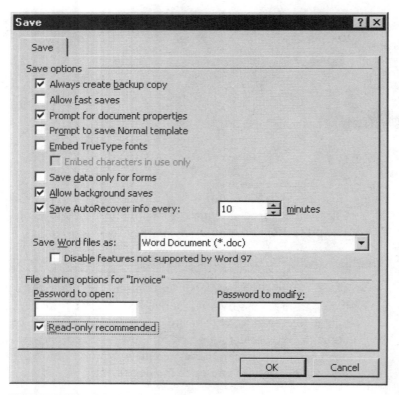

Check the *Read only recommended* check box and close the *Options* dialog box by clicking the *OK* button. Click *Save* to save the document.

When you open the document, a recommendation for read only mode appears and is activated by clicking on *Yes*. This will only prevent unintentional overwriting of the original text. If you click *No* the document will be opened without any protection.

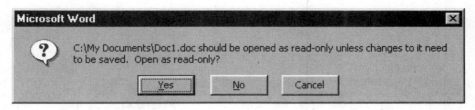

The *Cancel* button closes the dialog box without opening the read only recommended file.

Saving with Password Protection

Since the *Read-Only* protection can also be rejected, this mode does not totally protect the file content. For this reason *Word* offers you another protection mode: Step 2 provides password protection. The password protection can only be deactivated by someone who knows the correct password.

Options

To save a file with a password select *File/Save As* and click the *Tools* button and *General Options*.

Password protection

Set a password in the *Password to Open* text box if you want to allow only authorized users to make changes and save the document again with its original name. Without this password the file can only be opened later on as read only and has to be saved under a new name.

Your password is displayed using '*' characters so that those who are present while you are entering your password cannot read it. A good password contains more than four characters, contains letters and numbers and does not correspond to your name or your wife's/husband's one.

Number combinations of birthdays or the like are also risky. Such passwords can very easily be guessed. When you are choosing the password, be careful about writing letters in capitals. Confirm your password by clicking the *OK* button.

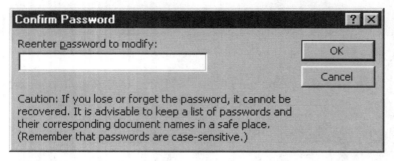

Confirm Password   ? X

Reenter password to modify:

[   ]   [OK   ]

                                                         [Cancel]

Caution: If you lose or forget the password, it cannot be
recovered. It is advisable to keep a list of passwords and
their corresponding document names in a safe place.
(Remember that passwords are case-sensitive.)

Fig. 3.27:   Confirm password

For security reasons *Word* displays a new dialog box in which you have to re-enter the same password. Again confirm by clicking the *OK* button. If the passwords are not identical, an error message will appear and you will have to enter your password again. Once you have done this, click *Save* in the *Save As* dialog box to finally save the file.

Password

Close the file and try to open the document, for example by selecting it on the *File* menu. The *Password* dialog box will appear, waiting for you to type in the correct password.

Enter the password and confirm by clicking the *OK* button. *Word* opens the document and gives you full access.

Password-protected

To open a *Password to modify* protected document, type in the password and click the *OK* button. If you do not enter the password, and have made some changes to such a document, you will have to save the document under another name.

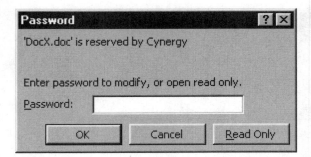

Fig. 3.28: Prompting for password when opening the file

Saving File Versions

Word 2000 provides a way to save different versions of your documents within one file.

Different variations and proposals can be saved in the original file and it can be decided later which file version will be used.

You can create these different file versions automatically when closing the file or you can set the saving time of a version yourself.

Setting File Versions Automatically

If you want *Word* to save the current version as well when closing a file, but without overwriting the original version in the process, select *File/Versions* and check the *Automatically save a version on close* check box. Close the dialog box by clicking the *Close* button.

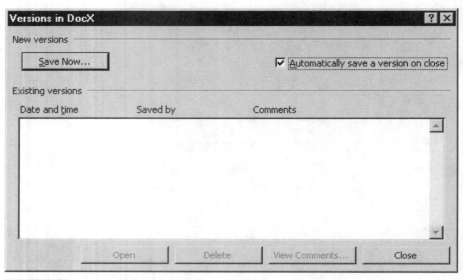

Creating versions automatically

Saving File Versions Manually

If you do not want *Word* to create the versions automatically, but wish to determine the version yourself, select *File/Versions* and click on the *Save Now* button.

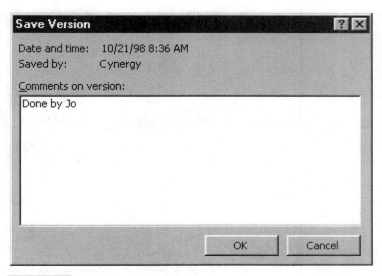

Fig. 3.30:   Enter a comment on the version

Afterwards you will be given the opportunity to insert a comment on the current version which will later be displayed in the dialog box and can be helpful when you are deciding which version you want to open.

After entering your comments click the *OK* button.

Opening File Versions

If several versions of a document have been saved, this will be indicated by a special icon on the status bar.

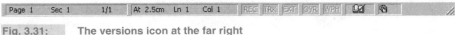

Fig. 3.31:   The versions icon at the far right

To access the saved versions double-click on the *File Versions* icon or select *File/Version*. The list box will display all versions.

157

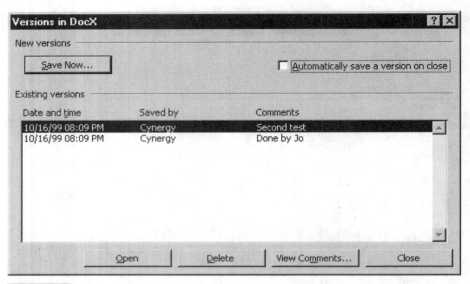

Besides the creation date and time of the version, the author and the comments are also saved and displayed in the list box. To enable you to read a long comment in its entirety, click the *View Comments* button.

Automatic version

When using the automatic version you will not be given an opportunity to insert a comment. That is the reason why, in this case, *Automatic Version* is displayed instead of the comment.

Open version

To open the version, click on the name of the desired version first and then on the *Open* button.

Delete version

Saving more than one version in a file does, of course, increase the size of a document. Therefore, you should make a point of regularly checking which versions you do not require any longer. Delete the file versions not longer needed by clicking the *Delete* button in the *Versions in Document xy* dialog box.

Deleting and Renaming Word Files

If you went on creating new files indefinitely, the capacity of the hard disk or diskette would quickly be filled up and the documents folder would soon be too unwieldy to handle.

Delete and rename in Windows

It may occasionally happen that a file name is no longer appropriate or precise enough, either because it cannot be distinguished from other files created later or because it does not fully describe the file content. In such cases you can rename the file.

The delete command and the command for renaming, however, do not belong to the *Word* commands, since this is part of Windows' job. However, with the introduction of *Windows 98*, it became possible to change the names of documents and even delete files in the *Save As* and *Open* dialog boxes.

Before calling-up the dialog box you should close the file you want to delete or rename. Then select either *File/Open* or *File/Save As*.

In the dialog box, right-click on the name of the file that you want to delete or rename. If the file is not displayed, you should first open the folder the file is stored in.

To rename it, select the *Rename* command in the shortcut menu. The original file name will appear with a blue background and you can overwrite it with the new file name. Do not omit the dot and the *DOC* suffix at the end of the name. A file that you want to call:

```
Protocol
```

should thus be entered correctly as:

```
Protocol.doc
```

Suffix

If you forget to enter the suffix, Windows will point this out to you and you'll be given a chance to add it. Finish the new name entry by pressing the *Enter* key ⏎.

To delete a file, you can also right-click on the file name in the *Open* or *Save As* dialog box and select the *Delete* command on the shortcut menu. You can also left-click on the file name with your mouse and then select the *Delete* icon.

Windows does not immediately delete a file upon selecting the delete command, but relocates it to a reserved storage space for safety reasons, called the *Recycle Bin*. Now you also have to confirm that the file can be moved to the *Recycle Bin*.

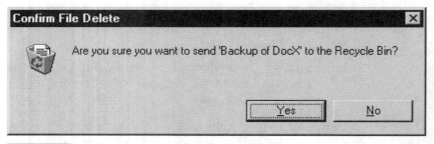

Fig. 3.33:   Deleting a file

Click the *Yes* button to confirm the relocation. Only after emptying the *Recycle Bin* or after you have deleted the file in the *Recycle Bin* is it finally eliminated from the storage medium.

As long as the file is in the *Recycle Bin,* you can still undo the *Delete* command. Open the *Recycle Bin*, select the file name and click *Restore* in the *File* menu.

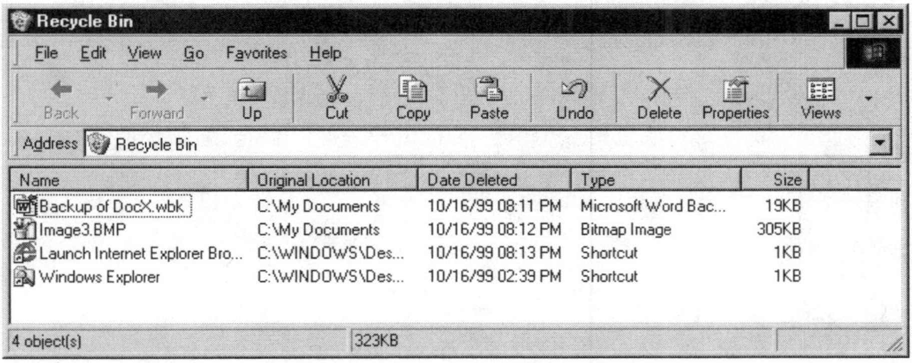

Fig. 3.34: The contents of the recycle bin

To empty the *Recycle Bin* immediately after you have deleted a file, to ensure that the file cannot be restored by anyone else, right-click the *Recycle Bin* icon on the desktop and select *Empty Recycle Bin* on the shortcut menu.

4. Formatting

Formatting in *Word* means applying certain formatting attributes to a text. Some examples of these formatting attributes are:

- Font

- Font size

- Font color

- Font style, e.g. *Bold* or *Italics*

- Effects, like *Shadow*, *Embossing*, *Engraving*

- Line spacing

- Print layout

- Borders and shading

- Background

- Paragraph splitting

Some of these formatting attributes can be applied to single characters, while others can only be applied to an entire paragraph. *Word* is a paragraph-oriented processing program, and therefore most of the formatting functions are related to paragraphs and are stored in the paragraph marks.

Differences Between Paragraph and Character Formats

A formatting attribute applicable only to characters, i.e. to one word or to one text section only, is termed character formatting. Character formatting attributes are *Bold*, *Italics* and *Underlined*.

Since *Word* organizes the text in paragraphs, you can also set formatting for an entire paragraph. This is called paragraph formatting. Examples of this are *Line spacings*, *Alignment*, *Spacing Before* and *After* a paragraph, and *Indentation*.

Formatting categories

In *Word* the different formatting commands are divided into categories which are easy to differentiate. For example, you will find the following formatting categories: *Font*, *Paragraph*, *Tabs* and *Section formatting*. A font formatting can be applied to a single character. Paragraph formatting concerns an entire paragraph, while a section formatting applies either to an entire document or a particular section of it. Tab formatting applies only to the tab stops within the selected paragraphs.

Format menu

Formatting commands are located on the *Format* menu. To set a font formatting, select the desired characters and choose the *Format/Font* command. If you want to format a paragraph, it is necessary the insertion cursor is in the relevant paragraph. Then select *Format/Paragraph*. If several paragraphs are to be formatted at the same time select the relevant paragraphs beforehand. The most important paragraph and font formatting styles are:

Font formats

Font, font size, font styles (bold, italics, underlined), superscript and subscript

Paragraph formats

Alignments (left- or right-aligned, centered, justified), left/right indents, line spacing

Tabs

The rules for formatting paragraphs also apply to tab formatting. In *Word* you can set different tab stops for each single paragraph, and generally a tab format concerns an entire paragraph.

Section formats

Section formatting implies working with the basic properties of a document, such as paper format, margins or headers and footers. A document usually consists of only one section. If there are several, the insertion cursor has to be located in the desired section in order to perform the section formatting. For example, you could create different headers or footers or change from portrait to landscape mode.

Quick Formatting

When talking about formatting, it can basically be said that all roads lead to Rome. There are usually several ways to apply a certain formatting, not only one in particular. Some of the different methods to apply formatting include:

- Buttons on the *Formatting* toolbar

- Key combinations

- Dialog box options

Formatting toolbar

For most daily correspondence the formatting commands on the *Formatting* toolbar are sufficient. They can be used very easily, since a click on a button or the selection of a list item suffices.

Formatting with the ruler

Another way of applying formatting quickly with the mouse, especially for indents or tab stops, is by using the horizontal ruler.

Shortcuts

Shortcut keys come in handy for the advanced user who wishes to work very quickly and effectively. Using shortcut keys, formatting is speeded up even more during text insertion.

**Formatting with
a dialog box**

In case formatting cannot be executed with the help of the *Formatting* toolbar, open the dialog box of the corresponding category via the *Format* menu.

Buttons on the *Formatting* Toolbar

By default, *Word* displays both the *Formatting* and *Standard* toolbars containing the most important program commands that can be called-up by using the mouse.

The most important formatting commands are on the *Formatting* toolbar. They represent a shortcut for document formatting using the mouse.

Fig. 4.1:   The *Formatting* toolbar

ScreenTip

The names of each single button on the *Formatting* toolbar will appear approximately one second after you place the mouse over the button in question. *Word* will then display a *ScreenTip*. If the *ScreenTip* does not appear on your screen, select the *Toolbars* command on the *View* menu and choose the *Customize* command from the submenu. Check the *Show ScreenTips on toolbars* check box on the *Options* tab page. If you check the *Show shortcut keys in ScreenTips* check box, the shortcut keys – when available – will also be displayed on the *ScreenTip*. Close the dialog box by clicking the *Close* button.

The following summary lists all the control elements on the *Formatting* toolbar, their names in the *ScreenTip* and their description:

	Name	Description
Standard	*Style*	applies a style
Times New Roman	*Font*	changes the font
12	*Font Size*	changes the font size
F	*Bold*	formats selected text in bold
K	*Italics*	formats selected text in italics
U	*Underline*	underlines selected text
	Align Left	left-aligns selected text
	Center	centers selected text
	Align Right	right-aligns selected text
	Justify	aligns the selected paragraphs with both the left and the right margins
	Numbering	numbers selected text
	Bullets	adds bullets to selected paragraphs
	Decrease Indent	decreases indent of a paragraph
	Increase Indent	increases indent of a paragraph
	Outside Border	adds or removes a border around the selected text
	Highlight	highlights selected text in color
	Font Color	colors selected text

Quick Formatting with the Ruler

Usually many *Word* formatting commands have to be further specified in the corresponding dialog boxes. If you want to format certain paragraphs, tab stops or tables by visual estimate, it is usually unnecessary to call-up the command on the *Format* menu and then to set formatting options in the corresponding dialog box.

Display the ruler

Once you are acquainted with the usual formatting methods, you can also execute certain formatting with the mouse via a special *Word* feature, the *Ruler*.

If the ruler is not visible, open the *View* menu and select the *Ruler* command. Anybody who has ever worked on a typewriter will now have a certain 'déja vu' feeling.

Horizontal and vertical ruler

In the *Print Layout* view *Word* displays two rulers simultaneously, a horizontal and a vertical one. In the *Normal* view only the horizontal ruler is displayed, since in this view page borders are not displayed. Page margins, indentation, tab stops and tables in the current paragraph are displayed on the ruler. In addition to that, the ruler comes with a centimetre/inch scale.

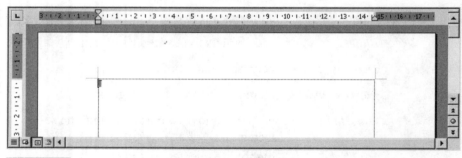

Fig. 4.2: Rulers displayed in the *Print Layout* view

You will find markers on the left end of the ruler. The upper triangular marker shows the indent of the first line while the one below shows the indent of the subsequent lines. With the square marker it is possible to move both triangles while keeping the same gap between them. Indents can be changed by dragging the markers with the mouse , but only in 0.25cm steps.

The triangular marker on the right end of the ruler sets the right indent. The transition between the grey and the white ruler area in both rulers represents the page margins can which can be changed by dragging the mouse.

Exact position

If you press the ⎡Alt⎤ key while making the ruler markers slide, the exact position of the marker will be indicated between two arrows. Now you can move the triangular markers and carry out a more precise adjustment.

Tables

If you place the cursor in a cell of a table, the table lines and columns will be displayed with the so-called *Adjust Table Row* and *Move Table Column* markers. By resorting to them, you can fix both the cell height and width with the mouse. An easy way to enter more precise formatting is by double-clicking one of the markers, which will call-up a dialog box.

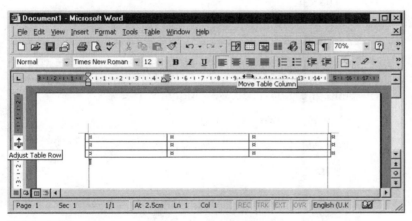

Fig. 4.3:   An activated table and ruler markers

Tab stops are also displayed on the ruler. You can create, move and delete tab stops. The little grey lines at the bottom edge of the horizontal ruler represent the default settings of tab stops.

Setting tabs

User-defined tab stops can be created by clicking the [L] button on the left of the horizontal ruler and then by clicking again at the desired position on the ruler to set the tab.

Move or delete tabs

Tab stops can be moved by holding down the mouse button. If you drag a tab stop downwards and out of the ruler, then the tab stop will be deleted.

While altering settings for margins, indents or tab stops with the control elements on the ruler, be careful in always pointing at the marker very precisely. In certain cases the mouse pointer changes in shape. You can then make the changes, mouse button held down. Changes made with the ruler by using the mouse are limited to a precision of 0.25cm. In case you must be more accurate and precise, work either with dialog boxes or press the (Alt) key.

Formatting with Shortcut Keys

If you prefer not to use the mouse when you are editing your text or if you want to apply formatting even while entering it, you can use shortcut keys.

Font Formatting

- Bold   [Ctrl]+[B]
- Italics   [Ctrl]+[I]
- Underline   [Ctrl]+[U]
- *Font* list box   [Ctrl]+[⇧]+[F]
- *Font Size* list box [Ctrl]+[⇧]+[P]
- Increase font size [Ctrl]+[⇧]+[>]
- Decrease font size [Ctrl]+[⇧]+[<]
- Capitalize letters [Ctrl]+[⇧]+[A]

- Change case   ⌂ + F3
- Underline words   Ctrl + ⌂ + W
- Double-underline   Ctrl + ⌂ + D
- Hide   Ctrl + ⌂ + H
- Small caps   Ctrl + ⌂ + K
- Subscript   Ctrl + =
- Superscript   Ctrl + ⌂ + +

Switches

Most shortcut keys operate like switches. If you press once, formatting is applied; if you press a second time, formatting is removed. Shortcut keys for increasing or decreasing fonts do so by one point at a time whenever you press the key combination. The key combination to change the case switches the selected character sequence from *All capital letters*, *All small letters*, *First letter capitalized*. Other shortcut keys related to font and character formatting are:

- Open *Font* dialog box   Ctrl + D
- Remove manual character formatting   Ctrl + Space
- Font icon   Ctrl + ⌂ + B
- Review text formatting   ⌂ + F1
- Copy format   Ctrl + ⌂ + C
- Paste format   Ctrl + ⌂ + V

If you have problems memorizing shortcut keys, you can make the shortcut key for the corresponding button be played on the *ScreenTip*. Select *Tools/Customize* and check both the *Show ScreenTips on toolbars* and *Show shortcut keys in ScreenTips* check boxes on the *Options* tab page. This will help you memorize the shortcuts in a very short time.

You can set additional key combinations or buttons for font and character formatting by customizing *Word* or by adding them to the toolbars. For more information see Chapter 15. Many paragraph formats can be set or cleared again with key combinations:

Alignments and Indents

- Center   `Ctrl`+`E`
- Justify   `Ctrl`+`J`
- Left Align   `Ctrl`+`L`
- Right Align   `Ctrl`+`R`
- Left indent   `Ctrl`+`M`
- Remove left indent   `Ctrl`+`⇧`+`M`
- Increase hanging indent   `Ctrl`+`T`
- Reduce hanging indent   `Ctrl`+`⇧`+`T`

Line Spacing

- Single-spacing   `Ctrl`+`1`
- Double-spacing   `Ctrl`+`2`
- 1.5-line spacing   `Ctrl`+`5`
- Spacing before one line   `Strg`+`0`
- Remove paragraph formatting   `Ctrl`+`Q`

Styles

- *Regular* style   ⎡Ctrl⎤+⎡ ⬦ ⎤+⎡N⎤
- *Heading 1* style   ⎡Alt⎤+⎡1⎤
- *Heading 2* style   ⎡Alt⎤+⎡2⎤
- *Heading 3* style   ⎡Alt⎤+⎡3⎤
- *List Bullet* style   ⎡Ctrl⎤+⎡ ⬦ ⎤+⎡L⎤

Font Formatting

The font, together with all its properties, has a fundamental impact on the appearance of a document. All attributes characteristic to the font can be altered through
character formatting.

To change the formatting of an already entered text, select the text beforehand. An exception to this rule is the
case of character formatting when you want to apply it to
a word. In this case click the word and subsequently apply a character formatting.

Changing Font and Font Size in Word

If you are writing a letter in *Word*, the processing program applies the default font in the default size without
any special formatting.

Default font   By default *Word* uses the *Times New Roman* font in the *12
Point* font size. Each character entered in *Word* can be
formatted in any available font and font size.

For texts that have already been entered, select the desired characters, text paragraphs or the entire text with
⎡Ctrl⎤+⎡A⎤. Then select the *Font* command on the *Format*
menu to call-up the *Font* dialog box.

The current font and the applied font size are displayed in the *Font* and *Size* list boxes. The *Preview* box shows how your document will look like with the selected option. All available fonts are listed in the *Font* list box.

If that is the case of a scalable *TrueType* font, you will get notice of it in the *Preview* box (in the *Font* list box on the toolbar you will find the font marked with the **T͞T** symbol in front of the font name). Select the new font in the *Font* list box with the mouse. If necessary, use the scroll bar to scroll through the list of installed fonts.

Select a new value (measured in *Point* size) from the *Size* list box. Finally, confirm by clicking the *OK* button.

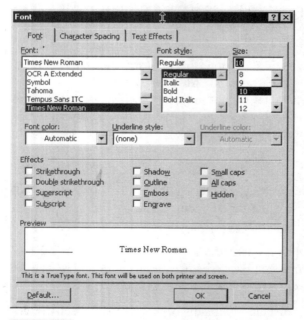

Fig. 4.4:   The *Format/Font* dialog box in Word

You can format your text more quickly by using the *Font* and *Font Size* drop-down boxes on the *Formatting* toolbar. If the toolbar is not already visible, choose *Formatting* from the *Toolbars* submenu on the *View* menu. Open the drop-down boxes and select your new settings.

Intermediary font sizes

The font size can also be typed directly into the *Font Size* box. To this purpose, click in the text area and overwrite the value by entering a new one measured in *Point* size. Then press the *Enter* key ⏎ to confirm the font size.

Font formats in shortcut menus

You might want to apply this procedure when you are setting values not listed in the font size list. The maximum possible value is 1638 Point - this value corresponds to a letter about 58cm high!

Both font and font size can be set either before or during text insertion and remain valid until you apply a different formatting. The *Font* command on the shortcut menu is also available to you if you select a text and right-click the mouse.

Font Formatting in *Word*: bold, italics and underline

In the previous section we have already explained how to set both font and font size in *Word*. You will now learn how to format text paragraphs, single characters or an entire text in **Bold**, *Italics* or <u>Underline</u>.

Before you can apply font styles to a text you first have to select the text.

The *Bold*, *Italics* and *Underline* font styles are applied either by clicking the relevant buttons or by selecting the *Font* command on the *Format* menu. If you want to format a text paragraph with the *Bold* font style, first select the paragraph. In the *Font* dialog box select the *Font style*

Font style

command. In the *Font style* list box select *Bold* on the *Font* tab page.

Using the same procedure you can format selected characters in *Italics*, *Bold Italics* or you can also remove formatted styles by choosing the *Regular* font style.

Fig. 4.5   The *Font style* list box

Preview

The *Preview* box shows you how your document will look like with the options selected. You can have your selected text displayed in the *Preview* box or, alternatively, the name of the selected font will be automatically displayed with its corresponding character formattings, if no text has been selected.

Underline

Select the *Underline* font style from the *Underline* list box. You can select *Single*, *Words only*, *Double*, *Dotted* underline in addition to several other styles, such as dot-dash, wave, etc. Set all the font formatting desired and click *OK* to confirm the formatting.

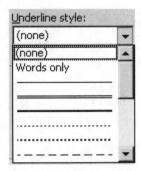

Fig. 4.6: The *Underline* drop-down list in the *Font* dialog box.

Select *(none)* in the *Underline* drop-down list to clear an already applied underline.

Buttons

Your work will be speeded up if you use the buttons on the *Formatting* toolbar. For bold text paragraphs, click the *Bold* button **B**. The *Italics* button *I* displays characters that you select in italics, and the *Underline* button **U** will underline them.

Effects

For more elaborate formatting, such as double underlining, call-up the *Format/Font* dialog box. For strikenthrough texts check the *Strikethrough* check box in the *Effects* option group.

You will find more options in this options group box, such as *Engrave*, *Outline*, *Emboss* and *Shadow*.

WYSIWYG

The document will be printed exactly the way you see it on the screen – regardless of your printer. This is called *WYSIWYG* and stands for *What you see is what you get*.

Highlighting Text Sections

Some documents are edited by several people, while in the case of other texts you might not know how to phrase particular text sections.

In both cases it is convenient to be able to highlight the relevant parts in order to be able to distinguish them from the rest of the text.

Of course you can always give the text a different color by calling up *Format/Font*, but this procedure is relatively complex and takes a lot of time.

Word as a text marker

It is much easier if you highlight the important text parts by using a kind of "electronic markers". In Word it is possible to highlight paragraphs with different colors. Since the available colors are very fluorescent, they look like text markers. This feature is called *Highlight* in *Word*.

To highlight certain parts of your text so that they stand out from the surrounding text, select the text or the element you want to highlight. Then click the drop-down button of the *Highlight* button on the *Formatting* toolbar and choose the color you want. Check you have actually highlighted the section by clicking once again and eliminating the selection.

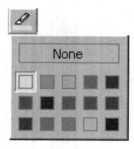

Fig. 4.7: Available highlight colors

You can now select the next element you want to high-light in your document. To highlight it with the currently selected color, just click on the *Highlight* button. Choose *None* from the drop-down list to cancel the high-light. Highlights are printed too! They appear as a grey background when printed on a black and white printer.

Highlighting can be very useful to the person receiving a document for on-screen checking of the document parts.

Apply a light color to highlight document parts that are to be printed on a black and white or a dot-matrix printer.

To change the highlight color click on the drop-down button next to the *Highlight* button and then choose the color your want. Select the text or the elements that you want to highlight now, and click the *Highlight* but-ton.

To cancel all highlights (but not the actual text) select *Tools/Options* and clear the *Highlight* check box on the *View* tab page.

When you are formatting an online document, you can apply the animated character formatting on the *Anima-tion* tab page. You can, for example, create a fluorescent text or a marching ant box around your selection.

To remove all manual character formatting you have ap-plied to a character range, select it again and press the Ctrl+Space key combination.

Paragraph Formatting

Word, like any other word processor, works with so-called paragraphs. A paragraph is created whenever you press the *Enter* key ⏎.

If you are entering text, all the characters will automatically belong to the same paragraph until you press the *Enter* key ⏎.

If you create empty lines by pressing the *Enter* key ⏎, you create paragraphs and, even though they are empty, they will determine how a text will look like.

Aligning Text in Word

You can change the *Alignment*, *Spacing* or *Indentation* of lines in a paragraph. Each paragraph can be formatted individually. With paragraph formatting you can easily create individual text sections standing out from the surrounding text. The alignment of text in documents is usually uniform, not considering centered headings in left aligned letters or lists with a ragged edge in otherwise justified formatted documents.

If you want to align several paragraphs to or between the margins, select them first. To align a single paragraph place the insertion cursor anywhere within the paragraph. The entire document can be quickly selected by pressing the Ctrl+A key combination.

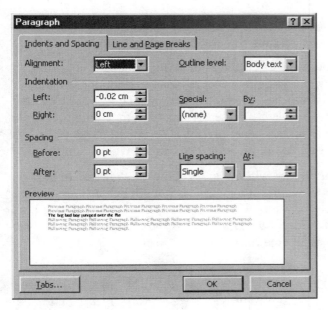

Fig. 4.8: The *Paragraph* dialog box and the alignment

If you want to work with a dialog box, select the *Paragraph* command on the *Format* menu. Open the *Alignment* drop-down list. It displays the items *Left*, *Right*, *Centered* and *Justified*. The default item is always *Left*. What does the word *Alignment* actually mean?

Left align

The lines of a paragraph are always aligned with regard to either the left and right margins or to the center of the page. If you want to align one or several paragraphs to the left margin, choose *Left* in the *Alignment* drop-down box in the *Paragraph* dialog box. The selected text will then be aligned along the left margin while the text on the right side will appear with an uneven, or ragged, edge.

Right align

If you want to align the text with regard to the right margin, select *Right* in the *Alignment* drop-down box in the

Paragraph dialog box. The selected text will be then aligned along the right margin.

Centered

If you want to center a line with regard to both the left and right margins, choose *Centered* in the *Alignment* drop-down box in the *Paragraph* dialog box. Centered alignments are frequently applied to headings, while normal text is generally left-aligned. Right-alignment is for example used in case of dates or invoice numbers.

Justified

To align text with regard to both the left and right margins, as we have done in this book, click *Justified* in the *Alignment* drop-down box in the *Paragraph* dialog box. Confirm the *Paragraph* dialog box by clicking *OK* or b by pressing the *Enter* key ⏎ to set the alignment.

Buttons

You can align one or several selected paragraphs more quickly with the *Align Left* button ▤, the *Center* button ▤, the *Align Right* button ▤ and the *Justify* button ▤ on the *Formatting* toolbar. Alternatively, you can place the cursor in the paragraph you want to align and choose the *Paragraph* command from the shortcut menu.

Setting Text Flow in Paragraphs

Word, as we know, manages text by paragraphs. For documents of more than one page *Word* provides an automatic page break if the last line of a paragraph does not fit on the page anymore.

Widow / Orphan

When creating documents consisting of more than one page, you have to observe a few rules. For example, you should generally avoid printing the last line of a paragraph by itself at the top of a new page. In the publishing sector, it is called the *orphan*.

Likewise, you should try to avoid having the first line of a new paragraph start at the bottom of a page - the so-called *widow*. And if you have very long tables, it is sometimes also advisable to prevent their being separated into paragraphs or lines.

Line and Page Breaks tab

Word can perform this job automatically as it is part of paragraph formatting. However, you have to choose the settings for the relevant paragraphs by yourself.

Select all the paragraphs you want to format. If you only want to format one paragraph, place the insertion cursor in the paragraph. Then select *Format/Paragraph* and activate the *Line and Page Breaks* tab.

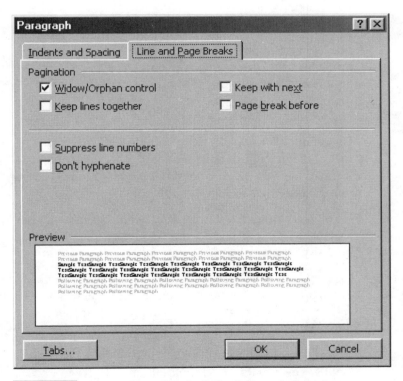

Fig. 4.9: Line and page breaks in the *Paragraph* dialog box

Widow/Orphan control

Check the *Widow/Orphan control* check box to prevent *Word* from printing the last line of a paragraph by itself at the top of the next page, or the first line of a paragraph by itself at the bottom of a page. *Word* will then print at least two lines of the paragraph at the top or bottom of a page respectively. This option is activated by default.

Keep lines together

Select the *Keep lines together* check box to prevent a page break within a paragraph.

Keep with next

Select the *Keep with next* check box to prevent a page break between the selected paragraph and the following paragraph.

Page break before

Page break before inserts a manual page break before the selected paragraph so that the selected paragraph is always printed as the first paragraph on a new page. Confirm your changes by clicking *OK*.

Setting Line Spacing for Paragraphs

By default *Word* works with a single line spacing. It refers to the amount of space between lines in a paragraph. 'Single' denotes the line height of the text in the typesetting measurement unit called *point*.

If you are writing a text with a *12-point* font size, the line spacing by default is *12 point*. However, this value can be easily modified.

Setting line spacing

Line spacing can be set separately for each paragraph. This applies only to paragraphs having several lines. To set the line spacing of a single paragraph, place the insertion cursor anywhere in the paragraph.

Line Spacing

If you want to change the line spacing of several paragraphs, you should select them all at once. Then choose the *Paragraph* command from the *Format* menu.

If necessary, activate the *Indents and Spacing* tab page. Open the *Line spacing* drop-down box and select the item you want, then confirm by clicking the *OK* button.

Line spacing:

Single ▼
Single
1.5 lines
Double
At least
Exactly
Multiple

Fig. 4.10:   Setting line spacing

- *Single*
  The font size determines the line spacing.

- *1.5 lines*
  One-and-one half times the font size determines te line spacing.

- *Double*
  Twice the font size determines te line spacing.

- *At Least*
  The point value displayed in the *At* text box is the minimum point size for the spacing, i.e. for a larger font it will naturally be more, but if using a smaller font it will not decrease the spacing to less than this value.

- *Exactly*
  The point value displayed in the *At* spin box is exactly sticked to, i. e. it is neither increased nor decreased.

- *Multiple*
  The value displayed in the *At* spin box is multiplied

by the single line spacing value to get the new line spacing.

Indent Text from the Left or the Right Margin

Important text paragraphs in letters are frequently moved a little bit inside from the left edge of the page. In word processing this procedure is called *Indent*. It is a paragraph formatting generally applied to all the lines of a paragraph, regardless of the position of the insertion cursor in the paragraph.

Basically you can indent paragraphs from either the left or the right margin. The first line sometimes plays a special role as far as indents go.

First line indent and hanging indent

For example, newspapers frequently use *First line indent* as a means of separating paragraphs. The *Hanging Indent* is a variation of this - it leaves the first line unchanged along the left margin but indents all the following lines of the paragraph.

If you want to indent only one paragraph, simply click anywhere within the paragraph. If you want to indent several paragraphs simultaneously, select them beforehand.

Select the *Paragraph* command on the *Format* menu and, if necessary, activate the *Indents and Spacing* tab.

To indent text from the left or right margin, enter the desired value, in centimetres, into the *Left* or *Right* spin boxes in the *Indentation* group box. You can also increase the value by the spin buttons. Check your changes in the *Preview* box.

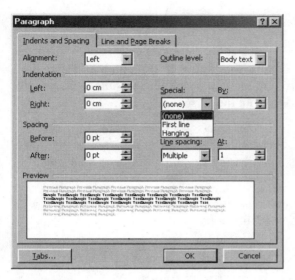

Special

If you select *First line* in the *Special* drop-down box, only the first line of a paragraph will be indented by the value you selected in the *By* text box. If *Hanging* is selected, only the subsequent lines will be indented by the value selected in the *By* text box. Confirm by clicking the *OK* button to set the indentation.

Increase and decrease indentation

Indentation from the left margin can be increased by 1.25cm values by clicking the *Increase Indent* button on the *Formatting* toolbar. Click on the *Decrease Indent* button to decrease the indent by 1.25 cm values.

Negative indents

If you insert negative values into the *Left* or *Right* spin boxes, the paragraph will extend beyond the margins of the page. By this method you can also enter text beyond the page margins.

Creating Lists

While writing business letters it is often necessary to have certain text sections, for example, schedules and product lists, stand out from the surrounding text.

Of course you can select such text parts in *Word* and manually choose another font with a particular font size, or you can apply styles like *bold*, *italics* and *underline*.

However, we wish to show you how to create lists and mark important paragraphs so that they stand out with just one click of the mouse button.

Bulleted and Numbered Paragraphs

Word offers two numbering formats allowing you effectively create lists in your letters and documents. These numbering formats are named *Numbering* and *Bullets*. You can add numbers and bullets to a paragraph if you want to draw the attention of the reader.

Numbering and bullets

To convert one or several *Word* paragraphs to a bulleted item, first select the paragraph or paragraphs and then right-click with your mouse the *Bullets and Numbering* command on either the *Format* menu or the shortcut menu.

Select the bullet style you want and confirm the *Bullets and Numbering* dialog box by pressing the *Enter* key ⏎ or by clicking the *OK* button.

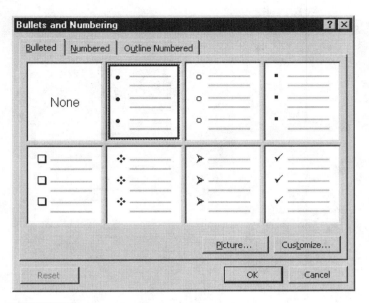

Fig. 4.12: Bullet formats

Bullets button ☰ It is much easier to apply bullets by clicking on the *Bullets* button ☰ on the *Formatting* toolbar. *Word* automatically indents bulleted items. If the paragraph is several lines long, the text of the subsequent lines will always be aligned. To remove bullets from selected paragraphs click the *Bullets* button ☰ again.

If you do not want to use the black dot but a different bullet format, select *Format/Bullets and Numbering*, and choose one of the seven styles with the mouse. Then select the *Customize* button.

Set the indentation value in the *Text position* group box to '0' if you do not want any indent, although this is not a good idea in case of paragraphs that are several lines long.

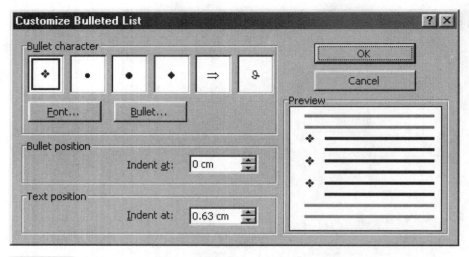

Fig. 4.13: Selecting additional bullet formats and indentation

If you want to use a different character, select it in the *Bullet character* option group.

Bullet position The indentation value for bullets can be specified in centimetres in the *Indent at* text box in the *Bullet position* group box and can be increased or decreased with the spin buttons. You can select an indent value for the text in the *Text position* group box. Confirm your changes by clicking the *OK* button.

Customize Bullet Characters

Customize If you want a bullett character different from the default one – the black bullet – select *Format/Bullets and Numbering* and choose one of the seven styles available by clicking on the bullet or numbered list style you want.

If you do not like any of the suggested bullets or numberings, select a bullet whatsoever and then click the *Customize* button. The *Customize Bulleted List* dialog box appears and presents further bulleting options in the *Bullet character* group box.

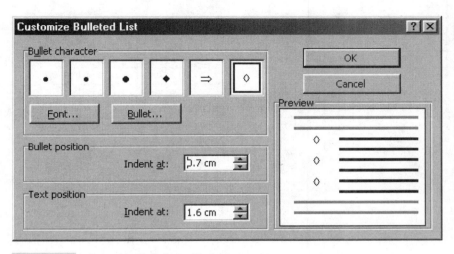

Fig. 4.14: Selecting bullets and indents

If one of these bulleted formats suits you, select it and confirm by clicking the *OK* button.

Font size and
Color

The selected bullet style will become the standard bullet style that you can also apply now by clicking the *Bullets* button ≣ on the *Formatting* toolbar.

You can modify the bulleted formatting style in many ways in the *Customize Bulleted List* dialog box: for example, if you wish to change the color or the size of a bullet, click the *Font* button. There you will find all possible formats you can apply. View your settings in the *Preview* box.

To use a completely different bullet character open the *Symbol* dialog box by clicking the *Bullet* button.

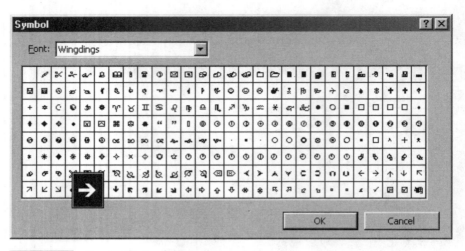

Select the desired font in the *Font* drop-down list box. We recommend the *Symbol* or *Wingdings* fonts because they contain many symbols. A magnified preview of a character is displayed by holding the mouse button down onto the character. Once you have selected a character, click the *OK* button.

The chosen character will appear in the *Preview* box of the *Customize Bulleted List* dialog box after you click *OK*. If you want to turn this font into your default font, click the *OK* button again.

Creating Numbered Paragraphs

Advantage of automatic numbering

In *Word* you can automatically number paragraphs, lists or items. If you do not want to use numbers, you can choose characters instead. The advantage of automatic numbering is that, when changing a text by adding or deleting new text for instance, or even when rearranging the order of already numbered items, *Word* automatically adjusts the numbers accordingly.

Numbering ▤

To add numbers before items or lists, select the paragraphs you want to number. Then click the *Numbering* button ▤ on the *Formatting* toolbar. *Word* automatically inserts a numbered list starting with number '1'. To insert a new numbered paragraph at the end of those already numbered, simply press the *Enter* key ↵.

When doing this, *Word* creates a new paragraph with the next appropriate number. By pressing the *Enter* key ↵ twice, however, *Word*'s automatic numbering will be halted.

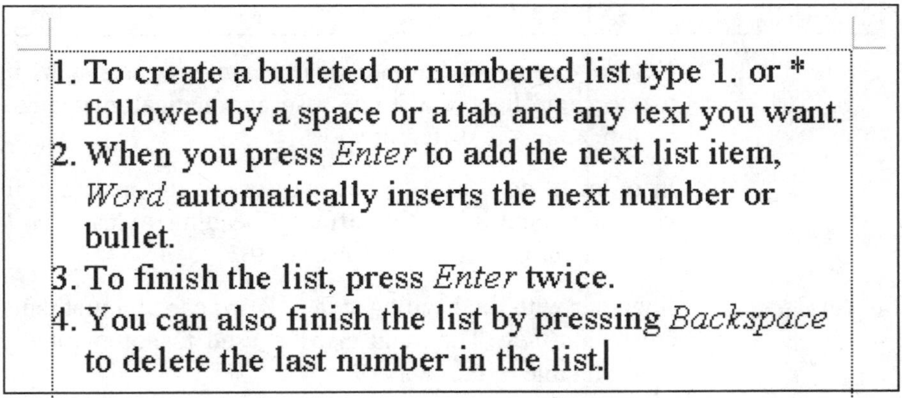

1. To create a bulleted or numbered list type 1. or * followed by a space or a tab and any text you want.
2. When you press *Enter* to add the next list item, *Word* automatically inserts the next number or bullet.
3. To finish the list, press *Enter* twice.
4. You can also finish the list by pressing *Backspace* to delete the last number in the list.

Fig. 4.16: Numbered paragraphs in Word documents

The text following the number is automatically indented by *Word*. In this way the lines of your paragraph are correctly aligned even though the paragraph itself consists of several lines.

To remove the numbering, select the relevant paragraphs. Then click on the *Numbering* button ▤ on the *Format* toolbar. *Word* removes the numbers of the selected paragraphs, and automatically adjusts the numbering of the subsequent paragraphs.

A single number can be removed as follows: click between the number and the text which follows and press the ⌫ key. To restore the previous situation, click once again the ⌫ key.

Should you number your lists manually, *Word* will change the numbering automatically. If a section begins with '1.' or '*' with a subsequent space or a tab stop, *Word* automatically inserts the next number if you press the *Enter* key ⏎. To end the list of numbered items, press the *Enter* key ⏎ twice.

Creating Numbered, outlined paragraphs

Not only can *Word* automatically number paragraphs in lists or item lists, but it can also automatically organize your headings in different ways.

In order to do this, you have to format the headings in your document using the different heading styles (*Heading 1*, *Heading 2* through *Heading 9*).

Table of contents   Together with the heading styles, *Word* can automatically create outlines. They can also be used to automatically create a table of contents.

If you have a document with headings of different levels that you have formatted with the *Heading 1*, *Heading 2* to *Heading 9* styles, you will be able to create an attractive visual or numerical outline.

To do this, place the cursor in any heading you like and select the *Bullets and Numbering* command on the *Format* menu. Activate the *Outline Numbered* tab page in the relevant dialog box.

1　How To Modify This Report

1.1　How to Delete Graphics

To delete a graphic, click on each object (in Page Layout View) to select, and press Delete. To delete the Return Address frame, click on the text to reveal the bounding border of the frame. Click on the border, and press Delete.

To lighten or darken the gray shaded areas, click to select the frame, and choose Drawing Object from the Format menu. Experiment with the options to achieve the best shade for your printer. To change the shading of the earth, double-click on the graphic to activate the picture. Click in the gray area of the picture, and choose Drawing Object from the Format menu. Choose a new shade, and choose Close.

1.1.1　How to Create a Footnote

To create a footnote, choose Footnote from the Insert menu and click OK.

1.2　How to Force a Page Break

In general, the best way to force a page break is to first insert a blank paragraph, and choose Break from the Insert menu. In the dialog box, click the Page Break button, and then OK.

Fig. 4.17:　　An example of a headings outline

Select one of the available outlines with the mouse and confirm by clicking the *OK* button. *Word* will then execute indentation and numbering and display all the headings in the text accordingly.

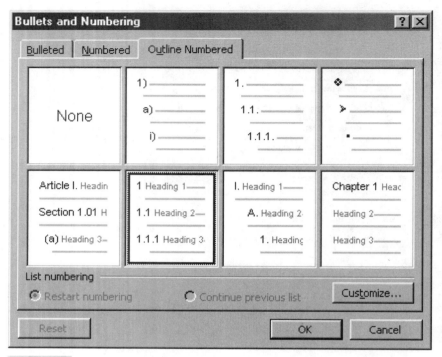

Fig. 4.18:   Selecting an outline format

Raising or lowering a heading

If you find out that one heading or another is on the wrong level, place the insertion cursor in the corresponding section after the bullet or the item number, but just in front of the heading text.

Each time you press the *Tab* key ⌨ the selected heading will move down by one level, the indentation will be increased accordingly and any automatic numbering will automatically be readjusted. To raise the level of a heading use the key combination ⌨+⌨: The indent will be decreased accordingly and any numbering adjusted automatically.

Outline view 🔳

It is even more convenient to work in the *Outline View*. It is a special view that displays the text outlined by heading level. You can change to *Outline View* by selecting the *Outline* command on the *View* menu or by clicking the *Outline View* button 🔳 on the horizontal scroll bar. The levels can be increased or decreased by clicking buttons.

Hide and display levels

If you only want to display all headings up to the third level, click the ③ button. A click on the ① button collapses the displayed levels to show only the *Heading 1* style, etc. Click the Show All Headings (Alt+Shift+A) button 🔘, if you want to display the entire text again.

Moving heading levels up or down

By clicking the *Promote/Demote* buttons ◀▶ you can move the selected paragraph to the next higher or lower heading level.

Moving levels

By using the *Move Up/Move Down* buttons ▲▼ you can rearrange the text. This will also automatically move all sublevels stored in the currently selected level. It applies to copying or moving selected headings with the mouse or the *Copy/Paste* and *Cut/Paste* commands. *Word* automatically adjusts the indentation and bullets as well as the outline numbering.

Customizing Paragraph Numbering

Numbered paragraphs are often required within a list or within numbered items in documents. This brings into special focus products or particular items making them stand out from the rest of the text. *Word* offers a special automatic formatting tool called *Numbering* to create numbered lists.

To format one or several paragraphs in *Word* with automatic numbering, select the paragraph or paragraphs you want to number and then click on the *Numbering* button

⊞ on the *Formatting* toolbar. *Word* automatically inserts a numbering scheme beginning with number '1'. To insert new numbered paragraphs at the end of a numbered list simply press the *Enter* key ⏎.

Word automatically indents the paragraphs containing numberings. If the paragraph is several lines long, this ensures that the lines following the first one are all aligned with it.

To remove a single numbered item or a complete numbered list, select the relevant paragraphs and click the *Numbering* button again.

If you want to insert a numbering style other than Arabic numerals, or if you do not want to begin with number '1', place the insertion cursor in one of the numbered sections and select *Format/Bullets and Numbering*.

If necessary, activate the *Numbered* tab page and click one of the seven available numbering formats, for instance, Roman numerals or the alphabetical list. *Word* changes the automatic numbering accordingly as soon as you confirm your choice by clicking the *OK* button.

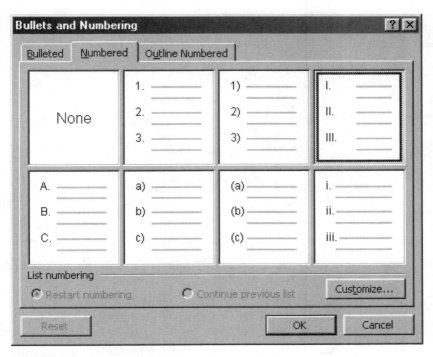

Fig. 4.19: Select numbering style

Start at

If none of the seven numbering styles available in the *Bullets and Numbering* dialog box is what you are actually looking for, or if you want to change the starting number, you can go about this by selecting any numbering format and then by clicking the *Customize* button. The *Customize Numbered List* dialog box appears. To alter the starting number click the *Start at* box and enter the number you want to begin the numbering with. Confirm by clicking the *OK* button.

The *Number style* drop-down box contains further numbering styles. The automatic numbering will take your settings into account. A preview of the changes made will be shown on the right in *Preview* in the dialog box.

199

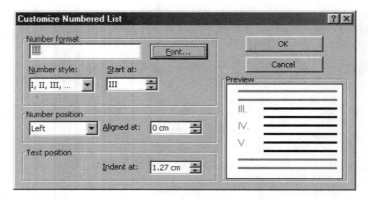

The *Customize Numbered List* dialog box

The selected numbering style will become the default style you can call-up by clicking the *Numbering* button ⊫ on the *Formatting* toolbar.

The *Customize Numbered List* dialog box offers you further options to customize your numbered list style: you can select font, font style and size of the characters used for numbering. Click the *Font* button and select the relevant dialog box. Format the numbering style accordingly and confirm by clicking the *OK* button.

Alignment

The indentation for the numbering style can be specified, in centimeters, in the *Aligned at* text box in the *Number position* group box, or it can be increased and decreased by using the spin buttons. In the *Number position* drop-down box you can align the text with the *Left*, *Right* or *Centered* items.

Indent at

In the *Indent at* text box in the *Text position* group box you can enter the value of the indent you wish to have between the number and the beginning of the text. Confirm your changes and close the *Customized Numbered List* dialog box by clicking the *OK* button.

Borders and Shading

Creating Paragraphs with Borders

Perhaps you already know that in *Word* you can also draw simple geometrical objects such as rectangles. We will talk about this function in Chapter 10. In this section we will discuss formatting paragraphs with borders. The result may look the same as drawing a rectangle. The difference between the rectangle and the border feature is that here we are dealing with paragraph formatting.

Borders and
Shading
dialog box

Paragraph formatting refers first to the current or to several selected paragraphs. With the *Borders* paragraph formatting feature, you can create a text that is good-looking and well-organized. You have two options: you can either work with a dialog box or you can work with a special toolbar. First, we will introduce you to the *Borders and Shading* dialog box that can be called-up with *Format/Borders and Shading*.

Setting borders

Before you proceed, place the insertion cursor in the paragraph you want to give a border to. If you want to place a border around several paragraphs, select them simultaneously. The quickest way to give paragraphs a border is by opening the *Borders and Shading* dialog box and selecting one of the available borders in the *Setting* option group. If you have selected only part of a paragraph, it will be bordered.

Border style

You can begin by selecting the desired *Style* and *Width* of the border and then by clicking the *Box* button in the *Setting* option group. Confirm by clicking the *OK* button.

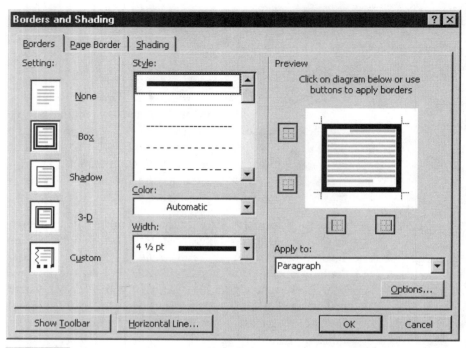

Fig. 4.21: The *Borders and Shading* dialog box

The border is influenced by all settings, even those applied to the paragraph. It extends to the right and left margins of the text.

Options for borders and shading

You can determine the distance of the border from the text in the *Border and Shading Options* dialog box. Open the dialog box by clicking the *Options* button in the *Borders and Shading* dialog box. Enter the value in points in the text boxes in the *From text* group. All four pages can be individually adjusted.

Border style

In the *Preview* box you can specify on which sides of the selected paragraphs borders will appear. Always select the *Style* or *Width* of the border in *Border style* and then switch on or off the borders in the *Preview* group which you want to be visible. *Word* displays all changes graphically. To apply the formatting to the paragraph or paragraphs click the *OK* button.

Borders

The second way to format borders is by using the *Borders* feature. Use this feature by clicking on the *Border* button ▣ ▾ on the *Formatting* toolbar.

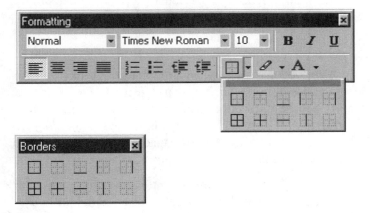

Fig. 4.22:   Borders

Click the *Outside Border* button ▣ in *Borders* to apply a box to the current paragraph. Click the *No Border* button ▣ to remove a border.

If you want to separate several selected paragraphs (or table cells) with a border, click the *Inside Border* button ▣.

If you use the *Borders* option a lot, you can insert it as an icon on the toolbar on your screen. Click the grey edge at the top of the list and drag it away with the mouse button held down.

Single borders

For single borders click on one of the following buttons: *Top Border* ▢, *Bottom Border* ▢, *Left Border* ▢ or *Right Border* ▢. Borders between two selected paragraphs or table cells can be inserted by clicking the *Inside Horizontal Border* button ▦, while borders between table columns can be inserted by clicking the *Inside Vertical Border* button ▢.

Previously used border

If you want to reuse the previously applied border simply click the ▢▾ button again.

Adding Shading to the Text Background

In *Word* you can also add a colored or grey background to paragraphs to achieve a visual effect. The background color can be used either as paragraph formatting or font formatting. In the former case it is known as *Shading*. In the latter case it makes the text stand out from the rest. The difference lies in previous selections.

Paragraph formatting always refers to the paragraph where the cursor is or to several selected paragraphs. The *Shading* paragraph format enables you to create an good-looking text and to achieve a clear overview. If you have selected one or more words, the formatting applies only to the selected text.

Borders and Shading dialog box

There are two ways, either by working in a dialog box or with a special toolbar. We will first introduce you to the *Borders and Shading* dialog box. Open it by calling-up *Format/Borders and Shading*.

First of all, to add a colored shading to a paragraph, place the insertion cursor in the respective paragraph or, if you want to color more than one paragraph, select the ones you want. In order to add a shading color to a paragraph, activate the *Shading* tab page.

Border style

Select a color by clicking the respective button on the color list. Select the pattern style in the *Style* drop-down box in the *Patterns* option group. You can also select a color from the *Color* drop-down list. Confirm by clicking the *OK* button.

The shading is influenced by all settings, even those applied to the paragraph. It extends to the right and left margins of the text.

By clicking the *Tables and Borders* button ⊞ on the *Standard* toolbar you can display the *Tables and Borders* toolbar.

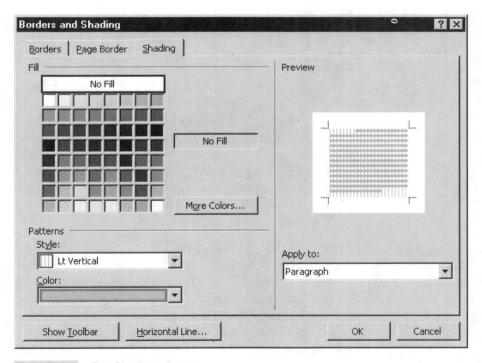

Fig. 4.23:   The *Shading* tab page

Shading color

You will find the *Shading Color* button ◢◣ on the *Tables and Borders* toolbar. Click on the arrow on the drop-down button to open the *Shading Color* popup menu with buttons which allow you to select the background color of the text. To apply once again the last color you have used, simply click on the button.

No fill

If you want to remove a shading color select the *No fill* item on the button menu.

You can also activate the *Shading* tab in the *Format/ Borders and Shading* dialog box. A transparent background appears as *None*. Click this item to remove the shading.

Copying Formatting

Generally text is first entered in *Word* and then formatted. It happens quite often that certain character or paragraph formatting is required again in other parts of the document. In that case those who are already acquainted with styles will not have any problem. Almost everybody else will find the going tough once in a while if they have to plough through the menus for character and paragraph formatting each time. The more time it takes to carry out the work steps, the easier it is to make mistakes.

Character and paragraph formatting

Word, however, allows format copying. As this discriminates between character and paragraph formatting, you should be careful when selecting the part of the text with the formatting you want to copy. If you want to copy only the character formatting, such as *Font*, *Font Size* and *Style* (*Bold*, *Italics* and *Underline*), then select only one text paragraph or simply click on a formatted word. Important: when selecting character formats to be copied, do not select the paragraph mark '¶'.

Paragraph mark '¶' If, on the contrary, you want to copy only the paragraph formatting (line spacing, indentation, paragraph spacing or fixed tabs, etc.), then select only the paragraph mark '¶' of the formatted paragraph. To copy both paragraph and character formattings of a paragraph select the text as well as the paragraph mark '¶' of the formatted paragraph.

Format painter ◇ To copy the formatting click the *Format Painter* button ◇ on the *Standard* toolbar.

Mouse pointer ▲I Your mouse pointer will change into a little brush ▲I. With this you can select the text paragraph you want to apply the format to.

Double-click Format Painter To apply the same copied format to several text sections one after the other, double-click the *Format Painter* button ◇ on the *Standard* toolbar. You can then select all the text parts one after the other and apply the copied formats to them with the mouse pointer ▲I. When you are finished, click the *Format Painter* button again or press the Esc key to switch off the format copying feature.

Formatting with the keyboard If you prefer working via the keyboard, you can use the following keyboard combinations: select the original and copy the format with the Ctrl+◇+C key combination. Select the new text section and apply the copied format with the Ctrl+◇+V key combination.

5. Setting up Pages and Sections

In the last chapter, we introduced you to different ways of formatting fonts and paragraphs in a document. In this chapter, we will have a look at the last category of *Word* formatting, i.e. properties which can only be applied to a whole page or to single sections of a document respectively. They include:

- Margins

- Paper Size

- Page Numbers

- Headers and Footers

- Footnotes

- Line Numbers

- Newspaper Columns

As a rule, most of these formats are used throughout the whole document in order to make it appear uniform. There are, however, situations in which a change in this formatting is desirable, for example:

- when the first page of a letter is to be printed with margins different from those of the following pages;

- when each chapter of a document is to receive a different header;

- if it is to be noted on all pages but the last one that another page follows;

- when the heading of a column is to be printed above two newspaper columns.

What are sections?

In all of these cases, the document has to be divided into *sections*. By now you already know why a document is divided into sections in *Word:* it is because you want the page layout in each section to be different.

Therefore, it is easy to deduce that a section is a part of a document with a unified page formatting.

If the page format is just one for the whole document, then the latter consists of only one section. This is what happens in the case of default settings.

How is a new section created?

If you want to change the page format, start a new section. Either insert the section break manually, or select the text paragraph for the new section so that *Word* automatically inserts the section break.

Page Setup

In *Word*, as soon as you create a new document on the basis of the *Normal.dot* document template (*File/New* and *Blank Document*, or by clicking on the *New* button ⬜), the *Word* program processor uses certain default settings for paper size, alignment, and for margins where no text can be written.

However, you can change all of that. All the settings mentioned are determined in the *Page Setup* dialog box which you open by choosing the *Page Setup* command in the *File* menu.

The Print Preview

In order to check the current page settings, or in order to adjust certain formatting, open the *Print Preview*. You will see the text displayed exactly as it will be printed out by the selected printer.

Print Preview 🔍

In order to display the text in the *Print Preview*, choose *File/Print Preview* or click on the *Print Preview* button 🔍 on the *Standard* toolbar.

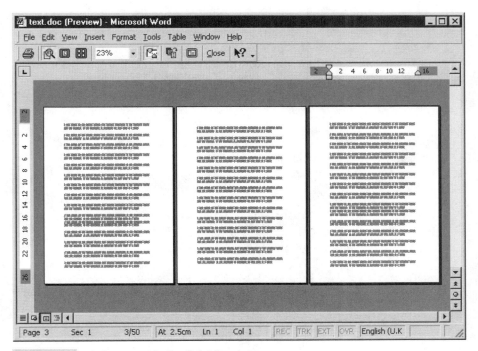

Fig. 5.1:   A document in the *Print Preview*

In the *Print Preview*, you can display one or several pages at the same time, with or without rulers. In addition, a special toolbar provides you with buttons allowing you control the view.

▪ 🖨 *Print*
   Activate this button in order to print the document directly from the print preview.

- *Magnifier*
  With this button you can switch between the magnifier and the editing mode. In the magnifier mode you can enlarge a certain section of a page by clicking on it.

- *One Page*
  This button displays only one page of the document.

- *Multiple Pages*
  When you click this button, you can select (from a grid) the number of pages you want to display at the same time, either next to each other and/or underneath each other.

- *Zoom*
  This drop-down list enables you to reduce or increase the size of the displayed page.

- *Ruler*
  A click on this button shows or hides both the horizontal and the vertical rulers. You need the ruler to change the margins.

- *Shrink to Fit*
  Click this button to make *Word* shrink the size of the document's contents so that the number of pages will be decreased by one.

- *Full Screen*
  Hides all superfluous screen elements. Deactivate this view by clicking [Esc].

- *Close*
  Closes the *Print Preview* and returns to the previous view.

■ **[?]** *Context Sensitive Help*
Click this button and then a screen element so as to display an explanation of the element.

Mouse pointer in the shape of a magnifier

In the *Print Preview*, the mouse pointer takes the shape of a magnifier. Click wherever in the document to magnify the text therein. Click once more into the document in order to return to the previous size. A plus sign appears in the magnifier when the display is reduced in size; on the contrary, a minus sign appears when it is enlarged.

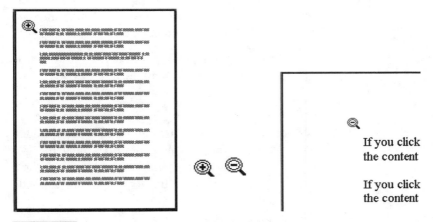

If you click the content

If you click the content

Fig. 5.2: Mouse pointer to magnify and to reduce the size

Active page

Even though several pages are displayed in the *Print Preview*, only one page is the active page. You can recognize it by its border, which appears thicker. In addition, the horizontal ruler is shown only on top of the active page.

Scrolling through the Print Preview

In the *Print Preview* you will see a horizontal and a vertical scroll bar. In the latter, click the *Next Page* button [≢] or the *Previous Page* button [≜] if you want to browse by page through the document. As an alternative, you can use the [PgDn] and [PgUp] keys.

Rulers

With the help of the rulers and the mouse, you can change the page margins. For more details see further down in this chapter.

Changing the Margins

One of the page properties you basically set once and then adjust according to your needs, is setting the page margins. You can change them either in the *Page Setup* dialog box or in the *Print Preview*. While the dialog box allows for more exact values and the setting of a default values, the *Print Preview* makes it possible to adjust margins with regard to the current document content.

Print Preview

A fast way to change margins, or headers and footers, is by dragging them with the mouse in the *Print Preview*.

Changing the Margins in the Print Preview

Let's say you created a document and had a definite idea of how big it would be, but now the document has become either shorter or longer, and you are looking for a way to adjust the margins so that its length corresponds to your estimate.

Print Preview 🔍

In order to adjust the margins with regard to the document contents, choose *File/Print Preview* or click the *Print Preview* button 🔍 on the *Standard* toolbar.

If the rulers are not displayed, click the *View Ruler* button 🔲. Point the position in the ruler where the white and the gray ruler areas meet. The mouse pointer will change into a double-headed arrow, and the margin line will appear. Next to the mouse pointer a *ScreenTip* will display the name of the margin.

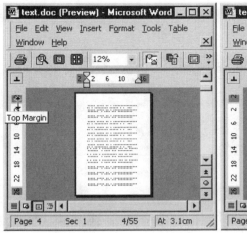

Fig. 5.3: Changing margins with the mouse

Drag the margin and the line to another position. When you change the left or right margin on the horizontal ruler, you should always make sure that the mouse pointer is in the shape of a double-headed arrow. Otherwise you might move the indents instead of the margins!

Undo

Since the *Standard* toolbar is not displayed in the *Print Preview*, choose *Edit/Undo* if you want to undo a change in the margins which has not yielded the desired result.

Maybe you have already had the rather frustrating experience of finding that your document contents are spread, unfortunately, in such a way that the last few lines spill over onto the final printing page. You may now be trying to squeeze these lines onto the previous page by reducing the margins. *Word*, however, offers you a more sophisticated solution.

Click the *Shrink to Fit* button ▓. *Word* will then try to reduce the number of pages by one, by changing the font size step by step. If this formatting of the document contents is not possible, then *Word* will display the following message:

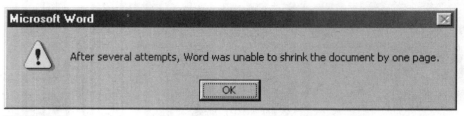

Fig. 5.4: The *Shrink to Fit* action was not successful

In this case, adjust the document contents by yourself either by changing the margins or through other formatting.

Changing the Margins in the Dialog Box

To change the margins of a document in the dialog box, choose *File/Page Setup* and, on the *Margins* tab page, use the corresponding text boxes at the left.

Top
Bottom
Left
Right

Double-click one by one the centimetre values in the *Top*, *Bottom*, *Left*, and *Right* text boxes, and overwrite the preset values with new ones in centimetres. You can also use the *Tab* key ⌨ to jump from one text box to the next to overwrite the values. You need not enter *cm* for 'centimetres'. If you delete a character of the measurement unit, you will get a warning message. So make sure that you enter the values correctly. If you use the spin buttons, the values will be changed in steps of 0.1 cm.

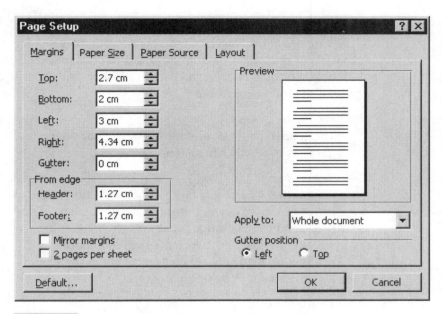

The *Page Setup* dialog box in *Word*

From edge

To the right of the text boxes you will see a preview of your changes in the form of one or two stylized miniature page(s). The options available in the *From edge* group box will be described later in the section on headers and footers.

Mirror Margins

Gutter

If you work with facing pages as is the case in this book, after selecting the *Mirror margins* check box you can determine the so-called *Gutter* in the text box with the same name. The gutter is the space added to the margin on the inner side of the page which provides for the necessary binding allowance.

Apply to

On the *Margins* tab page and on all other tab pages of the *Page Setup* dialog box, you find the *Apply to* drop-down list box. The items in this list depend on the document contents and on whether anything has been selected prior

217

to opening the dialog box. If the settings you change in the *Page Setup* dialog box are supposed to be valid for the whole document, you do not have to change the default *Whole document* item. All in all, you can choose one of the following items:

■ *Whole document*
The settings will be valid for the whole document, regardless of whether it contains one or more sections.

■ *Selected text*
This option will be displayed only if a section of the text was selected before opening the dialog box. *Word* will then insert a section break before and after the selection. The text between the section breaks is newly formatted. The text before and after the section breaks remains in its original format.

■ *This section*
The new settings are applied exclusively to the current section. This item appears in the list only if the document consists of at least two sections.

■ *This point forward*
The new settings are valid from the cursor position onwards. *Word* inserts a section break just before the cursor position. The text above the section break remains in the original format.

Paper Size and Orientation

Landscape

If you want to change the paper orientation, switch to the *Paper Size* tab page and, in the *Orientation* option group, click one of the two radio buttons, either *Portrait* or *Landscape*.

Paper Size

In the *Paper Size* drop-down list box you can change the *Letter* default setting to other preset formats, such as *Le-*

gal, *Executive*, or *A4*. The *Custom size* item enables you to define individual paper sizes by specifying the *Width* and *Height* in the corresponding text boxes.

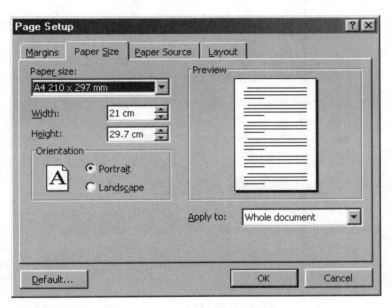

Fig. 5.6:   Defining paper size and orientation

You can also enter the different measurements directly into the text boxes. In this case *Word* automatically switches over to *Custom*.

Paper Source

On the *Paper Source* tab page, select the tray of your printer offering the selected paper size. The items in the dialog box depend on your printer. Here you can also determine the paper source for the *First page* and the *Other pages* separately. You could, for example, use cardboard/manila paper for the title and insert it manually, and then normal paper for the following pages by the default tray.

Layout

The *Layout* tab page is used to define headers and footers and is described in detail later. Confirm your changes by clicking *OK*.

Determine the settings of margins, paper size and orientation before you start typing your document.

It is true that afterwards you can change the page settings. However, in that case there will be new page breaks, and this might mean you have to format the document once again.

Changing the Default Settings for Margins or Size

After installing *Word* or *Office* respectively, *Word* uses the default settings for both paper size and margins.

▓ The A4 format corresponds to 29.7 cm x 21 cm

▓ The default orientation is *Portrait*

▓ The top margin is 2.5 cm

▓ The bottom margin is 2 cm

▓ The left margin is 2.5 cm

▓ The right margin is also 2.5 cm

Default

If you want the changes you made on the various tab pages in the *Page Setup* dialog box to become the new standard for all new documents in the future as well as for the current one, then click the *Default* button.

Since this will be a fundamental change of settings, *Word* displays a message box with a message asking you to confirm the change. Click the *Yes* button.

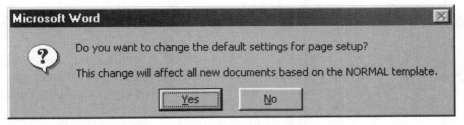

Fig. 5.7: Changing the default settings

Inserting Page Breaks

When you enter your text into a *Word* document, *Word* uses automatic line breaks. At the end of a page, *Word* automatically creates a new page, if the text does not fit on the current page anymore. This is called *automatic page break.*

Page break

Sometimes you may want to show only certain information on one page, and display the text which follows on the next one, such as might be the case with the covering page of a report or a thesis, or with paragraphs of a contract that belong together, or just specific sections in a document. What is the problem, some of you may ask? I will just keep pressing the *Enter* key ⏎ until *Word* moves on to the next page. This is exactly what you should *not* do.

Why not a page break by pressing the *Enter* key?

Word handles documents by paragraphs. Every time you press the *Enter* key ⏎, it creates a new paragraph. Well, you *can* actually create page breaks in this way. But what if you modify the text later on? As soon as you insert additional text on the first page, increase the font size or apply a different font, *Word* automatically creates new line breaks. This may result in new page breaks as well. The previously inserted empty paragraphs may shift to the next page, and the text of the document will then start

221

somewhere in the middle of the new page and you will have to delete the empty paragraphs manually.

Page break with Ctrl + ↵

If you want to make your text continue on a new page, insert a manual page break. Now *Word* can, to some extent, react to changes in formatting or text and maintain the page breaks at the right place. Position the cursor where you want the page break to be set, and choose *Break* on the *Insert* menu. In the dialog box having the same name, confirm the already selected *Page break* radio button by clicking *OK*. You can insert a page break even more quickly by pressing the [Ctrl]+[↵] key combination.

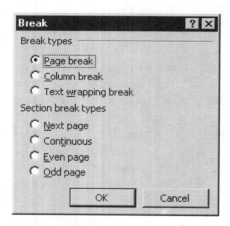

Fig. 5.8: Inserting a manual page break

Deleting a page break

In a document, manual page breaks are displayed by a dotted line with the description *Page Break*. In case you want to delete the page break again, click onto the selected *Page break* – the cursor blinks at the beginning of the line – and press the *Delete* key [Del].

Using Section Breaks to Format the Document

Sec 1

Normally, a *Word* document consists of one section. This is shown in the status bar at the bottom of the screen as *Sec 1*. The same settings with regard to paper size, orientation, number of columns, as well as headers and footers are applied throughout the section. Every time you want to change one of these settings within a document, you need to have at least two sections and sometimes even more.

If you want, for example, to print the first page of a document in the *Landscape* orientation and the following pages in the *Portrait* orientation, insert a section break after the first page. You would also insert a section break if, within the document, you wanted to switch from a one-column to a two- or even more than two-column text.

Sometimes, *Word* inserts section breaks automatically when certain functions are called-up, for example when fixing different headers and footers for even and odd pages, or when setting different headers and footers for the first page.

Inserting a Manual Section Break

To insert a manual section break at the cursor position, open the *Insert* menu and click the *Break* command. The *Break* dialog box opens.

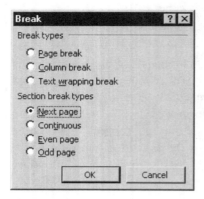

Fig. 5.9:   Inserting a section break

Word distinguishes between various sorts of section breaks which are displayed in the document as dotted double lines with the *Section Break* label.

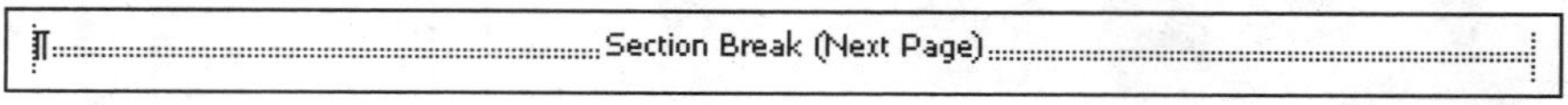

⁋ ·· Section Break (Next Page) ··

Fig. 5.10:   A section break in a document

If the section break is not displayed in the *Print Layout* view, click the *Show/Hide* ¶ button ¶ on the *Standard* toolbar to show the nonprinting characters.

Next page

With the *Next page* option, *Word* inserts a section break by breaking the page and beginning the new section on the following page.

Continuous

With the *Continuous* option, *Word* inserts a section break and begins the new section on the same page.

Even page
Odd page

If you click the *Even page* or *Odd page* radio buttons, *Word* inserts a section break and begins the new section on the even or odd page respectively. In order to insert a section break, click the radio button with the desired option, and then click *OK*.

Deleting Manual Section Breaks

In order to delete a section break, select the dotted double-line with the *Section Break* label, and then press the *Delete* key `Del`. If the section break is not displayed in the *Print Layout* view, click the *Show/Hide* ¶ button ¶ to show the nonprinting characters.

If you delete a section break, the section formatting of the text section above will be deleted as well. This text will become part of the following section and will take on its formattings.

Copying Section Formatting

In order to "transfer" a formatting from one section to another (for example page margins or columns in a newspaper style), first open the *View* menu and switch to *Normal* view. Then select the section break at the end of the section containing the formatting to be copied. Copy the section break to the new position in one of the following ways: you can use the *Edit/Copy* command on the menu, then position the cursor at the new location in the text, and choose the *Edit/Paste* command on the menu. You can also click the *Copy* button on the toolbar, position the cursor at the new location in the text, and then click the *Paste* button on the toolbar. The formatting will then be applied to the text above the new section break.

Saving Section Formatting for Future Application

If you want to use the formatting of a certain section in other documents, you can define the section break as an *AutoText* item and insert it by using the shortcut text and the `F3` key to duplicate the section format. For more information on the *AutoText* item, see Chapter 9.

Headers and Footers

When working on a document, you generally move only in the document area containing normal text. That is what the area between the upper, lower and the left and right margins is called. In *Word*, it is also possible to place text or other objects outside this area.

Headers and footers

In *Word*, text inserted outside the document area into the upper or lower (or left or right) margins, is called a header or a footer. The characteristic of headers or footers is that the text inserted there will be displayed and printed out on every page of the document, even though it has been inserted only once.

That is why headers and footers are always used for information which should appear on every page, such as:

- Page number
- Number of pages
- Indication of following pages
- Date of document creation
- Author
- Title of a chapter
- A company's name and its logo.

This is only a small sampling of the many ways in which headers and footers can be used. It is up to you to decide what text, graphic symbol or other object is to be displayed there. We should add that, for some of the examples mentioned above, *Word* offers automatic functions and buttons enabling you to insert this information.

Inserting Page Numbers in a Header or Footer

In certain documents, you need page numbers. Such documents can either be a letter which is several pages long, or a contract, a treatise or more complicated texts such as manuscripts. Inserting page numbers manually would be an awkward and tedious task, and it could easily mean mistakes. Not to mention that manually inserted page numbers could be a distinct disadvantage for *Word*. If you were to change the document so as to make it shorter or longer, the page numbers as normal text would not be automatically updated.

Automatic page numbering

Word can do this job for you much more efficiently if you use the automatic page numbering function. With it, you can insert the current page number quickly and easily into a specific place.

If you change the total number of pages in the document, or change their order, *Word* takes this into account and updates the page numbering automatically. As a rule, specific locations in the document are used to insert page numbers.

Word inserts the page number in the header or the footer, even if you have never used these areas before. To insert page numbers into a document, choose the *Page Numbers* command on the *Insert* menu. The dialog box with the same name appears on the screen.

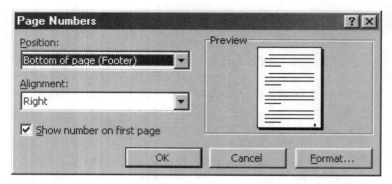

Fig. 5.11:   Inserting page numbers

Now you can determine where to insert the page numbers by choosing from the *Position* drop-down list. Select the *Bottom of page (Footer)* item, if you want to display the page numbers in the lower margin.

Top of page (Header)

Select the *Top of page (Header)* item, if you want *Word* to insert the numbers in the upper margin above your text. With these settings you fix a vertical orientation for the document.

Alignment

In the *Alignment* drop-down list you can set the horizontal position of the page numbers within the header or footer. The positions available depend on the current document settings. Basically, you can place the page number at the *Right*, at the *Left*, or in the *Center* of the page. If your document is printed on both sides of the page, you can also choose between *Inside* and *Outside*.

If you do not want the page number to appear on the first page, clear the *Show number on first page* check box. Then click *OK*. Page numbers are displayed in light grey in the *Print Layout* view at the insertion point, since headers and footers represent text panes of their own.

(PAGE)

Page numbers are inserted into the document as a field function (PAGE), and before any saving or printing, they are automatically updated. You can even do this manually by double-clicking the page number or by pressing the F9 key.

Deciding upon the Page Number on the First Page of the Document

You can enter the current page number in the header or footer and *Word* adjusts the page numbers automatically according to any change in the document. You can also decide (and then change your mind once again) whether to display a page number on the first page of your document, as well as to set additional page number formatting.

Why shouldn't a document start with page number '1'? The answer is very simple: as a rule, you never include covers and tables of contents in the counting. These items follow a different number formatting. Students writing their assignments or theses know this only too well. The same happens when you divide an extremely long document into several files.

Deciding page
number for
first page

In this case, you want the first page of the second chapter to begin with the page number directly following the last page of the first chapter. With *Word*, it is no problem to set the page numbering of the first page. To insert page numbers, choose *Insert/Page Numbers*. In the dialog box with the same name, determine the *Position* and the *Alignment* of page numbers and then click the *Format* button.

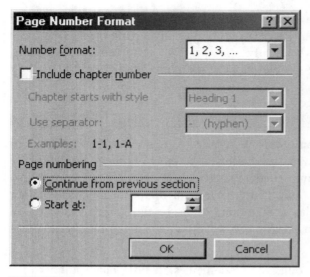

Configuring page numbers

In the *Page Number Format* dialog box, select the *Start at* radio button in the *Page numbering* option group and enter the page number, or use the spin button.

Continue from previous section

If your document consists of several sections, you should define the page numbering separately for each section. For the section following section 1, click the *Continue from previous section* button, otherwise *Word* will start each new section with '1'. For section 1, however, you can use the *Start at* button to decide the first page number. Confirm your changes by clicking the *OK* button.

Close

If you have already set the position and alignment of page numbers earlier on, then close the *Page Numbers* dialog box by clicking *Close*.

Inserting Headers and Footers into the Document

In *Word*, headers and footers are special panes on top of or below the actual text on a page, presenting additional information which is displayed and printed out on each document page. This implies that these panes are ideally suited to contain the company's name and/or its logo, as well as the title of a composition or any information about the page such as the page number. The areas for the headers and footers lie outside the margins and cannot be written into directly. We will first look at how you can insert headers and footers into a document.

View/Header and Footer

Choose *View/Print Layout* in *Print Layout* view. Then open the *View* menu and select *Header and Footer*. *Word* displays the *Header* pane with the label which is normally not visible. The insertion cursor will blink there. You can now type in your text which can be formatted in whatever way you like. Instead of text, however, you can just as well insert a table or a graphic object into the header. Basically, there are three positions available to you, *Left*, *Right* or *Center*, which you can jump to by pressing the *Tab* key ⇥ .

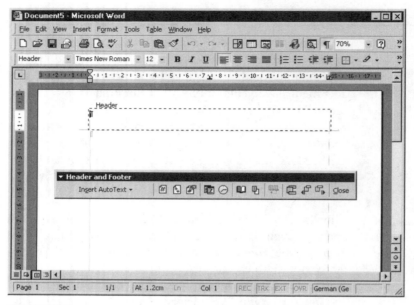

Fig. 5.13: Inserting headers and footers in the *Print Layout* view

Switch between header and footer

Everything you insert into the header will later on be displayed and printed out on each page of your document. With the *Switch Between Header and Footer* button you can move to the footer and insert the desired entries there. After you have completed the changes to the header or footer, click on the *Close* button.

How to create different headers and footers for different documents will be explained later in this chapter.

Using the *Header and Footer* Toolbar

While talking about the switching from the header to the footer, we introduced you to the new *Header and Footer* toolbar you can use to move between various headers and footers, or when you want to insert certain information by using the corresponding buttons.

■　　| Insert AutoText ▾ |

This drop-down list contains several items for *Auto-Text* functions you can use to insert information such as the current page number or the total number of pages, the file name and path, or the date of document creation, as well as the name of the author.

■　　⊞ *Insert Page Number*
Inserts the current page number as a field.

■　　🗎 *Insert Number of Pages.*
Inserts the total number of pages as a field.

■　　⊡ *Format Page Number*
Opens the *Format/Page Number* dialog box.

■　　⊞ *Insert Date*
With this button you insert the date of document creation as a field.

■　　⊖ *Insert Time*
This button inserts the current time as a field.

■　　⊡ *Page Setup*
Opens the *Page Setup* dialog box.

■　　⊟ *Show/Hide Document Text*
Shows or hides the normal text.

■　　⊞ *Same as Previous*
Cuts or re-establishes the link to the header of the previous section.

■　　⊟ *Switch Between Header and Footer*
Displays the footer or changes back to the header.

■　　⊒ *Show Previous*
Displays the previous header or footer.

■　　⊒ *Show Next*
Displays the next header or footer.

■ `Close` *Close Header and Footer*
Closes the header or footer pane, thus finishing the editing, and returns to the document text

By clicking the *Switch Between Header and Footer* button ⌕, you jump from the header to the footer, and vice versa.

With the *Close* button `Close` you return to the normal text after you have entered all information to the header or footer.

In the *Print Layout* view, the information in the headers and footers is now displayed in light grey. If you want to change a header or footer, double-click on its area or, on the *View* menu, select the *Header and Footer* command. In the *Normal View*, headers and footers are not displayed. When you work in *Normal View* and select the *View/Header and Footer* command, *Word* automatically switches to the *Print Layout View* and displays the header or footer pane.

Insert Page Number

With the *Insert Page Number* button 🔢 you can insert the corresponding page number of each page at a given position in the header or the footer. If you want to insert the total number of pages, too, click the *Insert AutoText* button and select the *Page X of Y* item.

Creating Different Headers and Footers for Different Pages

Documents with many pages often contain headers and footers in which information about the text contents is displayed. In the simplest case, a header may contain, for example, the topic of a report or the address of the author. Note that *Word* as a rule prints out the same header/footer on every page of the document.

Let's turn to the advanced header and footer options. Look at the pages of an ordinary book, for example. The left – or the even-numbered – pages are normally aligned to the left, while the right – or the odd-numbered – pages are aligned to the right. Even if the difference is minimal, the corresponding headers and footers are totally different.

To create such different headers and footers, you have to prepare your document before you start to write. On the *File* menu, select the *Page Setup* command and activate the *Layout* tab page.

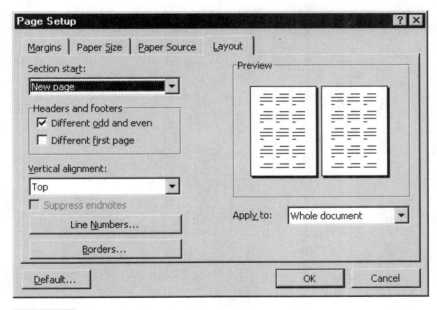

Fig. 5.14:   Creating different headers and footers

In the *Headers and Footers* option group box, select the *Different odd and even* check box if you want to create different headers and footers on pages printed on both sides.

Different first page If the first page is to receive a different header or footer (or no header or footer at all), check the *Different first page* check box. You also need this option, if you do not want the first page to show any header or footer, but want to assign them only to the following pages. Select the desired options, and confirm by clicking *OK*.

To edit the different headers and footers, insert two page breaks into the document by pressing the shortcut keys `Ctrl`+`↵`. In order to switch into the headers and footers panes in the *Print Layout* view, choose *View/Header and Footer*.

Word moves into the header and footer panes and displays the *Header and Footer* toolbar. With the help of the three buttons *Switch Between Header and Footer*, *Show Previous*, and *Show Next* you can now move between the various headers and footers.

At the top border of the header or the footer, the corresponding label is displayed, and the cursor blinks in the pane.

The label depends on the option you chose on the *Page Setup/Layout* tab page. Each pane can now be filled and formatted with individual information, independent of each other.

The same holds true for the footers. Here too, you can use different information or formatting.

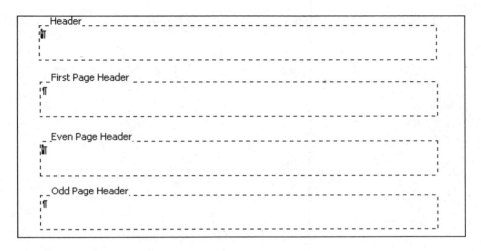

Fig. 5.15: Different headers in *Word*

1,25 cm from
paper edge

the Position of the Headers and Footers

By default, *Word* places the headers and footers in the page area above and below the document text. For documents created on the basis of the *Blank Document* style, *Word* prints the information in the headers and footers 1.25 cm from the upper or lower edge of the paper sheet on each document page.

Therefore, the headers and footers panes lie within the top and bottom margins, which *Word* has set at 2.5 cm for the upper and 2 cm for the lower edge of the page in the *Normal.dot* template. Since we have now referred to the edges of the paper, you should already know where to set the position of the header and footer.

In the *File* menu, choose the *Page Setup* command, and in the dialog box with the same name activate the *Margins* tab page.

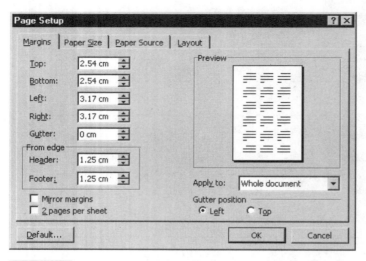

Fig. 5.16:   Setting the position of the header and footer

In the *From edge* option group, enter the value for the *Header* or the *Footer* distance, or change the settings by using the spin buttons. The unit of measurement is centimetres, but you do not need to add *cm* for centimetres - *Word* will do that for you. You should pay attention, though, not to accidentally delete a character of the measurement unit. So either enter the measurement only, or type it out fully with 'cm'. Confirm the settings by clicking *OK* for the changes to become active.

If the footer is not being printed

Certain printers are not capable of printing all the way down to the paper position of 1.25 cm, measured from the outer edge. This is the case with inkjet printers. If you work with an inkjet printer, change the settings for the footers, since otherwise they will be not, or only partially, printed. Check for this in the *Print Preview* before printing out for the first time. Control that the headers and footers do not overlap with the margins.

Creating Documents of Several Columns

In *Word*, you generally create only single column documents. The borders of this 'column' are formed by the margin settings. Creating a *Word* document comprising several columns in the style of a newspaper is almost child's play. This formatting is very suitable for small publications or brochures.

Assigning the Number of Columns

Newspaper columns throughout the whole document

Before you insert columns into a document, switch to the *Print Layout* view. If you want to format the whole document in newspaper columns, choose the *Select All* command from the *Edit* menu, or press the ⌈Ctrl⌉+⌈A⌉ key combination.

Newspaper columns only in parts/sections

If, on the other hand, you want to format only part of the document in columns, select only this part. If you want to format an entire section of your document in several columns, just click anywhere in the section. In order to format several sections in columns, select the sections accordingly.

Column ▦

There are two ways available to insert newspaper columns: you can either use your mouse and a dialog box, or you can click on a button.

Let's look at the mouse method first: on the *Standard* toolbar, click on the *Columns* button ▦. A drop-down palette with several icons will appear.

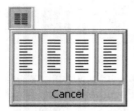

Fig. 5.17: Selecting the number of columns needed

By dragging the mouse across the displayed column icons, select the number of columns you want to use. *Word* will immediately divide your document into that many columns.

In case your document does not contain any text yet, you will not be able to see much of your columns, of course. Choose *Tools/Options* and activate the *View* tab page. In the *Show* option group select the *Text boundaries* check box, and click *OK*. Now you can clearly see the boundaries of the columns you created.

If the ruler is not visible, you can display it by going into the *View* menu and choosing *Ruler*. In order to visually change the column width and spacing, drag the column mark on the horizontal ruler to the desired position.

While dragging, press and hold down the Alt key. *Word* then gives you the corresponding column width in centimetres. Columns are separated from each other by a space.

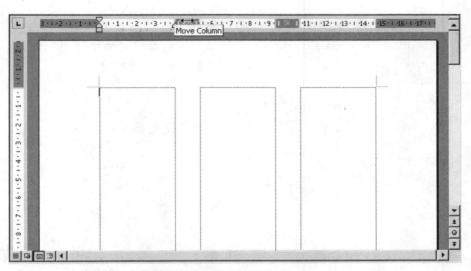

Fig. 5.18:   Ruler and text boundaries in a multiple column document

Since you cannot extend a column so as to make it overlap the adjacent column by using the mouse, it may be advisable to first reduce the width of the adjacent column. If the columns are all of the same width, this will change the widths of them all. If the columns are of differing widths, only the column you are dragging will be changed in width.

Presets

In order to precisely determine the column width and the spacing in-between, select the *Columns* command on the *Format* menu, and choose the desired options in the dialog box. In the *Presets* option box, select the desired number of columns.

Width and spacing

In the *Width and spacing* option group, enter the relevant values into the *Width* and *Spacing* text boxes for the corresponding column, or change the preset values by using the spin buttons.

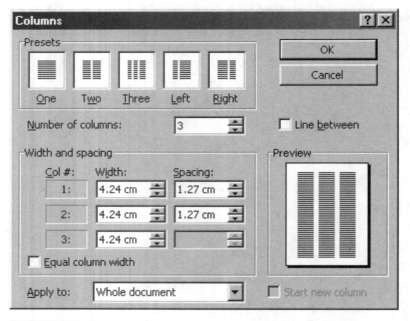

Formatting the columns via the *Columns* dialog box

If you want the columns to be identical in width, check the *Equal column width* check box.

Newspaper columns cannot be created in headers and footers, in notes or in frames. For these text areas, you need to use a table instead.

Removing Newspaper Columns

In order to remove newspaper columns, click anywhere within a column, then click the *Columns* button ▦ and by dragging the mouse, select the only-one-column layout.

Working With Footnotes

Footnotes and *endnotes* are notes or source references as-signed to certain passages in a text. Behind the last word typed, *Word* enters the so-called note reference mark, a superscript number of this appearance[27], which indicates the number of the corresponding footnote.

At the bottom of the page containing a note reference mark in the text, the relevant number will reappear with the corresponding text. Footnotes are displayed and printed.

Inserting Footnotes and Endnotes into Text

Footnotes and endnotes

Footnotes are used primarily in scientific texts, for example, for book references. A special kind of footnote is the endnote which is printed only at the end of a document. Except for their location, however, there is no difference between footnotes and endnotes, as for the method of both insertion or formatting.

To insert a footnote or endnote, position the cursor after the word in the text you want to assign a footnote or endnote to, and click. Don't press the space bar after the word.

Now open the *Insert* menu and choose the *Footnote* command.

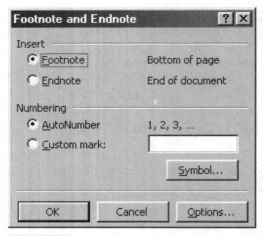

Fig. 5.20: The *Footnote and Endnote* dialog box

AutoNumber

If you want to insert a footnote, click on the *Footnote* radio button in the *Insert* option group in the *Footnote and Endnote* dialog box. To insert an endnote, select the corresponding *Endnote* radio button. In the *Numbering* option group, select the *AutoNumber* radio button, and close the dialog box by clicking *OK*. *Word* automatically inserts a *footnote symbol* after the word.

Note reference mark

A note reference mark is a superscript number[1] indicating the term a footnote was designed for. Note reference marks in an ongoing text are automatically numbered consecutively.

Footnote pane

After the insertion, *Word* switches to the footnote pane. In the *Print Layout* view, *Word* jumps to the end of the page.

In the *Normal* view, the window is divided in two sections, and in the lower portion the *Footnotes* pane is displayed.

In both cases, the cursor blinks behind the note reference mark in the footnote pane.

Enter the text of your footnote in that space. A footnote can be of any length and can also contain any textual and graphic elements which are allowed in normal text.

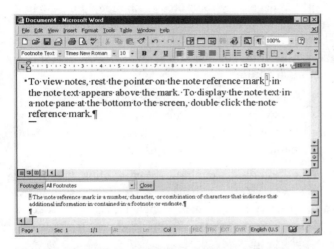

Fig. 5.21: Footnote pane in the *Normal* view (top), and in the *Print Layout* view

After you have inserted the footnote text, click into the normal text if you are in the *Print Layout* view, or click on the *Close* button <u>Close</u> if you are in the *Normal* view. *Word* then closes the footnote pane, and returns you to the document text.

Enter all the necessary footnotes or endnotes into the text in this way. *Word* automatically takes care of the correct numbering. If you insert a foot- or endnote in between two existing foot- or endnotes, *Word* will adjust the numbering accordingly.

Footnote separator

When you insert a footnote, the normal text is delimited by a footnote separator. You can also edit this line in the footnote pane in *Normal* view by selecting the icon with the same name in the drop-down list box.

Editing a footnote

To edit a footnote or endnote, double-click the corresponding note reference mark. *Word* switches into the footnote pane, where you can then change the text as needed. In order to remove a footnote, delete the note reference mark in the text.

Foot- and endnotes can be copied or moved within the text.

ScreenTip displays footnote text

The contents of footnotes and endnotes are displayed in every view (including the *Print Layout* and the *Web Layout* views) in a *ScreenTip* if you place the mouse cursor over a note reference mark.

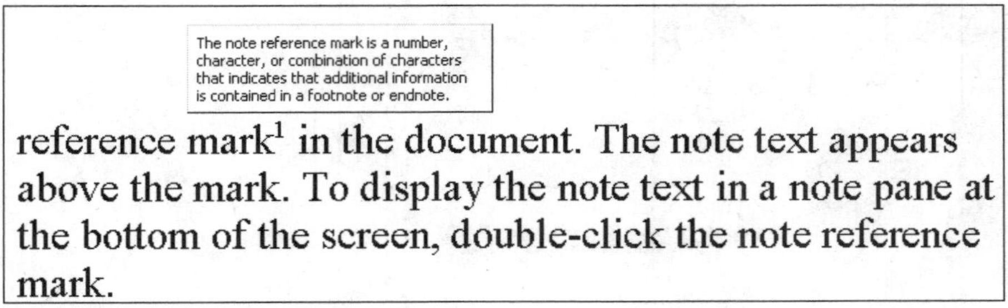

The note reference mark is a number, character, or combination of characters that indicates that additional information is contained in a footnote or endnote.

reference mark[1] in the document. The note text appears above the mark. To display the note text in a note pane at the bottom of the screen, double-click the note reference mark.

Fig. 5.22:   The *ScreenTip* for a footnote

Changing the Numbering of Footnotes and Endnotes

By default, the numbering of footnotes starts with '1' in each document. Endnotes, however, start with 'i'. Let's see how to define a different numbering for the first footnote or endnote, and how to use other numbering formats or symbols.

To insert a footnote or endnote, position the cursor right after the word in the document you want to assign the foot- or endnote to, just as you would do for default numbering. From the *Insert* menu select the *Footnote* command.

In the *Footnote and Endnote* dialog box, click the *Options* button. In the *Note Options* dialog box activate the *All Footnotes* tab page. If you want to change the format of an endnote, activate the *All Endnotes* tab page instead.

Number format   In the *Number format* drop-down list you can choose one of six different number formats. The *1,2,3* format is set as default, and it numbers the footnotes using Arabic numerals. The *a,b,c* and *A,B,C* formats imitate the number format using letters of the alphabet, one in small letters and one in capital letters. If more than 'z' footnotes are contained within the document, *Word* will continue the numbering with *aa, bb, cc*.

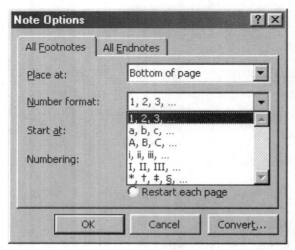

Fig. 5.23: Numbering format for footnotes

Next, in the *Number format* drop-down list, there are the Roman numerals *i,ii,iii* in lower case – hence, footnote number 18, for example, would become *xviii*. The *, †,‡,§ Number format* consists of only four symbols and if there are more than four footnotes, they will have to be used more than once.

Start at

In the *Start at* text box, you can determine the starting number or symbol that is to be used for the first footnote in the document. This way, you can use consecutive numbers even in documents consisting of several chapters.

To do this, select the *Continuous* radio button. If you decide not to use continuous numbering but would rather prefer the footnote numbering begin again with '1' on each new page, select the *Restart each page* radio button.

New note reference mark

You can choose completely new reference marks for footnotes or endnotes by clicking on the *Symbol* button in the *Footnotes and Endnotes* dialog box, and by choosing a symbol from the *Symbol* dialog box.

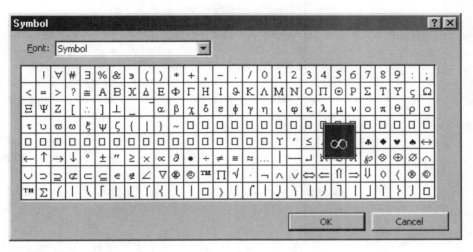

Fig. 5.24: Choosing customized numbering symbols

First, in the *Font* drop-down list, select the desired font. Fonts such as *Symbol* or *Wingdings* are recommended since they offer a wide range of different symbols. By clicking a particular symbol, an enlarged view of the symbol chosen is displayed. When you select a symbol and confirm it by clicking *OK*, it is copied into the *Footnote and Endnote* dialog box and appears in the *Custom mark* box. Click *OK* once more in order to close the dialog box and use the new note reference mark in your document.

Editing or Deleting Footnote or Endnote Separators

Every time you insert footnotes into a document, *Word* sets the footnote apart from the normal text by a so-called *footnote separator* which is also printed. This line is displayed in the *Print Layout* view above the footnote in the final printing position at the bottom edge of the page.

However, any attempt to select the footnote separator in the *Print Layout* view is bound to fail. The separator can neither be selected nor changed or deleted.

Formatting footnote separator

If you want to alter the shape of the footnote separator, or if you want to get rid of it, switch into the *Normal* view by choosing the *Normal* command on the *View* menu. Double-click a note reference mark in the text. The *Word* window is divided into two panes with the lower pane displaying the footnotes.

However, you will not find the footnote separator displayed there anymore. What can you do? The answer is very simple: click the *Footnotes* drop-down list, and select the *Footnote Separator* item. The footnote separator will then be displayed in the footnote pane.

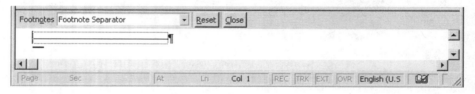

Fig. 5.25: The footnote pane in the *Normal* view

Delete footnote separator

Highlight the line. In order to delete the footnote separator, simply press the *Delete* key Del. If you want to edit the line, use for example the *Tables and Borders* button on the toolbar.

Formatting the separator

When formatting the separator you have all the possibilities you have during normal text formatting. After you have completed the task, close the footnote pane by clicking the *Close* button. The new footnote separator will be used. You can then switch back to the *Print Layout* view if necessary.

The *Line Style* box displays the border line you last used. Click on the drop-down button to the right in order to open the *Line Style* palette from which you can choose a new line to format the footnote separator.

Deleting Footnotes or Endnotes

In case you do not need a particular footnote anymore, you can remove it from the document quite simply without changing the numbering of the remaining footnotes. *Word* automatically executes it and controls that the numbers of the remaining footnotes are adjusted according to the new sequence.

In order to delete a footnote, select the note reference mark and press the *Delete* key Del. Do not try to remove the footnote text in the footnote pane independently of a note reference mark, otherwise you will only get an error message.

Inserting Line Numbers into a Text

If you want to refer to a certain line in a document such as a manuscript or a contract, for example, you can insert line numbers into the document. *Word* then prints the line numbers in the left margin or on the left-hand side of columns formatted in the newspaper style.

Show/hide line numbers

Word automatically counts every line in the document, except for the rows in columns, including footnotes, endnotes, text boxes, foot- and endnotes. You can, however, decide which line numbers are to be displayed. Likewise you can decide to hide the line numbers of certain paragraphs. You can either number the lines of the whole document, or just a part of it.

Number interval

Moreover, you can display line numbers at certain intervals, for instance, every tenth line – i.e. in every line which is a multiple of 10. If you do not want certain lines to be numbered, for example headings or empty lines, you can leave the line numbering out for these elements and afterwards resume the numbering in the following lines.

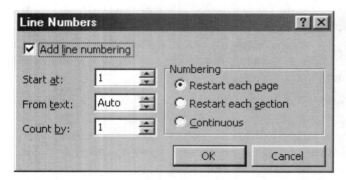

Fig. 5.26:   Adding line numbers

Switch to the *Print Layout* view. In order to add line numbers to the whole document, open the *Edit* menu and choose the *Select All* command. In order to add line numbers to only a certain part of the document, select the lines in the text which you want to be numbered. To add line numbers to an entire section, click into the relevant section, or select several sections.

Line numbers

To add line numbers, choose the *Page Setup* command on the *File* menu. Then activate the *Layout* tab page, and click the *Line Numbers* button. Select the *Add line numbering* check box, and choose the desired options.

Restart or
continuous

By selecting *Restart each page* or *Restart each section*, *Word* begins counting afresh with each new page or each new section. If you want to number the lines continuously throughout the entire document, select the *Continuous* radio button.

Start at

Use the spin buttons to enter the first number in the *Start at* box, and, if you want to display the line numbers at intervals (for example, by tens), enter the corresponding interval into the *Count by* box. Confirm by clicking *OK*.

Apply to

If you want to insert the line numbers into only a certain section of the document, open the *Apply to* drop-down list in the *Page Setup* dialog box and choose the *Selected text* item. Then close the dialog box by clicking *OK*.

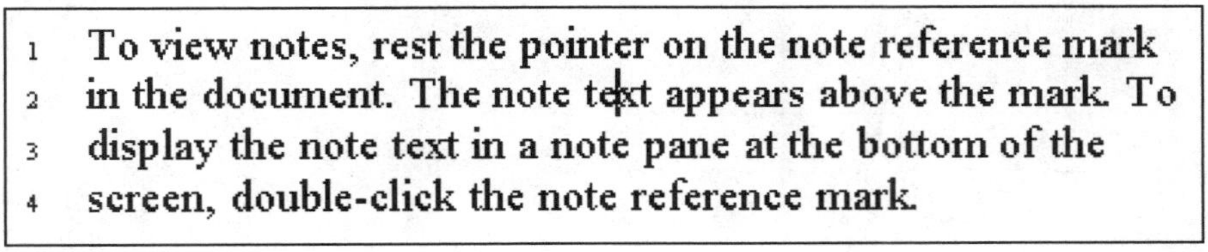

1	**To view notes, rest the pointer on the note reference mark**
2	**in the document. The note text appears above the mark. To**
3	**display the note text in a note pane at the bottom of the**
4	**screen, double-click the note reference mark.**

Fig. 5.27:   Line numbers

Suppressing Line Numbers

If a document contains headings or empty lines, the line numbering can be interrupted with regard to these elements.

For example, lines 1 to 23 are already numbered, but they are followed by a heading for which the line numbering is to be interrupted. The numbering of the following lines should continue with number '24'.

Suppressing line numbers

If you want to interrupt the line numbering in certain paragraphs, switch to the *Print Layout* view. Then select the paragraphs in which the line numbering is to be interrupted. On the *Format* menu click the *Paragraph* command, and then activate the *Line and Page Breaks* tab page. Now select the *Suppress line numbers* check box. Confirm by clicking *OK*.

Fig. 5.28:   Interrupting the line numbering for certain paragraphs

Formatting Extensive Documents

In this chapter we have talked about page formatting of a document of one or more pages. This kind of formatting is obviously useful only when a document contains more than one page.

Apart from formatting documents several pages long, *Word* also supports the formatting of very large documents, using some practical functions such as:

- The *Outline* function, to organize a document

- *Bookmarks*

- Commands to quickly move within the document and to find specific passages

Displaying and Using the *Outline* View

Word can display a document in many different ways. The way a document is displayed in *Word* is called a *view*. Different views are used while performing different tasks. Some views can display a document whose formatting is of little importance, while others display the document in the actual layout it will later be printed in. Still other views are used only for very specific tasks, such as to present an overview of the headings, or to combine several documents into one file.

What can the
Outline view do?

The *Outline* view is a special view displaying the text organized according to heading levels. In order to be able to do this, however, certain conditions have to be fulfilled beforehand.

Outline view ▣

In order to change to the *Outline* view, select the *Outline* command on the *View* menu, or click the *Outline* button ▣ to the left of the horizontal scroll bar. The *Outline* view presents the structure of the document in its different levels. In order for *Word* to be able to do this, however, the document must have been previously outlined with the formatting styles *Heading 1* to *Heading 9,* since in the *Outline* view, *Word* uses only the heading levels.

The outline levels displayed can be expanded and collapsed by using different buttons. In this view, you can portray a lengthy document in a very clear manner. Furthermore, you can easily change the position of text in a long document.

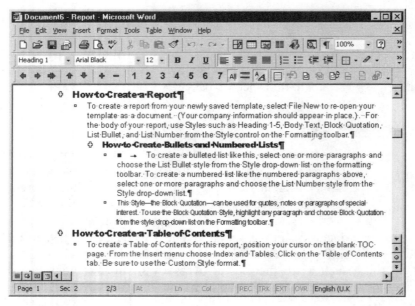

Fig. 5.29: A document in the *Outline* view of *Word*

To reduce the levels displayed, use the numbered buttons on the *Outlining* toolbar which is automatically inserted underneath the *Formatting* toolbar.

Fig. 5.30: The *Outlining* toolbar

If, for example, you want to show only the headings up to the third level, click the **3** button. A click onto the **1** button reduces the displayed levels to those paragraphs which have been formatted with the *Heading 1* style, etc.. Click the *All* button **All** to display the whole text again.

The different levels are also indicated by various indents. The more a text is indented in the *Outline* view, the lower is its position in the structural hierarchy. Plus or minus signs in front of the heading levels indicate whether the section contains more sections on lower levels. Click a plus sign in order to display the heading levels which lie beneath the current level. Click a minus sign to hide the levels beneath the current one.

Show Formatting

With the *Show Formatting* button, you can show or hide the text formatting. Click the *Show First Line Only* button if you want to display only the first line of the text in each section.

Promote/Demote

With the *Promote/Demote* buttons you can promote or demote the selected level to the next higher or lower heading level respectively. With the *Move Up/Move Down* buttons you can change the order of the text in such a way that it automatically moves along with all the sublevels you have created within it. This also happens in the case of copying or moving headings with the mouse, or when using the clipboard commands *Edit*, *Copy*, *Paste* and *Paste Special*.

Document Map and *Outline* View

You can combine the *Outline* view with the *Document Map*. If the *Document Map* is not automatically displayed when you call-up the *Outline* view, select either *View/Document Map* or click the *Document Map* button in order to display it.

The document is then divided into two window panes. On the left, you will see the section headings, while on the right, you will see the heading hierarchy of your document. Use the left part of the window to quickly move to a certain heading in the document without having to hide all the sublevels in the outline window. Simply click the corresponding heading in the map window.

In the *Document Map*, like in the *Outline* view, a minus sign is displayed in front of a heading containing one or more sublevels. Click the sign to hide the sublevels. If you do hide them, the minus sign changes into a plus sign. Click it again if you want to show the hidden elements.

Jumping to specific document pages

In the long run, moving to different pages in long documents by using the *Page Down* `PgDn` or *Page Up* `PgUp` keys can be rather tedious. Therefore, *Word* offers you alternatives for jumping to specific document pages.

One way to get to a certain page is by using the scroll box in the scroll bar. If you drag the scroll box upwards or downwards with the mouse button pressed down, you get a *ScreenTip* at the mouse pointer showing the current page number, and if the page contains a heading, this is shown as well. When you reach the desired page, release the mouse button, and *Word* jumps to this page.

Go to

Alternatively, *Word* offers you a command by means of which you can jump to a specific passage in a document. On the *Edit* menu, select the *Go To* command.

A faster way to activate the *Go To* command is by pressing the `Ctrl`+`G` key combination or the `F5` key. Either way, the *Find and Replace* dialog box will open and the *Go To* tab page will be activated. In the *Go to what* list box the *Page* item is selected.

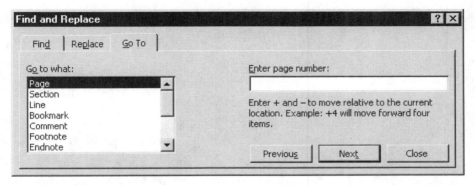

Fig. 5.31:   Jumping to a specific page

Into the *Enter page number* box on the right, enter the desired page number, and press *Enter* ⏎ or click *Go To*. *Word* now jumps to the corresponding page. If you want to move ahead by 10 pages, for example, enter '+10' into the *Enter page number* text box. If on the other hand, you enter '-4', you will jump four pages back from where the cursor is currently positioned in the document.

If you have inserted page numbers, you should be careful. When you change the starting number of the first page, the *Go To* command either jumps to the actual page number or to the relative page number. *Word* always jumps to the position which is available first (for example, page 4 means page 104 in a text which starts numbering from 100.)

Browse Document for Objects

In *Word 2000* you can resort to the vertical scroll to jump to specific passages in a document. Click the *Select Browse Object* button ⊙ located in the vertical scroll bar with the other buttons.

A menu opens offering buttons with which you can search for or jump to specific passages in the document.

In the button area below you will find a description of their different functions.

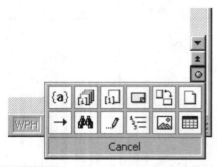 

The buttons and the choice

If you point to one of the buttons, a description of the button you have selected will be displayed underneath it. The buttons search the document for certain objects such as pages, headings, pictures, graphic objects, tables, fields, or footnotes.

After you have selected a button, you can jump from object to object by clicking the buttons above or below the *Select Browse Object* button

Inserting and Using Bookmarks

In long documents, you often waste a lot of time looking for particular text passages. If you know the page number containing the information you are looking for, you can use the *Go To* function in order to quickly jump to the corresponding page. For the function we are going to introduce you to now, you also need the *Go To* command.

What are bookmarks?

First, define what are known as *Bookmarks* in your document - they will be helpful when you want to jump to particular text passages. Bookmarks are very useful to find a certain point in your text, for example to select an element as a reference point for a cross reference, or to mark a page section to create an index. You can also assign a bookmark to selected text, graphics, tables or other elements. To set a bookmark, select the relevant text passage or the relevant object, and then choose *Insert/Bookmark*. A dialog box opens. Enter the name of the bookmark without using any spaces, and click on the *Add* button.

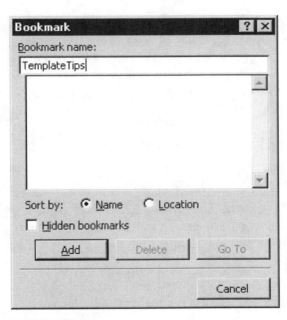

Fig. 5.33: Inserting a bookmark into a document

Repeat the procedure for all elements or text passages you want to mark. In order to jump to a bookmark, select again the *Insert/Bookmark* command and, choose the desired bookmark in the list.

Sort by

In the *Bookmark* dialog box, the *Sort by* option group allows you choose the sorting order. You can sort the names of bookmarks in alphabetical order by clicking the *Name* radio button. If you click the *Location* radio button, you will view the list of bookmarks as they were inserted into the document.

Displaying bookmarks

Inserted bookmarks are displayed on the screen as square brackets – not printed, however – if you have activated the *Bookmarks* check box in the *View* tab page via the *Tools/Options* menu.

Edit/ Go To/ Bookmark

Alternatively, you can jump to bookmarks by choosing the *Edit/Go To* command. In the *Go to what* list box select the *Bookmark* item, and in the *Enter bookmark name* drop-down list box select the desired bookmark or type in its name. Then click the *Go To* button.

Inserting a Table of Contents

If your document contains organized headings, you can easily create a table of contents automatically.

To do this, select the *Insert/Index and Tables* command at the position you have chosen for the table of contents, and activate the *Table of Contents* tab page.

In the *Formats* list box select the desired format for the table of contents. In the *Preview* box, you can view how the selected format will modify the table of contents.

Show page numbers

If the table of contents should display the page number next to the heading, as it is normally the case, check the *Show page numbers* check box. If you display the page numbers, you can choose whether you want the page numbers to appear right next to the headings, or to be aligned on the right side of the page, by selecting or clearing the *Right align page numbers*.

Tab leader

If you right-align the page numbers, you can insert leader elements between the heading text and the page number, and this will make the association easier to the reader. Select the leader element from the *Tab leader* drop-down list.

Show levels

In the *Show levels* box you can specify how many heading levels you want to be shown in the table of contents.

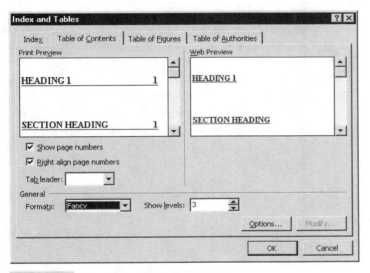

Fig. 5.34:   Creating a table of contents

After you have confirmed the selected options by clicking *OK*, *Word* inserts the table of contents at the selected insertion point. The table of contents is inserted as a field.

If you later change the document so as to affect the table of contents, you can update it by clicking into it and pressing the F9 key.

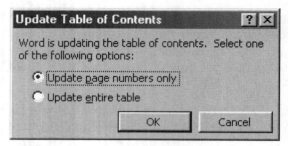

Fig. 5.35: Update table of contents

If you want to change only the page numbers but not the formatting, select the *Update page numbers only* radio button in the *Update Table of Contents* dialog box. If you have inserted a new heading on a level you want to show in the table of contents, choose the *Update entire table* option button. Click *OK* to update the table.

6. Printing, Faxing and Sending

During the installation of Windows 98 you will be asked to identify your printer. This won't be the case if you have bought a new PC on which Windows 98 has already been installed. In that case your printer hasn't been set up yet, because the dealer obviously doesn't know what printer model you're going to use. For *Word* you will definitely need a printer since without it, word processing is not very useful. You will now learn how to install your new or any other printer using Windows.

Installing a Printer

When you install a printer, something known as a 'printer driver' will be copied onto your hard disk, either from the Windows setup CD or from the floppy that came along with the printer. A printer driver is a small program that prepares the data contained in a document for a particular printer. The printer installation will set the necessary information for the printer you're using in the Windows *Control Panel*.

New printers can be installed under Windows 98 at any time. Use a Windows function to install the necessary driver program which will control the printing out of the data.

Installing a Printer with Windows 98

To install a printer choose *Settings/Printers* from the *Start* menu or open the *Printers* folder via *My Computer*. Double-click on the *New Printer* icon in the *Printer* folder to start the *Add Printer Wizard*. The first step of the wizard window can be immediately confirmed with *Next*.

Local Printer

In the second step you will be asked if the printer to be installed is directly attached to your computer. For a stand-alone system select the *Local printer* radio button and click *Next*. In the dialog box displayed below, you can then select the printer manufacturer and the printer model.

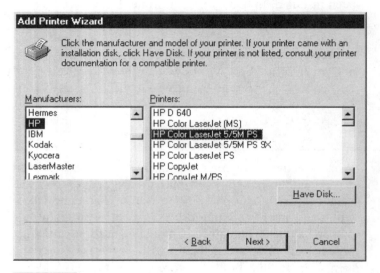

Fig. 6.1:   Wizard for installing a printer

Manufacturers and Printers

Select the corresponding entry in the *Manufacturers* list box. In order to select entries which are not immediately visible, use the scroll bar or just type the first letter of the manufacturer's name. The *Printers* list box at the right side of the dialog box will display all the available printer drivers of the selected manufacturer. Select the specific model of your printer and click *Next*.

Floppy

If you do not find the manufacturer's name or model in the list, you will need to use the floppy provided by the manufacturer which you can access by clicking the *Have Disk* button. Then click *Next* to proceed to the next step.

Available ports

Select the entry *LPT1: ECP Printer Port* in the *Available Ports* list box. Click *Next* again and either give your printer a name or accept the proposed name.

Default printer

If you have only one printer or if you want to print mainly with this printer, choose the option *Yes* in the lower part of the dialog box to set this printer as your *Default Printer* in *Windows 98*. Click *Next* again. Now you're given the option to print a test page. To do so, simply click *Finish*. Wait for the printout and answer the question whether the page has been printed properly. In case you don't want to print a test page, select the *No* radio button and click *Finish*.

Windows 98 will copy only the necessary driver from the setup CD-ROM. The new printer will then be added to the *Printers* folder as a new icon.

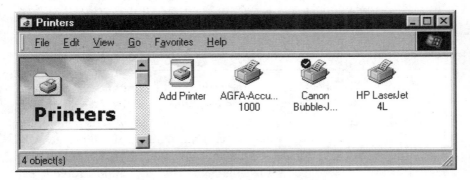

Fig. 6.2:   The Printers folder with different installed printers

Selected printers in the *Printers* folder can be configured at any time via the context menu or the *File/Properties* item.

Checking Printer Settings

Having a printer that works properly is especially important when working in *Word*. After a new printer has been installed, Windows 98 and programs like *Word* generally use the default settings of the driver. Adjust the properties of the printer driver to ensure your printer is working correctly. The properties can be viewed or modified at any time from the *Printers* folder in Windows 98.

Start/Settings/
Printers

All you have to do is to choose *Settings/Printers* from the *Start* menu, or alternatively you can open the *Printers* folder with a double-click on *My Computer* and the *Printers* folder. Select the icon of the printer you are using.

Properties

Click on *Properties* in the *File* menu. The properties available on the different tabs of the *[Printer name] Properties* dialog box will depend on what type of printer you have. To get an overview of all the different options you can access, have a look at the contents of the tabs.

Printing a Test Page

To check whether the printer is working properly, change to the *General* tab and click the *Print Test Page* button. If all the information printed on this test page is legible, the printer is working fine. Then confirm the message with *Yes*. If some sections are unreadable or if the small *Windows* logo is missing, it means that some problem occurred. Click *No* and follow the *Windows 98 Print Troubleshooter*.

Details tab

The printer port can be changed and viewed on the *Details* tab; use the *Print to the following port* drop-down list box for this purpose. The current printer driver is displayed in the *Print using the following driver* drop-down list box.

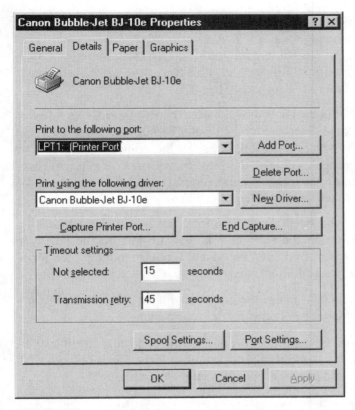

Fig. 6.3: Viewing the properties of the printer

Graphics tab

In order to change the appearance of the printout, activate the *Graphics* tab page. The number of available options depends on the capacity of your printer, but the option group called *Dithering* and the *Intensity* slider are common to all printer drivers in Windows 98.

Printer driver settings

In case you didn't install any Windows 98 printer driver, this tab page may be arranged in a completely different way or it might not appear at all. If this happens, follow the manufacturer's description of how to configure your printer.

Most of the Windows 98 printer drivers have the following dithering options: *None*, *Coarse*, *Fine*, *Line art* and *Error diffusion*. The *Error diffusion* option creates a very differentiated printing result even in black and white with a laser printer.

But in the end you will have to choose from all the different possibilities and try them out. The *Intensity* slider gives you control over the brightness of the printout. Confirm your changes and start the printout with *OK*. It is advisable to make test printouts and compare the results which can be obtained using different settings.

What's This

If you need to get help for other items on the tabs, first click on the *Help* button [?] and then on the item you need to find out more about. Changes in the printer properties will affect every document printed on the printer.

File/Page Setup

You can change the properties for an individual *Word* document by choosing *File/Page Setup*.

Device options

For laser printers the setting of the available printer memory is especially important. Use the *Device Options* tab in the printer properties dialog, to configure it.

Viewing Documents Before Printing in the Print Preview

The *Print Layout* view in *Word* is a very good example of the successful representation of a document on-screen. Depending on the *View* option selected, the paper edge and page margins may be displayed.

The way the document or letter is displayed depends on the enlargement factor.

In a larger magnification the scroll bars can be used to scroll easily from the beginning of a document to the end, should you want, for example, to check the layout of the text on the page before printing. But this still falls short of a real overview. By displaying your document with the *Print Preview* you'll get the overview you're looking for. Here you can see one or more pages of a document in their entirety.

Print Preview 🔍 Click the *Print Preview* item on the *File* menu or click on the *Print Preview* button 🔍 on the *Standard* toolbar. The key combination to use if you want to switch between your current view and the *Print Preview* is `Ctrl`+`F2`. *Word* displays the document in such a way that the whole page is contained within the preview window. The layout of text on the page can be easily judged in this manner.

For further information on how to use the *Print Preview* have another look at Chapter 5.

Printing Documents with Word

Click the *Print Preview* button 🔍 on the *Standard* toolbar, or choose *File/Print Preview*, to check the document once more before printing it out. Click on the *Print* button to open the dialog box of the same name. The printing procedure is the same for all *Windows* applications.

Printing Quickly

The fastest way to print is to click the *Print* button 🖨 on the *Standard* toolbar. The document will then be printed using the default settings of the *Print* dialog box, that is to say, the entire document will be printed in one go.

Using the *Print* Dialog Box

To print a document from the *Normal* or *Print Layout* views in *Word*, call up the *Print* dialog box by choosing the *Print* item on the *File* menu.

271

Default printer

To print without making any changes to the default settings, simply press *Enter* ↵ or click the *OK* button. In case there is more than one printer installed on your system, the name of the printer which is set as the default printer will be displayed in the *Name* drop-down list box of the *Print* dialog box by default.

Selecting the printer

In case you want to use a printer other than the default printer, open the drop-down list and choose the printer you want. To configure the printer, click the *Properties* button.

Page range

In the *Page range* option group choose which parts of the document you want to print. More about printing only certain text sections will be explained later in this chapter.

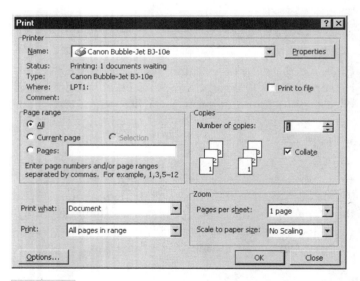

Fig. 6.5:   The *Print* dialog box

Copies

In the *Copies* options group enter the number of copies you want to print in the *Number of copies* box. Check the *Collate* check box if your printer has such a feature.

Zoom by printing

Changing the size of the screen with the *Zoom* drop-down box in the *Standard* toolbar will not affect the printout. For checking purposes you can also print several pages on just one sheet of paper. To do so, in the *Press* dialog box in the *Zoom* option group choose the number of pages per sheet you want to print. If your printer uses A4 paper, as is usually is the case, and if you need to print a little brochure on A5 paper, which is half the size of a A4 sheet, you can then choose to print two pages next to each other on a single sheet of paper. From the *Pages per sheet* drop-down box select the *2 pages* item. If you want to print an A5 sheet individually on an A4 sheet later, you have to choose the *Scale to paper size* option. The size of the font and the graphics will then be adjusted in order to fit properly into the page. You can proceed in the same way if you have A3-size paper, which is twice the size of a A4 paper. In this case you can decrease the size of the page to fit into an A4 sheet. It works just like the zoom function of a photocopying machine.

Click on *OK* to begin the print out.

Printing Only Selected Text

Press the *Print* button 🖨 on the *Standard* toolbar to print a document; the default settings of the *Print* dialog box will be enabled.

Page range

In order to print a document from the *Normal* view or the *Print Layout* view, choose *File/Print* to call up the *Print* dialog box. Use the *Page range* options group to change the page range.

Current page

If you only want to print the current page, select the *Current page* radio button. But be aware that the current page is the one where the insertion cursor is blinking. This is not necessarily the one displayed on the screen.

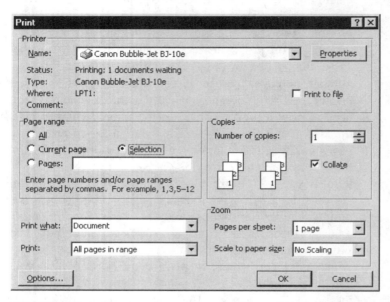

Fig. 6.6:   The *Print* dialog box with the *Selection* radio button selected

Selection

If you want to print only a selected section of your text, click the *Selection* radio button. This option is not available if there is no text selected when you activate the dialog. You cannot select the text with dialog box open, so you have to take care to first select the desired passage and then open the *Print* dialog box.

To print specific pages, or one or more sections, or a range of pages in more than one section, click the *Pages* radio button. Your entry in the box next to it will depend on what you want to print.

Non-contiguous pages

For a number of non-adjacent pages, enter the page numbers separated by a comma. If page numbers are separated by a hyphen, *Word* will print all the pages between and including the start and the last page. You can also specify a section to be printed. For example, to print pages 4 to 7 within section 2, enter: p4s2-p7s2

Printing sections

To print an entire section enter 's' for section together with the number of the section. Enter for example: s3 to print the entire third section. Non-contiguous sections can be printed if you indicate each section separated by a comma. If you enter, for example, s3,s5, then only section 3 and section 5 will be printed.

Printing a range of pages across sections

To print a range of pages across sections, you have to type in the range of pages together with the corresponding section numbers. Separate the beginning and the end of your selection with a hyphen. For example, to print pages 2 and 3 throughout sections 2 to 5, enter 'p2s2-p3s5'.

Printing on Both Sides of a Page

In case you want to print a multiple-paged document and save space and paper, you can choose to print your document on both the front and the back sides of the paper. You don't need a special deluxe printer to do this. In the *Print* drop-down list on the bottom right side of the dialog box, first select the *Odd pages* entry and click *OK* to print all the pages on the front side, then select the *Even pages* entry in the same drop-down list. Now turn the pages upside down and start the printing process a second time. This time all the even numbered pages, i.e. the other side of the page, will be printed.

Background Printing

Usually the printing of documents happens in *background*. *Word* prepares the document first, saves it in a temporary file and lines it up in the print queue. *Word* then lets you get on with your other work almost immediately. That way it is possible to print large documents while you are working on a different text or editing other documents.

Tools/Options

In principle *Background printing* is a noble thing, but there might be certain circumstances when you wish you could switch off this function. The process of printing documents can be quite long and drawn out, because *Windows* needs to use its multitasking capacity for the background printing and normally printing does not have a very high priority. In case you want to speed up the printing process, choose the *Options* item from the *Tools* menu.

Print tab

Change to the *Print* tab and clear the *Background printing* check box. Confirm with *OK*.

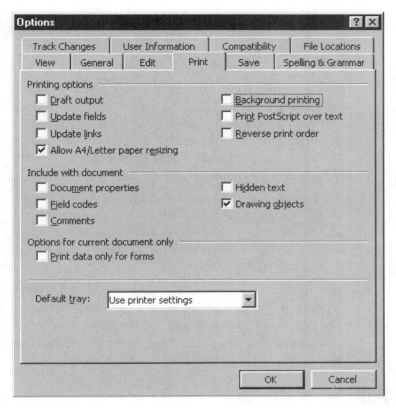

Fig. 6.7:   **Turning off background printing**

Word will then give its full attention to printing the documents. During the preparation and also during the printing you will see the *Printing* message indicating the progress of the printing procedure.

With the background printing deactivated *Word* is blocked during the time of printing. You will have to wait until all the pages of the document have been printed before continuing your work.

Canceling the Printing Job

After typing a text into a document, and after formatting it, you will normally print out the *Word* document. Before that should always remember to save the document.

If you don't follow this advice, and a major error does occur during printing, then your document might not be available any more. Admittedly, these errors occur only very rarely, but nevertheless they do occur, and it could just happen to you and to your document ...

Default print

To print out the entire document on the default printer without changing the properties or the page range, just click on the *Print* button 🖨 on the *Standard* toolbar. If you want to define what should be printed, activate the *Print* dialog box with *File/Print*.

After you have set all printing parameters, click *OK* to start the printing job. Depending on the configuration of *Word* the printing job will begin in the background or, if the background printing feature is disabled, the *Printing* dialog box will appear. See Figure 6.8.

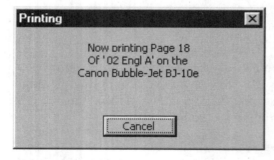

Fig. 6.8:   The *Printing* dialog box

In case this dialog box is displayed you will have to wait until the printing of all the pages is completed before you can continue working with *Word*. The first line of the dialog box shows the current status of the printing job. Here *Word* displays which page of your document is currently being printed.

Cancel

In the second line you can see the name of the document which is currently being printed. The third and last line of the message shows the name of the printer in use. If you realize, after having called up the print command, that there is a mistake in your document or that you forgot to add a section to the document, you can still cancel the foreground printing job by clicking on *Cancel*.

Cancel the print queue

This message will not appear if you are using the default *Background printing* setting, but you will still see the progress while the printing job is going on in the form of a small icon in the status bar. A little printer will appear there. While the data is being sent to the print queue, the little printer will eject papers: . In small documents of only a single page this icon can be very easily ignored, because it will only appear for a very short time. To cancel a background printing job simply click on the printer icon.

Display in the taskbar

Windows 98 will also display the printing job on the taskbar. A printer icon 17:25 -next to the current time displays the activity of the jobs in the queue. A double click on the icon opens the dialog box showing all the jobs in the print queue. You can also cancel the printing of a document from there.

If you stop the foreground printing just as the printer is about to print a page, this page will be printed anyway in most cases, before *Word* becomes available for other tasks again. But such details depend on the printer you are using and the printer driver installed.

Windows 98 Print Queue

By default *Word* prints documents in background: the document is prepared and saved in a temporary file before it is placed in the print queue. This print queue normally stays hidden, since it is a multitasking function of Windows 98 operating system.

Why a print queue?

The print queue manages the printing jobs of the different Windows applications. Printing jobs from *Word* are put into this queue and are taken care of independently of *Word*.

Double-click on

If there are printing jobs standing in the print queue, a little printer icon 🖨 17:25 is displayed in the *Windows 98* taskbar just to the left of the clock. After finishing all the printing jobs this icon will disappear again from the taskbar. To look at the jobs in the print queue, double-click on this printer icon. A dialog box with the name of your default printer will be displayed, containing a list of all the pending printing jobs and their status.

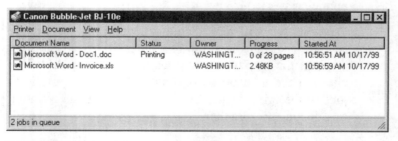

Fig. 6.9: Printing jobs in the print queue

Pause Printing

Using the print queue you can stop the printing procedure, change the order of the printing jobs or cancel a job completely. You can use this function to respond to errors during printing. In the case of a paper jam in your printer, for example, choose *Printer/Pause Printing*. You have time to correct the paper jam problem and then choose *Printer/Pause Printing* again to resume printing.

Retry

With certain types of printer error, you will get a particular message. If everything is OK with your printer, and there was only a break while printing, click the *Retry* button to go on with the job.

Cancel

When a serious printer error occurs, stop printing with the *Cancel* button. Then solve the problem and start the printing process once more with *File/Print*.

Cancel Printing

When a problem occurs, printing jobs can also be halted via the print queue dialog box. To do this, select the document currently being printed in the list box and choose *Cancel Printing* from the *Document* menu. This way you only have to reprint the pages in the document where the error occurred and which therefore did not print correctly. You can also interrupt any other printing jobs which have not yet started by choosing *Purge Print Documents* from the *Printer* menu.

You will only see the print queue if you did not deactivate the background printing in *Word*.

Faxes

There is a variety of ways to send a fax using the computer. For the method explained here, your fax-modem has to be connected to the PC and the telephone line. The modem has to be switched on. If your modem is correctly configured in the *Control Panel* and if the software *Microsoft Fax* program is installed, then you can send faxes from *Word* or any other Windows application.

The only requirement is that the program needs to be able to address a Windows printer. Since this is no problem in *Word*, sending faxes is very easy.

Creating Faxes with the New Fax Wizard

Word helps you with the creation of a fax. You will be led step by step through the process needed to send your fax.

In order to send a file as a fax, choose *File/Send to* and select *Fax Recipient* from the submenu. This will start the *Fax Wizard*. It will help you step by step with the preparations and the actual sending of the fax.

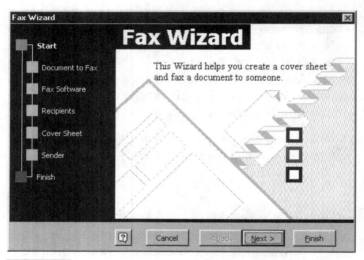

Fig. 6.10:   The Fax Wizard

In the first dialog box called *Fax Wizard*, the steps which the wizard will take you through are displayed. This screen is just for your information. Click on the *Next* button.

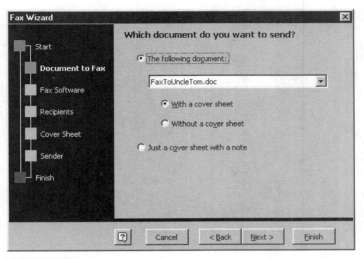

Fig. 6.11:   Fax with or without a cover sheet

On the next page you'll be asked which document you want to send. The active document from which you have given the fax command will be displayed by default. Open the drop-down list to select a different document. The list will only display open documents.

Cover sheet

Using the corresponding radio button, select whether you want to send the document with or without a cover sheet. You can also choose to send just the cover sheet with a note. Click again on *Next*. The next page will ask you which fax program you intend to use. You can choose either to send the fax from the PC or to make a printout and send the fax from an ordinary fax machine.

Choosing the fax software

In order to send your fax from the PC you have to choose which software you want to use for this. Click the *Microsoft Fax* radio button to use this program, or choose the second radio button and select from the drop-down list the corresponding fax driver. Click *Next* to continue.

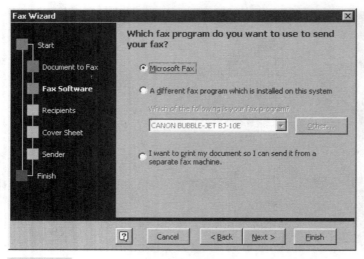

Fig. 6.12:   Choosing the fax software

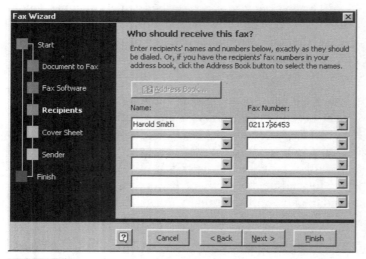

Fig. 6.13:   Choosing the recipients

The next page will ask you for the recipients' name. Enter the *Name* of the recipient and the *Fax Number* into the corresponding boxes.

Address book

A name that has already been used before can be selected from the drop-down list. If you want to use a name from one of the address books, click the *Address Book* button and choose the name from there. *Word* will then automatically add the saved fax number to the corresponding box.

In case you want to send the fax to more than one number, repeat this procedure for each box. After having chosen the recipients, click on *Next* to go to the next page of the *Fax Wizard*.

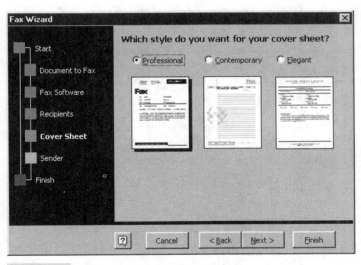

Fig. 6.14:   Choosing a cover sheet style

On this page you need to choose the style of your cover sheet. Decide between the three possibilities and click again on *Next*.

Address book

The next page will ask you the name of the sender. Enter the necessary information into *Name, Company, Mailing Address, Phone* and *Fax* boxes or open the address book, and select an entry if you have saved the address in there.

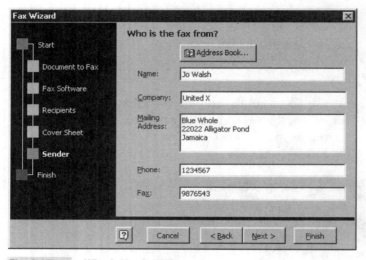

Fig. 6.15: Who is the fax from

With one more click on *Next* you will have completed your fax. The last page gives you information on any possible errors that might have occurred.

Read through this and end the *Fax Wizard* with the *Finish* button.

Changing the cover sheet

The cover sheet will be displayed and you can give it a final touch-up. You can, for example, select the topic of the fax and overwrite it.

Send fax now

The *Fax Wizard* toolbar will be displayed automatically. Click on the *Send Fax Now* button after you have made your final changes to the cover sheet.

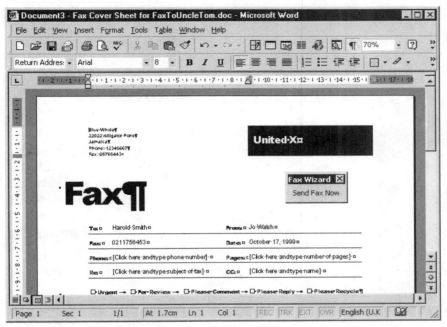

Fig. 6.16: Fax cover sheet and the toolbar

After *Word* has successfully sent the fax you will get a message you should acknowledge with *OK*.

Sending Documents

If you are using *Word* in a team and a network has been established, you can use *Word* in connection with *Outlook* to send documents to other participants on the network or via Internet. You will have the choice of sending the document as HTML file or as an attached file to a single user or to more recipients.

Send Files to E-mail Recipients

To send a document via E-mail, open the document and choose *File/Send To/Mail Recipient*. In addition an E-mail header is inserted above the document. The same result is achieved through the *E-mail* button of the *Standard* toolbar.

The document can be edited in the usual way and then sent in HTML format, also used in Internet environment. However, not all E-mail contacts can receive files in HTML format. If you know that a user cannot receive the HTML format, make a note of that in his address. When the *Send E-Mail using plain text only* option is marked for a contact in the address book, you will be informed of that when sending a formatted message to him.

Once you have completed your E-mail, click the *Send* button.

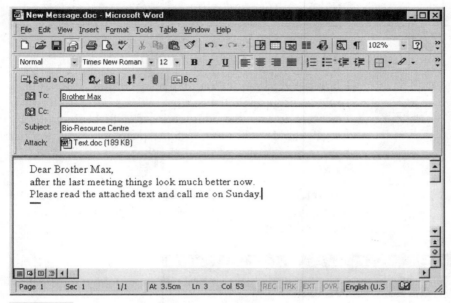

Fig. 6.18: Sending a document

After the mail has been sent, you will automatically be returned to the *Word* environment.

Sending a file as attachment

In the previous version of Word, files to be sent by E-mail were attached to a normal e-mail message (text only). You can do the same thing with Word 2000 too, using the command *File/Send to/Mail Recipient (as Attachment)*.

The file is attached and an E-mail header is displayed as well, in which the recipient name must be entered, or selected from the address book and an accompanying message can be typed. At the end, click on *Send*. To open and read the file, the recipient needs now Word 2000.

Sending a File to Routing Recipients

To send a document as a *Routing Slip*, open the document and choose *File/Send To/Routing Recipient*.

To

Click the *Address* button and select in the *Show Names from the* drop-down list box the address book from which you want to take the addresses. After that select one by one all the desired names of the recipients from the list box on the left side of the dialog box and click on the *To* button.

The selected names will be displayed in the *To* list of the dialog box. After you have summarized the names, activate the *OK* button.

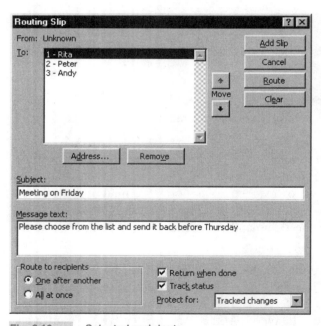

Fig. 6.19:   Selected recipients

Order

You can change the order of the recipients in the *To* list box with the help of the *Move* arrow buttons. Move the selected recipient up or down the routing list. If you click the *One after another* radio button, the document goes to recipients in the order they appear in the *To* list.

Message text

If necessary, overwrite the *Subject* and type the text of your mail into the *Message text* box.

Route to recipients

In the *Route to recipients* options group you can choose whether you want to send the documents to *All at once* or *One after another*.

Route

To add the routing slip to the document and send it according to the currently selected options, click the *Route* button. This button is unavailable if the *To* list is empty.

7. Tables

Word offers you a very simple and effective way to arrange any given document horizontally or vertically in tables. In this manner you can align texts, numbers, graphics, or diagrams, to give a few examples, in whichever way you like.

The creation and handling of tables in Word is very easy. Every Word table consists of a grid of columns and rows. The intersection of a column and a row creates what is known as a cell. Anything can be placed into a cell. Unlike in previous Word version, in Word 2000 you can now place one table inside another table.

Tables

In Word, a table is constructed by an arrangement of rows and columns similar to a spreadsheet program.

The smallest element of a table is a cell, created by the intersection of rows and columns.

Whereas in earlier versions of Word the table grid was only an aid which could not be printed out but could only be displayed on-screen, the Word 2000 version offers a special grid which can be inserted automatically and which will then be printed by default.

You can also hide this grid in case you just wanted to use it as an aid while arranging and editing your table.

Inserting Tables in Documents

There are two methods of creating a table within a document. One of these methods is by dragging the mouse and the other is by using a dialog box. To proceed with it, set the cursor in the position in your document where the table should be inserted. Then click the *Insert Table* button 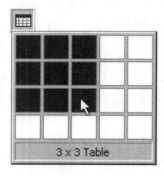. *Word* will immediately display a button menu which represents a table grid.

Point to the first cell and, while holding down the left mouse button, drag the mouse cursor to the right until the desired amount of columns has been selected. Do the same thing moving downwards to select as many rows as you wish. In the lower part of the dialog box you will see information about the table size *[Rows] x [Columns] Table.*

Fig. 7.1: Defining the table size with the mouse

If you selected too many cells, move the mouse back until you reach the desired amount of rows and columns. *Word* will insert the table only when you release the mouse button.

Inserting a table

Another way is to create a table with the *Table* menu. From the submenu choose the *Insert* command and then the *Table* item. A dialog box will be displayed.

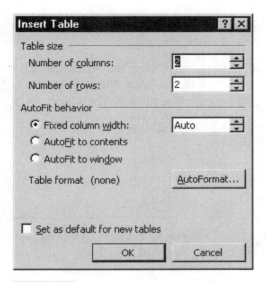

Fig. 7.2: The *Insert Table* dialog box

Enter the number of columns you want to have in the *Number of columns* text box of this dialog box. Enter the required number of rows into the *Number of rows* box. It is possible to enter an individual number into the *Fixed column width* box if you do not want *Word* to automatically adjust the table width to your margins. Choose *AutoFit to contents* if you want to adjust the width of columns on the basis of the cell content or *AutoFit to window* if you want to adjust the content to fit in the window. The last command item has the same effect as *Fixed column width: Auto*. As soon as you confirm with *OK*, *Word* will insert the table in your document.

No Border

The actual gridlines will not be printed, but they can be a valuable aid to make it easier for you to edit the table. However, on top of this support grid there is a border which will be printed. If you don't want this border to be printed, select the table and choose, from the *[border name]* *Border* drop-down palette on the *Tables and Borders* toolbar, the *No Border* button ▦ ▾.

If you have disabled the border, the actual gridlines of the table become visible. If the helping lines are not displayed in your table, choose *Table/Show Gridlines*.

Using the same command, the displayed gridlines can be hidden again. If you show the ruler with *View/Ruler*, you will see the column and row marks on the ruler when the text cursor is placed within the table.

Moving in a Table

In order to move from one cell to the next, press the *Tab* key ⇥ once. The same key will also bring you from the last cell in one row to the first cell of the next row. You can also just click into any cell to move there. To quickly move to the beginning or to the end of a row or column you can use the following key combinations:

- Beginning of a row   Alt + Home

- End of a row   Alt + End

- Top of a column   Alt + PgUp

- End of a column   Alt + PgDn

Within a cell use the normal key combinations to move between entire words or between lines and paragraphs.

Selecting Table Items

Select a cell by moving the pointer to the left edge of the cell until it changes to a right-pointing arrow, and then click to the left of the end-of-cell mark. Even if the mark is not displayed as in Figure 7.3, you can recognize the position because the cursor changes into an arrow pointing right.

Select a column by pointing at the top gridline of the column and clicking the mouse after the cursor has taken the shape of a downward pointing arrow.

In order to select any given section of a table, click into the first cell and drag the mouse to the last cell required.

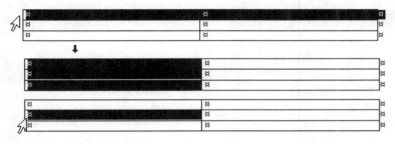

Fig. 7.3:   Selecting rows, columns and cells

Selecting items

Instead of using the mouse, you can also use commands to select certain table contents. To do so, click in the *Table* menu and from the submenu choose *Select*.

Deleting or Inserting Rows or Columns

You can enlarge a table or delete table items as easily as you can insert a table into a document. It is possible to add rows, columns or single cells as well as delete rows, columns or cells.

In order to be able to comprehend everything that will be explained below, it is better if you display the formatting marks. To do so, click the *Show/Hide* button ¶ on the *Standard* toolbar in order to see all those unprintable marks on the screen.

Tab key ⌨

Every time you press the *Tab* key ⌨ you normally move one cell to the right, but if you press the same key at the end of a row in a table, the cursor will jump to the first cell of the next row.

Add another

empty row

Pressing the *Tab* key ⌨ in the last cell of the last row will automatically add another empty row.

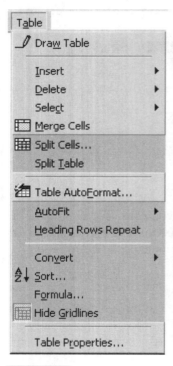

Fig. 7.4:   The *Table* menu

You can also add table rows or table columns with the help of commands from the submenu of the *Table/Insert* command. A faster method is to simply click on the buttons whose function changes depending on the kind of table item you have selected.

Select the necessary number of cells, rows or columns. Always heed the following rule: New table columns will always be inserted to the left of the selection, while new table rows will always be inserted above the selection. To insert the selected table sections click on the following buttons which will appear as soon as you select the corresponding item. These buttons will be displayed in the position where the *Insert Table* button was before.

- ⬛ ▤ *Insert Rows*
  will insert the selected number of rows above the first selected row. If the cursor is located directly below the table, the new row will be inserted below the last row.

- ⬛ ▥ *Insert Columns*
  will add the selected number of columns on the left side of the selected column. If the end-of-row marks right to the last column are selected, it will insert the column behind the last column.

- ⬛ ▦ *Insert Cells*
  will insert the selected number of cells on the left side of the cursor. The existing cells will be shifted downward or to the right, depending on your choice.

- ⬛ Warning: If you did not select anything and if the cursor is simply on a cell, on the screen you will only see the *Insert Table* button. This button allows you to insert a new table inside the current cell.

Insert commands

Word immediately inserts the desired amount of columns or rows into your table. As an alternative method, you can choose the *Insert* command from the *Table* menu. If you want to insert only one column or only one cell, you do not even need to make a selection. Besides you can use the menu command to determine on which page of the current selection you want to insert the new element.

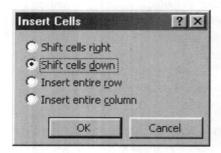 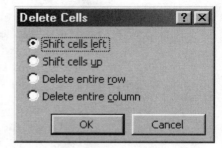

Fig. 7.5:   Dialog boxes before inserting or deleting cells

In order to delete sections of the table, select the rows, columns or cells you want to delete, and choose *Rows*, *Columns* or *Cells* respectively from the *Table/Delete* submenu. Before deleting cells you will be prompted to specify in which direction *Word* needs to shift the remaining cells.

Creating Tables with the *Tables and Borders* Toolbar

In the *Standard* toolbar of *Word 2000* you will see the *Tables and Borders* button ▦. With this button you can call up the toolbar of the same name.

Fig. 7.6:   The *Tables and Borders* toolbar for editing tables

You can use this toolbar to create new tables and to enlarge or edit existing tables. The buttons are:

- *Draw Table*
  With this button and the help of the mouse you can create not only horizontal and vertical table lines but also single cells.

- *Eraser*
  With this button you can delete unnecessary lines very easily.

- *Line Style*
  Choose from this list the line style for the next border or line you want to assign to a table item.

- *Line Weight*
  Choose from this list the weight of the line for the next border or line you want to draw.

- *Border Color*
  From the color palette, select the color for the next border or the next line you want to insert.

- *Outside Border*
  Assign borders or lines to the selected table cells at the corresponding positions, as indicated on the button.

- *Shading Color*
  Choose a shading or fill color to assign to the selected table item.

- *Insert Table*
  Insert a table or single table item in the existing table. Click on the triangle on the right of the button in order to open the corresponding menu.

- *Merge Cells*
  This button combines the selected cells within a row or column into one cell.

- ▦ *Split Cells*
  This button splits the selected cells into a specified number of rows or columns.

- ▯ *Align Top* palette
  This button aligns the cell content within the cell borders.

- ⊞ *Distribute Rows Evenly*
  This button sets all the selected rows to the same row height.

- ⊞ *Distribute Columns Evenly*
  This button sets all the selected columns to the same column width.

- ▤ *Table AutoFormat*
  This button opens the *Table AutoFormat* dialog box to format tables automatically.

- ▥ *Change Text Direction*
  With this button you can change the direction of the text flow from horizontal to vertical and the other way around.

- ↕ *Sort Ascending*
  This button sorts the contents of the table columns from the smallest to the largest value, for example from 1 to 9, or from A to Z.

- ↕ *Sort Descending*
  This button sorts the contents of a table from the largest to the smallest value, for example from 9 to 1 or from Z to A.

- Σ *AutoSum*
  This button automatically inserts a formula field containing the sum of the cells which are above or to the left of the selected cell.

Drawing Tables

If you create a table with the *Insert Table* button or with the *Insert Table* command on the *Table* menu, you will notice that all the rows inserted are of the same height and all the columns inserted are of the same width. Moreover, every single row and every single column contains the same number of cells.

Word has got a function which allows you to draw your tables using the mouse. With this method you can easily create a table with varying row and column sizes, as well as tables with a variable number of cell partitions. You can also apply these changes to existing tables.

To draw a new table, choose the *Table and Borders* button ▣. The toolbar with the name *Tables and Borders* will open.

Draw table

Immediately after displaying the toolbar, the *Draw Table* button ✐ will be enabled. Later on you will have to click this button to activate the drawing tool. You can also activate the drawing tool with the corresponding item on the *Table* menu.

Once the drawing tool is activated, the mouse pointer will turn into a drawing pen. Hold down the mouse and drag a rectangle which will become the table. Then insert lines by dragging the desired column lines and row lines within the table.

To deactivate the drawing function, either double-click on the table, press the pencil button again, or simply press the *Escape* key ⌈Esc⌋ on your keyboard.

If you make a mistake and draw a wrong line, activate the *Eraser* button and with the *Eraser* mouse pointer click the table lines you have accidentally inserted. As long as you click the mouse button, the line will appear as a bold line.

Keep the mouse button held down to check if you are deleting the right line. You can also drag the *Eraser* mouse pointer in order to simultaneously delete several adjacent lines.

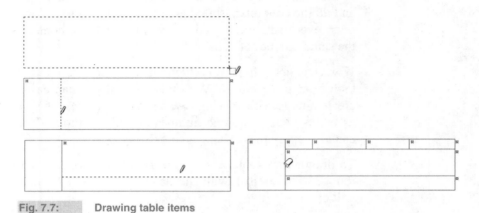

Fig. 7.7:   Drawing table items

 **Tip!** Another convenient way to erase lines is to hold down the shift key ⌂ while drawing. The *Pencil* mouse pointer changes to the *Eraser* pointer.

Setting Row and Column Widths of the Table

As long as *Word* tables use uniform row heights and column widths, adjusting column width and cell heights isn't hard at all. But if you drew you own table, the procedure becomes more difficult.

Changing column width in the ruler

The easiest way is to correct or adapt the column width directly in the table. To do so, point at the gridline between the columns so that the cursor changes to the split pointer shape ◄‖►. Hold the left mouse button down, and change, by visual approximation or based on cell content, the width of the column.

Changing row height

For the row height you proceed in exactly the same way. Point on the gridline of the desired row and move it with the split pointer +‖+ to the position you want.

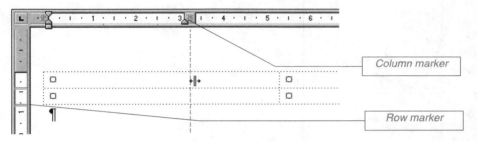

Fig. 7.8: Changing the column width with the mouse

If you select beforehand a particular area of either rows or cells, any changes in their size will be applied only to the selected area. The column width and the row height can also be influenced with the ruler.

To display the ruler, choose *View/Ruler*. Set the cursor at any position within the table to display the column and the row markers on the ruler.

You can now move the column or the row marker while holding down the left mouse button and change the positions of the gridlines in the table.

Additionally, pressing the *Alt* key Alt will display the height of the row and the width of the column in centimetres on the ruler allowing you to continuously adjust them.

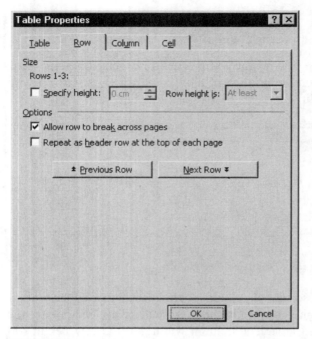

Fig. 7.9:   Set exact height and width in the dialog box

In case you want to set the row height or the column width exactly and not by visual approximation, select the respective columns or rows and choose from the *Table* menu the *Table Properties* item.

Depending on the selection, *Word* will now automatically display the corresponding *Row* or *Column* tab page in the *Cell Height and Width* dialog box. You can then enter the desired width or height in centimetres. For columns, this would be in the *Width of column X* text box.

To change the formatting of other columns, click the *Previous Column/Next Column* buttons to display the corresponding column.

Height of the rows X (-Y)

To change the height of rows, activate the row tab and choose in *Height of rows X(-Y)* the *Exactly* or *At least* entry. With the *At least* entry, *Word* will later adapt the height to the amount of rows in the table, while with *Exactly*, the exact height will be maintained.

Specify the *Row height* in the *At* box, in points. With the *Previous/Next Row* buttons you can make changes to other rows. Once you have made all changes confirm with *OK* to apply the changes to the table.

You can simultaneously change column and cell size by dragging the little square at the end of the table. You can only see it when you set the mouse pointer at the bottom of the table.

A square at the beginning of the table allows you to change the position of the table.

Adapting the Column Width Automatically to the Cell Content

By default, *Word* uses uniform row heights and column width determined by the current font size and margins. But of course this can be modified. In this section you will learn how you can adapt the column width to the widest content of your cells.

Large tables

Changing the column width by visual approximation or according to the cell contents, using the split cursor +‖+, can be difficult. Particularly when creating large tables, the contents cannot be displayed completely, so you have to scroll up and down to figure out whether the widest cell content fits into a row or if the text is wrapped into several rows. For this, *Word* provides you with an automatic function.

Double-clicking to AutoFit

The fastest way to use the *AutoFit* function is directly in the table. Point on the right gridline of the column to be changed. The cursor will then change to a split pointer ◀‖▶. Double-click to adapt the column width automatically to accommodate the widest cell content.

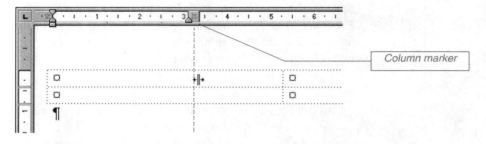

Column marker

Fig. 7.10: Optimizing the column width with the mouse

Centering Table Headings Across Several Columns

A table is always made up of rows and columns. For this reason, at first glance, it seems impossible to place a heading across the entire table or to center it on top of the table. But *Word* offers a function to center a heading across the whole table.

You have to first select the desired cells or the first row of the table. Now you can merge the cells of that row or the selected range to one single cell.

Merging cells

If you want to center the heading across the entire first row, you can quickly select all those cells by clicking into the *Selection* bar on the left side of the row.

Then choose the *Merge Cells* item from the *Table* menu. If that item is disabled and greyed, it means that you probably only selected one cell. You can now enter your heading and center it within the merged cells.

Fig. 7.11: **Merging table cells**

The text already contained in merged cells will be separated by a paragraph mark. You can enter now the headline for your table, and if you want, click on the *Center* button ≣ on the *Formatting* toolbar so that the heading will be centered.

It is also possible to undo the merging of the cells. Select the cell and choose the *Split Cells* item in the *Table* menu. In *Number of columns*, enter the number of columns you want to split the cells into and confirm with *OK*.

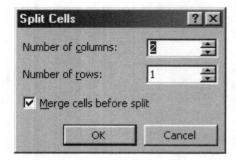

You can also call up the *Merge Cells/Split Cells* functions with buttons. To merge several selected cells click on *Merge Cells* on the *Tables and Borders* toolbar ▣.

You can also merge vertically placed cells without any difficulty. If you want to split merged cells again later on, you can do that by clicking the *Split Cells* button ▣. When you do so, the *Split Cells* dialog box appears. You can then enter the number of columns into which you want to distribute the cell.

Displaying Headings of Tables on Every Page

If you work in *Word* with large tables, which span more than one page of your document, you will find that, already on the second page, you have trouble remembering which information is entered or is supposed to be entered into which column. Checking the column headings by scrolling back and forth can drive you crazy, can't it?

If you want the column heading of a *Word* table to be displayed and printed on each page, you have to select the column headings and choose the *Headings Rows Repeat* item on the *Table* menu.

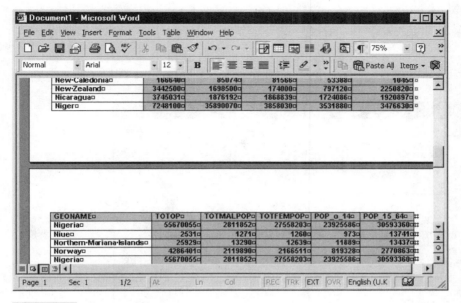

Showing the heading on every page

And that's about all there is to it. If your table does not fill more than one page, this heading will remain invisible. This is different in the case of multiple page tables. There, the first cell of every column will contain the heading of the column and this heading will also be printed. As soon as you insert enough rows to make pagination necessary, *Word* will again automatically create the corresponding headings for the columns on the following page.

Sorting Tables

The fastest way to sort a table is with the help of the *Tables and Borders* toolbar. Click the *Sort Ascending* button to sort the cell contents from the smallest to the largest value, or from A to Z. To sort the other way around, choose the *Sort Descending* button, which will sort from the highest to the lowest value, or from Z to A.

In case you want to sort a table using more than one criteria, choose instead the button the *Table/Sort* item.

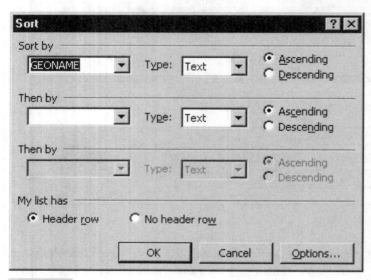

Fig. 7.14:   The *Sort* dialog box

If you want to sort the table using more than one sorting key, you can choose up to three keys from the drop-down lists. Make sure that *Word* has recognized the correct type of data in the *Type* drop-down list for the column you want to sort.

My list has

Word can usually recognize automatically whether a table contains a heading or not. If this is not the case, select the correction radio button in the *My list has* option group. Depending on this choice, the headings will be included in or excluded from the sorting process.

Sort column only

If you want to establish more sorting options, click the *Options* button in the *Sort* dialog box and make the desired choices. With the *Sort column only* check box you can sort the contents of single columns while the other table columns remain unchanged. This option is only available if a single column was selected before opening the dialog box.

With the *Case sensitive* check box you can decide whether or not the case should be matched. By default, *Word* does not take into account upper and lower case.

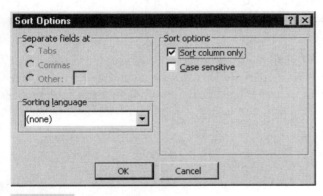

Fig. 7.15: Sort options

Sorting language

In case you would like to sort tables in different languages, you can select the corresponding language in the *Sorting language* drop down list. After choosing the sort options, close the *Sort Options* dialog box with *OK* and start the sorting process with *OK*.

Borders and Shadings for Table Formatting

When you insert a table in *Word*, the rows and columns are automatically displayed with a gridline which can be changed or deleted accordingly. If you delete it, it will be displayed as a grey gridline. These gridlines will not appear on the printout.

To change a gridline structure you can either use the *AutoFormat* tool in *Word* or read on in this section for how to perform this formatting manually.

First select the entire table, or certain columns or rows, or even just a single cell. Then click the *Borders and Shading* item on the *Format* menu to call up the *Borders and Shading* dialog box.

Setting

The fastest method is to assign a border format to the selected table range in the *Setting* options group on the *Borders* tab.

Style

First select the desired style, color or width and then click on the *Box* item in *Setting* to create an outside border, on the *All* item to apply lines having the same breadth to the table or on the *Grid* item to apply thin inner lines and thicker external lines.

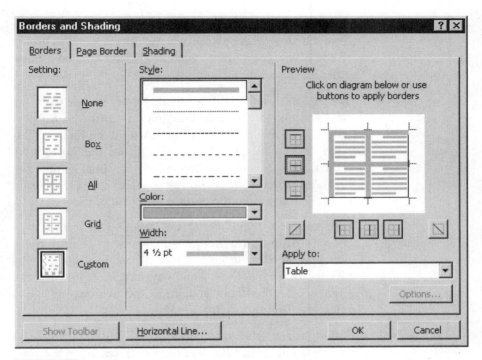

Fig. 7.16: The *Borders and Shading* dialog box

In the *Preview* option group on the *Borders* tab page you can add horizontal borders above, below and at the center, as well vertical borders left, right, and at the center of the table. First select the line style and the width you want and then in *Preview*, click on the button that corresponds to the edge you want to be visible in your table. *Word* will immediately display all the settings in the *Preview* box. To assign the formatting to your table, you have to confirm by clicking *OK*.

Shading tab page

Table sections can be highlighted either with color or with different shades of grey to make them appear more prominent. You can find this function on the *Shading* tab page of the *Borders and Shading* dialog box.

Change to the *Shading* tab page and choose a grey value from the *Style* drop-down list in the *Patterns* option group. If you have a color printer you can also use colored fillings. After making changes, confirm with *OK*.

The second method of formatting borders involves the *Borders* palette of the *Border* button. Open the *Borders* palette with a click on the drop-down button on the right-hand side of the *Border* button 🔲▾ on the *Formatting* toolbar. By default, the *ScreenTip* for this button will display *Outside Border*; however, the name of the button cleverly depends on the current selection of the tool.

First choose a *Line Style* and a *Line Weight* from the respective drop-down lists ¾ pt ▾ on the *Tables and Borders* toolbar. Since *Word* does not display this toolbar by default, you may have to show it first. Choose *View/Toolbars* and, from the overlapping menu select the *Tables and Borders* item.

Among many other new buttons, the *Tables and Borders* toolbar contains the *Borders* button. If you open the *Borders* palette with a click on the drop-down button on the right-hand side of the *Border* button 🔲▾ and move over the palette's title bar, you can click and drag it anywhere you like.

It will be converted into a floating toolbar. Click on the *Outside Border* button to put a frame around the selected part of your table. To remove the border, use the *No Border* button. If you want to format the table to display gridlines choose the *Inside Border* button.

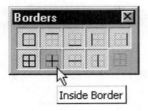

Fig. 7.17: The *Borders* palette

Likewise, for single lines click the *Top Border*, *Bottom Border*, *Right Border*, *Left Border*, *Inside Vertical Border* and *Inside Horizontal Border* buttons. For line attributes such as shading, coloring, line style and line width use the *Tables and Borders* toolbar. Like the *Borders* palette, you can drag this palette and keep it floating.

Performing Calculations in a Table

Word can calculate table contents automatically. Of course the available functions are not as sophisticated as in the *Microsoft Excel* spreadsheet program, but for most of your work the functions in *Word* will do.

Word uses calculation formulas based on a particular syntax. For simple functions such as the calculation of a sum, *Word* will guess what you're looking for and spontaneously propose the respective function.

To calculate sums of rows or columns in tables, click the cell that should contain the total, that is either the cell to the right of the row or the cell beneath the column you want to total.

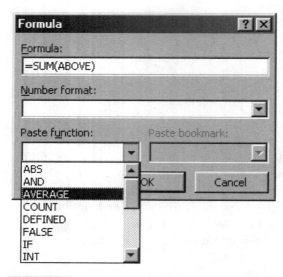

Fig. 7.18: Choosing a function of Word

Subsequently, choose the *Formula* command on the *Table* menu. In the *Formula* text box of the *Formula* dialog box, *Word* automatically displays the SUM(ABOVE) for column sums and SUM(LEFT) for row sums. If both interpretations are possible, then *Word* will choose to sum up the column. Confirm with *OK*, and *Word* will place the result into the selected cell.

If you later on change the cell contents, the cell which contains the formula will automatically update the result in connection with certain actions, for example with saving and printing. You can manually update the result by selecting the cell and pressing the F9 key.

Sum Σ

An even faster way of calculating the sum of rows or columns is by clicking the *AutoSum* button Σ on the *Tables and Borders* toolbar.

Cell addresses

If you want the calculation to include only particular cells, specify the respective cells in the formula. The addresses, in the form of A1 for the first cell in the first column, are not displayed in *Word*, though you may be used to this technique from an *Excel* table or other spreadsheet programs.

To address the fourth cell in the fifth column you just have to know that the cell has an address of 'E4'. Yes, that can be somewhat laborious. For more complex tables you are advised to switch to *Excel* and import the finished table into *Word*.

In the *Paste function* drop-down list in the *Formula* dialog box, readymade formulas are available. The following rules have to be applied:

- A formula always starts with an equal '='sign.

- Functions entered with the *Paste Function* drop-down list need to have cell references and operators in brackets.

- A cell address consists of a column letter followed by a row number, and several addresses need to be separated by commas.

- Continuous cell contents are written with a colon to separate the first cell address and the last cell address.

- Calculation operators are '*' for multiplication, '+' for addition, '-' for substraction and '/' for division. The normal algebraic rules apply.

When you make incorrect cell references or divide by zero you'll get the respective error message within the cell.

Using Tables as Data Sources for Mail Merge

After creating the main document for mail merge with fixed letter elements and variable elements in the form of merge fields, you will need a data source containing the receiver's data for the mail merge.

You can use a normal *Word* table containing all the necessary data in separate columns as your data source.

Create a new empty document and choose *Insert Table* from the *Table* menu. In the *Insert Table* dialog box enter the required number of columns and what you estimate to be the required number of rows into the respective text boxes Close the dialog box by clicking the *OK* button. *Word* will insert the table into the document. The insertion cursor will blink in the first cell of the table. Enter all required column headings into the respective cells in the top row, such as first name, surname, job, etc.

Address¤	City¤	Region¤	Postal·Code¤	Country¤	Phone¤

Fig. 7.19: Entering column headings

Enter the necessary information about the receivers of the mail merge into the cells below the headings, and save your table. For further organization and editing of the table contents, you can use the *Database* toolbar, which can be displayed from *View/Toolbars*.

Fig. 7.20: The *Database* toolbar

With the buttons on this toolbar you can conveniently organize your addresses in the table. Click the *Data Form* button ![icon], and the *Data Form* dialog box will appear. This dialog box lets you view existing records. To enter new data click the *Add New* button [Add New]. You can then enter new data into the empty form. *Word* uses the column headings of your table as the text box labels.

To navigate through the records, use the buttons on the lower part of the *Data Form* dialog box. The box in the center [1] displays the current record number. Clicking the button ◄ will take you to the first record, while the button ► will do the opposite and take you to the end of the records. The two buttons ◄ and ► move backwards and forwards one record at a time. The *Find* button enables you to search for particular records.

Address¤	City¤	Region¤	Postal·Code¤	Country¤	Phone¤
Obere·Str.·57¤	Berlin¤	¤	12209¤	Germany¤	030·0074321¤
Avda.·de·la·Constitución·2222¤	México·D.F.¤	¤	05021¤	Mexico¤	(5)·555-4729¤
Mataderos··2312¤	México·D.F.¤	¤	05023¤	Mexico¤	(5)·555-3932¤
120·Hanover·Sq.¤	London¤	¤	WA1·1DP¤	UK¤	(171)·555-7788¤
Berguvsvägen··8¤	Luleå¤	¤	S-958·22¤	Sweden¤	0921-12·34·65¤
Forsterstr.·57¤	Mannheim¤	¤	68306¤	Germany¤	0621-08460¤
24,·place·Kléber¤	Strasbourg¤	¤	67000¤	France¤	88.60.15.31¤
C/·Araquil,·67¤	Madrid¤	¤	28023¤	Spain¤	(91)·555·22·82¤
12,·rue·des·Bouchers¤	Marseille¤	¤	13008¤	France¤	91.24.45.40¤
23·Tsawassen·Blvd.¤	Tsawassen¤	BC¤	T2F·8M4¤	Canada¤	(604)·555-4729¤
Fauntleroy·Circus¤	London¤	¤	EC2·5NT¤	UK¤	(171)·555-1212¤
Cerrito·333¤	Buenos·Aires¤	¤	1010¤	Argentina¤	(1)·135-5555¤
Sierras·de·Granada·9993¤	México·D.F.¤	¤	05022¤	Mexico¤	(5)·555-3392¤
Hauptstr.·29¤	Bern¤	¤	3012¤	Switzerland¤	0452-076545¤
Av.·dos·Lusíadas,·23¤	São·Paulo¤	SP¤	05432-043¤	Brazil¤	(11)·555-7647¤
Berkeley·Gardens¶	London¤	¤	WX1·6LT¤	UK¤	(171)·555-2282¤
Walserweg·21¤	Aachen¤	¤	52066¤	Germany¤	0241-039123¤
67,·rue·des·Cinquante·Otages¤	Nantes¤	¤	44000¤	France¤	40.67.88.88¤
35·King·George¤	London¤	¤	WX3·6FW¤	UK¤	(171)·555-0297¤

Fig. 7.21: A Word table as a database

More information about *Data Forms* can be obtained in Chapter 11. You can exit the *Data Form* dialog box any time with [Esc] or by clicking *OK*. The new records are not saved until you save the document containing the table.

Converting Tables to Text

The contents of *Word* tables can be converted to normal text at any time. *Word* will remove the gridlines and the table structure and display the contents as normal text.

Word uses particular control characters to separate the various cell contents. These controls are selected before the conversion. This ensures that the column and row contents are properly displayed after the conversion.

To convert a table, first select the whole table or part of it. Then choose the *Convert* command and the *Table to Text* item from the submenu.

If the command appears greyed, it is not available. You have then probably selected parts of the table that cannot be converted. In the *Convert Table to Text* dialog box you can determine the type of separator to be used after conversion.

With the default *Tabs* setting *Word* will use tabs for the separation of cell contents after conversion. The different rows will be displayed as separate paragraphs.

Using these settings you obtain a virtual representation of the table in the form of normal text. Convert and close the dialog box by clicking the *OK* button.

Fig. 7.22:   Converting a table to text

Word will then separate cells by applying tab stops.

You can choose different separators in the *Convert Table to Text* dialog box. If you choose *Paragraph marks* as a separator, the cell contents will be displayed in separate paragraphs. If you want to specify the separator yourself, choose the *Other* radio button and type the separator yourself. Close the dialog box by clicking the *OK* button and the table will be converted. If you do not like the result, you can use the *Edit/Undo* command.

Shifting Tables and Text wrapping

Word inserts tables in such a way that you can change their position on the screen as you like. If you set the mouse pointer on the table, a little square will appear at the beginning and at the end of it. The square at the beginning allows you to change the table position in the screen. Click on this square to drag the table to a new position.

If the table is not arranged to take the complete row width, you have to decide the way normal text should be arranged around the table. Call the *Table Properties* dialog box. You can either use the *Table/Table Properties* command or double click the square before the table. On the *Table* tab page you can set the alignment of the table as well as the *Text wrapping* of the paragraphs around the table. On the preview you can see how the text will be arranged as regards the table.

Splitting Tables to Display Text Before or In Between

Sometimes when you've finished a table you realize that it would have been wiser to display the data in two separate tables. But you cannot insert text in between the table once it has been created.

If you press the *Enter* key ⏎ within a cell, you add a paragraph within the cell. If you press the *Enter* key ⏎ at the end of a row (behind the last cell and not inside it), you get a new empty row. To insert an empty line in a table, or to split a table into two, you need a particular command. Click in the row above which you want to insert a line or where you want to split the table.

Split Table

Now choose the *Split Table* item from the *Table* menu. *Word* inserts an empty paragraph which perhaps you do not see immediately on the screen because, for instance, in the *Table* tab page of the *Table properties* dialog box you ticked the *Around* check box in the *Text wrapping* option group. Change to the *None* option, or shift the lower part of the table: as soon as you set the mouse pointer on it, its position square will be displayed.

Ctrl + ⇧ + ⏎

If you prefer working with the keyboard, place the insertion cursor in the line above which you want to insert a line and press the Ctrl + ⇧ + ⏎ key combination.

Converting Text in Tables

Text in *Word* documents can be converted into a table in certain situations. You have to separate the sections of the text by the respective separators before conversion enabling *Word* to assign the right parts of the text to the various cells.

The best will be if you use tabs as separators, since *Word* uses them anyhow to separate column contents. For a new row in a table, use a paragraph mark, created by pressing *Enter* ⏎. In other words, the contents that should appear next to each other later can be separated by pressing the *Tab* key ⇥, while contents that should appear on top of each other should be separated by pressing *Enter* [↵].

Instead of tabs you can also use commas or any other character which can be inserted with the keyboard.

Converting text into a table

Subsequently, highlight the section of the text that you want to convert into a table. Choose the *Convert Text to Table* command in the *Table* menu. If the command is greyed, then you have selected text passages that cannot be converted.

The *Convert Text to Table* dialog box normally displays the correct number of columns and rows in the respective text boxes.

Fig. 7.23: Converting text into a table

Separator

If your text contains paragraphs with a varying number of separators, enter the required number of columns manually so that *Word* can create the necessary empty cells. If you used a separator other than a tab, enter it into *Separate text at* with the *Other* radio button. If you want *Word* to automatically distribute the columns over the available space between the page edges, confirm with *OK*. If you want a different column width you can determine that in *Column width*.

If you don't like the result, choose *Edit/Undo*. Check your text for unnecessary or unwanted separators or paragraph marks. Correct these mistakes and try the conversion again.

Tabs

While creating documents you will often need vertically aligned text columns, for example for lists, product overviews, or bills. For this kind of alignment use the tab stops or tabs in *Word*.

Using Tabs in Word 97

A tab is a jump marker in the document that can be user-defined?. The insertion cursor automatically jumps to these markers, or tab stops, when you press the *Tab* key ⌧. Pressing the *Tab* key ⌧ again takes you to the next tab stop, etc.

Default tabs   If you do not set any user-defined tab stop, *Word* uses default positions with a default distance of 1.27 cm. With every press of the *Tab* key ⌧ the insertion cursor moves 1.27 centimeters, or one tab stop to the right. Default tab stops are displayed in the ruler as light grey lines.

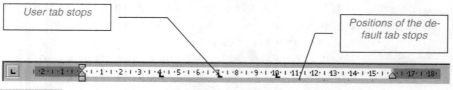

User tab stops

Positions of the default tab stops

Fig. 7.24:   Default tab stops and user tab stops on the ruler

Enter some text and press the *Tab* key 🔄 to make the insertion cursor jump to the right. Enter more text and press 🔄 again, etc. When you repeat this procedure on the next line, the text will be positioned at the same points as on the previous line. The default tab stops can be replaced by your own tab stops any time.

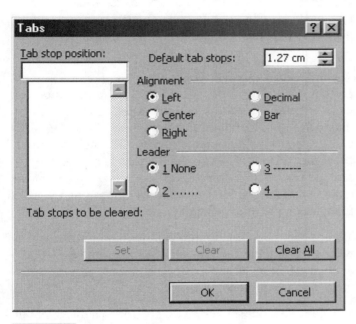

Fig. 7.25:   The *Tabs* dialog box

If you want to replace them, select the paragraphs in which you want to apply the tabs and choose *Format/ Tabs*. In the *Alignment* option group choose the required tab alignment. Later in this section you will learn more about the different tab alignments.

Enter the value in centimetres for the first tab into the *Tab stop position* text box. Now click the *Set* button. The new tab position is displayed in the *Tab stop position* list box.

Repeat this procedure for all required tabs. Close the dialog box and set all tabs by clicking the *OK* button. Now type your text and align it by using the *Tab* key ⌧ .

The *Tabs* dialog box can also be used to remove unnecessary tabs. Select the unwanted tab in the *Tab stop position* list and click the *Clear* button. To delete all user-defined tabs click the *Clear All* button. The tab stop distance of the default tabs can be set in the *Default tab stops* spin box.

Alignment ⌧

The ruler also displays your own tabs. For the default *Left* tab, *Word* uses a small 'L' at the tab position. But there is more you can do with the ruler. The tabs can be dragged with the mouse and moved by visual approximation. To switch to other tab types click the *Tab* button ⌧ at the left end of the horizontal ruler until you see the type of tab you need. You can use this button to move indent marks if you meet difficulties in grasping the little triangles on the ruler using the mouse.

Then move the mouse to the point in the ruler where you want to insert the tab and click with the mouse. User-defined tabs can be moved to a different location using the left mouse button.

You can also double click an empty row in a document to set tab stops, here too the alignment depends on the setting options you set in the corresponding box.

You can easily delete tab marks by dragging them out of the ruler. To simplify the alignment of tabs, *Word* temporarily displays a dashed line in the document while moving the tab.

The Different Types of Tabs

There are four alignments available: *Left*, *Right*, *Center* and *Decimal,* and additionally a *Bar tab*.

Alignment

In order to determine the tab alignment through a dialog box, select the paragraphs you want to align and choose *Format/Tabs*. Select the desired radio button in the *Alignment* option group.

Left will, after you press the *Tab* key ⎆, align the text on the right side of the mark, while *Right* will align the text on the left side of the mark. *Center* keeps the center of your text on the position of the tab stop. *Decimal* aligns any numbers or text around the first decimal separator that appears, which is the point by default.

Bar

The last option in the *Alignment* option group is not really a type of alignment at all. It just creates a vertical line in the height of the paragraph at the tab stop position.

Determine the alignment and set all required tab stops for your document. Every paragraph can have its own set of tab stops. Close the dialog box by clicking the *OK* button.

Using the mouse you can also set the tab stops directly in the ruler. First choose the alignment of the tab by clicking the *Tab* button 🔲 on the left-hand side of the ruler until it shows the required alignment:

▪ *Left-aligned*: ⌊

▪ *Right-aligned*: ⌋

▪ *Centered*: ⊥

▪ *Decimal*: ⊥·

▪ *Bar Tab:* ▮

Then point with the mouse at the position in the ruler where you want to place the tab.

Using Tabs with Leaders

Tabs can be of great help in creating lists with vertically aligned text.

What are leaders?

If your document is a product list or a price list, you will use the tab to enter the price at a fixed and uniform distance from the product.

Here a line or a even dashed line from the product item to the price would help to give more clarity to the document. A similar example would be the table of contents of a larger document such as a thesis.

In *Word*, those connecting lines of different styles assigned to a tab are called *leaders*. To assign a leader to a tab, select the paragraph where you want the leader to appear.

Then choose *Format/Tabs*. In the *Tabs* dialog box enter the value and the alignment to assign to tab stops.

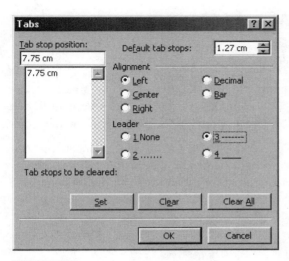

Assigning leaders to tabs

Leaders

In the *Leaders* option group, choose the line style you would like to assign to the particular tab. Then click the *Set* button. Repeat the procedure for all tabs needed. Set the tabs and close the dialog box by clicking the *OK* button. Type your text now and align it using the *Tab* key [⇆]. Only then will the leaders be shown.

Leaders can also be set later, once you have assigned tab stops with the ruler. If you double click a tab stop mark on the ruler, the *Tabs* dialog box will appear. Select from the list a desired tab stop to which you want to assign a given leader.

Removing leaders

In this way you can also remove a set leader. To do so in the *Tab stop position* list select the tab from which you want to delete the leader. Then choose the *1 None* radio button in the *Leader* option group and click the *Set* button.

Inserting Vertical Lines between Text in Columns

Besides the four alignments you'll find a fifth option, the vertical line called *Bar Tab*.

This last option in the *Alignment* option group is not really a type of alignment. It just creates a vertical line in the height of the paragraph at the position of the tab stop.

Select the paragraphs where you want to insert the *Bar* and choose *Format/Tabs*. In the dialog box which appears, enter the position for the first vertical bar into the *Tab stop position* text box. Choose the *Bar* radio button and click the *Set* button.

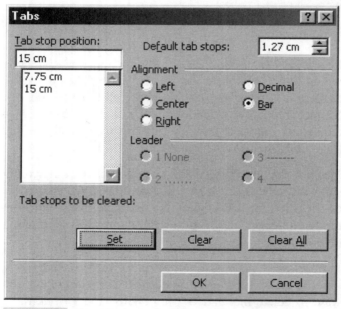

Fig. 7.27: Inserting a vertical Bar

Repeat these steps for every vertical line you want and close the dialog box by clicking the *OK* button.

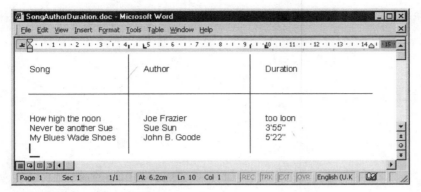

Fig. 7.28:   Vertical lines in a table

In *Word 2000* you can also set *Bars* by using the ruler. To do so click the tab stop button on the left side of the ruler until the *Bar Tab* appears.

8. Styles and Templates

After you have become familiar with the fundamentals of formatting, you will start using them a lot in different ways. You will hardly use some of them at all, while others might become close companions in your daily work.

Formatting with the help of the buttons on the toolbar or with the key combinations already described immediately speeds up the process and makes the creation of your documents easier.

Nevertheless you are bound to reach the point where you will be looking for ways to make your daily formatting procedures even faster.

In this chapter, we will introduce you to two powerful features: *Styles* and *Templates*. It is important to study these tools carefully because they can speed up your work tremendously.

Templates

Imagine a *Template* as a sample file in which you will find all the elements you might need in connection with a particular kind of document, such as:

- Ordinary Correspondence,
- Bills,
- Fax Forms,
- Orders.

These are only a few examples. If you are looking for more illustrations, you should go through the tab pages in the *New* dialog box. There you will find all the *Templates* offered in *Word*.

Creating a Document on the Basis of an Existing Template

Every time you start *Word*, an empty new document will appear where you can type in your text. This blank document is based on the *Blank Document (Normal.dot)* template. One could say that this is a kind of default *Word* document that contains an A-4-size page in portrait layout with certain margins and the *Times New Roman* font in 12-point size, as well as other settings.

New You can also call up the same document type by clicking the *New* button on the *Standard* toolbar. In case you do not want to work with this template but want to use one of the existing *Letters & Faxes* templates, for example, then open the *File* menu, choose the *New* item and change to the tab containing the corresponding templates. For letter or fax templates, change to the *Letters & Faxes* tab page. If you want to create a memo, change to the *Memos* tab.

Wizard The other tabs offer templates for *Professional Resumes* and *Web Pages*, to name just two. The exact number of templates, as well as which ones, depends on the options selected at the time of installation. Select the entry which comes closest to the actual document you want to create. Selecting any available wizard icon will call up a wizard program in which you will have to make additional choices for the document (for example, *Personal Record*).

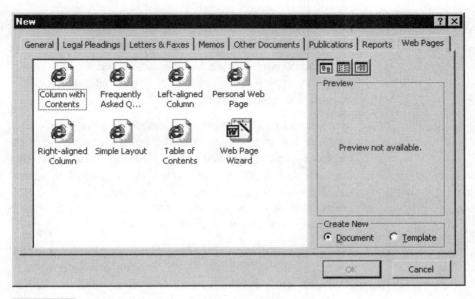

Fig. 8.1: Thematically sorted templates in the *New* dialog box

Confirm the dialog box with *OK* or ⏎, to open a new document based on the chosen template. Now click on the specially selected text areas and overwrite the default, or enter new text into the corresponding places.

Creating a Template

A *Template* is a sample document which will be used as the basis for new documents. It contains all the necessary *Styles*, toolbars and *AutoText* entries for certain types of documents.

Let's say the *Template* contains a blank sample of a letter, a fax or some other kind of document which you use often. All text formatting is saved within a template. All you have to do is to type the actual text into a document based on a certain template and you needn't bother with the formatting anymore.

Creating New Templates

Templates can be created in two different ways. Using the first method, you create a new document and then do all the necessary typing and formatting. After that you save the document as a sample template.

Template

The second method is to first choose *File/New* and activate the tab page containing the template which comes closest to what you need for your work. Then select the template and in the *Create New* option group box select the *Template* option. Finally, click the *OK* button. Of course it is also possible to create a template on the basis of a *Blank Document* on the *General* tab.

Template x

With a right-click on the *Blank Document* icon you open a context menu. Choose *Open* to open a new template. You can see that a document has been opened on the basis of a template, but by looking at the title bar you can also see that it is not an ordinary document. You will find *Template x* written there.

Now insert the text which appears identically in all of your documents, for instance, the name of the company, the address, the bank account number or other such items which need to be repeated in other documents.

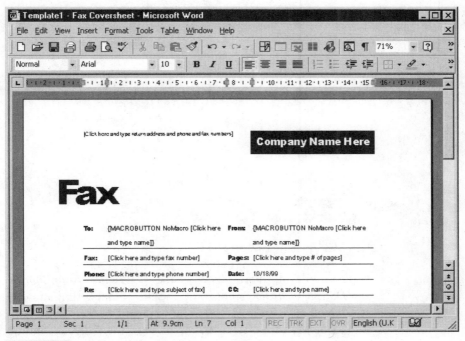

Fax

Fig. 8.2:   Creating a new template

Format the text the way you want it and add headers or footers if required. Define all necessary *AutoText* entries. You will need to rearrange toolbars or create your own styles which will be incorporated in the documents you want to create using this template. *Word* offers all the same options that it offers for the creation of a document.

Once all the required elements have been inserted in the template, choose *File/Save As*. Now enter a name for the new template. In the *Save as type* box the default type will be *Document Template (*.dot)*.

Fig. 8.3: Saving your own template

Template folder

In addition, *Word* displays the *C:\Windows\Application Data\Microsoft\Templates* template folder automatically. If you save your template here, it will be displayed subsequently in the *General* tab page of the *File/New* dialog box. These subfolders are identical to the corresponding tabs in the *New* dialog box. You can also create you own template folder where you can save your templates. This new folder will be then displayed as new tab page in the *New* dialog box.

Close the *Save as* dialog box by clicking *Save* and close the document on the screen with *File/Close*.

Template Folder

A template can also be created from a pre-existing formatted document. To do so, open the document and make all the necessary changes. For example, delete all the unnecessary text sections. Save the document with *File/Save As* and choose the *Document Template (*.dot)* file type in the *Save as Type* drop-down list box to save it in the corresponding template folder. Now the template can be used to create other documents. This can be done by going to the *New* dialog box and selecting the corresponding tab page there.

DOT

Unlike *Word* documents which are saved with the DOC (*Word Document*) extension, templates are saved with the *DOT* (*document template*) file extension.

Normal.dot

Word 2000 saves the *Normal.dot* general-purpose template in the *C:\Windows\Application Data\Microsoft\Templates* folder. More templates of *Office 2000* are saved in the subfolders of the *C:\Programs files\Microsoft Office\Templates* folder. Not all the templates in the *Office 2000 Suite* can be used in *Word 2000*.

In the standard installation, the template subfolders *Letters & Faxes*, *Memos*, *Other Documents* and *General* are available to *Word 2000*. You can save your own templates there.

Creating New Tabs for Your Own Templates

As described above, *Word* automatically places templates in the *Templates* folder with the following path:

C:\Windows\Application Data\Microsoft\Templates

Creating folder

This folder contains templates of the *General* tab page. In order to keep track of your own templates, you might like to save them all together in a particular folder. To display this folder on an extra tab page in the *New* dialog box , create a new folder in the *Templates* folder. You can do so directly in the *Save As* dialog box.

New folder icon

Choose *File/Save As* and open *C:\Windows\Application DataMicrosoft\Templates*. Now click the *Create New Folder* button ⬜. Write a suitable name that the new tab will have in the *New Folder* dialog box.

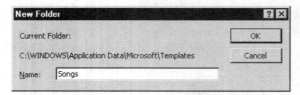

Fig. 8.4:   Name the new template folder

If you confirm with *OK*, the new folder will be created with the entered name. If you want to save the current template in this folder, open this folder in future by double-clicking on the folder icon. If the dialog box was open only in order to create this folder, then click on *Cancel* to close it.

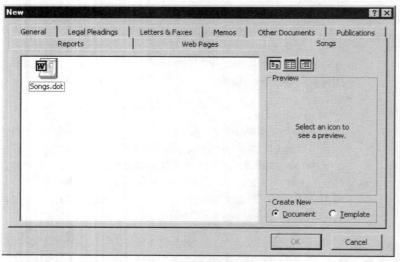

Fig. 8.5:   The folder in the hierarchy and in the *New* dialog box

Do not be disappointed if you open the *New* dialog box now and you do not see your tab there. It will not display the newly created tab page until at least one template has been saved in the folder.

If this tab page does not appear in the dialog box even after creating a file, check the template path referred to earlier on your computer. Choose *Tools/Options* and the *File Locations* tab page. In the *File types* list select the *User templates* item and click the *Modify* button in order to check the complete path in the *Modify location* dialog box.

Using Templates for New Documents

When you create new documents on the basis of a template, a copy of that template is opened.

Default template If you want to use your own templates or those that are provided with *Word,* you cannot use the *New* button. Instead, open the *File* menu and choose the *New* item.

In the *New* dialog box all the available templates are displayed on different tabs.

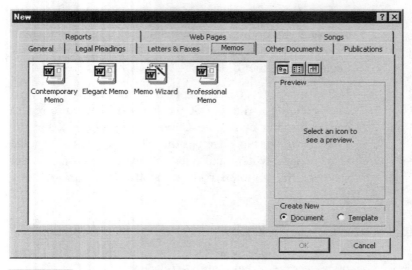

The *Memos* tab and list of templates in the *New* dialog box

The number of the available tabs depends on the installed options. You can also create new templates and tabs on your own.

Choosing a tab page

Go to the tab page containing the desired template and select the template. Now create a document based on this template by clicking the *OK* button.

Opening and Modifying Templates

Every template that you have created as well as every template supplied by *Word* can be opened or modified just like any normal document. First you have to let *Word* know that you want to open a template.

To open or modify a template, it is necessary to close all documents based on this template. To open a template choose *File/Open* and select the *Document Templates (*.dot)* entry in the *Files of type* drop-down list box.

When you change the file type, the *Templates* folder will unfortunately not be displayed automatically as it is when you are saving. Change to the *C:\Program Files\Microsoft Office\Templates* folder and to the corresponding subfolder that contains your template. As an alternative method you can display the templates by choosing the *General* tab page in the *File/New* dialog box. Then select the template and click the *Open* button.

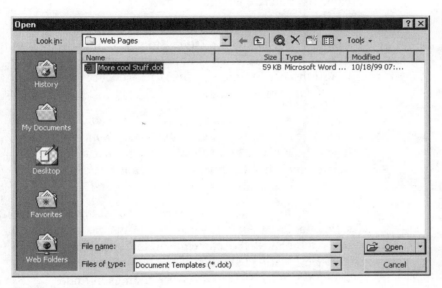

Fig. 8.7:   Opening a template

Make the desired changes and save the modified template by choosing *File/Save* or by using the *Save* button 🖬. You can then close the open template with *File/Close*.

Copying Template Contents for Other Documents

Word saves certain elements of a document in the template on which it is based. This can include new or modified styles and toolbars, *AutoText* entries and macros.

This will not create any problems for beginners for a long time, since normally only documents created with the default *Word* template are used. A document using this template is automatically created after starting *Word* or by clicking on the *New* button ▢.

Why copy template contents?

All changes to existing styles or custom toolbars and *AutoText* entries will then be available in all documents using the standard template.

This will not be the case, however, if you have defined custom styles or changed styles, toolbars, *AutoText* entries or macros in a different template and you would now like to use those customized formats in a document based on *Normal.dot*, or vice versa.

If, for example, you have changed or extended the content of one of the letter templates which came with *Word*, it will henceforth be available only in that template and not in any other template, and obviously not in a document based on a different template.

In order to make those user-defined styles, modified styles, toolbars, *AutoText* entries and macros available to other templates, the contents of the template in which they were defined should be copied into the templates in which you may want to use these settings in future.

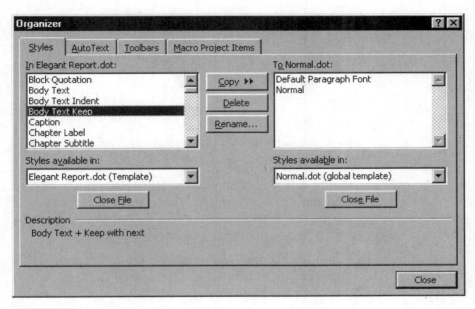

The *Organizer* dialog box

**Templates and
Add-Ins**

Open a document based on the template containing the desired elements and select the *Templates and Add-Ins* item in the *Tools* menu. Then click the *Organizer* button in the dialog box.

Choose tab

Now change to the required tab page, which will be either *Styles*, *AutoText*, *Toolbars* or *Macro Project Items*. The corresponding tab will display the current template on the left under *Styles available in*. In the box above that, all the saved contents will be displayed.

**Close File,
Open File**

Word will now presume that you did not save these entries in the standard template *Normal.dot* and will offer you this template in the right part of the dialog box as a copy target. In case you want to copy certain template contents from the current document into a different template, click on the *Close File* button on the right side of the dialog box. The button will then change the label to *Open File*. Click on this button again.

The *Open* dialog box will show the contents of the *C:\Windows\Application Data\Microsoft\Templates* template folder.

Select the particular template and click on *Open* in order to display its contents on the right side of the *Organizer* dialog box.

Select

On the left side of the dialog box, select all the desired elements in the template. To save time you can hold down the multiselection key Ctrl and click on all the entries you wish to copy one after the other.

From time to time you might choose to scroll through a large number of entries with the help of the scroll bar. If you move the mouse downwards, the contents of the list box will also be moved down and selected automatically.

Copy

Click on *Copy* to insert the selected template contents into the other template. Repeat this procedure as many times as needed in order to copy other contents on the various tabs.

When you have finished, close the *Organizer* dialog box by clicking the *Close* button. Now the custom or modified styles, the toolbars, *AutoText* entries and macros are also available to be called up or used in the other template.

Installing Additional Templates

In the standard installation of *Word*, only the most often used files, templates, Help files and converter programs are copied. To save hard disk space, *Word* does not copy all the supplied templates or Help files. The standard setting is carried out in such a way that most templates will be installed on your hard disk only after you call them for the first time. By calling this element you are required to insert the CD, all further steps will be carried out automatically. If one of the tab pages is not displayed, it means that you did not carry out the standard installation and you should therefore repeat installation. You must follow the same procedure if you want to delete any element from the hard disk, e.g. because of memory shortage. Again in this case you must proceed manually.

Control Panel

To change the *Word* templates on your system, choose the *Settings* item on the *Start* menu. In the submenu which appears select the *Control Panel* item. In the *Control Panel* double-click on the *Add/Remove Programs* icon and activate the *Install/Uninstall* tab in the *Add/Remove Programs Properties* dialog box.

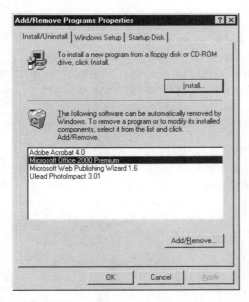

Fig. 8.9: Installing additional Word templates

Insert the CD program in the corresponding drive and select the entry *Microsoft Office 2000 Premium* or *Microsoft Word*. Then press the *Add/Remove* button. The setup program will start in *Maintenance mode* and you can change the settings with the *Add or Remove Features* button.

If, for example, you do not have the tab page for *Reports*, click on the plus sign in front of the *Microsoft Word* item in the *Update features* dialog box and click again the plus sign in front of *Wizards and Templates*. Now all templates will be displayed. Click the *Reports* symbol and choose one of the following settings:

- *Run from My Computer* copies the files in your program folder which is why this feature makes it necessary to have a sufficient amount of memory on your hard disk.

- *Run from CD* requires you to insert the CD the first time you try to use a non-installed template. In this way you do not overburden the hard disk but you do need to insert the CD Rom in the drive in order to carry out the installation. If you change a template you have to save it in your folder.

- *Installed on First use* is the default installation for most templates and this option carries out the installation in such a way that elements do appear on the screen, but they will be copied on the hard disk only when you try to use them. In this case you will be required to insert the CD-Rom.

- *Not Available* deletes an element from hard disk. As a result it will no longer be displayed but you can choose to install it any time you want to.

In case you cannot find the entry of *Word* in the list box on the *Install/Uninstall* tab, or you get an error message after clicking *Add/Remove*, you have to start the *SETUP.EXE* setup program from the main folder on the CD.

Styles

During your search for new formatting options, in the *Format* menu or by calling up the *ScreenTips* of the items of the *Formatting* toolbar, you might already have come across the *Style* entry. You have most probably wondered what this means exactly.

What is a style?

A certain formatting that is used frequently can be stored in a style. In a *Style* character, paragraph, border and shading, language, and tab formats can be stored under a particular name.

You can use your own styles or the styles supplied in *Word*. In this way complex formatting can be assigned to any paragraph in your document with a single mouse click.

One result will be a reduction in the amount of time it takes you to complete the complex editing of documents that look good. It also ensures the same formatting of every paragraph in order to achieve a uniform style. *Word* will automatically apply any changes you make in your styles to the other paragraphs created using the same style.

Formatting Documents with Styles

Before you can apply a *Style*, you first have to have a document based on the template in which the desired style is saved.

351

Styles are saved in templates

Choose *File/New* and change to the corresponding tab page. Now double-click on the desired template to create a document based on it.

The text can then be entered. In order to assign a style to a paragraph, put the cursor into the paragraph to be formatted. If the style is supposed to be assigned to several paragraphs at a time, first select all the paragraphs concerned.

***Style* list**

Now open the *Style* drop-down list box on the far left side of the *Formatting* toolbar by clicking on the drop-down button. Use the scroll bar if necessary to scroll through the available styles more quickly. Select the desired style. The corresponding formatting saved in this style will be applied to the current paragraph (or to all the selected paragraphs).

Fig. 8.11: The *Style* drop-down list box

In the *Style* drop-down list box, different types of styles are displayed. Paragraph styles contain all kinds of formatting which generally affect whole paragraphs and are displayed together with a paragraph mark ¶. Other types of styles are character styles. In the *Style* drop-down list they appear with an **a** symbol and are only allowed to contain character formatting.

In the *Style* drop-down box the name of the style appears in the actual formatting, and in addition information about font size, paragraph formats and alignments is provided.

The *Style* Dialog Box

In the various *Word* templates, the most diverse kinds of styles are saved. In case you want to have a look at these styles, choose *Format/Style*. In the left list box of the *Style* dialog box, the *Styles* available in the template will be displayed. On the right side in the dialog box you will see in the *Paragraph preview* box a preview of the paragraph and in the *Character preview* beneath that, a preview of the characters. Below that you will find a *Description* of the style.

In order to be able to get an overview of such a large list, you have the option of using certain filters for the entries. To check the display of the list of styles, open the *List* drop-down box and choose one of the following entries:

- *All styles*
  displays all the styles contained in the template, the ones applied as well as those which are not in use.

- *User-defined styles*
  displays only the styles defined by yourself, without showing the styles that come with *Word*.

- *Styles in use*
  displays only the styles that are currently being used in the document.

On the lower half of the dialog box you will see different buttons. You can modify, delete, or apply the style that you have selected in the list by using those buttons. Additionally you will find a button to create new styles and another to organize them.

Delete Formatting

You can write paragraphs based on a certain style, and in addition, you can make your own modifications to the formatting whenever you want to. In case you want to delete those modifications in a paragraph, you have to select the affected characters or the whole paragraph and press the key combination `Ctrl`+`SPACE`. The formatting, saved in the paragraph style will be restored. In this way subsequent formatting can be quickly and easily removed.

Creating Styles by Selection

To apply exceptional formatting to a document is a time-consuming task. In case you frequently need to use a certain formatting, you already know that you can save it in a style. With the help of a style, complex formatting can be selected with a single mouse click and applied to paragraphs in a document.

This not only reduces the amount of time you will spend on this but it also makes sure that every single paragraph will have the same formatting. Subsequent modifications to the style are automatically applied by *Word* to all the other paragraphs formatted in the same style.

This makes a lot of sense, especially for a long document or for company correspondence. With the style function you will quickly and safely get a grip on those terrifying demands.

Choosing styles To use a style, first create a document on the basis of the template in which you want to use the new style. Styles are always saved in the template and will for this reason only be available to documents based on the same template.

Now enter all the paragraphs which are often used in this document and format them accordingly. All the character formatting is at your disposal. Select the desired font and font size, as well as the font style.

Then apply the corresponding paragraph styles to the paragraphs. Set the alignment (Align Left, Center, Align Right or Justify), define the indentation, set the line spacing or the tab positions. As you can see, the style does not curb your creativity at all.

What caution is necessary ?

While creating a style you should remember that the style is generally related to a paragraph. So if you want to create a style from a pre-formatted text, the paragraph should be formatted in a uniform manner. The paragraph should, for example, contain only one font or one font size.

The simple reason for this is that in order to assign a style, all you have to do is to put the cursor inside the respective paragraph. *Word* is obviously not able to distinguish by itself which characters in the paragraph are to be formatted in a different font style.

The formatting of your paragraph can now be used as a style. To do this, place the cursor in the respective paragraph.

Click on the *Style* drop-down box

Then go to the *Formatting* toolbar and click on the name in the *Style* drop-down list box, to highlight the style you have been using up to now. Overwrite this selection with the name of your first customized style.

```
Document Labe ▼
```

Fig. 8.12:   The *Style* drop-down list box in the *Formatting* toolbar

Confirm with the
***Enter* key** ⏎

The name of the style can be as long as 255 characters. These may include spaces and upper and lower case as well, all of which will be respected. Enter the name and whatever you do, do not forget to press the *Enter* key ⏎.

Now you have created the first style based on a formatted paragraph. The new style name will henceforth be found in the *Style* drop-down list box and is available for further use.

Repeat this procedure for all formatted paragraphs for which you want to create separate styles.

Apply the style

In case you want to apply the style, click on the paragraph or the selected paragraphs which are supposed to be formatted in that style. Open the *Style* list and select the appropriate style.

Note: Character styles cannot be created via the *Style* drop-down list box.

Modifying a Style in the *Style* Drop-Down Box

To modify a style, select the style to be modified from the *Style* list. Then modify the formatting of the current paragraph as you wish, and select the paragraph. Click on the current style entry in the *Style* list box and press *Enter*. The *Modify Style* dialog box will appear.

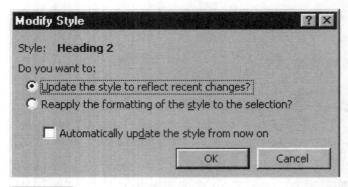

Fig. 8.13:   Modifying a style

Word recognizes that you are about to modify the style. Select the *Update the style to reflect recent changes* radio button. Then click *OK* to modify the style.

Automatically
update

If you select the *Automatically update the style from now on* check box, the definitions of a style are automatically changed without displaying the *Modify Style* dialog box. To switch off this function again choose the *Style* item on the *Format* menu, select the style and click *Modify*. In the *Modify Style* dialog box clear the *Automatically update* check box and confirm with *OK*.

Set Styles in the Dialog Box

You can also use the *Style* dialog box to save certain formatting which is going to be used more often as a style.

Word will automatically apply subsequent modifications of the style to other paragraphs using the same style.

First, create a document based on the template in which you are going to use the new styles in future. Styles are always saved in the template and are, for this reason only available in documents based on the same template.

Choose the *Style* item on the *Format* menu. On the left side of the *Style* dialog box the names of the styles in the template will be displayed. If you want to display only certain styles, open the *List* drop-down box.

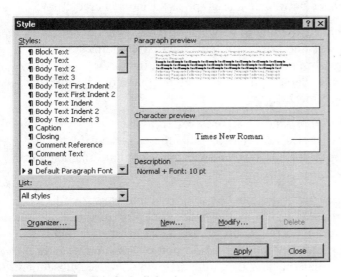

Fig. 8.14: The *Style* dialog box

The default entry *Styles in use* shows only those styles which are being used in the current document. The *All styles* entry gives a list of all styles available to the document. The *User-defined styles* entry gives a list of all the user-defined styles. On the right side of the dialog box you can see a *Preview* of the paragraph style in the upper box and of the character style in the box below. In *Description*, all the formatting information is displayed.

Modify
New

Click on the *Modify* button to modify an existing style. In order to create your own new style, click *New Style*. In the *Modify Style* dialog box enter a name for the styles.

Go to the *Style type* drop-down list box to choose whether you want the new style to be a *Paragraph* style or a *Character* style. When modifying a pre-existing style, this button will be disabled. But what exactly is the difference between a paragraph style and a character style?

¶

Paragraph style

a

Character style

Word distinguishes between different types of styles. One type is the paragraph style which contains all sorts of formatting and which generally affects the whole paragraph. Paragraph styles will be marked with the paragraph mark ¶.

The other kind of style is called a character style. Character styles are marked with the **a** symbol in the *Style* drop-down list box and can only contain character formatting.

Character style

Character styles can be useful if you always want to write particular terms in the same font, for example, or the same font size. To do so, use a character style and it will be possible to change the format of those terms later on. This can be an incredible help in case of subsequent changes to your document.

Choose format

After you have chosen the *Style type* the formatting process can begin. To start with, go to the *Format* button to open a popup menu.

From this menu choose the desired formatting type: *Font, Paragraph, Tabs, Border, Language, Frame* and *Numbering*. Each of these items opens the corresponding dialog box of the *Format* menu.

Select one of these formatting entries, set all the options in the corresponding dialog box and confirm with *OK*. Click again on the *Format* button if you want to change the formatting of a different category.

Proceed in the very same way, as many times as necessary, until all the desired formatting has been assigned to the style.

To find out which formatting has already been assigned to the new style, you have to go back to the *New Style* dialog box. There you can see all the various settings in the *Description* box.

Add to template

In case you want to save the new style not only in the active document but also in the template, in order to make it available to other documents as well, select the *Add to template* check box.

Confirm the *New Style* dialog box with *OK*. The new style will be displayed in the *Styles* list box.

You can now create more styles or you can exit the *Style* dialog box by clicking on *Cancel*.

In case *Word* gives you a message asking you if you would like to save your modifications in the template, you should confirm with *Yes* if you want to save the styles.

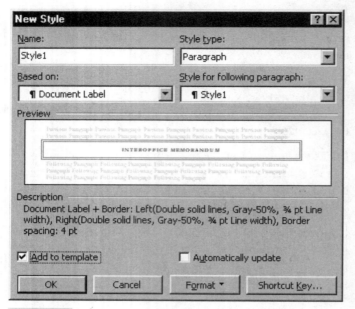

Fig. 8.15:   The *New Style* dialog box

Assigning Styles to Key Combinations

Normally you apply either your own styles or styles offered by *Word* by using the *Style* list box. But most of the time your hands are already on the keyboard while you are working with *Word*. For this very reason there is a convenient way to avoid having to keep moving your hands back and forth between the keyboard and the mouse.

An alternative is to assign your styles to certain key combinations and so quickly create homogeneous documents with the help of the styles. You need to open a document on the basis of the template in which your styles are saved, if you want to assign a keystroke to your style.

Format/
Style

Choose *File/New* to change to the corresponding tab and create a new document by double-clicking onto the name of the desired template. Now select the *Style* item on the *Format* menu. On the left side of the *Style* list box, the names of the styles in the template are displayed. If you want more styles to be displayed, open the *List* drop-down box.

Select the particular style in the *Styles* list for which you want to assign a key combination and click onto the *Modify* button.

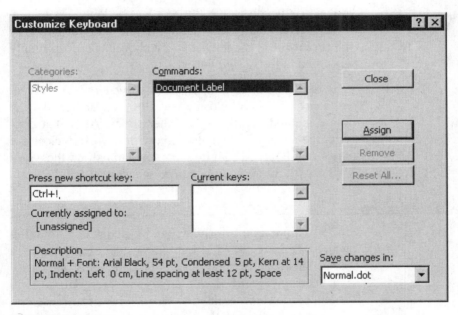

Fig. 8.16: Assigning styles to key combinations

Shortcut key

In the *Modify Styles* dialog box click on the *Shortcut Key* button. A new dialog box called *Customize Keyboard* will open. The cursor will blink in the *Press new shortcut key* text box. Now enter the key combination you want to use in future to call up this style, for example Ctrl+!.

Look at the message below the *Press new shortcut key* box. Only if it reads *[unassigned]* is the key combination still available. Make sure not to use any shortcuts already used by *Word*. The *Word* shortcuts are very useful and you will not be able to access the predefined commands with the keyboard anymore if you accidentally replace them with your own key combinations.

Assigning shortcuts

Select the desired template in the *Save changes in* drop-down box if you would like to save the key combination in a different template. Afterwards the shortcut will only be accessible in the template you choose. Confirm finally by clicking the *Assign* button.

Current keys

The key combination will be displayed in the *Current keys* list box. Now close the dialog box and repeat the same method described for other styles. After that confirm the *Modify Style* dialog box with *OK*. Now close the *Style* dialog box. From now on you can call up the saved styles with the key combinations whenever you like.

Organizing Styles

In *Word*, paragraph formatting and character formatting which are in regular use can be saved in the form of a style. This enables you to call them up quickly and easily whenever you want. In this section we are going to look at one of the shortcomings of *Word*, which can cause you certain difficulties in the use of customized or modified styles.

Word saves particular items in templates, styles being one of them. This fact will not be a problem as long as you are only working with documents based on the *Word* standard template which are created right after the start of *Word* or by clicking the *New* button 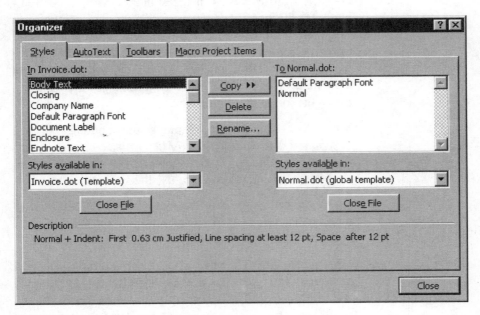.

Styles of other templates

All modifications to existing styles or any custom styles you have created are available in each of those documents. This is different if you have defined styles, regardless of whether they are your own or ones which have been modified, stored in a different template but which you now want to use in a document based on *Normal.dot*, or vice versa. If, for example, you have saved one or more custom or modified styles in a letter template, you will have access to them only in this template and not in any other.

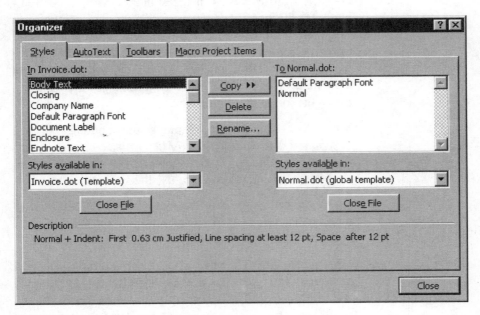

Fig. 8.17: Organizing custom and modified styles

365

To make your own or modified styles available to other templates as well, you have to copy the styles from the original template in which they were created to the template in which you now want to use them. To do this, open a document based on the template in which the desired style is contained. Then select the *Style* item from the *Format* menu.

Click on the *Organizer* button in the *Style* dialog box and change to the *Styles* tab. All the other tabs will show the items available in this template.

Close File
Open File

The current document name will be displayed in the *Styles available in* drop-down list box. The styles in the current template will be displayed in the list box on the left side of the tab. *Word* will now presume that you have not saved those entries in the standard *Normal.dot* template. It will therefore offer you this template on the right side of the dialog box as a copy target. In case you want to copy your styles from the current template into a different template, click on the *Close File* button and, right after that, on the new *Open File* button you will find on the right side of the dialog box.

The *Open* dialog box displays the contents of the *C:\Windows\Application Data\Microsoft\Templates* template folder. Change to the subfolder which contains the template in which you want to use the style

Open

Select the corresponding template and click on *Open* to display the styles saved in this template on the right side of the *Organizer* dialog box.

Select

Now select all the desired styles. For multiple selection press the Ctrl key and one by one click on every style you want to copy. If necessary you can make use of the scroll bar if too many entries are displayed.

You can select a range of entries by holding down the mouse button and dragging it downwards through the list, which will be automatically scrolled as you are doing this. Click on *Copy* to copy the selected styles to the other template. Repeat this method with other templates if necessary. End the session in the *Organizer* dialog box with *Close*. The custom as well as the modified styles will now be available in the other template and logically also in any other document based on the template.

Concatenating Styles

If you already became familiar with styles or are even used to working with them, you should explore one more method of speeding up your daily work.

After studying this chapter you already know how to create a style and how to apply it. To apply a style you either select the name of the style in the *Style* drop-down box or in the *Style* dialog box, or you press the corresponding key combination.

If you are in the process of defining a particular type of document, you will notice that you have to repeat the following procedures again and again:

- Entering the text of the paragraph and confirming with *Enter* ↵.

- Selecting a style from the list box.

- Entering the text of the next paragraph and confirming with *Enter* ↵.

- Assigning the next style.

Whenever we have to repeat the same procedure over and over again, for example when we always use the same item in the same manner, the PC or in this case *Word* in fact, can be used to make this work a lot easier. Fortunately *Word* offers a simple way of doing this.

If you are creating a document in which all the styles are always used in the same order, you can connect or link these styles in a sequence. Then you only need to call up the first of the connected styles in order to call up all the others automatically if you end your paragraph as usual with the *Enter* key ⏎.

To connect styles you need to create all the styles that you always use in the same order. Choose *Format/Style* and select the name of the first style that begins the concatenation from the *Styles* list box. Then click the *Modify* button.

Style for following paragraph
Open the *Style for following paragraph* drop-down list box and select the name of the next style that *Word* is supposed to automatically call up.

Confirm with *OK* and select the second name from the *Style* list box. Again click *Modify*. Then select the name of the style for the third paragraph from the *Style for following paragraph* drop-down list box, which will thus become the third style in the chain.

Repeat this method carefully until all the desired styles have been connected in the desired order.

Close the *Style* dialog box with the *Cancel* button.

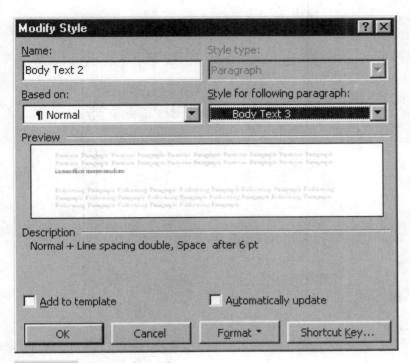

Fig. 8.18: Connecting styles

In order to assign the sequence of styles, type the text for the first paragraph and assign the first style from the *Style* drop-down list box to it.

If you end your paragraph now with *Enter* ⏎ as usual, *Word* will automatically call up the next style for the second paragraph, and so on.

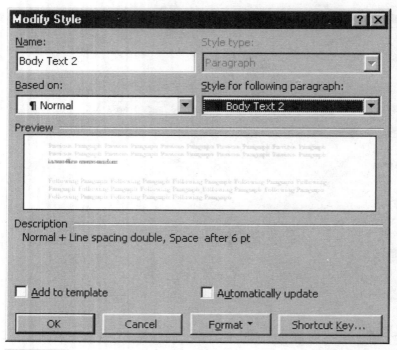

Fig. 8.19: Resetting a connected style

You can of course also reset a connected style. Go to *Format/Style* and select the name of the particular style.

Then click the *Modify* button and select in the *Style for following paragraph* drop-down list box the name of the current style again.

Close the *Modify Style* dialog box using *OK* and the *Style* dialog box with *Close*.

Printing Styles

You can print out the list of styles saved in your current document, or rather in the template on which this document is based. It can be interesting or necessary to compare the styles of the current document with the styles of a different template in order to decide which of those styles you want to copy and which ones you do not. To print the list of styles and the formatting specifications saved therein, choose *File/Print*.

Print

Open the *Print* drop-down box in the lower left corner of the *Print* dialog box and select the *Styles* entry.

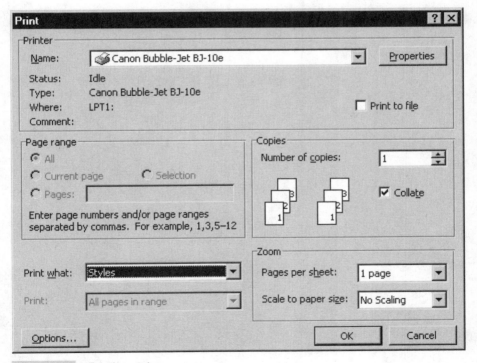

Fig. 8.20:   Printing styles

Select *OK* to start the printing process. *Word* will print your styles in alphabetical order. Only the custom and modified styles will be printed.

9. Automatic Functions

Despite the fact that *Word* is already quite an easy-to-use word processing program, you still have to do most of the manual work like entering text, checking the completed layout, etc., by yourself. Other tasks, like the correction of typing mistakes, the formatting and the pasting of recurring sections of text, can be left to *Word*. In this chapter we will summarize the automatic functions. By automatic we mean that *Word* can do the respective processes by itself, if the necessary preparations have been made. These functions are prefixed with 'Auto' and include:

- Automatic Spelling and Grammar Checking
- AutoCorrect
- AutoText
- AutoFormatting
- AutoSummarize
- Automatic Thesaurus
- Automatic Sorting
- Automatic Hyphenation

Spelling and Grammar Checking

You may have wondered why certain words in your document are underlined in red or green, or you might have already heard about the automatic spelling and grammar function that checks as you type, but wondered why your mistakes weren't automatically corrected. You will now find the answer to both these questions.

Spelling check as You Type

Not only is *Word* equipped with a spelling checker, but also with a grammar checker. The spelling and grammar checkers are activated immediately after installation. As you type, *Word* uses wavy red underlines to indicate spelling errors and wavy green underlines to indicate possible grammatical errors.

Underlined words

With the automatic spelling check, unrecognized words are underlined with a wavy red line. We use the term 'unrecognized words' on purpose, because not every word underlined with a red wavy line is necessarily a typing mistake. We also say that unrecognized words are 'marked' and not automatically corrected. In *Word* the automatic correction of often repeated typing mistakes is called *AutoCorrect*. This function will be described in more detail later on in this chapter. For the moment, we will look at the function that checks the spelling in your document.

Word uses wawy red underlinse to inidcate spellling errors

Fig. 9.1:   Unrecognized or wrongly spelled words are marked

Manual correction

The *Automatic spelling check* is activated by default. All unrecognized words are marked with a red underline. The words are marked as unrecognized only after you have pressed the space bar. You can correct the marked mistakes immediately. If you replace the word with the correctly spelled term that *Word* recognizes, the underline will disappear.

Active checking

As long as the automatic spelling check is active, a small icon is visible in the status bar. If an unrecognized word is found after the check, this 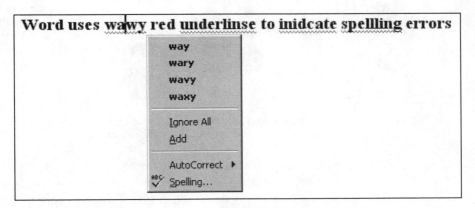 icon will appear.

Use Word to correct

You will find *Word's* help useful in correcting the marked words. Point the cursor on a word marked in red and click on the right mouse button. In the context menu, different commands and correction proposals will be available. Choose an option from the suggestions available and click on the selection of your choice to replace the word. The correction will be made only in this particular place. If you want this same correction to be repeated automatically in future, then instead of choosing the correct word, choose *AutoCorrect* in the shortcut menu, as explained below.

Word uses wawy red underlinse to inidcate spellling errors

> way
> wary
> wavy
> waxy
>
> Ignore All
> Add
>
> AutoCorrect ▶
> Spelling...

Fig. 9.2: Spelling and Grammar shortcut menu

Ignore All

Choose *Ignore All* to delete the marks of all instances of a word which is spelled correctly in your document but which you do not want to include in the dictionary. This function can be used for words that *Word* does not know, but which you use only once in a while.

Add

If you want to insert the term marked in red into the user dictionary, click *Add*. This can be helpful in the case of words which are not recognized by *Word*, but which will occur frequently in your documents. By adding them to the dictionary once, you will save time by not having to deal with them over and over and again.

AutoCorrect

Choose *AutoCorrect* to open an overlapping menu wherein the correction proposals are listed once again. After choosing the desired suggestion, *Word* 'remembers' it and automatically makes this correction in future.

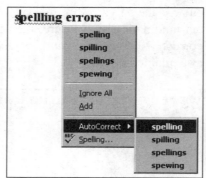

Fig. 9.3:   Left: The mistake will only be corrected in the actual position.
              Right: The correction will be done automatically in future

To start the spell checker for the current document manually, choose *Spelling and Grammar* from the *Tools* menu. A dialog box will open which contains more buttons and which will also enable you to select a spelling dictionary.

Tip!

You can move from mistake to mistake more quickly and, at the same time, see the correction proposals in the context menu if you double-click on the  icon in the status bar.

Deactivating the Automatic Spelling check

The automatic spelling check will mark any unknown words in a document with a wavy red underline as you type. This means that typing mistakes can be spotted at once and quickly corrected if so desired. In texts which employ a lot of technical terms, the marks made by the automatic spell checker can be rather distracting, and apart from that, the processing of your document is slowed when the spelling check is active in the background.

Check spelling as you type

For this very reason you can disable the spelling checker during typing, or customize it to suit your personal needs. To do so, choose the *Options* command on the *Tools* menu. Change to the *Spelling and Grammar* tab. Deactivate the spelling checker by clearing the *Check spelling as you type* check box.

Hide spelling errors in this document

Clear the *Hide spelling errors in this document* check box to get rid of the red wavy lines under the potential mistakes in your document without sacrificing the functionality of the spelling checker. Always confirm your changes with *OK*.

Shortcut menu

A faster way of doing this is via the shortcut menu. Right-click on the icon for the spelling checker or, in case this icon is disabled or not visible, right-click on the position in the status bar at which this icon is usually displayed.

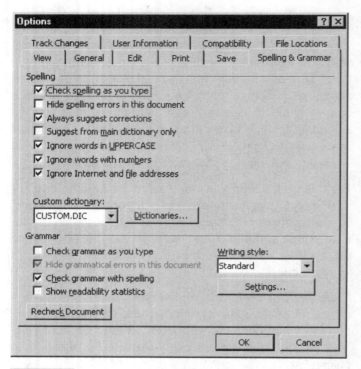

Fig. 9.4: The *Spelling and Grammar* tab page

To hide or show the red wavy lines under the words, clear or check the *Hide spelling errors in this document* check box respectively. With the little check mark in the corresponding check box, you can determine whether the function is working or not. The dialog box containing all these options can be called up by selecting the *Options* item in the *Tools* menu.

Checking the Spelling of Your Document Manually

Word uses the automatic spelling checker while you are typing by default. Unknown terms are then marked with red wavy underlines. You can correct those terms using the replacements suggested in the context menu. In case you have disabled the checking while you type, you can still correct mistakes in your document afterwards 'by hand', so to speak.

Spelling and Grammar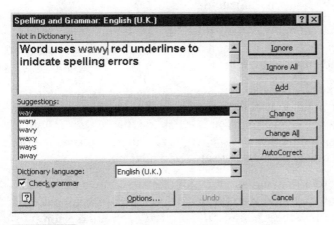

This method can be used to correct only a selected portion of your document, or even just a single word. To do so, start the spelling checker manually by clicking on the *Spelling and Grammar* button on the *Standard* toolbar. Another way of starting it is by choosing the first item, *Spelling and Grammar*, from the *Tools* menu. Another way, and probably the easiest of all, is just to press the F7 key. *Word* will then show the *Spelling and Grammar* dialog box in the currently selected language. It will immediately check the text with the help of the built-in spelling dictionary in *Word*. A term which is not found in the dictionary in the way you have spelled it will halt the checking process. The unrecognized word will be displayed together with different suggestions for the way in which it could be corrected.

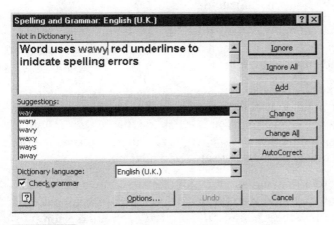

Fig. 9.5: The *Spelling and Grammar* dialog box

We will explain the functioning of the grammar checker later on in this chapter. First let's take a look at the different ways to correct spelling errors.

Not in dictionary

The first unrecognized word the checker comes across with will be marked in red in your text and will, at the same time, be displayed together with its context in the *Not in Dictionary* list box. The name of this box can also be '*Repeated word*' or '*Capitalization*' depending on the type of mistake you have done.

Ignore

There are different buttons available for the correction of unrecognized words. In case the marked term is spelled correctly, you simply have to choose *Ignore*. The term will remain unchanged and the next time it appears in your document it will be displayed as a possible error.

Ignore All

This may not be a problem unless the correctly spelled term is used quite often in your document. In that case, choose *Ignore All* instead of the *Ignore* button. This will remove the red underline whenever the same term occurs throughout your document.

Suggestions

If a term really is spelled wrong, take a look at the *Suggestions* list. If the correct term has already been selected, you need only press *Change*.

Change

If the correctly spelled suggestion is displayed in this list, but not yet selected, you have to select this suggestion manually and afterwards click on the *Change* button. Now the incorrectly spelled word will be replaced in your document by the suggestion you have chosen.

Change All

In order to avoid having your attention drawn to the same error over and over again in the current document, you can click the *Change All* button to correct the error automatically throughout the whole document.

Delete

Delete All

In case you have accidentally repeated a word in the document, this repetition will also be pointed out to you. The labels on the buttons will change from *Change* to *Delete* and from *Change All* to *Delete All*.

Correcting manually

If there is no appropriate correction available in the *Suggestions* list box, click on the position of the error in the *Not in Dictionary* box and correct the mistake manually. You can move back and forth and within the box using the → and ← keys. When you have corrected the term, press the *Change* button.

Undo

Press the *Undo* button to undo the corrections you have already done. The *Undo* button can be used several times in a row in order to undo more than one step.

AutoCorrect

Typing mistakes that are shown by the spelling checker and repeated over and over again, such as common typing mistakes, can be corrected as mentioned above. To ensure that they will be corrected automatically in future, press the *AutoCorrect* button after making the correction. You will find out more about *AutoCorrect* in connection with the spelling check functions later on in this chapter. By using this feature, the mistake will be corrected automatically whenever it occurs during the typing process.

After the spelling check is complete you will get the following message.

Fig. 9.6:   Message at the end of the spelling check

Similar messages will appear when the checker reaches the end of the document or the end of the marked words.

The rest of the document can be checked by pressing the *Yes* button. If the checking should stop at that point, press the *No* button.

Grammar Check

Green wavy underlines

Grammar checking is activated along with the spelling check by default immediately after installation, and the suspected mistakes are marked with a green wavy underline. Unlike the spelling check feature, which always marks only single words, the grammar checker looks at whole sentences and underlines ambiguous ones.

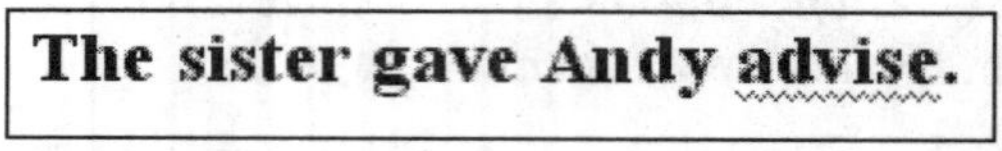

The sister gave Andy advise.

Fig. 9.7: Marking grammar mistakes

If you are already familiar with the automatic *Check spelling as you type* function, you will not have any difficulty with the automatic grammar check. If a mistake is spotted, it can be manually corrected right away.

Grammar context menu

A right-click onto a sentence marked with a green wavy underline opens the context menu which displays a list of suggestions for the correction. A description of the mistake as well as the commands for the correction will also be shown.

The sister gave Andy advise.
advice
Ignore Sentence
Grammar...

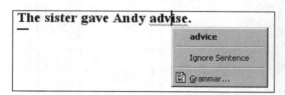

Fig. 9.8: The grammar checking context menu

Read the brief description of the mistake which the grammar checker will show you. The phrases that have led to the mistake will be displayed prominently in the description.

Accept the suggestion

In the list below, *Word* shows suggestions as to how the mistake can be corrected. In case the marked section of text is grammatically incorrect, and a good suggestion for its correction is given, click on the suggested phrase in the shortcut menu. The error will be corrected and the marks will vanish.

Ignore Sentence

If the sentence marked does not contain a mistake, you can choose the *Ignore Sentence* item on the shortcut menu. In this case, too, the green wavy underline will disappear, but the sentence will remain unchanged.

Grammar

By choosing the *Grammar* item you call up the dialog box for the spelling and grammar checker. You will find more buttons for editing your mistakes here.

Deactivate the Automatic Grammar Check

It is more than likely that users with little experience will make quite a few typing mistakes at first. The document they are working on might also contain a lot of terms unknown to them, depending on the content. This will unavoidably lead to many red and green wavy underlines.

Extras/Options

Genuine grammar mistakes as well mistakes which *Word* proposes will occur relatively seldom. Even so, if you want to hide the green wavy underlines or to deactivate the grammar checker, choose *Tools/Options* and activate the *Spelling and Grammar* tab. Clear the check box *Check grammar as you type* in order to switch off this function completely. You would do this if, for example, you wanted to check the text manually once it has been entered.

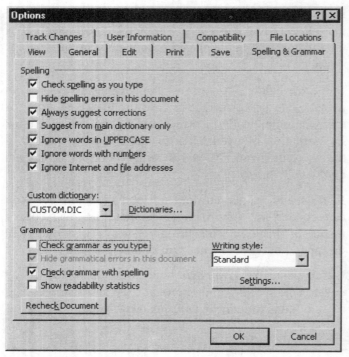

Fig. 9.9: Deactivate grammar check

Grammar marks

Select the *Hide grammatical errors in this document* check box if would like the marks to be hidden, but still want the grammar checker to go on with its work. Close the dialog box with *OK*.

It is also possible to use the context menu to hide the marks of grammatical errors. Right-click on the icon in the status bar and choose the *Hide Grammatical Errors* command.

Separate Grammar and Spelling check

Normally *Word* checks the spelling and the grammar in a document simultaneously and marks words that it does not recognize in red, and sentences that are inconsistent with the rules of grammar in green. The manual checking with the help of the dialog box proceeds in the same way. This can be confusing, especially when you are not yet familiar with these functions.

On the *Spelling and Grammar* tab in the *Options* dialog box as well as in the *Spelling and Grammar* dialog box, a check box allows you separate these two functions of spelling and grammar checking.

Grammar checking

Clear the *Check grammar* check box in the *Spelling and Grammar* dialog box to deactivate the grammar check for the moment.

Simultaneous grammar and spelling check

If you want to disable the function from outside of the dialog box, choose *Tools/Options* and deselect the *Check grammar with spelling* check box on the *Spelling and Grammar* tab. Close the dialog box with *OK*.

Using the Dialog Box to Manually Correct the Grammar

Should you have deactivated the *Check grammar as you type* function, you can still use the grammar checker either for the whole document or for a marked section of it.

The way to go about this is to select the *Spelling and grammar* button 🔲, or choose the *Tools/Spelling and grammar* command.

In the *Grammar* box at the top of the *Spelling and Grammar* dialog box, *Word* shows the sentence with the suspected mistake and displays the cause of the problem in green letters.

Suggestions Below that, in the *Suggestions* box you will find the description of the mistake and possible solutions for it.

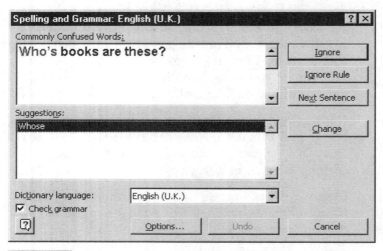

Fig. 9.10: The *Spelling and Grammar* dialog box

Ignore If a passage is grammatically correct but has been marked as a mistake, press the *Ignore* button to clear away the green wavy underlines.

Ignore Rule Choose the *Ignore Rule* button to ignore the rule which determined the sentence in question to be marked as possibly wrong.

Change To change a sentence, select the correct suggestion made by *Word* and click on the *Change* button, or click into the box containing the erroneous sentence and correct the grammatical error manually.

Next Sentence The *Next Sentence* button takes you to the next sentence, leaving the current sentence as it is. This means that if there is an error in the grammatical structure, you will have to correct it manually.

Undo

You will find the *Undo* button in the dialog box of the grammar checker too. Using this button you can undo the most recent editing steps you have made one by one.

Spelling Check of Technical Terms

The spell checker in *Word* shows you all the words in your document that are unknown to it. If you use *Word* to write technical literature, every third word of these correctly spelled but special terms might be marked with a red wavy underline, or shown as an unknown word during the manual check. In the long run, this can be rather annoying. The integrated dictionary is of course not capable of containing all these technical terms, but fortunately the spelling check tool has the capacity to 'learn'. This chapter describes how you can add the correctly spelled terms that are not found in the dictionary so that in future they are not shown as unrecognized anymore. The only thing you have to do is to 'teach' these unknown words to *Word*.

Open the dialog box

You can do this by clicking on the *Spelling and Grammar* button ABC in the *Standard* toolbar in order to start the manual spelling check of your document. You can also choose the *Spelling and Grammar* item in the *Tools* menu or simply press F7.

Add

The manual spell checker will display technical terms in the *Not in Dictionary* box. If the technical term is spelled correctly but is still displayed, and if this is a term which you will be using quite often in future, then press the *Add* button.

CUSTOM.DIC

These terms will be added to the custom dictionary CUSTOM.DIC. This custom dictionary will be automatically created the first time you choose the *Add* button.

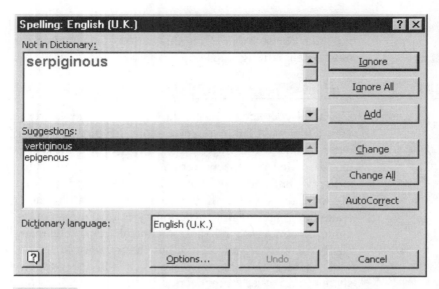

Fig. 9.11:   Manual spelling check of unknown 'technical terms'

The automatic spelling checker marks any unrecognized technical terms with a red wavy underline as you type. You can also add marked but correctly spelled words that will be used more than once in your document with a right-click. Select the *Add* command in the context menu and the technical term will be added to the custom dictionary CUSTOM DIC.

Fig. 9.12:   Automatic spelling check of unknown words

If a word has been added to the custom dictionary, *Word* remembers the word even after the correction process is over, unlike the *Ignore All* command which is valid only for the current checking session. Repeat this method for all correctly spelled technical terms and little by little build up your personalized dictionary. The spelling of all the technical terms which are of importance to you will be retained and *Word* will not mark or display them as errors anymore. *Word* will, however, still check the spelling of these terms.

Make sure that only words which are spelled correctly are added to the custom dictionary using the *Add* command, or *Word* will not be able to recognize certain spelling mistakes in your document afterwards.

Dictionary for Different Spelling Possibilities

Many words have more than one spelling. This is not likely to change merely by rewriting the rules over and over again. In fact this can even lead to more confusion instead of more freedom. The term 'program' for instance can also be spelled 'programme'. 'Color' is another word which you will often find spelled as 'colour'.

The list of words which can be spelled in more than one way is endless, but you might have settled on your own choices or you might have to adhere to the rules prevalent in your company. This is a problem for the spelling checker, which accepts both spelling options in most cases. This won't help much if you want to stick to one particular spelling. Here's what you can do in such a case.

The custom dictionary cannot be edited

If the dictionary of *Word* contains more than one way of spelling a word, you have to delete whichever spelling option you do not want to use. If for example you want to use the word 'program' exclusively, then the term 'programme' should be deleted. Unfortunately the custom dictionary of *Word* cannot be edited, but there is another way to tell *Word* not to accept 'programme' as the correct spelling.

Exclude dictionary To do this you have to create an exclude dictionary in which you will enter all the terms that you would like to be recognized as wrongly spelled in future. In order to create such a dictionary, you first have to create a new document. Click on the *New* button ⬜ on the *Standard* toolbar. Enter every term that you want to exclude one by one and after each entry, press the *Enter* button ⏎.

Fig. 9.13: Example for an exclude dictionary in Word

Sort Tex*t* Once this is done, the list has to be sorted alphabetically. This can be done by selecting the list with the *Select All* combination $\boxed{\texttt{Ctrl}}+\boxed{\texttt{A}}$ and then by selecting the *Sort* command from the *Table* menu. In the *Sort Text* dialog box choose the *Paragraphs* option in the *Sort By* drop-down list, and select the *Text* option in the *Type* drop-down list. Now select *Ascending* and click *OK*.

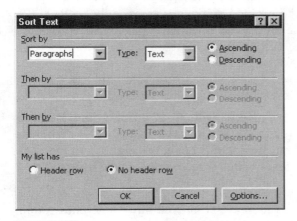

Fig. 9.14: Alphabetical sorting of the exclude dictionary

You should save this sorted list as a *Text Only* file in a specific folder. Choose the *Save As* item from the file menu and type in the file name.

MSSP2_EN.EXC

Now change to the target folder. The dictionary will be saved under the same folder and the same name as the main dictionary, but it will have a different extension. If, for example, you want to create an exclude dictionary for the English MSSP3_EN.LEX, call it this way and save it under following folder:

C:\PROGRAM FILES\COMMON FILES\MICROSOFT SHARED\ PROOF.

File type

Text Only

Select *Text Only (*.txt)* in the *File type* drop-down list box. Confirm by clicking *Save*. The document will then be saved in such a way that it can be used by *Word*. Close the document with *File/Close*.

From now on, the spell checker will display the words found in the exclude dictionary as wrongly spelled. The exclude dictionary can be modified or expanded later on without any difficulty.

AutoCorrect

Everybody who works with *Word* makes typing mistakes from time to time. Many mistakes can be attributed to the method of entering that is being used, although there are certain mistakes which a person may make over and over again.

You may already have wondered how sometimes certain words are automatically completed or corrections in your typing are automatically made to your document by *Word*. What's responsible for these automatic completions or corrections is a tool called *AutoCorrect*.

The present version of *Word* is able to automatically correct most of the common mistakes made while typing, like inverting letters. But maybe you are not yet aware of this function, even though it is active by default and might already have corrected more than one of your typing mistakes. You do not believe us? Well then, instead of typing the word 'and', type in 'adn' and press [Space-bar]. 'This is magic – a miracle – that's impossible!' But yes, it is possible, and it's called *AutoCorrect*!

This function checks the words automatically while you are typing. It proceeds in a manner similar to that of the automatic spell checker. Finish the word with a spacebar, a punctuation mark (full stop, comma, semi-colon, question mark, or exclamation point) or a separation mark like Tab, or press the *Enter* button. *Word* will then check the word for a mistake in no time at all. It will immediately correct the error if it finds a mistake in the typed word.

How does *AutoCorrect* recognize the mistakes in a word? The method used by this tool is again similar to the one used by the spell checker. The *AutoCorrect* function refers to a list of words with their probable typing mistakes. It will compare your word with this list and find the correct version. Obviously it will only recognize mistakes that are included in this list.

Difference between spell checker and AutoCorrect

The spell checker can only recognize and mark a mistake. But the *AutoCorrect* function has access to the list of the correctly spelled terms, and so it can correct the mistake immediately.

Typing Mistakes are Automatically Corrected

Dialog box and *AutoCorrect* tab

AutoCorrect is always running in the background by default. In case the example of the 'adn' correction didn't work, or if you want to look into the list of terms which will be corrected automatically, choose the *AutoCorrect* command on the *Tools* menu.

The automatic functions of *Word* are collected in the *AutoCorrect* dialog box. This might lead to some confusion, as the actual *AutoCorrect* is only found on the *AutoCorrect* tab.

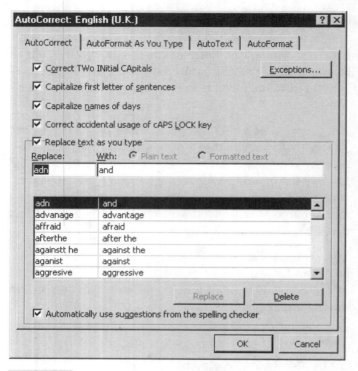

Fig. 9.15: The *AutoCorrect* dialog box with the *AutoCorrect* tab

To switch on *AutoCorrect*, check the *Replace text as you type* check box. Clear the check box to deactivate the function.

List of corrections

You can go through the list of preselected definitions of mistakes and their correction using the scroll bar. On the left side you will find the wrongly typed terms which will automatically be replaced by the terms or signs shown on the right side.

Replace

If you would like to enlarge the list by adding some words which you know you frequently mistype, you can enter the wrongly spelled word into the *Replace* text box.

Add individual typing mistakes

Now enter the word as it should be spelled into the *With* box. To add this new word to the list, press the *Add* button. Repeat this procedure for each and every bothersome typing mistake that has been slowing you down again and again. Once all the words have been entered, close the dialog box by pressing the *OK* button.

Adjust *AutoCorrect* to Your Personal Needs

AutoCorrect is a very handy tool. As we mentioned in the paragraph above, most common typing mistakes can be automatically and completely eliminated straightaway while you are typing. *AutoCorrect* is also able to avoid starting the beginning of sentences or lines in lower case, or to correct the mistakes that crop up if the *Caps Lock* key has been activated by accident.

TWo INitial CApitals

Document texts are very different and *Word* has a multitude of features to suit each one. However, the *Auto-Correct* function may cause some corrections that you do not want. There might be specific terms used by your company which need to begin with two capital letters and then continue with small letters for the remainder of the word. Somebody might use initials or special keys which are incorrectly interpreted by *AutoCorrect*. For example, it will convert ':)' to ☺.

Try typing '(C)' and you will immediately realize that it is necessary to adapt the *AutoCorrect* to meet your personal needs. Choose the *AutoCorrect* item on the *Tools* menu. If you want to abandon the corrections of words beginning with two capital letters, you have to deselect the *Correct TWo INitial CApitals* check box.

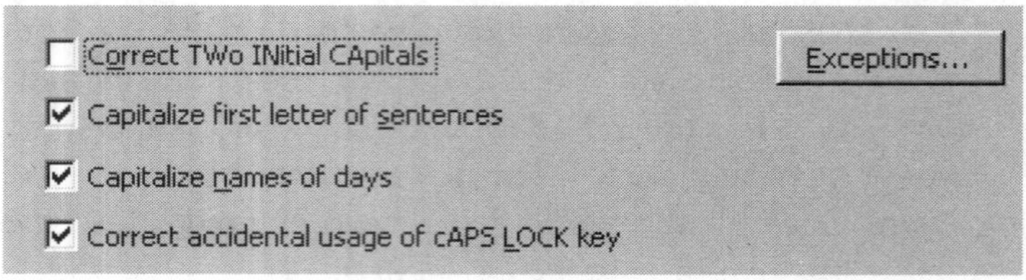

```
☐  Correct TWo INitial CApitals                    [ Exceptions... ]
☑  Capitalize first letter of sentences
☑  Capitalize names of days
☑  Correct accidental usage of cAPS LOCK key
```

Fig. 9.16:   Adapting AutoCorrect

Capital letters

In order to deactivate the correcting function for capital letters at the beginning of a sentence, just deselect the *Capitalize first letter of sentences* check box.

**Accidental usage
of cAPS LOCK key**

If you need the *Caps Lock* function for certain special terms in your document and are annoyed by the automatic correction of this key, then deselect the *Correct accidental usage of cAPS LOCK key* check box. Close the dialog box after the modifications by clicking *OK*.

Setting Exceptions for AutoCorrect

If in principle you appreciate the automatic correction facility, and are only rarely annoyed by some terms, you can define such terms as exceptions for *AutoCorrect*.

Exceptions

For this purpose choose *Tools/AutoCorrect*, activate the *AutoCorrect* tab and click on the *Exceptions* button.

First Letter

On the *First Letter* tab page you can enter all the abbreviations which contain a period so that the function will not put a capital letter after these words when they occur.

INitial CApitals

On the *INitial CAps* tab you can enter all the technical terms which are supposed to begin with two capital letters. You do not need to type in terms having more than two capital letters, because *Word* will not correct them anyway.

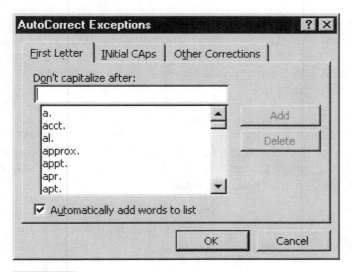

Fig. 9.17:   Set exceptions for AutoCorrect

Type your exceptions into the *Don't correct* text box and click *Add*. In order to delete a wrong term from the list, you have to first select the entry and then click *Delete*. Always confirm your changes at the end of a session with *OK*. The *AutoCorrect* dialog box can also be closed with *OK*, if you do not intend to make any other changes in it.

Deleting AutoCorrect Entries

In certain documents such as user's guides, manuals or while presenting descriptions of different kinds of mistakes, it can be necessary to use spellings or key combinations that are uncommon. Since *Word* is not able to distinguish between words spelled incorrectly on purpose and accidental typing mistakes, it will of course correct those spellings too as soon as *AutoCorrect* detects them. To avoid these corrections, you can delete the particular spellings or special key combinations that are responsible for the automatic corrections from the list.

Searching abbreviation

To avoid undesired corrections of supposed typing mistakes (for example, ':)' will be corrected as ☺), select *AutoCorrect* from the *Tools* menu, and search in the *AutoCorrect* list for the abbreviation or term responsible for the problem.

Delete

The scroll bar can be used for this purpose. Select the unwanted correction entry and click the *Delete* button. Repeat this procedure as many times as you need to and then confirm the session at the end with *OK*. Click *OK* again to come out of the *AutoCorrect* dialog box.

Switching off the function

Deselect the *Replace text as you type* check box if you want to switch off this function completely, but still wish to use other *AutoCorrect* options.

Accepting *AutoCorrect* Entries Automatically

You will now learn how you can check your text for typing mistakes and define individual terms as *AutoCorrect* entries on the spot.

AutoCorrect will save the entry you make, and will make sure that in future this same typing mistake is recognized and corrected by *Word* even as you type. For this combined method of correction, check the text with the spell checker in *Word*. To start the spell checker, press the F7 key.

Another way of going about it is to select the *Spelling and Grammar* item on the *Tools* menu. Now use the methods described earlier in this chapter to edit your document.

If an oft-repeated individual typing mistake appears in the *Not in Dictionary* text box of the *Spelling and Grammar* dialog box, and the *Suggestions* list box contains the correctly spelled term in its dictionary, all you need to do is to select the correct term in *Suggestions* and click on *AutoCorrect*. This will enter the typing mistake into the *AutoCorrect* list.

AutoCorrect

Fig. 9.18:   This button creates new AutoCorrect entries

That's all you need to know about this function. The spelling checker will now jump ahead to the next un-known term. Repeat this method when you want to enter more of your frequent typing mistakes into the list. The corrections can also be entered directly into the text box. Click *AutoCorrect* to enlarge the list available to *Auto-Correct*.

Fig. 9.19:   AutoCorrect entry in the context menu

If you prefer working with the automatic *Check spelling as you type* function, you can also add the corrections to the *AutoCorrect* list via the context menu. In the context menu, choose *AutoCorrect* and click on the correct spelling in the overlapping menu.

You can browse the *AutoCorrect* list and make any changes you need. Choose *Tools/AutoCorrect* to display the list. In order to correct new documents automatically, including typing mistakes which you have entered individually, select the *Replace as you type* check box.

AutoText

In *Word*, you can save recurring phrases or text passages like embellishments or contract paragraphs under an abbreviation sign in order to recall them whenever you need. This function is called *AutoText* and can save you a lot of time in your daily work with *Word*. All you have to do is to type the abbreviation characters along with one special key, and the text attached to this character sequence will appear at the point where the cursor is in your document.

Using Readymade AutoTexts

In many documents standard text passages like salutations and greetings are used quite often. *Word* has a wide variety of such standard phrases that you can easily call up.

For this purpose, *Word* checks what you type, and determines whether or not a sequence of characters you have entered is the same as one of the *AutoText* entries. If such is the case it will propose the *AutoText* as a *ScreenTip* in the way that is illustrated in the following figure.

Show ScreenTip

show   **Show ScreenTip**

Fig. 9.20:   AutoText ScreenTip

You can accept such a proposal by pressing *Enter* ⏎. However, not all glossary items cannot be called up in this way. For that you can use a special command. Place the insertion cursor at the correct location in your document and select *Insert/Autotext*. In the submenu which appears, select the category of *AutoText* from which you want to select an entry.

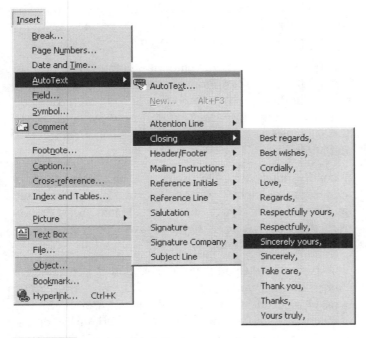

Fig. 9.21:   Standard AutoText

Word organizes *AutoText* entries into different categories. These categories are created on the basis of the styles in which they will afterwards be used. For every category, one menu item will be shown, which in turn will open up a submenu containing the actual *AutoText* entries.

Go to the *Salutation* category, for instance, to choose between private and official salutations.

Saving and Calling Up Embellishments as AutoText

To define a new *AutoText* entry, you have to open a document on the basis of a template in which you want to use the abbreviations later on. You can also set *AutoText* entries during your day-to-day work, if you see that you are using a particular text passage quite regularly. Simply type in the respective text and format it.

An *AutoText* entry can even contain tables, graphics, or icons. There is no restriction on the length of an *AutoText* entry. But there are two important things you have to remember. Firstly, the *AutoText* will only be saved in the current template or in the *New Document (Normal.dot)* global template.

AutoText entries burden the memory

Secondly, many *AutoText* entries in one template are a burden on the memory. If you create a document based on a template in which you have created *AutoText* entries, the whole *AutoText* glossary will be loaded in future along with the template.

Now type the text you want to save under a character or abbreviation. If you want to format the text in a certain way, choose this formatting beforehand. Select the text passages and choose the *AutoText/New* command on the *Insert* menu.

Add AutoText entry

The beginning of the selected text section will be displayed by default in the *Please name your AutoText entry* text box in the *Create AutoText* dialog box. Accept this proposal or overwrite it with a different name. This name can have up to 32 characters and should make sense to you so that you can easily remember the abbreviation.

The fewer letters you use for the characters of an abbreviation, the faster you can call up the *AutoText* afterwards using the keyboard. It does not matter if you use lower or upper case letters for your abbreviations. Press the *OK* button to confirm. Repeat this method for all texts which you want to save as *AutoText*.

Word might ask you at the end of your task whether you want to save the changes in the template. In this case, always confirm with *Yes*, otherwise your *AutoText* entries will be lost.

Calling Up AutoText

Some ways of calling up a saved *AutoText* entry have already been described above. To call up your own *AutoText* entries you can use the same methods used for the predefined *AutoText* items of *Word*.

Suppose you have saved the *AutoText* shown on Figure 9.22 under the name *take*; in future it will be enough to type 'take' for *Word* to propose the content of the *AutoText*.

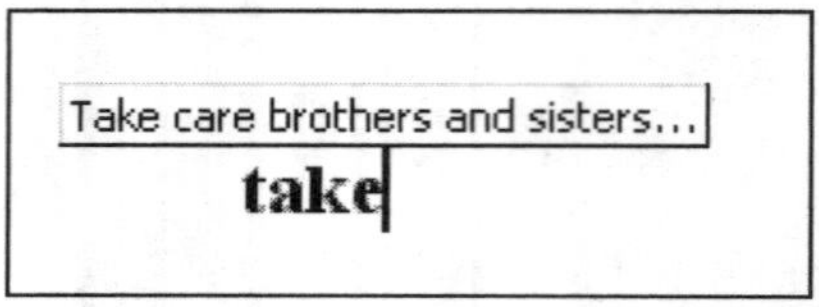

Take care brothers and sisters...

take

Fig. 9.23: Autotext of Figure 9.22

There are several more ways of calling up an *AutoText* entry.

Choose *AutoText/AutoText* from the *Insert* menu. Select the abbreviation of the text you need in the list. Check the text saved under this abbreviation in the *Preview* box and click on *Insert*.

An even faster method to get the particular *AutoText* you want is to enter the abbreviation directly into the text and press the F3 key.

Insert/
AutoText/
Normal

Another method lets us do the same thing via the menu. Choose *Insert/AutoText* and from the submenu, select the *Normal* item if your document has not been created using a special template.

After that, select the name of the *AutoText* category from the submenu.

Fig. 9.24: AutoText on the *AutoText* tab

Creating and Calling up AutoText from the Toolbar

You may have noticed the *Show Toolbar* button on the *AutoText* tab before. You can display a new toolbar either by clicking on this button or by choosing *View/Toolbar/AutoText*. This new toolbar contains special buttons for working with *AutoText*.

Fig. 9.25: The *AutoText* toolbar

You can use the buttons on this toolbar to create or call up *AutoText*.

■ ◄ *AutoText*
The first button on the toolbar will open the *AutoText* tab page in the *AutoCorrect* dialog box, where you can add, insert, rename and delete *AutoText* entries.

■ New... *New*
This button opens the *Create AutoText* dialog box. To be able to get to this button, you first have to select a text passage. Enter a name into the *Please name your AutoText entry* text box and confirm with *OK*. You have now created a new *AutoText* entry.

■ All Entries ▾
The *All entries* button contains all the *AutoText* entries. A click on this button opens a menu with all *AutoText* categories and submenus that show all *AutoText* entries.

You can close the toolbar by clicking the *Close* button ☒ .

Renaming an AutoText Entry

If you create a new *AutoText* entry and realize that you have already used the corresponding abbreviation for an earlier entry, you will find yourself in trouble.

When to rename

Of course it is possible just to save the new entry under a different name or to delete the old *AutoText* entry in order to save the new text passage under the abbreviation you had used before.

Insert/AutoText/
AutoText

However, *AutoText* entries can also be renamed after they have been created. If you want to rename an entry, you have to select the *AutoText* item on the *Insert* menu, and in the submenu choose *AutoText* again.

Add

Select the entry in the list which you want to rename and click on *Insert*. Select the inserted *AutoText* in the document and now once again select *Insert/AutoText/AutoText*. Go ahead and type in the new name and click on *Add*.

Now write the text you want to save under the name of the *AutoText* entry that you have just renamed. If necessary, format it. Once you have done so, select *Insert/AutoText/AutoText* once again and enter the original name of the freshly renamed *AutoText* entry, taking care to put in the exact spelling. Now click on the *Add* button. Confirm the message that appears with *Yes* to overwrite the former *AutoText* entry.

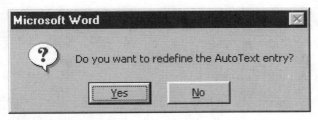

Fig. 9.26:   Defining a new AutoText entry

If you want to attach a new text to an existing *AutoText* abbreviation, and you no longer need the text which was saved before under this abbreviation, you can choose *Insert/AutoText/New* to overwrite an existing *AutoText* entry. Confirm with *OK* and *Yes*.

Deleting AutoText Entries

It is a very good idea to save text passages, salutations, embellishments or contract paragraphs that frequently occur in your documents using this function of *Word*. The so-called *AutoText* entries can save you a lot of time and typing in your daily work with this program.

But a large number of *AutoText* entries is also likely to be a burden on your memory. If you create a *Word* document based on a template which contains *AutoText* entries, a whole glossary of entries will be loaded along with the document or the template.

You might notice after some time that certain *AutoText* entries have not been used for a while and do not seem to be of much use any more. You should go ahead and delete these unnecessary text entries from your template, especially if you do not have much memory in your computer. Even apart from the possible memory problem, it is a good idea to limit the size of the list to something which you can easily manage.

To search for *AutoText* entries in order to make changes or delete some of the entries, first create a document based on the template containing the entries with *File/ New*. On the *Tools* menu choose the *AutoCorrect* item and select the *AutoText* tab.

Delete

Go through the list of abbreviations using the scroll bar and select those abbreviations whose meanings you can no longer remember or which you want to delete. You can see the saved text in the *Preview* box. Delete the *AutoText* entries you selected by clicking on the *Delete* button. Repeat this procedure as often as necessary to delete all the superfluous text entries. Close the *Auto-Correct* dialog box clicking on *OK*.

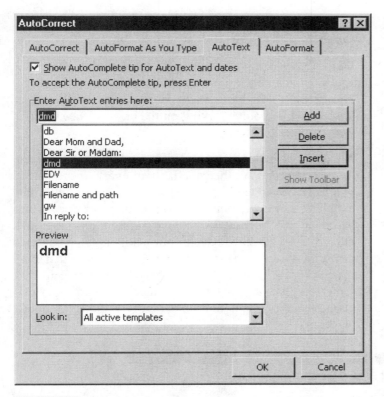

Fig. 9.27: Deleting superfluous text in a glossary

At the end of a *Word* session you will get a message asking whether you want to save the changes you made in the template. Confirm this by clicking on *Yes*, otherwise the time you spent deleting the extraneous entries will have been in vain.

Using AutoText Entries in Other Document Templates

The saving of often used embellishments and the calling up of text passages has been assumed by *Word* with the *AutoText* function. In this section we concentrate on a peculiarity found in *Word* that can sometimes lead to a certain bewilderment while working with *AutoText*.

Word saves certain elements in the template file, like styles, changes in toolbars, macros and finally the *Auto-Text* entries. This effect won't cause you any problems as long as you are only working on the basis of the standard *Word* template.

All changes in toolbars, styles and all the user-defined *AutoText* entries are thus available in every document. If you have saved certain *AutoText* entries in a different template, however, but want to use them in documents based on the *Normal.dot* or vice versa, then things are different. If you have saved your salutations or contract paragraphs as *AutoText* entries in one of the letter templates provided, then they will only be available in this same template and not in any other template. This obviously makes them unusable in other kinds of documents.

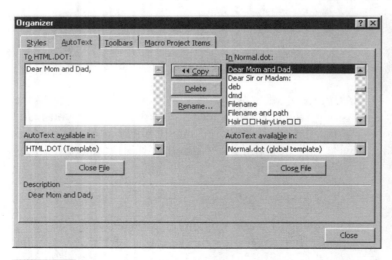

Fig. 9.28:   Organizing AutoText entries

Templates and Add-Ins

To make the *AutoText* entries available in other templates as well, you have to copy the entries from the template in which you created them to the template in which you want to use them in future. In order to do this, you first need to open a document based on the template in which you have saved your *AutoText* entries. Now select the *Templates and Add-Ins* item on the *Tools* menu.

AutoText tab

In the dialog box that is called up, click on the *Organizer* button and change to the *AutoText* tab page. The other tabs show all the other elements saved in this template. On the lower left side of the *AutoText* tab you will find a drop-down list called *AutoText available in*. This displays the current template. In the list above it all the saved *AutoText* entries will be displayed.

Opening other templates

Word assumes that you have not saved these entries in the standard template *Normal.dot* and offers you this template in the right part of the dialog box as a copy target. To copy the *AutoText* entries from the current template into another template, click the *Close File* button at the right-hand side of the dialog box. Then click on the same button again, which will now be called *Open File*.

Templates

The *Open* dialog box shows the content of the *Word* template folder, usually *C:\Windows\Application Data\Microsoft\Templates*.

Open

Mark the corresponding template and click on *Open*. Now you can see the saved *AutoText* entries in this template in the list on the right side of the *Organizer* dialog box.

Mark

Now select all the desired *AutoText* entries from the list at the left of the dialog box. To select multiple items, hold down the Ctrl key and click on each entry you want to copy. To select all or many entries in a row, keep the mouse button held down, and move the mouse downwards. The contents of the list moves along with you, selecting all the entries automatically.

Copy

Click on *Copy* to copy the entries onto the other template. Of course you will need to repeat this procedure for each template that you need. Close the *Organizer* dialog box by clicking *Close*. The *AutoText* entries are ready to be called up in the respective template.

Printing Lists with *AutoText* Entries

Reading material that is printed is easier and more efficient than going over the same content directly on-screen. This holds true for the *AutoText* entries as well. If you have saved a lot of embellishments which can be called up by *AutoText*, then you had better go in for a printout of a complete list of your *AutoText* entries. Only if you know what the abbreviations of your entries stand for will you be able to make use of the *AutoText* function in your day-to-day work.

Opening documents or templates

In order to make a printout of the *AutoText* entries, open a document using the template from which you want to print the *AutoText* entries. The best way to do this is by choosing *File/New*. Activate the tab of the respective template, select the template and confirm the procedure with *OK*. Another way is to open the template in which the *AutoText* entries are saved directly. If you are going to use this method, do not forget to change the *File type* in the *Open* dialog box to *Templates (*.dot)*.

The *Print* item on the *File* menu is used to call up the *Print* dialog box. It may be necessary to choose the name of the particular printer on which you are going to print out your list. The printer can be selected in the *Name* drop-down list box. Open the *Print what* drop-down list on the bottom left of the dialog box, and select *AutoText entries* before confirming the dialog with *OK*.

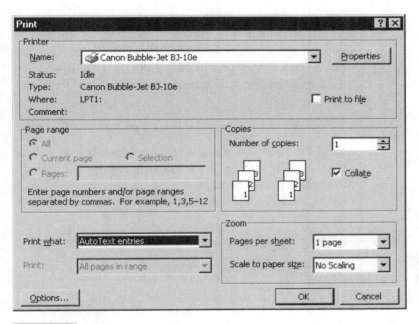

Fig. 9.29: Printing only AutoText entries

Word will then print the *AutoText* entries. The abbreviation of an entry will be printed in bold. Below that the corresponding text will appear. If an entry contains graphics they will also be printed along with the text.

Using the same technique, you can also print out document properties, comments, styles or key assignments.

Activating and Deactivating AutoComplete

The *AutoComplete* function in *Word* can recognize a sequence of characters as the name of an *AutoText* entry. It can give a tip with the content of the *AutoText* and it will insert the text after you have pressed the *Enter* key ⏎.

If this function isn't working then most probably you will have to activate it first. Another possibility is that the sequence of characters matches more than one *AutoText* entry. You can decide whether or not the function is activated by selecting or clearing a check box in the *AutoText* dialog box.

Choose *Tools/Autocorrect* and activate the *AutoText* tab.

Select the *Show AutoComplete tip for AutoText and datas* check box if you want *AutoComplete* to display the *ScreenTip*. If you want to deactivate this function, deselect the check box. Then close the dialog box with *OK*.

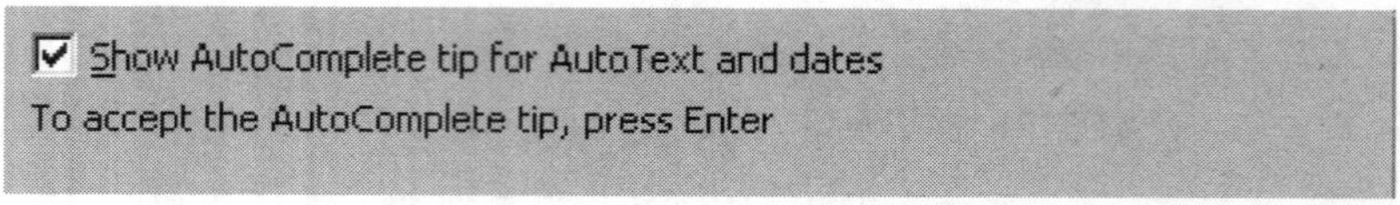

☑ S̲how AutoComplete tip for AutoText and dates
To accept the AutoComplete tip, press Enter

Fig. 9.30: The ScreenTip for AutoText is controlled by this check box

You can still insert *AutoText* entries even if the *AutoComplete* function is not activated. You just have to use the menu or enter the name and press F3.

Using the Automatic Hyphenation

Word automatically writes the word at the end of a line onto a new line if there is not enough space left on the line. When a word is very long this means that a rather long and empty space will appear in the text. Such gaps are disturbing, especially when they occur in justified paragraphs. In the first chapter we already looked at one of the methods to manually hyphenate words in your text.

Hyphenation

Word has an built-in automatic hyphenation function at its disposal, which affords you the comfort of a fast and automatic procedure that accompanies you while you type. This function is not activated by default. To activate the automatic hyphenation of words at the end of a line, select the *Language* item in the *Tools* menu and choose *Hyphenation* from the submenu.

The *Hyphenation* dialog box appears. Select the *Automatically hyphenate document* check box and confirm the dialog box with *OK*. The text will now be automatically hyphenated.

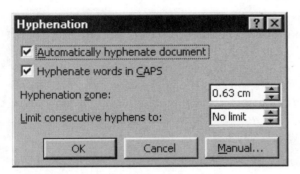

Fig. 9.31: The *Hyphenation* dialog box

The automatic hyphenation will be active even for new text entered into the current document. For other documents you have to activate the automatic hyphenation function once again.

Terms with capital letters

If you want to configure the automatic hyphenation, call up the *Hyphenation* dialog box again. Now clear the *Hyphenate word in CAPS* check box if you do not want to break terms spelled with capital letters.

Hyphenation zone

The *Hyphenation zone* box will allow you to choose the distance from the right margin within which the text of your document is supposed to be hyphenated. *Word* will then break only the terms that extend beyond this zone. A narrower hyphenation zone will lead to a smoother right-margin, but the number of terms that need to be hyphenated will, of course, increase.

In the *Limit consecutive hyphens to* spin box you type in the maximum number of consecutive text lines that can be hyphenated. Should this number be reached, *Word* will stop hyphenating.

Finding Synonyms with the Thesaurus

In addition to the dictionary for the spell checker, *Word* also has a special dictionary containing terms and their equivalents, i.e., words with the same or with a similar meaning. These words are called synonyms. The *Word* function responsible for finding or using synonyms is called the *Thesaurus*. We will now take a closer look at this function.

Thesaurus:
Dictionary with
synonyms

Do you like to create documents with more variation of expression, or do you prefer a higher standard of precision in the terms that are used? Well, then use the *Thesaurus*. To do so, select a term that you have already used a few times in your document and open the *Tools* menu. Select the *Language* item and click the *Thesaurus* item in the submenu. The key combination for the *Thesaurus* is ⇧ + F7.

Meanings

In the *Thesaurus* dialog box, the selected term is displayed in the *Looked Up* drop-down list box. Underneath it in the *Meanings* list box you will find a list of different meanings that the term in the *Looked Up* box can have.

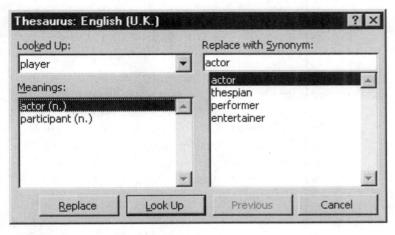

Fig. 9.32: The *Thesaurus* dialog box

The functioning of the *Thesaurus* is dependent on the language that you chose in *Tools/Language/Set Language*. If you are using a language other than English (United Kingdom), *Word* will look up the terms in the *Thesaurus* of the chosen language.

Replace with Synonym

Thesaurus also helps you to look up the meanings of identical words. Try this out by first selecting the term with the meaning that comes closest to the one that you are looking for. In the *Replace with Synonym* list, you will then find different terms with a similar or identical meaning to the term in question.

Replace

The first term in the *Replace with Synonym* list is the first choice that *Thesaurus* offers as an alternative. To use this term instead of the one you have typed, click on *Replace*.

The *Thesaurus* will close and your term will be replaced. If you would rather have a different term to replace your word, select that term in the *Replace with Synonym* list and then click on the *Replace* button. In case you do not want to replace the term by any of those offered in the

Thesaurus, click on *Cancel*. The *Thesaurus* dialog box will be closed and you will return automatically to your text.

Look Up

It might be interesting to go through the list of the different meanings of your word. If you find a word that seems to come close, you can look up the synonyms of that word as well. Select the word and click on the *Look Up* button. The term in the *Replace with Synonym* text box now becomes the original word. Another method of doing this is to double-click directly onto a term in one of the lists. The term will then become the new original.

Replace with Synonym

Open the *Looked Up* drop-down list box to get a history list containing all the terms you looked up during the session. In this way, you can trace back to your original word.

Looking up

In the *Replace with Synonym* text box it is also possible to enter a term directly. Click on the *Look Up* button and the term becomes the original. This way the *Thesaurus* can be used as an electronic dictionary of synonyms.

AutoFormat

There is still another automatic function which can format documents with a completely automatic procedure. It is correspondingly called *AutoFormat*.

Automatic Formatting of Documents with *AutoFormat*

In the following section you will soon find out how much the reality differs from the claim. It is unfortunate that the *AutoFormat* function cannot bring about miracles. Things that work out well for tables fail for most of the documents.

But the best is if you try out this function on your own to get an impression of how the *AutoFormat* function works in documents. The only real advantage of this function is for writing letters.

Create a letter and do not use any kind of formatting whatsoever. Now open the *Format* menu and select the *AutoFormat* item. The *AutoFormat* dialog box appears.

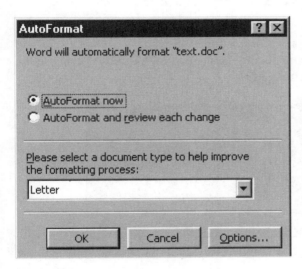

Fig. 9.33:   Start automatic formatting

With a click on the *Options* button you configure the *AutoFormat* function. You can also call up the dialog box via *Options/AutoCorrect* and the *AutoFormat* tab.

In case *Word* recognizes particular text passages, you can choose whether *Headings, Lists, Automatic bulleted lists* and *Other paragraphs* should be automatically assigned to an integrated *Word* style. Confirm your choice with *OK*.

Letters

Choose the type of document you want from the drop-down list box in the *AutoFormat* dialog box, so that

Word can use the correct formatting. If you have created a letter that is supposed to be automatically formatted, choose the *Letter* item.

AutoFormat now

If you want the *AutoFormat* procedure to happen fully automatically, select the *AutoFormat now* option button.

AutoFormat and review each change

To control the changes *AutoFormat* makes in your document, select the *AutoFormat and review each change* option button.

Start the *AutoFormat* function with *OK*. Then *Word* will examine the document and display in the second case the following messages:

Fig. 9.34:   Accept All and Reject All

Accept All
Reject All

The *Accept All* button in the *AutoFormat* dialog box accepts all the autoformatting *Word* wants to apply to your document. It does not take much imagination to figure out that the *Reject All* button rejects all the proposals.

Reviewing changes

Click on the *Review Changes* button and *Word* will display all the changes made to the text one by one. In the *Review AutoFormat Changes* dialog box you can reject a formatting change with the *Reject* button. Using the *Find* buttons, you can jump to the previous or the following change. Clicking on *Cancel* will end the review. To accept all the formatting changes in one go, click *Accept All*. Clicking *Reject All* cancels the *AutoFormat* session.

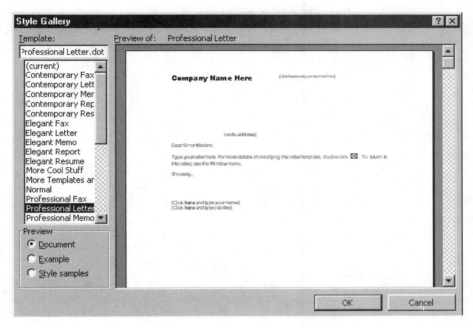

Click the *Style Gallery* button to open a dialog box that displays all the available templates on the left side, with a preview of the current document using the currently selected template on the right side. Changing the style in the left box will apply the formatting saved under this template to your document.

Confirm this change with *OK* in order to return to the document. The styles assigned by *Word* are displayed on the *Formatting* toolbar in the *Style* drop-down list box.

Automatic Formatting of Tables with *AutoFormat*

Unlike the automatic formatting of texts, the *AutoFormat* function works astonishingly well for *Word* tables. This function really is one of those features described in the *Microsoft* advertisement. It makes a perfectly styled and attractive table with border, frames and shadings out of an uninspired list or table containing only nonprinting gridlines, and it does it quickly with a simple mouse click.

First create a table in your document, or convert a list created with tabs into a table. Refrain from using any kind of formatting while doing this. Now choose the *Table Auto-Format* command from the *Table* menu. The *Table Auto-Format* dialog box contains a list with the available formats on the left side.

On the right side you will get a preview of the currently selected format applied to a sample table. Select in the *Formats* list the format that seems to be most appropriate for the contents of your table and one whose design you like.

If necessary, scroll through the options with the help of the scroll bar to find formats which are not displayed. Look at the preview of the selected format in the *Preview* box.

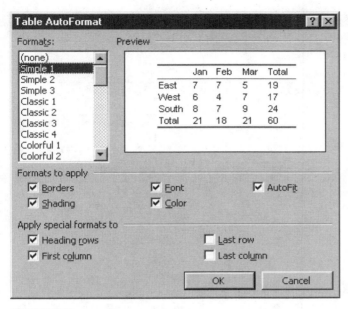

Choose the formatting items you want to use by selecting or clearing the various check boxes in the *Formats to apply* group box.

AutoFit

Clear the *AutoFit* check box if you have already set a fixed width for the columns in your table.

Color

If you do not intend to use a colour printer, you can clear the *Color* check box.

Apply special formats

The *Apply special formats to* option group is dependent on the content of your table. *Word* can automatically recognize the headings for your table in the document if *Heading rows* is checked, but these have to be arranged on the first line.

Select the corresponding check boxes for all the options you wish to use. Confirm with *OK* in order to assign the *AutoFormat*.

Monday	Tuesday	Wednesday	Thursday
Scale practice	Clean up	Scale practice	Scale practice
Big band rehearsal	-	-	Big band rehearsal
-	Ear training	Piano class	-

Monday	Tuesday	Wednesday	Thursday
Scale practice	Clean up	Scale practice	Scale practice
Big band rehearsal	-	-	Big band rehearsal
-	Ear training	Piano class	-

Fig. 9.37: A table before and after assigning an AutoFormat

An *AutoFormat* can be immediately cancelled with *Edit/Undo*. In order to delete the *AutoFormat* at a later time, choose *Table/Table AutoFormat* and select the *(none)* option.

If the *Tables and Borders* toolbar is visible, you can call up the *Table AutoFormat* dialog box much more quickly with the help of the *Table AutoFormat* button ▦.

AutoSummarize

Word has an automatic function called *AutoSummarize*. This function is supposed to be able to automatically summarize the contents of your document.

But this function does not work very well in most cases. Nevertheless, it might be good to give it a try and test this function. You can make your own judgement as to whether this function is useful to you or not.

Tools/Auto-Summarize

Open the *Tools* menu and choose *AutoSummarize*. Depending on the size of the current document, it might take some time before the dialog box is displayed.

There are different ways to summarize the document.

- *Highlight key points*
  This is the default choice. It highlights the contents of the summary and displays the rest of the document dimmed.

- *Insert an executive summary or abstract at the top of the document*
  This choice will insert a summary at the beginning of the document.

- *Create a new document and put the summary there*
  Choose this option in order to create the summary in a new document. Both documents will be linked.

- *Hide everything but the summary without leaving the original document*
  This option displays only the summary and hides the rest of the document

Length of summary

In the *Length of summary* area, by default *Word* proposes to bring the length of the summary down to 25% of the original document size. To set the value yourself, click on the drop-down button to open the list of choices.

Update document statistics

By selecting the *Update document statistics* check box you can apply the contents of the summary to the *Document Properties* dialog box.

425

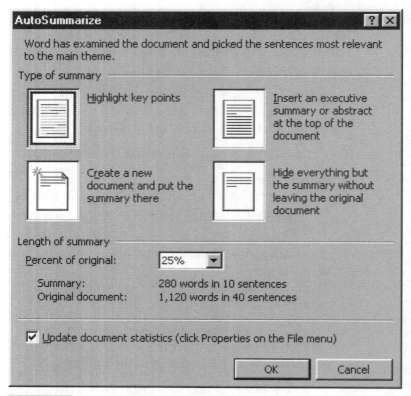

The *Autosummarize* dialog box

Select the options for the summarizing function and confirm the dialog box with *OK*. Depending on the type of summary, the corresponding toolbar will be displayed together with the summary.

Fig. 9.39: The *AutoSummarize* toolbar

Use the *Highlight/Show Only Summary* button ▨, in order to hide or show the text which is not part of the summary.

With the arrow buttons on the percentage scroll bar, you can enlarge or shrink the automatic summary.

Click the *Close* button to hide the toolbar and the automatic summary.

Sort Lists or Texts Automatically

For the contents of certain *Word* documents, alphabetical order would be very much appreciated. A good example of this would be lists of customers, orders or products. In addition, in tables which use article numbers, a numerical sorting can often be very helpful. As you might have already guessed, *Word* offers an automatic function for this task. With this feature you can sort texts or tables according to different criteria.

Sorting tables

The only assumption that the sort function makes is that the contents of the text which have to be sorted are separated either by paragraph marks or, in the case of tables, by columns containing similar contents. Select the text or column of a table to be sorted and choose the *Sort* command on the *Table* menu.

Sort by

In the *Sort Text* dialog box you will have to choose your selection from the different possible sorting criteria. Do this in the *Sort by* drop-down list box. In order to sort tables, always select the entries in the columns whose lines are supposed to be sorted.

To sort paragraphs in alphabetical order, choose the *Paragraphs* entry. This will sort the paragraphs by the first word of each paragraph.

Choose the *Column 1* item in the *Sort by* drop-down list box to sort texts with columns by the first column of each paragraph.

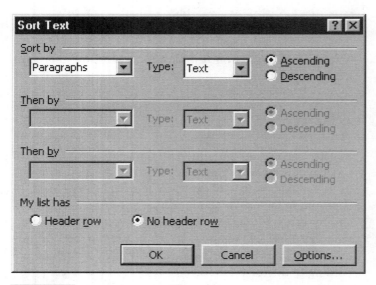

Fig. 9.40: Sorting texts alphabetically by paragraphs

Type

In the *Type* drop-down list box set the type of data that is supposed to be sorted. *Word* is able to sort text alphabetically, numerically or by date. This sorting can be done either in ascending order (A to Z or 0 to 9) or in descending order (Z to A or 9 to 0).

Entries starting with special keys or punctuation signs like !, #, $, % or '&', will be listed first. Next come the entries starting with numbers and finally, the entries beginning with letters.

While sorting by number, the function of *Word* ignores all other characters. The numbers can be located at any point in the paragraph. Dates will be treated by *Word* as numbers having three parts.

Then by

If necessary, select another sorting order in the *Then by* drop-down list box. All in all you can work with a maximum of three sort orders. The amount of sorting orders available depends on the contents of your paragraphs or the contents of the table cells. With more than one order you can sort lists and tables first alphabetically, for example, and then again by numbers and/or dates if it suits your purpose.

Ascending

Descending

Click on the *Ascending* option and *Word* will sort starting with the first letter of the alphabet, the smallest number or the oldest date. Choose *Descending*, and the sorting procedure will begin with the last letter of the alphabet, the largest number or the most recent date.

Header row

Select the *Header row* button in the *My list has* option group box to exclude the first line of a list or the heading of a column from the sorting procedure. In case you have chosen the *Headings* command in the *Table* menu in order to be able to format more that one line as a header, *Word* will skip those lines while sorting.

Sorting by dates

If you are sorting by date, *Word* will accept the following signs as date delimiters: hyphens, forward slashes (/), commas, and periods. Additionally, *Word* recognizes colons (:) as valid time separators.

If *Word* cannot recognize times or dates, the corresponding element will be inserted at the beginning or the end of the list (depending on whether you have been sorting in an ascending or in a descending order).

In case two or more elements begin with the same character, *Word* continues the sorting process by comparing the next character ('Aa' before 'Ab', etc.).

Undesired sorting

After selecting the sorting options, you can start the sorting process by clicking the *OK* button. If you realize, as soon as the sorting is over, that you did not get the result you wanted, make use of the *Undo Sort* button  or click on the *Undo Sort* item in the *Edit* menu, to cancel the sorting.

Tip! If you have chosen to display the *Tables and Borders* toolbar, you can use the ⬆ and ⬇ buttons to sort tables more quickly.

10. Special Effects for Online Documents

Word documents may consist of not only plain text or tables but of other objects such as graphics, drawings or WordArt objects as well. These are text objects with special effects, so-called AutoShapes, or maps and many other things.

Word 2000 provides you with various toolbars to insert graphics and other objects. You can design these objects; and they can be shaded and displayed in 3-D format. In this version you have the new option of using page borders if you prefer a simple but effective design.

When importing objects you should remember that they require much more memory than plain text.

In this chapter you become acquainted with formatting methods for graphics and special effects.

Insert and Edit Pictures

Inserting pictures or drawings into *Word* documents makes them much more attractive. In this chapter you will learn how to insert the supplied ClipArt from the *Microsoft Clip Art Gallery* as well how to use a drawing from *Paint*, the Windows drawing program, in *Word*.

Inserting Pictures in Your Document

Here we will show you how graphic files of different programs can be put into your *Word* documents. Locate the cursor at the position where the graphic should be placed.

Next choose the command *Picture/From File* on the *Insert* menu. In the *Insert Picture* dialog box, choose the folder that contains the saved graphic file. If you wish to insert a bitmap that came with *Word*, change to the *C:\Program Files\Common FilesMicrosoft Shared\ClipArt* folder and select one of the subfolders.

Then click the *Preview* button 🖳 if necessary and select the file name of a graphic file in the left list box. The contents of the graphic file will be displayed in the preview box on the right.

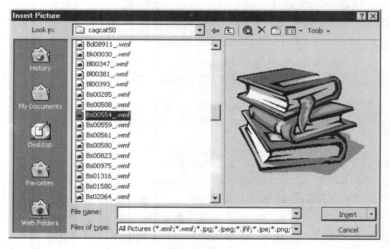

Fig. 10.1: The *Insert Picture* dialog box

If you want to save disk space and keep the size of your *Word* document as small as possible, click on the spin box of the *Insert* button and select the *Link to file* command. Click the *OK* button to insert the graphic file into the document. If you click on the bitmap, you will see resizing handles. By keeping the mouse button pressed over one of the resizing handles, you can change the size of the graphic.

Files of type

In the *Files of type* drop-down list box in the *Insert Picture* dialog box you will find a list of the graphic formats that *Word* can import.

Importing *Paint* Graphics into Word

The Windows drawing program *Paint* is a good tool with which to create simple pixel graphics. If you know how to use this program already, you can create small graphics in *Paint* instead of using the *Word* drawing tools.

Select ▣

In this section you will learn how to quickly and easily import drawings or graphic elements from the *Paint* drawing program into *Word*. In order to do this, we use the Windows *Clipboard*: Open the *Paint* drawing program from *Start/Programs/Accessories* and draw the required bitmap. <u>Important</u>: Select the section you want to import with the *Select* button ▣.

Now select the *Copy* command from the *Edit* menu in *Paint* or press the key combination Ctrl+C. Change to *Word*, locate the cursor on the point in the document where you wish to place the graphic, and choose the *Paste* command from the *Edit* menu or press the key combination Ctrl+V.

Paste 📋

The *Paint* graphic or the selected area will be inserted into your *Word* document. Another way to paste something in *Word* is to use the *Paste* button 📋 on the *Standard* toolbar. Click on the graphic and use the resizing handles that appear, if you wish to change the size of the graphic. If you would like to save the drawing as a bitmap, change to *Paint* and choose *File/Save*.

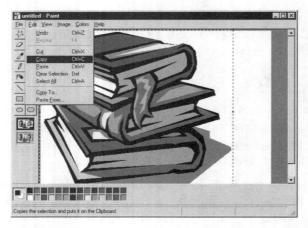

Fig. 10.2: Copy a picture in Paint and paste it into Word

Inserting ClipArt from the Microsoft ClipArt Gallery

If you have purchased the CD-ROM version of *Word* or the *Microsoft Office Suite*, you will find a lot of graphics on various topics. These graphics are called *ClipArt* in *Word* and they can be inserted into any document.

Word uses the *Microsoft Clip Gallery* to organize and manage its *ClipArt*. The *Microsoft Clip Gallery* provides a preview of the graphics, sorted by category. If you want to get an overview of the pictures that are stored in the gallery or if you want to insert a ClipArt into your document, click the mouse on the position where you want to insert the picture, and choose *Insert/Picture* and the *ClipArt* command.

Microsoft Clip Gallery 3.0

The *Microsoft Clip Gallery 3.0* is starting. On the various tabs, *ClipArt*, *Sounds* and *Videos* are provided, any of which can be inserted into documents. To insert the pictures, sounds and videos you may need the setup CD-ROM, because these items will not necessary be loaded from the hard drive but directly from the CD according to the kind of installation which has been carried out.

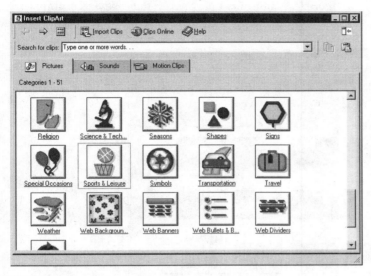

Fig. 10.3: Using pre-installed graphics in Word documents

Categories

By opening you will see an overview of different categories. Under the name of the tab page you will see the number of currently available categories and you may need to use the scroll bar to flip through all the categories. As soon as you click one of the Category symbols, all pictures relating to this category will be displayed.

If you click the ClipArt you want to use, a toolbar will appear. This will help you insert the ClipArt in the document, preview it, add it to favorites or search for other similar clips using keywords. Click the *Insert* button to insert the picture in the document. The ClipArt Gallery will not be closed and you can insert other pictures or close the ClipArt Gallery by clicking the *Close* button of the title bar.

To change to the Category overview, either click the *Back* button in the toolbar of the dialog box or the *All categories* button or press the key combination `Alt`+`Pos1`.

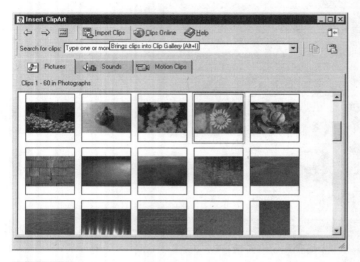

Fig. 10.4: Inserting ClipArt pictures

Word will insert the graphic. By clicking on the picture, you will get resizing handles which allow you to change the size of the ClipArt.

Changing the Position of Graphics in a Document

Unlike earlier versions of *Word*, *Word 2000* allows you to insert graphics of any size and form directly into the text without using a frame. If you open a document that contains frames from a previous version of Word, the frames will remain.

Drag the graphic to any position in the document with the mouse. The graphic will be placed in the paragraph by default. If you prefer to let the text flow above or around the picture, select the picture and choose the *Format/Picture* command, then switch to the *Layout* tab in the *Format Picture* dialog box. You can also call up the dialog box by double clicking on the picture. Here, on the *Layout* tab page, choose the one you prefer from the different wrapping styles and click on it.

Alignment

On this tab page you can also change the position of the graphic by aligning it to the left, in the center or to the right. If you changed the picture position by dragging it with the mouse, in the *Layout* tab page on the *Horizontal Alignment* option group you will find the *Other* radio button already checked. To make more precise adjustments to the alignment, click *Advanced*. You will now have two more tab pages at your disposal to set with millimetric precision the position or the wrapping properties of your picture.

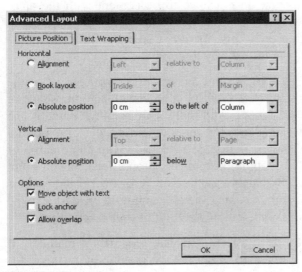

Fig. 10.5: Fixing the position in the dialog box

Horizontal
Vertical

In the *Horizontal* and *Vertical* spin boxes you can adjust the distance to the selected reference point.

By activating the *Move object with text* check box, you link the object to the following paragraph. If the paragraph is moved, then the graphic will follow. By checking *Lock anchor*, the graphic will be fixed by *Word* in its current position in your document.

After choosing your options, close the dialog box by clicking the *OK* button and you will return to the *Layout* tab page.

Changing the Size of the Graphic in the Document

Word usually inserts graphics and ClipArt from the clipboard, as well as bitmaps, in their original sizes. The exceptions are text boundaries like side margins or table cells. But you do not have to be content with the automatically inserted size. You can change the size of inserted graphics to just about any size you want. Using the mouse is the fastest way to do this.

Resizing handles

How to do it? Click on the graphic. *Word* provides you with eight *resizing handles*. You can change the shape of or scale the bitmap with these little handles. Point at one of the resizing handles on a corner of the graphic and keep the mouse button pressed. Now you can enlarge or reduce the graphic, keeping its proportions. If you point at one of the handles in the middle of one of the borders you can, while keeping the mouse button pressed, expand or compress the graphic lengthwise or horizontally.

Do not try to restore the original proportions manually if you have stretched or shrunk the graphic by mistake. Instead, select the graphic, choose the *Picture* command on the *Format* menu, or double click the graphic, and activate the *Size* tab.

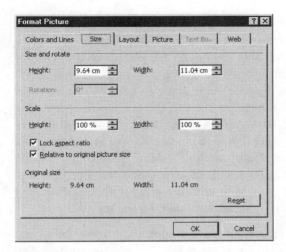

Formatting graphics in the dialog box

Reset

In the dialog box, click the *Reset* button and confirm with *OK*. The graphic is now restored to its original size and proportions. Remember: If you want to change the size of the graphic but to keep the proportions the same, use the diagonal resizing handles on the corners of the graphic.

You can also change the size in the dialog box by typing the numerical value into the *Height* and *Width* boxes in the *Size and Rotate* option group.

Height and width

If you want to change the graphic in proportion to its original size, type the required percentage ratio into the *Height* and *Width* boxes in the *Scale* option group.

If the Graphic is Displayed as a Small Bar Only

Is the graphic or ClipArt that you inserted into your document not displayed in its full size but as a small bar instead? You will now learn how to eliminate this un-pleasant effect

The reason why *Word* shows imported graphics and ClipArt in a document in the form of small bars is because of the unfavourable paragraph formatting of this type of object. If you inserted the graphic as a normal paragraph (as is usually the case) or if you chose the *In line with text* option in the *Layout* tab page of the *Format Picture* dialog box, and the paragraph in which the graphic has been inserted is formatted with a fixed line spacing, then *Word* resolutely maintains this line spacing no matter what the line contains. To check or to change the line spacing, click on the paragraph with the graphic that is displayed as a small bar. You can also click on the bar itself.

Now choose the *Paragraph* item in the *Format* menu and change to the *Indents and Spacing* tab. Change the entry *Exactly* in the *Line spacing* drop-down list box.

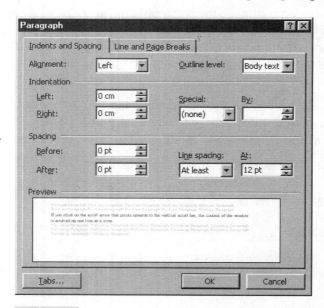

Fig. 10.7:   Set line spacing for inserted graphics

All entries are valid with the exception of *Exactly*. With the *Exactly* item, *Word* always keeps to the fixed line spacing, no matter what the actual size of the inserted graphic is. Change the *Line spacing* to *Single* or *At least*, for example, and confirm the changes with *OK*. Now the inserted graphic will be displayed in your document in its full size.

Another way to eliminate this problem is to let the graphic float over the text. Click on the visible portion of the graphic in your document. Select *Format/Picture* and choose the *Position* tab. Select the *Float over text* check box here. Close the dialog box with *OK*. Now using the mouse, you can drag the graphic which is displayed in its entirety to any position in your document.

How to Crop Graphics in a Document

In *Word*, imported or inserted graphics or photos are displayed in their original size if possible, but always in their entirety. Often only a part of a graphic is needed. In *Word* you can crop the graphic or cut out the parts you do not need. First select the graphic. You will see the eight resizing handles that allow you to change the size of a graphic as well as to crop it.

Crop

If you select a graphic, *Word* automatically displays the new *Picture* toolbar. Click the *Crop* button on this. The mouse pointer takes the shape of the crop tool. Click on one of the resizing handles and keep the mouse button pressed. Now the visible part of the graphic changes. Perhaps you will have to use more than one handle to get the required cropped effect.

Fig. 10.8:   Original and cropped graphic

The resizing handles in the corners will crop the height
and width of the graphic at the same time, while the resizing handles in the middle can only cut either the height
or the width. *Word* also provides you with the option of
fixing exact measurement for the cropping of a graphic.
Click the *Picture* command on the *Format* menu. Choose
the *Picture* tab. Here you can fill in the margins you want
to fix in the required text box of the *Crop from* option
group.

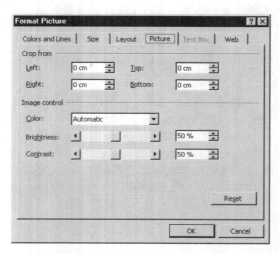

Fig. 10.9:   Cropping a graphic via the dialog box

Reset

By clicking the *Reset* button on the *Picture* tab you can always restore the full size of the graphic.

Setting Text Flow Around Graphics and Other Objects

Whether the text flows on the left, the right or on both sides of the frame depends on the text flow setting. The tools to work with inserted graphics are stored on the six tabs of the *Format Picture* dialog box. To get there, choose *Format/Picture,* double click the graphic or click on the *Format Picture* option in the shortcut menu of the graphic. As soon as you select a graphic, *Word* automatically displays the new *Picture* toolbar. Here you find, in the form of buttons, the most important tools and commands to edit photos or *ClipArt*.

The *Wrapping* tab

To set the text flow around the graphic, use the *Text Wrapping* Tab in the *Format Picture* dialog box. Here you can choose from various possibilities for text flow setting. To adjust the text wrapping more precisely click on the *Advanced* button and in the *Advanced Layout* choose the *Text wrapping* tab. Once you get acquainted with the basic option you will not have any difficulties in dealing with the advanced ones.

If the text should flow around the graphic, choose your option under *Wrapping Style*.

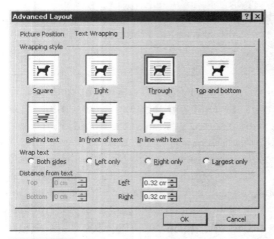

Setting the text flow

Wrap to

The *Tight* option allows the text to follow the shape of any graphic, and *Behind text* places the graphic as a waterselect behind the text. Further options are given in the *Wrap text* option group in the *Text wrapping* tab of the *Advanced Layout* dialog box. To reach this dialog box select the *Advance* button in the *Layout* tab of the *Format Picture* dialog box. Here you can choose whether the text should flow on both sides of the graphic or only on the left or right side.

Editing Graphics with the Toolbar

Usually *Word* displays the *Picture* toolbar automatically as soon as you insert or select a graphic. If this is not the case, due to your having previously switched off the toolbar, select the *Picture* check box on the *View/ Toolbars* menu or the *Show Picture Toolbar* command on the shortcut menu of the selected graphic to display the toolbar again.

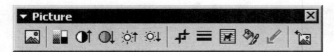

Fig. 10.11:   The *Picture* toolbar

In the toolbar you will find buttons to insert additional graphics, open the *Format Picture* dialog box, as well as options for setting brightness, contrast and other properties of the graphic.

- *Insert Picture*
  Activate this button to open the *Insert Picture* dialog box when you want to put another graphic or ClipArt into your document

- *Image Control*
  With this button you can display the graphic in *Greyscale*, *Black & White* or as a *Waterselect*.

- *More Contrast*
  Click on this button to gradually increase the contrast.

- *Less Contrast*
  Use this button to gradually decrease the contrast.

- *More Brightness*
  Activate this button to gradually increase the brightness.

- *Less Brightness*
  Click this button to gradually decrease the brightness.

- *Crop*
  With a click on this button you select or deselect the *Crop* mode. By pulling the drag points with the mouse you can change the displayed portion of the imported picture.

■ ≡ *Line Style*
Click this button to see a list of lines of varying shapes. By choosing the *More Lines* item from the list, you open the *Format Picture* dialog box with the *Colors and Lines* tab active.

■ *Text Wrapping*
With this button you open a menu with various text flow variations. Select the *Edit Wrap Points* menu item to display the handles on the outline of the graphic object.

■ *Format Picture*
A Click on this button opens the *Format Picture* dialog box.

■ *Set Transparent Color*
This option allows you to set a transparent color for bitmaps. By clicking the *Set Transparent Color* button the mouse pointer changes to a graphic pen. With this tool you click on the color you want to be transparent.

■ *Reset Picture*
If you click this button, all formatting you have applied to the graphic will be set back.

The shortcut menu gives you another way to format pictures. Click with the right mouse button on a graphic and choose the *Show Picture Toolbar* command or activate the *Format Picture* option to open the dialog box.

WordArt

From time to time the user wishes to have more freedom in *Word* regarding display of text. You may for a certain reason need to rotate the text by a certain angle or arrange the name of a company or a club in a circle. This is no problem if you have a graphics program. But *Word* does not leave you in the lurch. Although no *Word* functions are used for this purpose, an *OLE* program from the *Microsoft Office Suite*, *Microsoft WordArt* is available. This program allows you to get interesting font effects, distortions and mirror images of short text passages. But why not take a look at it right away?

Inserting WordArt Objects

Open a new empty document and select the *Picture/WordArt* command on the *Insert* menu. You can also open the *Drawing* toolbar by clicking the *Drawing* button on the *Standard* toolbar. On the Drawing toolbar you must choose the *Insert WordArt* button.

WordArt style

The *WordArt Gallery* will be displayed. You can choose your favorite style by clicking on it and confirming it with a click on *OK*.

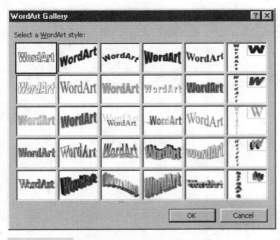

Fig. 10.12:   Choosing a WordArt style

447

The *Edit WordArt Text* dialog box will be displayed with the default text 'Your Text Here' Above this, there are drop-down list boxes which allow you to choose *Font* and *Size* as well as buttons to select the *Bold* and *Italic* font styles. You should now overwrite the default text, format your text as you like and click on the *OK* button to insert the text into your document.

Fig. 10.13: Program in a program: WordArt for text effects

Handles

The inserted WordArt object is automatically selected. On the edges and in the corners you will see the handles needed for enlarging or reducing the object. These resizing handles have already been introduced in the section on editing graphics.

Fig. 10.14: Selecting and applying font effects

In addition, the *WordArt* toolbar will be displayed. It contains buttons to format the WordArt objects.

Editing WordArt Objects with the Toolbar

The *WordArt* toolbar will be displayed after an object has been inserted and every time you select a WordArt object. If you want to manually make it appear, you can either choose *View/Toolbars/WordArt* or right-click a WordArt object and choose *Show WordArt Toolbar*.

- *Insert WordArt*
  Click this button to insert a new WordArt object.

- Edit Text... *Edit Text*
  With this button you open the dialog box to edit the WordArt text.

- *WordArt Gallery*
  Open the *WordArt Gallery* if you want to apply a different style to the selected WordArt object.

- *Format WordArt*
  With this button you open the *Format WordArt* dialog box.

- *Word Art Shape*
  A click on this button opens the WordArt shapes palette. There are some very interesting effects on the palette. For example you can give your text the shape of a STOP sign if you like, or a wave or a circle.

- *Free Rotate*
  This button activates the *Free Rotate* mode. The selected WordArt object gets circular handles. With these handles the WordArt object can be rotated in perspective.

- **Aa** *WordArt Same Letter Heights*
  With this button you can assign the same height to small as well as capitalized letters.

- **ab** *WordArt Vertical Text*
  This button allows you to switch from horizontal to vertical text flow and vice versa.

- **≣** *WordArt Alignment*
  A click on this button opens a menu offering different alignment options for your text.

- **AV** *WordArt Character Spacing*
  This button opens a menu to alter the character spacing.

With the buttons on the *WordArt* toolbar you can rotate font effects, change font attributes, add outlines, hachure, and shadows as well as special effects. These options are also available as commands in the *Format WordArt* dialog box.

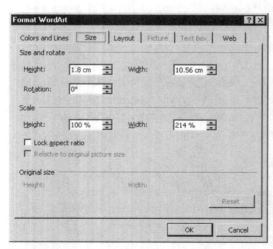

Fig. 10.15:   *Format WordArt* dialog box

In this dialog box you will find almost the same options as in the *Format Picture* dialog box that has been introduced to you earlier.

Fonts

The font can be chosen by clicking *Edit Text* on the *WordArt* toolbar. The *Edit WordArt Text* dialog box will be displayed. In the *Font* drop-down list box, all the fonts installed on your system are listed. Just have a look at them and see which ones you like.

If you want to go back to the text outside the WordArt object you simply have to click on the text somewhere outside the area of the WordArt object. You can move the object freely in your document. If you want to work on the WordArt object later, just click on the object. The *Word-Art* toolbar will be displayed again.

Drawing Objects and AutoShapes

Already in previous versions, *Word* provided a drawing function that allowed you to insert simple graphic elements such as lines, circles and rectangles as well as text boxes and callouts.

In *Word* you can access a huge number of default graphic elements called *AutoShapes*. You can shape drawing objects three-dimensionally with shadow effects, freely rotate them, change the outline with the mouse, as well as insert text into all kinds of two- and three-dimensional objects.

Drawing Lines in Word

There is more than one way to place additional lines in your document. One way is to use the *Borders and Shading* dialog box. But you can also draw the required lines directly into your document. There is only one thing you

451

need in order to do this: and that's a special toolbar. Click the *Drawing* button  in the *Standard* toolbar to open the *Drawing* toolbar at the bottom of the *Word* window. If necessary, *Word* switches automatically to *Print Layout* view.

Fig. 10.16: The *Drawing* toolbar

In the *Drawing* toolbar you will find buttons representing all the important drawing tools. If you are not familiar with the function of a button, place the pointer on the button. Approximately one second later, a *ScreenTip* shows you the label of the button. More information is displayed in the status bar if you click the button in question. On the left part of the toolbar you will find buttons for the various drawing functions.

Zoom your document

If you want to draw a line in your document it is useful to zoom your document first. Reduce it until the whole area you want to edit is visible.

Click on the *Line* button on the *Drawing* toolbar. Now point the mouse onto your document, The mouse pointer will change into a *Precision Select* crosshair + cursor.

Line Color, Line Style and Dash Style button

Click on the point where you want your line to start, keep the mouse button pressed and draw your line. If you release the mouse button the line will be displayed using the settings of the *Line Color* button, *Line Style* button and *Dash Style* button. More information on filling objects and setting the style, weight and color of a line will be explained later in this chapter.

15-degree increments	If you want to limit the angle setting of the line to increments of 15 degrees, then in addition to holding down the mouse button, keep the *Shift* key ⌷ pressed.
Select objects	To edit a *Word* drawing object you have to first select it. Click on the *Select Objects* button ⌷ in the *Drawing* toolbar and then on the line you have drawn.
Delete lines	*Word* displays a selected line with two handles. To delete unnecessary lines first select them and press the ⌷Del⌷ key or choose the *Cut* command in the *Edit* menu.
Changing the size of lines	Using the handles with the mouse button pressed, selected objects can be enlarged or reduced. The angle of lines can be changed in the same way.
Dragging lines	To drag a line, click on it, keep the mouse button pressed and drag it to the new position in your document.
	To draw freeform lines use the *AutoShapes* button. In the menu choose the *Lines* option and click the *Freeform* button.

Drawing Geometrical Objects in Word

Would you like to add a little drawing to your *Word* document, or do you want to design your company's own logo on your word processing program? That's no problem using *Word 2000*. As long as the drawings are based on simple geometrical shapes it's no problem to create small graphics directly in your document.

What makes this option so nice is the fact that you can draw directly into your document. But be aware that the drawing elements are at first always placed over the text. Now click on the *Drawing* button ⌷ in the *Standard* toolbar. The *Drawing* toolbar will be displayed at the bottom of your screen.

If necessary *Word* switches automatically to *Print Layout* view. In this section you will learn how to operate the buttons to create geometrical figures.

Fig. 10.17: The *Drawing* toolbar

In the *Drawing* toolbar you will find all important drawing tools in the form of buttons.

Circle and Oval ○

If you want to draw an oval, for example, click on the *Oval* button ○ on the *Drawing* toolbar. When you point with the mouse in your document you will notice that the arrow has turned into a crosshair cursor +. Now click, and keeping the mouse button pressed, draw your oval. To get a perfect circle you have to keep the *Shift* key ⇧ pressed at the same time.

The outline indicates the size of the object. If you release the mouse button the oval will be displayed using the settings of the *Fill Color* button ⬥, *Line Color* button ⬥, *Line Style* button ≡ and *Dash Style* button ≡.

Rectangle ▢

If you want to draw a rectangle, click the *Rectangle* button ▢ on the *Drawing* toolbar. Now click, and while holding down the mouse button, draw your rectangle with the crosshair cursor +. To get a perfect square or rectangle, you have to hold the *Shift* key ⇧ down at the same time.

Select Objects

To edit a drawing object you have first to select it. Click on the *Select Objects* button ⬉ on the *Drawing* toolbar, then on the outline of your object. If the object is filled you can also click on the object.

Edit objects

Word displays a selected object with a frame and eight selection handles. To delete unnecessary objects select them and press the [Del] key or choose the *Cut* command on the *Edit* menu. While holding down the mouse button over one of the handles, you can enlarge and reduce the objects.

With the resizing handles which appear on the sides of the selected object you can change the object's height and width. If you want to change its size while keeping the same proportions, i.e., changing the height and the width maintaining the same scale, then use one of the corner handles and keep the *Shift* key [⇧] pressed down at the same time. To drag drawing objects click on the object frame, hold down the mouse button and drag the object to the required position.

Editing Drawing Objects with Colors and Effects

All two- or three-dimensional geometrical drawing objects that have been generated with the buttons on the *Drawing* toolbar can be filled in with a color. In *Word* this color is called *Fill Color*. In addition you can color the outline, i.e., the line you were using to draw the object. This color is called *Line Color*. Last but not least you can set the *Line Style* and the *Dash Style* of the outline of your object.

Select Objects

Before you start editing you have to select the drawing object you want to edit. If you do not succeed with the normal text cursor, click the *Select Objects* button 🔍 on the *Drawing* toolbar and try again. To fill the objects with the color displayed on the button, click on the *Fill Color* button 🎨▾. To choose a different color click on the drop-down button right next to it. A color palette with every available color will be displayed.

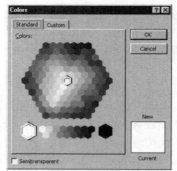

Fig. 10.18: Select *Fill Color* and the *Colors* dialog box

Fill Color    Click on one of the color buttons shown to color the selected object. This fill color will be assigned to the *Fill
Color* button and can be applied to other objects simply
by clicking on it. By selecting the *More Fill Colors* option in the *Fill Color* palette you open the *Colors* dialog
box. Here you can choose more colors or even mix them
yourself.

Fill Effects   By choosing the *Fill Effects* option you open the *Fill Effects* dialog box from which you can select gradients,
textures and patterns with which to fill your object.

Line Color   Click the *Line Color* button to set the outline color of
a selected object to the color shown on the button. To open
the *Colors* and the *Patterned Lines* dialog boxes click the
drop-down button.

Line Style   Click the *Line Style* button to open a palette with various line weights and styles. Select your choice using the
mouse.

Dash Style   To assign a certain *Dash Style* to a drawing object click
the *Dash Style* button. A palette of dotted and dashed
lines will be displayed.

Arrow Style ⇄

Click the *Arrow Style* button ⇄ to open a palette of various arrows. Choose your favourite style using the mouse.

If you want to change the settings for all new drawn objects, you can assign an already existing object all the formatting you want (fill color, line style and color). Then select the object and click the *Draw* button at the left side of the *Drawing* toolbar and choose the *Set Auto-Shape Defaults* command.

Features and Effects

In the following section we would like to give you a general view of some very interesting features that *Word* provides to give a document an attractive and unusual appearance in a simple way. Here are some examples of the new features and effects.

- *AutoShapes*
  These are default drawing objects you can insert in the desired size and edit as you wish.

- *3-D Effects*
  A special toolbar enables you to apply 3-D forms and to edit three-dimensional objects.

- *Shadows*
  Here too *Word* provides a special toolbar to apply shadows to objects and to vary their appearance.

- *Borders and Shading*
  This design option allows you to apply borders, lines and shading to the entire page.

AutoShapes

Word 2000 provides a new button called *AutoShapes* on the *Drawing* toolbar. With a click on this button you open a menu with a selection of default shape categories. If you select one option on the menu, a palette of specific shapes opens. You can get a *ScreenTip* by pointing on the shapes.

If while working you need the palette a lot, you can choose to display it as a separate toolbar. Open the overlapping menu and drag the palette by clicking on the grey bar on the upper border of the toolbar. This menu will be now displayed as a toolbar.

What are AutoShapes?

On the *AutoShapes* menu you can choose the most important basic geometrical shapes from thematically sorted submenus like *Block Arrows, Stars and Banners, Callouts* as well as *Lines*.

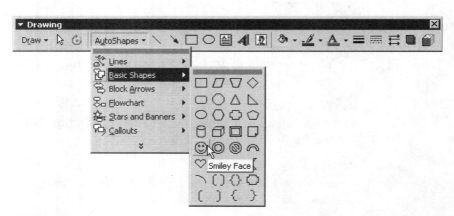

Fig. 10.19: AutoShapes

Click on one of the shapes and insert it in the desired size into your document. After placing it you can still change the size and the outline of the shape with the resizing handles.

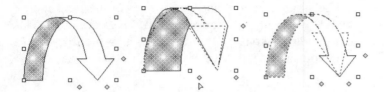

Fig. 10.20: An AutoShape is altered

To select an AutoShape all you have to do is click on it. Directly after inserting the AutoShape, it is automatically selected. A selected AutoShape is surrounded by handles. With these rectangular white handles you can change the size of the shape using the same procedure that has been described earlier in the section on pictures.

With the yellow rhombic handles you can change the outline of the AutoShape. If the pointer is placed on one of these handles it takes the shape of a triangular arrow.

You can apply fill colors, line colors, shadows and 3-D effects to AutoShapes. Click with the right mouse button on an AutoShape and choose *Format AutoShape* or select *AutoShape* in the *Format* menu. Both ways lead to a dialog box that offers options similar to those we have used to edit graphics and *WordArt* objects.

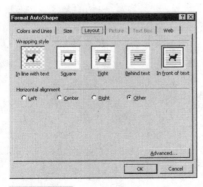

Fig. 10.21: The *Format AutoShape* dialog box

In the shortcut menu that you open with the right mouse button you can also choose the *Add Text* command. This option allows you to place text into an AutoShape. This way you can treat the AutoShape like a text box.

How to Insert and Link Text Boxes

Another interesting feature of *Word* is the option to link text boxes. Text boxes are inserted by using a button on the *Drawing* toolbar. Text boxes consist of one visible and one invisible rectangle. You can insert your text into the latter. Text boxes are used to place text wherever you want it in your document.

Text Box 🖳

You can add a text box to your document by clicking on the *Text Box* button 🖳 on the *Drawing* toolbar. Now you can place a rectangle of any size into the document.

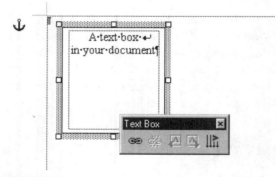

Fig. 10.22:   A text box

The *Text Box* toolbar

Immediately after inserting or selecting a text box the *Text Box* toolbar is automatically displayed. If it isn't shown, you can open it via *View/Toolbars/Text Box*. You can display the toolbar only if a text box is selected.

Linking text boxes enables you to let your text flow between more than one text box or between two- or three-dimensional AutoShapes.

To link text boxes the second text box has to be empty. Click on the first text box, then click the *Create Text Box Link* button in the *Text Box* toolbar.

Now click on the second text box. In the *Text Box* toolbar you also find a *Break Forward Link* button , two buttons to switch forward or backward between the text boxes and finally a button to change the direction of the text flow

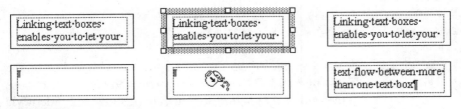

Fig 10.23:   Two text boxes before and after the link

3-D Effects

In *Word 2000* it is very easy to add 3-D effects to drawing objects, AutoShapes, text boxes and WordArt elements.

First click on the object, then on the *3-D* button in the *Drawing* toolbar. Now choose the 3-D shape you would like to apply to your object from those displayed in the palette.

To eliminate a 3-D effect choose the *No 3-D* option on top of the menu.

To edit 3-D objects *Word* provides a special toolbar Here you will find buttons for various settings of a 3-D object.

Fig. 10.24:   The *3-D Settings* toolbar

Fig. 10.25:   3-D effects

You can open the *3-D Settings* toolbar with a click on the last button *3-D*  in the *Drawing* toolbar. Here choose the option *3-D Settings*. You cannot show and hide it via *View/Toolbars*. In the toolbar you will find the following buttons:

- ▪ *3-D on/off*
  A click on this button switches the 3-D effect on or off.

- ▪ *Tilt Down*
  Click this button to tilt the perspective down step by step.

- ▪ *Tilt Up*
  Click this button to tilt the perspective up step by step.

■ ▥ *Tilt Left*
Click this button to tilt the perspective to the left step by step.

■ ▥ *Tilt Right*
Click this button to tilt the perspective to the right one step at a time.

■ ▥ *Depth*
With this button you open a menu with point values for establishing the depth of the perspective.

■ ▥ *Direction*
Click this button to get a palette of buttons to set the direction of the perspective.

■ ▥ *Lighting*
With this button you open a palette of buttons to set the direction of the object's lighting.

■ ▥ *Surface*
This button leads to a menu of object surfaces, e.g. *Wire Frame* or *Metal*.

■ ▥ *3-D Color*
With this button you open a color palette for the 3-D object.

The Shadow Effect

Another effect *Word 2000* can carry out, is the option to apply shadows behind drawing objects, AutoShapes, text boxes and WordArt elements. However you cannot simultaneously assign a shadow and a 3D-effect.

Shadow ▥

To apply a shadow to an object you have to select it and to click the *Shadow* button ▥ on the *Drawing* toolbar.

No Shadow

If you want to delete the shadow you have applied, choose the *No Shadow* option on top of the *Shadow* palette

Fig. 10.26: The palette of Shadow effects

There also is a toolbar to operate the shadow effects. To get to it, click the *Shadow* button on the *Drawing* toolbar and choose the *Shadow Settings* option.

Fig. 10.27: The *Shadow Settings* toolbar

The first button of the *Shadow Settings* toolbar switches the shadow on or off. The following set of four buttons fixes the direction of the shadow. The last button opens a palette from which you can choose the color of the shadow.

Page Borders

The *Page Border* option is another design feature of *Word*. It helps you to give an attractive touch to your document. With a single command you can apply a border to all the pages of your document, to every page except the first, to the first one only or to just a section of the page.

Choose *Format/Borders and Shading* and activate the *Page Border* tab. Now choose one of the buttons in the *Setting* option group, or set single lines with the buttons in the *Preview* section. By doing this you can, for example, apply lines only on the top and bottom of the page as you might do if you wanted to separate headers and footers from the rest of the text.

Style, color and width

In the *Style*, *Color* and *Width* list boxes you can fix more detailed settings for the lines of frames and borders.

Some very striking borders and lines can be found in the *Art* list box. Here you can choose from a large number of symbols that will give a shape to the border lines, e.g., Christmas trees, balls, birds, flowers, hearts and stars.

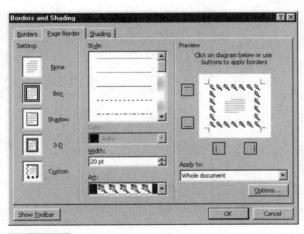

Fig. 10.28: Effects for page borders

If you want to give special attention to the position of the page border click the *Options* button.

By choosing *Text* in the *Measure from* list box you align the border with the page margin. Choosing the *Edge of page* option you align the border with the edge of the

465

page. The exact distance from either can be fixed in the *Top*, *Bottom*, *Left* and *Right* boxes.

Surround headers and footers

If you align the border with the text, you can determine whether or not the frame should surround headers and footers. If you decide that it should, then check the *Surround Headers* and the *Surround Footers* check boxes.

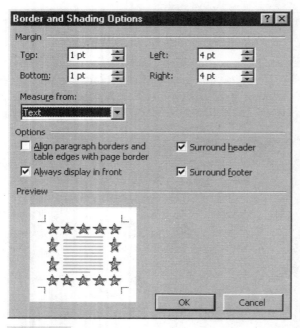

Fig. 10.29:   **Editing page borders**

After fixing all your page border options close the dialog box with *OK*. In the *Apply to* drop-down list box of the *Borders and Shading* dialog box, you can specify to which section of the document you want the border options to apply. Four options are available:

Whole document, This section, This section - First page only, This section - All except first page.

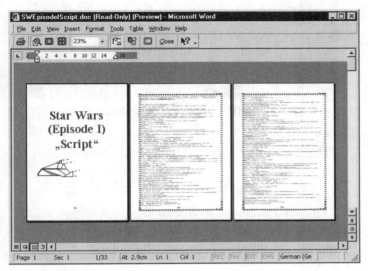

Fig. 10.30: A heart border

In Figure 10.30 you see an example of a page border which has been designed with an effect, aligned to the text, surrounding headers and footers.

Designing Online Documents

If you refer to a document as an *Online Document* it is understood that it will be displayed on the screen rather than printed out. A typical online document is a Web site on the Internet.

The Internet, and especially the WWW, the World Wide Web, is becoming more and more popular. The number of companies and individuals who are publishing their own homepages on the Web is increasing dramatically.

Microsoft did not want to be left behind. It has equipped *Word 2000* and the other *Office* programs with tools that

Online tools   enable you to edit online documents, to design Web sites, create hyperlinks and switch between hyperlinked pages. Special tools for online documents are:

- *Web Layout*
  This view helps you to optimize your document for online presentation but not for printouts.

- *Animation*
  These are moving font effects relevant only to the screen display.

- *Background*
  You can format the background with shadings, textures and patterns and pictures that are specially designed for the screen but not for printing.

- *Web Page Wizard*
  A tool to create Web pages.

- *Web toolbar*
  A toolbar that gives you access to the Web and switching between Web pages.

- *Insert Hyperlink button and command*
  An easy way to insert hyperlinks in Web pages and other documents. With a click you can open the linked document and display its contents.

- *Frame*
  By splitting the screen into two parts, on one side you can have an overview of the hyperlinks, and more precise information about them on the other side.

Web Layout

The usual view options, with the exception of *Normal* view that serves the purpose of fast entry, try to display the document as close to what the printout will look like as possible.

This does not help you at all if you want to create an on-line document. This document should be optimised mainly for the display. It will probably never be printed.

Therefore *Word* provides the *Web Layout* option in the *View* menu, which attempts to optimise the document for on-screen reading.

Web Layout view   Activate this view with a click on the *Web Layout View* button ▣ to the left of the horizontal scroll bar or choose *View/Web Layout*.

If the *Web Layout* view is active you can edit the layout by selecting the *Tools/Options* command and switching to the *View* tab. More detailed information on this can be found in Chapter 2.

Font Animation

To design a document with moving font effects, you have to follow the same procedure as in normal font formatting. Select the text section to which you want to apply the font effects and choose *Format/Font*.

Open the *Animation* tab page and select the effect of your choice in the *Animations* list box. The chosen effect will be displayed in the *Preview* box.

To remove an applied effect choose the *(none)* option from the list.

Fig. 10.31   Font animation

Applying a Background

Online documents will look much more interesting if you apply a background. If you want to try it out, choose *Format/Background*. With this command you open a color palette. Now choose one of the offered colors, or click on *More Colors* and mix your own color in the *Colors* dialog box, or open a dialog box with special effects by choosing the *Fill Effects* option.

The *Gradient* tab

In the *Fill Effects* dialog box you find four tab pages. On the *Gradient* tab you can select for example the *One color* option in the *Colors* option group to create a single color gradient.

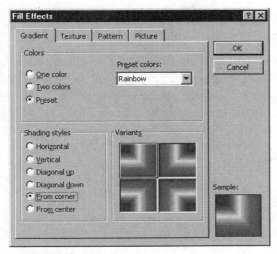

Fig. 10.32: Special *Fill Effects* for backgrounds

One color	After selecting the *One color* radio button you can choose the color you want from the color palette in the *Color 1* list box and adjust the contrast with the help of the *Dark/Light* scroll bar.
Two colors	If you choose the *Two colors* option an additional list box for choosing the second color is displayed.
Preset	The *Preset* option supplies a list of default designs. Here you will find premixed color options with names like *Early Sunset, Horizon, Fire, Rainbow, Silver* etc.
Shading styles	In addition you can choose the direction and the style of the gradient in the *Shading styles* option group. The gradient can start in the middle or from the edges, for example.
The *Texture* tab	The *Texture* tab offers various textures such as *Parchment, Granite* or *White marble*. The *Other Texture* button provides access to other graphic files. The graphic files

will be repeated several times in background, so that the whole file will be covered with it.

The *Pattern* tab

On the *Pattern* tab you can find a selection of background patterns. Choose your favorite pattern and click the corresponding button. The foreground and background colors of the pattern can be set separately. Choose from the *Foreground* and *Background* list boxes. The

The *Picture* tab

Picture tab allows you to insert a picture as a background. Click the *Select Picture* button and load a picture file.

Web Page Wizard

A document is called a *Web Page* if it is designed to be published on the World Wide Web, the multimedia aspect of the Internet. *Word* provides a special wizard to help you design Web pages. To do this, you have to have installed the Internet functions with the setup. If you omitted this option you have to start the setup again in order to install the Internet functions. To load the *Web Page Wizard* open a new document. Choose *File/ New* and select the *Web Pages* tab.

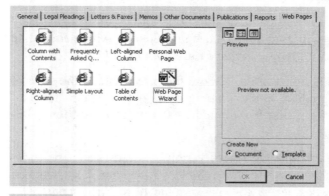

Fig. 10.33: The *Web-Pages* tab page

Select the *Web Page Wizard* icon and click the *OK* button. Now you just have to follow the instructions on the screen. Click the *Next* button. *Word* opens a dialog box to define the Web page titles and the save path.

Once you have made your choice click the *Next* button. The next dialog box gives you options of various visual styles for the navigation. By inserting frames the screen will appear split up. In one part you see the Website overview and the contents in the other part.

In the following dialog box you can define how many pages you want to have. You can insert blank pages, presentation pages or complete files in the Web page. After clicking the *Next* button you can order or change the names of the inserted pages.

In the last step you can set the Web page design, which is the document style in other words.

Once you have made your choice click the *Finish* button. You will get a sample with placeholders. All you have to do is insert your data.

Hyperlinks

The blue highlighted text passages are called Hyperlinks. That means they are linked to other documents. A click on such a hyperlink opens the linked document and displays its contents. Hyperlinks are usually used to provide further information.

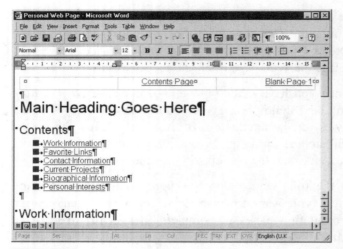

Fig. 10.34: A Web page with placeholders in *Web Layout* view

Web Layout view

If you create a Web page with the *Web Page Wizard* or one based on another Web page template, *Word* automatically switches to *Web Layout* view. In addition you find special features on toolbars and menus

■ Special buttons to edit Web pages

■ New commands for Web pages

■ Styles

Inactive or commands not on display are not available for this kind of document. Not all *Word* styles can be applied to Web pages.

If you want to publish existing documents on the Web, save them as HTML files. Be aware that while saving these documents, styles that are not supported by the Web page format might be lost.

The *Web* Toolbar

The *Web* toolbar provides access to so-called URLs, which are Internet addresses, and buttons to load Web pages.

Web Toolbar button 🌐

You can open and close the *Web* toolbar with the *View/Toolbars/Web* command. The buttons have the following functions

- ⬅ *Back*
  To go back to the last page.

- ⮕ *Forward*
  To jump ahead to the next page.

- ⊗ *Stop Current Jump*
  To cancel the page which is currently loading if, for example, it takes too long.

- 🔄 *Refresh Current Page*
  To load the current page again.

- ⌂ *Start Page*
  To show the start page.

- 🔍 *Search the Web*
  To display the search page.

- Favorites ▾
  Click this button to get a menu of various categories of saved Web pages like your favourite pages or the pages for the *Microsoft Services*.

■ Go ▾

With a click on this button you get a menu with options like *Start Page* and *Search Page*.

■ 🔲 *Show Only Web Toolbar*
With this button you close or open all toolbars with the exception of the *Web* toolbar.

■ http://www.user.com ▾

In this box you will find a list of the addresses of the documents you recently opened and the URLs of the Web pages you have visited.

Insert Hyperlink Button and Command

As you have seen in the section on creating a Web page, hyperlinks are highlighted text passages that allow you to open a linked file.

Hyperlinks in normal documents

But the insertion of hyperlinks is not limited to Web pages. It is also possible to link 'normal' documents, for example, to enable a colleague to work on your linked files in the company Intranet.

Before you insert a hyperlink you should save the document. To insert a hyperlink, either click the *Insert Hyperlink* button 🔖 in the *Standard* toolbar or choose *Insert/ Hyperlink*.

Write the name and path of the document or the URL of a Web page on a different Web server, in the *Type the file or Web page name* text box, or choose it from the list, or click on the *Browse* button and select the particular file in the *Link to File* dialog box. If you want to create a link to the Internet, you have to have access to it.

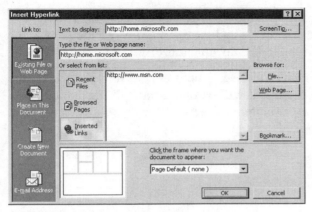

Fig. 10.35   The *Insert Hyperlink* dialog box

If the inserted document contains defined bookmarks, by clicking the *Bookmark* button you can set the precise point in the document you reach after clicking a hyperlink.

In the *Text to display* box, type the text to display in the document. If you do not type any text, the address will be inserted.

Close the *Inserted Hyperlink* dialog box with *OK*.

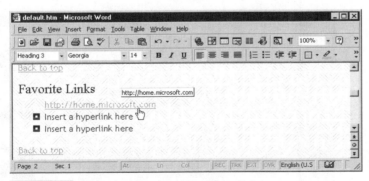

Fig. 10.36:   The mouse pointer on a hyperlink

As soon as you move the mouse pointer to a hyperlink, it changes to a hand and the *ScreenTip* with the path or the URL of the linked document is displayed.

With a click on the hyperlink, the linked page or the linked document will be opened and displayed. You can now use the buttons of the *Web* toolbar to switch between hyperlinked documents.

11. Letters, Mail Merge, Fields

Letters of all types are definitely the most often created documents in a word processing program. For this reason *Word* provides a special *Letters & Faxes* tab in the *New* dialog box, where you can find various templates for letters and faxes.

In addition, *Word* supports the creation and the mailing of letters with various functions:

- Address book to save and insert addresses
- Printing of single envelopes
- Printing of single labels
- Mail merge function

Envelopes and Labels

Before you start creating envelopes or labels you should decide if you want to use them one by one or with the help of the form letter tool. In the latter case you need only create a sample envelope or a sample label.

To work with the *Envelopes and Labels* printing tool make sure that your printer supports this option. Just take a look at the printer manual. Today most of the common printers are able to print envelopes and labels.

Creating Address Labels

There are two ways of creating address labels in *Word*. You can create and print a single address label or produce address labels with the form letter function for mailing to a group of customers. This section deals with both these options.

The process of creating single labels or labels for mail merge is of course similar. For single labels you do not have to add the field name of the data source. This data source makes sure that your address database is available for the creation of your labels.

To create single labels choose the *Envelopes and Labels* command in the *Tools* menu. Here activate the *Labels* tab page. With the button you can open the Outlook *Address book*.

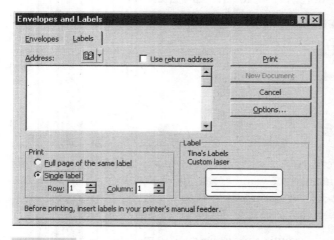

Fig. 11.1:   Creating single address labels

To print a label click the *Print* button.

Directly inserting addresses

As an alternative you can also insert an address you do not use often directly into the *Address* box. If you want to print a single label select the *Single label* radio button and use the *Row* and *Column* spin boxes to determine the position of the label on the page to be printed.

Do you want to create a label with your own address so you can paste it as a sender sticker on a parcel? Click the

Full page of the same label	*Use return address* check box and select the *Full page of the same label* option button.

Using Custom Label Sizes

In *Word* you can create your own label styles. You can use these both to print single address labels as well as mail merge labels.

For single labels choose the *Envelopes and Labels* command on the *Tools* menu and change to the *Labels* tab page. Click the *Options* button to bring up the *Label Options* dialog box. Select the correct printer type in the *Printer information* section and select the setting in the *Tray* drop-down list if necessary.

Label products Choose the correct option for the label you want to use from the *Label products* drop-down list box.

Now click the *New Label* button.

Label name Type the name of your label in the *Label name* text box. *Word* adds the name of the custom label to the *Product number* list. Now set the dimensions to be used for the label.

Page size In the *Page size* drop-down list choose the size of the label page. Set the gap between the first label and the top and left margin of the sheet in the *Top margin* and *Side margin* boxes.

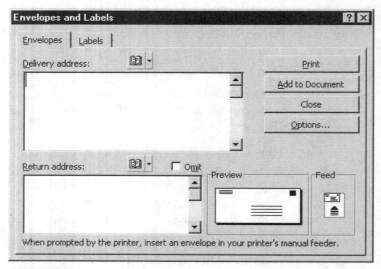

The Custom label

Vertical and horizontal pitch

The *Vertical pitch* indicates the height of a label including the gap in between the following label, the *Horizontal pitch* contains the width of a label including the gap in between the next label. *Label height* indicates the height of the label only, *Label width* the width only.

Number across, number down

Now set the number of labels you want to print on your sheet, next to each other and below each other. Type the figures in the *Number across* and *Number down* boxes.

After making all your modifications click the *OK* button.

Printing Single Envelopes

Letters are usually written in a style that prints the delivery address at a standard position. In this position the address is legible in the window of a window envelope, provided that the letter is folded properly.

Delivery address

There are of course situations where the address needs to be printed directly on an envelope. *Word* also supports this option with the help of a different feature. To print directly on an envelope, choose *Tools/Letters and Labels*. On the *Envelopes* tab page type in the delivery address in the *Delivery address* box or insert it from your address book.

Fig. 11.3:   The Address book button

To insert an address you have recently used, first click on the drop-down button next to the 🔲 button and then on the desired address. To select an address directly from the address book, click directly on the 🔲 button.

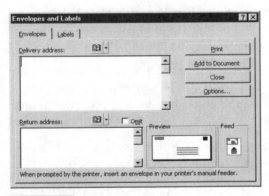

Fig. 11.4:   Printing an envelope

Return address

In the *Return address* box *Word* automatically inserts information from the user information. You can overwrite this entry or select the *Omit* check box if you do not want a return address to be printed on the envelope. You can also choose an address from the 🔲 button that appears above the *Return address* box.

Click on the *Options* button to choose the envelope size from the *Envelope size* drop-down list box. If you do not find the right entry there, choose the *Custom size* option and type the required dimensions into the *Width* and *Height* boxes.

Fig. 11.5:   Create a custom envelope size

Close the *Envelope Size* dialog box with *OK*.

Font and Position

In the *Envelope Options* dialog box you will find *Font* buttons and *From left* and *From top* boxes to format the delivery address as well as the return address.

Printing options

On the *Printing Options* tab you can select the *Feed method* and the *Feed from* options. If you changed the default setting a click on the *Reset* button will reset the default setting.

After setting your options for the envelope, click on the *Print* button to start printing.

Add to document

If you want to incorporate the envelope as page '0' in the document click the *Add to Document* button instead. After adding the envelope to the document you still have the option of printing it separately or together with the document.

Mail Merge Documents

If you are using *Word* in the office, you will from time to time create letters or other documents that you want to send to more than one address, e.g., to a number of clients or other people. In this case you should use the mail merge function. But even as a private user you might want to send the same letter or some other document to a larger number of people. This might be something like:

- A letter of application
- An invitation to a big party
- A request to submit a tender that should be sent to various dealers
- A letter of thanks after a big party.

Although mail merge is used mainly for letters, this function isn't limited to only this sort of document. It is also able to print:

- Labels
- Envelopes
- Catalogues

Creating a Form Letter in Word

In principle a so-called form letter is the same as any ordinary letter you write in *Word* . The difference between an ordinary letter and a form letter is that the latter is sent not just to one person but to many delivery addresses. The content is the same, only the address and the way you address the recipient is adapted to the particular person.

Main document

Mail merge letters are for example used for circulars or advertising letters. In *Word* all functions used to create form letters are summarised under the name *Mail Merge*. Mail merge allows you to print not only form letters but also address labels or envelopes. *Word* needs certain information for mail merge to work, not least of which is the so-called *Main document*.

Data source

This main document contains fixed elements that will be the same in each letter and variable elements that will be adapted in each letter according to the personal data of the receiver. In addition to the address data, further information can be inserted into form letters. Which information depends on the *Data source* of the letter.

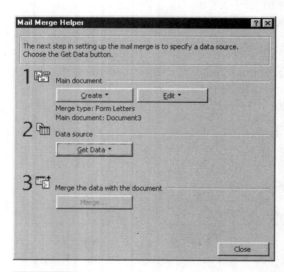

Fig. 11.6:   The Mail Merge Helper

The data source is the file or the document that contains the variable elements of the form letter. This data source can be a *Word* document that is built in a special way, such as a table, for example.

In *Word* you can also use data sources from other programs like the *Microsoft Access* database program, the *Outlook* scheduler that comes with the *MS Office Suite* or from the *Microsoft Excel* spreadsheet application. To be able to do this, the mail merge function of *Word* has special import filters.

But you can also create your data source with the *Mail Merge Helper*. This is a special tool that helps you with the creation of form letters. You will find it on the *Tools* menu in the *Mail Merge* option. *Word* allows you to insert the required data fields. You can later easily insert the data of the recipient into a data form. This *Word* function works like a small database.

Merge fields

The creation of a form letter is done in three basic steps. First create the *Main document*. This is a *Word* document that contains the text of the form letter. Later you add so-called *Merge fields* that read and insert the information from the *Data source*.

Data source

If you already have a database for the addresses of your customers or other clients, choose this in the second step as your data source. If this is not the case you can create the *Data source* in *Word* . The third step is to merge the data of the data source with the variable data in the main document. *Word* creates the corresponding amount of form letters based on the information in the data source and the merge fields in the main document.

Query options

These form letters can be printed and sent to your recipients. If you want to reduce the number of recipients by defining certain criteria and thus minimize the amount of form letters, you can filter the data source with *Query options*.

Create a Mail Merge Main Document

To create the main document of a form letter choose *Tools/Mail Merge*. Click the *Create* button in the *1 Main document* section and choose *Form Letters* from the pop-up menu. Then specify whether the current document will be the main document or whether a new one is going to be created. *Word* now inserts the merge type and the path of the mail merge main document below the buttons.

Creating a Data Source

After finishing the main document for the form letter with its fixed elements and before inserting the variable elements in the form of *mail merge fields*, you need a data source that provides the recipient or other client data.

As a data source you can either use existing sources from programs such as *Microsoft Access*, *Microsoft Excel* or *Outlook* etc., or you can create a new data source in *Word* .

If the *Mail Merge Helper* dialog box is not open choose the *Mail Merge* command on the *Tools* menu. In the *Mail Merge Helper* click on the *Get Data* button under *2. Data Source*. In the drop-down menu you can choose either to create a new data source or to open an existing one.

Open data source

If an existing data source is available and you want to use it, select the *Open Data Source* option. If the name of your data source is not displayed in the *Open Data Source* dialog box, choose the right folder from the *Look in* drop-down list. Now select the file name of your data source and click the *Open* button.

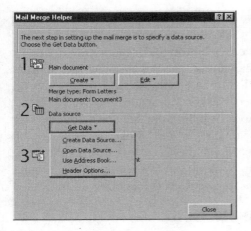

Fig. 11.7: Choosing the data source

Remove field name

To create a new data source choose the *Create Data Source* command instead. Select in the *Field names in header row* list one of the options which you do not need and click the *Remove Field Name* button to remove the field name.

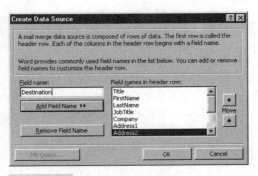

Fig. 11.8: Selecting the field names

Add field name

To create a new entry type, type it in the *Field name* text box and click the *Add Field Name* button. When your list is complete you can sort the selected entries with the

Edit data source

Move arrow buttons. Confirm with *OK* and save your data source in a folder of your choice. In the displayed dialog box click the *Edit* button under *Data source*. Choose the data source file name in the popup menu that appears. The *Data Form* dialog box with the field names you defined will be opened. Click in the first text box and insert the required information. To jump from one text box to the next press the ⬚ key or the ⏎ key. Make sure that you always type the entries in the *Title* text box in the same format, for example *Mr, Ms or Company*. Always make sure the spelling of your entries is identical.

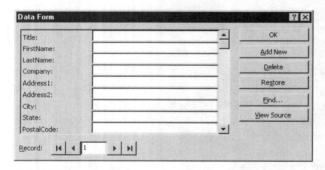

Fig. 11.9:   Data form to enter data

Empty data form

Once you have entered the first address, in other words the first record, click the *Add New* button. A new empty data form will be displayed. Enter all your records in the same way. To move between records use the buttons of the *Data Form* dialog box. The ▭ box in the middle indicates the number of the current record.

Jumping

A click on the ◄ button takes you to the first record, while a click on the ► button takes you to the end of the file. With the ◄ and the ► buttons you jump one record towards either the beginning or the end of the file respectively.

Find in Field

With the *Find* button you can search the records for entries in the data fields. Choose from the *In field* drop-down list in the *Find in Field* dialog box the field name in which you want to search for the entry. In the *Find what* box, type the entry which you are looking for.

Changing the data form

By clicking on the *Find First* button *Word* starts to search. If the entry is found the record will be displayed in the data form. Leave the *Find in Field* dialog box by clicking the *Close* button. You can now modify the data if necessary. With the help of the *Restore* button you can restore the previous entries of your record before they are saved. Once you have entered all your data close the *Data Form* with *OK*. Now you can insert the merge fields in your main document.

Fig. 11.10:   The *Mail Merge* toolbar

Word displays the empty main document of the form letter on the screen. Below the *Formatting* toolbar the *Mail Merge* toolbar is automatically shown. Now fill in the standard text for the form letter. Leave all the places where you want to put addresses or insert empty paragraphs as placeholders blank. All *Word* entry and formatting functions are available when entering your standard text.

Inserting Merge Fields into the Main Document

Apart from the data source, a so-called main document is needed for a form letter. This main document contains the subject of the form letter that should be sent to various recipients. For this purpose *Word* needs the name and address data in a special form, called merge fields. What might sound a bit difficult is actually pretty easy.

Open the main document

Open the main document if it is not the active document. You can get there either via the *Window* menu or by choosing the *Mail Merge* option on the *Tools* menu and selecting the *Edit* button in the *1 Main document* section.

The main document contains the text that you have created following the instructions given, which will be identical for all recipients. Is the main document still blank? No problem. To insert the merge fields for the recipient, place the insertion point at the desired position. If you work with window envelopes make sure that you have set the margins in such a way that the address is in the correct position and can easily be read through the window.

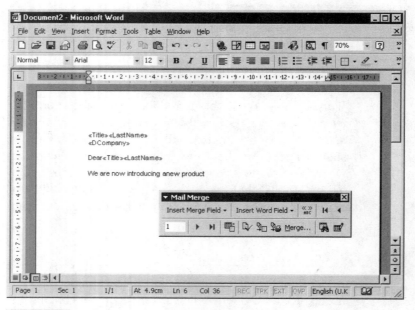

Fig. 11.11:   Inserting merge fields in the main document

To insert the name field, click the *Insert Merge Field* button on the *Mail Merge* toolbar. In the drop-down list you will find all available field names, e.g., FirstName, Address1, PostalCode, etc.. Click on the first field name you want to enter, e.g., *FirstName*. *Word* inserts the field name between angle brackets in the document. Then press ⌈SPACE⌉ to create the gap between the first and the last name and insert the second merge field *LastName*. Complete the address of the recipient in this way.

Fig. 11.12: Drop-down list of available field names

A typical address might look like this:

«Title»
«FirstName» «LastName»
«JobTitle»
«Company»
«Address1» «Address2»
«City»«State» «PostalCode»

Merging Form Letters

Once you have completed the main document of the form letter with its fixed elements and the variables in the form of mail merge fields, and you have opened or created a data source that contains data of customers or other recipients, you now have to merge these two form letter elements.

View merged data

Merge is the expression used in *Word* for the utilisation of the mail merge fields in the main document by the chosen data source. *Word* now exchanges field names like «FirstName» or «LastName» with the information in the data source, e.g., 'Arthur Miller'. If you want to preview the form letter along with the contents of its mail merge fields on-screen before you print, click the *View Merged Data* button ⟨⟩. The form letter with the data of the first record will be displayed. With the *Next Record* button ▶ you can move to the next record, and with the *Previous Record* button ◀ you can move back to the previous record.

The *Mail Merge* button Merge...

To merge the main document with the data source, open the *Mail Merge Helper* via *Tools/Mail Merge* and click the *Merge* button. You can also click the *Mail Merge* button Merge... on the *Mail Merge* toolbar of the main window. In both cases the *Merge* dialog box will be displayed.

Fig. 11.13:   The *Merge* dialog box

With the *Check Errors* button in the *Merge* dialog box you can find and correct mistakes after merging the data source with the main document. Choose the check method by selecting a radio button in the *Checking and Reporting Errors* dialog box and confirm with *OK*. You can also start the error checking with a click on the *Check for Errors* button ▤ on the *Mail Merge* toolbar.

If there is no error, confirm the message with *OK*. If a mistake is indicated, follow the instructions on the screen and check the mail merge fields in the main document.

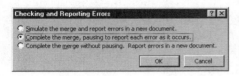

Fig. 11.14:   The *Checking and Reporting Errors* dialog box

Merge

To perform the final merge of the records click the *Merge* button. *Word* now reads the data from the data source and creates the corresponding amount of form letters. If you are using large data sources the progress will be displayed in the status bar. Each letter will be separated by a section break but displayed in a single document. In this way huge documents of several hundred pages can be created that might cause trouble especially if your system is slow and equipped with limited memory.

Records to be merged

If you want to merge only specific record numbers, select the *From* radio button in the *Records to be merged* group box of the *Merge* dialog box and insert the number of the first record into the *From* text box. Then insert the number of the last record into the *To* text box and finally click the *Merge* button.

When merging records

In the *When merging records* option group you can specify whether blank lines should be printed when data fields are empty or whether they should be omitted.

Printing Form Letters

Before printing form letters you should check the document with the *View Merged Data* button ![icon]. This option allows you to correct any possible mistakes. Before the printout, the data source and main document should be merged.

Merge to printer

Word then presents all form letters in the document *Form Letter X* separated by section breaks. To print all copies of the current form letter, click the *Merge to Printer* button 🖼 on the *Merge* toolbar. *Word* opens the *Print* dialog box. If you click the *OK* button *Word* prints one copy of the form letter for each record in the data source.

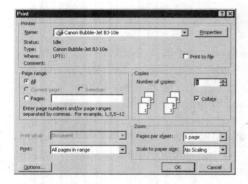

Fig. 11.15: The *Print* dialog box

Printing specific records

If you want to print only specific form letters of which you know the record number, click the *Mail Merge* button 🖼 on the *Mail Merge* toolbar. To merge only specific numbers of records click on the *From* option in the *Records to be merged* group box of the *Merge* dialog box and enter the number of the first record you want to print. Then insert the number of the last record to be printed into the *To* text box.

Printer

Now select the *Printer* option in the *Merge to* drop-down list box and click the *Merge* button. *Word* will send only the specified records to the printer.

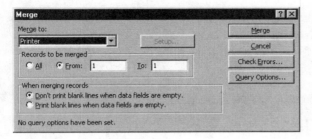

Fig. 11.16: Printing specific records

If you want to print only records of certain merge field contents, e.g., you want to send form letters only to persons living in a certain city, make this selection before you print.

If you start the printing process from the displayed document *Form letter X*, the whole document with all form letters will be printed by default. The selection of recipients always has to be specified before you merge the main document with the data source.

Inserting Different Titles

One of the characteristics of a form letter is that the same contents can be sent with a personalized address to various recipients. It becomes even more interesting if you start the form letter with a formal address like 'Dear Ms. XY' or 'Dear Mr. XY'. To do this you have to insert a so-called *Word Field*. This *Word Field* will check a specific data field in your record and insert the corresponding formal address.

In our example, your records need a field name called 'Title' with entries like 'Mr.' or 'Ms.'. *Word* cannot distinguish the male or female sex of the recipient by first name alone. If your records meet these conditions, place the insertion point in the main document of the form letter at the place where you want to insert the formal address. Now click the *Insert Word Field* drop-down button on the *Mail Merge* toolbar. Select *If ...Then ...Else* from the drop-down menu.

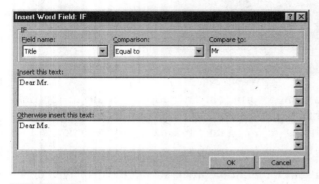

Fig. 11.17:   Inserting a Word Field into a form letter

Field name

Choose from the *Field name* drop-down list the field name of your choice. Mostly it will be the 'Title' field name, but you also find there all the other field names of your data source.

Comparison

compare to

From the *Comparison* drop-down list choose the *Equal to* operator and insert the correctly spelled term into the *Compare to* text box, *Mr.* or *Ms.* for instance. Make sure that you use exactly the same term you have used in your records. If you have used 'Mister' in your data source you cannot use 'Mr.' now. For *Word* 'Mr.' and 'Mister' are two totally different terms! Now click in the *Insert*

Insert this text

this text text box. Here insert the text that *Word* should print if it finds the field name you have specified in the *Compare to* text box in one of the records. In our example we fill in 'Dear Mr.'.

Otherwise insert

this text

In the *Otherwise insert this text* text box you insert the text in case the match is not found; in our example, to address a female person, e.g. 'Dear Ms.', and confirm with *OK*. *Word* inserts the *Word Field* with the text 'Dear Ms.' because the query has not yet been done. Insert a *LastName* merge field behind the *Word Field*. Because the name will be inserted in both cases it does not have to be a conditional field.

Three Different Titles

If you would like to have the option of a third title, a company for instance, you need a nested condition. A nested condition contains a further condition in the IF part or in the THEN part. In the following example it is assumed that the entries 'Mr.', 'Ms.' and 'Company' are saved in the *Title* field while the surnames of private persons are saved in the *LastName* field.

If...then...else

Place the insertion cursor where you want to insert the address in your main document and open the *Insert Word Field* drop-down menu. Again choose *If...Then...Else*. In the *Field Name* drop-down menu select *Title* and in the *Comparison* drop-down menu choose *Equal to*. In the *Compare to* text box type 'Company'. Click in the *Insert this text* text box and type:

```
Dear Ladies and Gentlemen,
```

Otherwise insert this text

The *Otherwise insert this text* text box should be left empty. Confirm with *OK*.

Now press the key combination Alt+F9 to make the condition visible. Click between the quotation marks of the still empty THEN part.

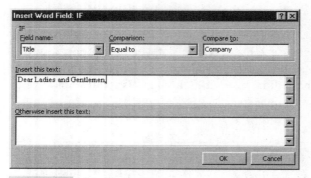

Fig. 11.18: The If condition

{ IF {MERGEFIELD Title } = "Company" "Dear Ladies and Gentlemen," "†" }

Fig. 11.19: The insertion point in the empty THEN part

Otherwise insert this text

Leave the insertion cursor at this position and select again the *If...Then...Else...* item from the *Insert Word Field* drop-down menu. Keep *Title* as the *Field Name* and *Equal to* as the *Comparison*. Into the *Compare to* text box type 'Mr.'. Into the *Otherwise insert this text* text box type:

```
Dear Mr.
```

Press the key combination ⌈Ctrl⌉+⌈F9⌉ and type into the braces:

```
MERGEFIELD LastName
```

At *Otherwise insert this text* you type:

```
Dear Ms.
```

Press again ⌈Ctrl⌉+⌈F9⌉ and type into the braces:

```
MERGEFIELD LastName
```

Compare your entries for the nested condition with the following figure:

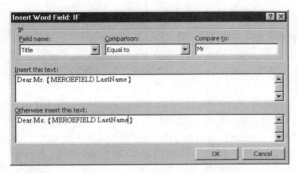

The entries of the nested condition

If everything corresponds confirm with *OK*. Now press Alt+F9 to switch back to the display of the field results. *Word* will now merge the records and compare the nested condition from left to right. It will insert one of three different entries, depending on the contents of the *Title* field:

- Title = 'Company': Dear Ladies and Gentlemen,
- Title = 'Mr.': Dear Mr. ...,
- Title = 'Ms.': Dear Ms. ...,

The clumsy procedure of inserting the *LastName* into the field is necessary since in the case of a neutral entry no name should be inserted. That's why the name has to be part of the condition. The *Comparison* drop-down list also offers you operators like *Less than or equal* and *Greater than or equal*. With these operators you can define other interesting *Word Fields* for the comparison of merge fields.

Filter Records for the Printout

Query options

After creating the data source and the main document of a form letter, the records of the data source should be merged with the main document. *Word* usually produces one letter for each record in the data source. In this section you will learn how to select only certain merge fields in the data source that conform to specific criteria and thus send form letters to selected recipients only. In *Word* selection criteria can be specified by selecting 'Query Options'. One of the simplest queries is, for example, to send letters to female or male recipients only. A more sophisticated query could include only specific postal codes or the a selection of customers with a particular interest. For all queries you need the corresponding merge fields in the data source of the form letter. You can only select the recipients by postal code if the data source contains the *PostalCode* merge field. If you want to send letters to customers with special interests you definitely need a merge field that contains this kind of information for each record. This could be a field called 'Interests', for example. You can see that the query options are directly dependent on the information available in the data source.

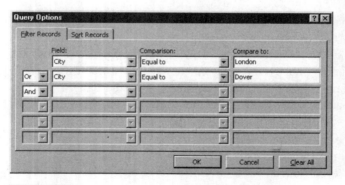

Fig. 11.21:   Filtering records for form letters

To set the query options for form letters you click the *Mail Merge* button on the *Mail Merge* toolbar of your

Query options

main window and then on the *Query Options* button in the *Merge* dialog box.

You can also open the *Mail Merge Helper* via *Tools/Mail Merge* and then click on the *Query Options* button. The *Query Options* dialog box will be displayed.

Field

Select the merge field you want to use for the query in the *Field* drop-down list. If you want to send form letters only to postal codes between 80000 to 90000, for example, select the *PostalCode* field name.

Greater than

Greater than or equal

Now select the *Greater than* option in the *Comparison* drop-down list and type '79999' into the *Compare to* text box to select all postal codes greater than 79999. You can also select the *Greater than or equal* operator and type '80000' in the *Compare to* text box.

AND

Now you will want to specify more conditions. Select the *And* option in the drop-down list on the far left of the second line and repeat the query on the *PostalCode* field. This time choose *Less than* from the *Comparison* list and enter '90001' into the *Compare to* text box to select postal codes up to 90000. Confirm with *OK*.

Merge

Click the *Merge* button in the *Mail Merge* dialog box or in the *Mail Merge Helper* dialog box. *Word* merges the form letters that correspond to your query options and creates a *Form Letter* document that contains all form letters with the final data and contents. To print the form letters, choose *File/Print*, select the printer options and confirm with *OK*.

Tip!

If you are familiar with this procedure you can also print right away. Select the *Printer* option in the *Merge to* drop-down list box in the *Merge* dialog box and click *OK* in the *Print* dialog box.

Special interest query can be made on *Interests of the customer*, *Regular customer*, *Marital status*, *Income*, etc. To simplify the query use numeral codes in your data source; for instance, insert a '1' for unmarried persons in the 'Status' merge field, a '2' for regular customers, a '3' for well-to-do customers, etc. This way you can set the *Comparison* option on *Equal to* to select only the desired number(s).

When to Use AND and When to Use OR

If you want to work with more than one condition when selecting the records, open the *Query Options* dialog box. Here you have two options in the drop-down list that link two conditions:

- AND
- OR

The default setting is always AND. What conditions should be linked with AND, and what conditions with OR?

Use AND if both conditions need to be fulfilled. Use OR if only one of the conditions has to be fulfilled. Here is an example to illustrate the link of two conditions:

- *Field*: City
  Comparison: Equal
  Compare to: Manchester
- *Field*: Title
  Comparison: Equal
  Compare to: Mr.

If you link the two conditions with AND, only the male citizens of Manchester will be selected. If you link the two conditions with OR, all citizens of Manchester and all male records, no matter in which city, will be selected.

Creating Labels with the Mail Merge Function

The mail merge function of *Word* can also be used to create address labels. In this case the contents of the labels are taken from the records in the data source. To create mail merge labels, open a new blank document and select *Tools/Mail Merge*. Click the *Create* button in section '1' of the *Mail Merge Helper* dialog box. Select the *Mailing Labels* command and click the *Active Window* button. Now click the *Get Data* button in section '2' of the *Mail Merge Helper* dialog box. If you want to use an existing data source select the *Open Data Source* command. In the *Open Data Source* dialog box select the name of the data source and click the *Open* button. To create a new data source choose the *Create Data Source* command in the *Get Data* drop-down menu of the *Mail Merge Helper* dialog box. When the data source is opened, confirm the message with a click on the *Set Up Main Document* button.

Label options

The *Label Options* dialog box will be displayed. Select the options for your printer in the *Printer information* section. Then choose the producer of your address label from the *Label products* drop-down list. In the *Product number* list, select the type of label.

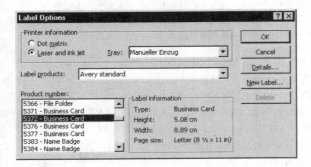

Fig. 11.22:   The *Label Options* dialog box

If you do not find a corresponding format in the *Product number* list, click the *New Label* button and define your own label. After choosing your label close the *Label Options* dialog box with *OK*. You will now get a blank sample label. Click the *Insert Merge Field* button and select the first merge field you want to print on the address label.

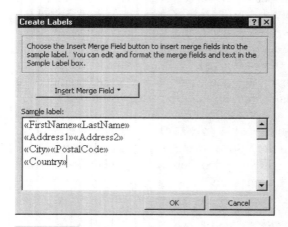

Fig. 11.23:   A sample label with merge fields

Insert all required merge fields into the sample label in this way, and close the dialog box with *OK*.

Print all records

If you want to print all records, click on the *Close* button in the *Mail Merge Helper* dialog box, then on the *Merge to Printer* button 🖶 on the *Mail Merge* toolbar.

If you want to print selected records only, click the *Merge* button in the *Mail Merge Helper* dialog box. Select the *From* option in the *Records to be merged* section of the *Merge* dialog box and insert the numbers of the records you want to select into the *From* and *To* text boxes. Select the *Printer* option from the *Merge to* drop-down list box and click the *Merge* button.

If you do not want to filter the records for printing by record number but rather by certain other criteria such as *City*, you can apply the query method described above to labels too.

Fields

You may have used fields or field codes in *Word* without being aware of it, for example when you were inserting the current date or page numbers. *Word* uses the so-called fields for this information. These are placeholders in your document that *Word* will automatically replace with certain information.

When creating form letters or other merge documents you will use fields as placeholders for various merge data such as names and addresses.

Inserting Fields into Documents

You can insert various fields that provide specific information into your documents. Often you will not realize that a field is used because you are using different commands or buttons and *Word* 'secretly' inserts the fields.

Date and time page numbers

The most commonly inserted fields contain the current date or page number. You can insert the current date via *Insert/Date and Time* and the page number via *Insert/ Page Numbers* or by clicking on the corresponding button on the *Header and Footer* toolbar. Information concerning the user or the document such as the name of the author, name of the document, date saved, etc., can be inserted by means of fields.

Fields are displayed in light grey

The information a field contains will be automatically updated by *Word*. But you can also change the entries yourself. Certain processes such as saving and printing automatically update the contents of certain fields. In documents by default *Word* displays the results of the field information. If you click on a field result *Word* displays the result in light grey. This way you will know immediately that this is not normal text but a field code.

To insert a field, place the insertion cursor at the position in the text where the field result should appear and choose the *Field* command from the *Insert* menu. The *Field* dialog box will be displayed.

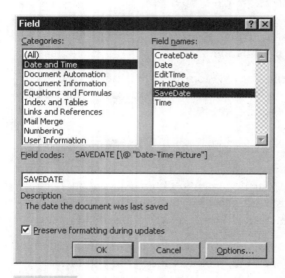

Fig. 11.24:   The *Field* dialog box

The *Categories* list contains various field types sorted by theme. Select one of the categories that comes closest to the desired information. If you want to insert for example the *Save Date* into your document, select the *Date and Time* category. In the *Field names* list box, select the *SaveDate* item from the available field names in the current category.

Description

If you need information about one of the fields click on the field name and read the explanation in the *Description* section. In our example you will be informed: *The date the document was last saved.* This is the right field for the last saved date. Other fields in this category such as *PrintDate* insert the date the document was last printed.

This list could go on endlessly for further categories. Select the desired field name under *Field names*.

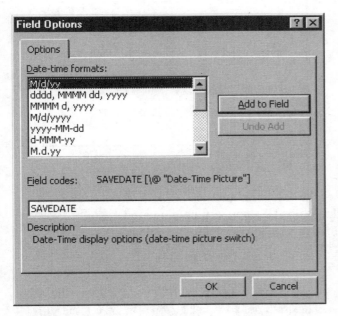

Fig. 11.25: Changing the format of the field result

If you want to check or change the formatting of the field, click the *Options* button. In the *Field Options* dialog box select one of the formats offered.

In *Word* the field code that sets the format of a field is called a 'switch'.

Click the *Add to Field* button to link the field with the field code indicated in the *Field codes* area and confirm with *OK*.

Close the *Field* dialog box with a click on the *OK* button to insert the field into the document. The field result will be displayed with the standard settings.

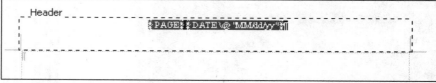

Fig. 11.26: Top, the results; bottom, the fields

Press the key combination ⇧+F9 to display the field code. With the same key combination ⇧+F9 you can also switch back to viewing the field results.

Tip!

If you are already familiar with fields and know the name of the desired field by heart you can insert the corresponding field more quickly: Press the key combination Ctrl+F9 and type the field name into the brackets.

Editing and Manually Updating Fields

Fields that are inserted into documents can automatically provide various kinds of information. Most often fields are needed to insert user and document information such as the name of the author, the name of the document, the date saved, etc. *Word* usually updates automatically the information contained in a field.

Updates

Specific commands such as *Save* or *Print* automatically update the content of the fields. This way you always have a printout or a saved file with updated information in all fields. But you can also update the fields manually. Select the field you want to update by clicking on the field result. *Word* then displays it with a light grey background.

The color indicates that it is not normal text but a field code. If the field code is displayed as *{CREATEDATE * MERGEFORMAT}* then press the key combination ⌂+F9 to switch from the view of the field code to the view of the field result.

Manual update

To manually update an inserted field, select it and press the F9 key. *Word* then updates the field result.

If you want to update all fields of the document at the same time, select the entire document with the key combination Ctrl+A and update all the fields by pressing the F9 key.

A summary of the most important key combinations for working with fields is shown below:

■ ⌂+F9
Switches the view of the selected field from field result to field code and vice versa.

511

- ▣ [Alt]+[F9]

  Switches the view of all fields of a document from field result to field code and vice versa.

- ▣ [Ctrl]+[F9]

  Insert field.

- ▣ [F9]

  Update field.

- ▣ [Ctrl]+[⇧]+[F9]

  Change field into its result text.

If fields or field results are updated, , you can set how to display them by using the options. Select *Tools/Options*.

The *View* tab

On the *View* tab page you will find the *Field codes* check box and the *Field shading* drop-down list. The *Field codes* check box switches from field code to field result.

In the *Field shading* drop-down list box you can choose if and when a field should be displayed with grey shading. If you confused the field shading with a selection, then you can deactivate this option by selecting the *Never* item.

The *Print* tab

The *Print* tab page contains the *Update fields* check box. Here you can specify that the fields are to be updated automatically before printing.

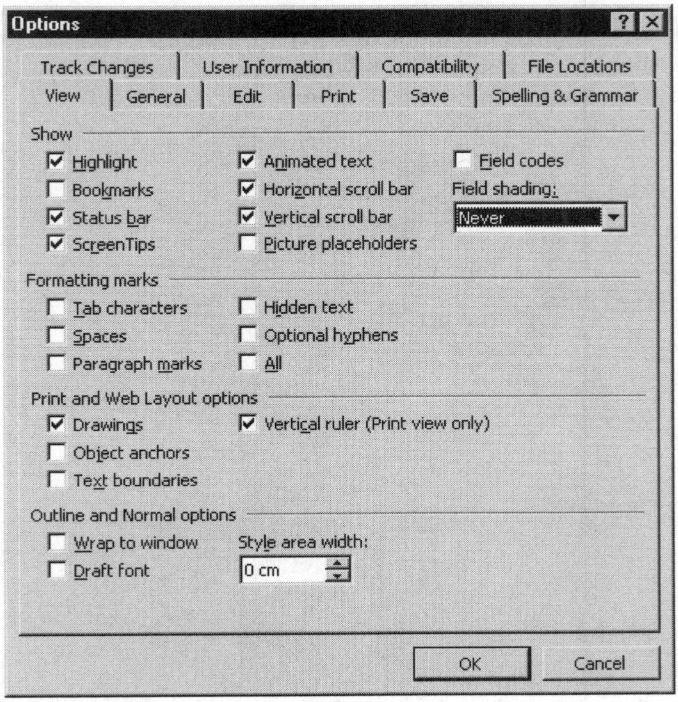

Options

| Track Changes | User Information | Compatibility | File Locations |
| View | General | Edit | Print | Save | Spelling & Grammar |

Show
- ☑ Highlight
- ☐ Bookmarks
- ☑ Status bar
- ☑ ScreenTips
- ☑ Animated text
- ☑ Horizontal scroll bar
- ☑ Vertical scroll bar
- ☐ Picture placeholders
- ☐ Field codes

Field shading:
[Never ▼]

Formatting marks
- ☐ Tab characters
- ☐ Spaces
- ☐ Paragraph marks
- ☐ Hidden text
- ☐ Optional hyphens
- ☐ All

Print and Web Layout options
- ☑ Drawings
- ☐ Object anchors
- ☐ Text boundaries
- ☑ Vertical ruler (Print view only)

Outline and Normal options
- ☐ Wrap to window
- ☐ Draft font

Style area width:
[0 cm ⬍]

[OK] [Cancel]

Fig. 11.27: Clearing the field shading

Include with document

With the *Field codes* check box in the *Include with document* option group, you can specify whether the field codes or the field results should be printed.

Usually field results are printed. That's why this check box should be cleared. Only for test printouts or when you are searching for mistakes in a form letter is it necessary to print the field codes. In this case select the *Field codes* check box.

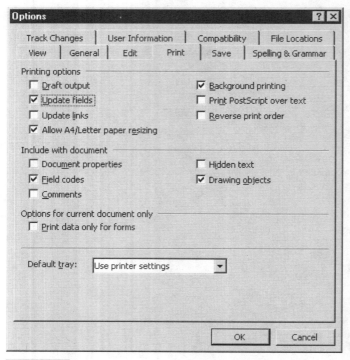

Fig. 11.28:   **Preparing the field codes printout**

12. Data Exchange

With the constant extension and improvement of the features of standard applications, people's expectations of the design and the production of text documents in *Word* and other programs is getting higher and higher.

Most users don't work with just one program anymore, but use *Word*, for example, in combination with other programs in the *Office Suite* such as *Excel* and/or *Access*.

Therefore, the exchange of data between different program components becomes more and more important. The different programs, especially the components of the *Office Suite*, provide various options for data exchange, that now is more or less standardized; therefore, this aspect should not pose any problem.

Loading Text from Other Programs in Word

Usually you open documents in *Word* that have been created with this program. But along with the installation of *Word*, conversion filters that allow you to open files that have not been created by *Word* are also supplied. Here we will confine ourselves to the opening of documents that have been created with other word processing programs.

File/Open

If you want to open such a document, choose the *Open* command from the *File* menu. In the *Open* dialog box select the drive that contains the desired document from the *Look in* drop-down list. With a double-click on one of the folders displayed in the big list box, you can switch to the subfolder where other files are saved. With the *Up One Level* button 🔁 you move up one level in the folder tree.

Files of type

Open the *Files of type* drop-down list box and select the entry corresponding to the file format of the file you want to open. For a *WordPerfect* document you select the *WordPerfect 6.x (*.doc, *wpd)* option; for documents created by other word processing programs, choose the corresponding product version number.

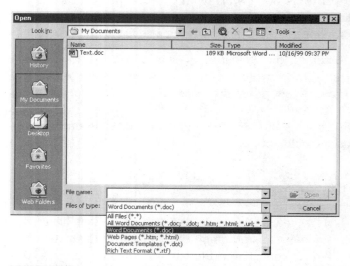

Fig. 12.1: Open documents from programs other than Word

All the files of the fixed file type in the chosen drive/folder are displayed in the big list box. Select the document you want to open and click the *Open* button.

Word loads the necessary conversion program and translates the contents of the file into a version which *Word* can understand. Then the document is displayed in a new window, where the title bar contains the document name.

Missing converter

If, after selecting a file, you get a message saying that *Word* cannot find the converter for the file, then the necessary converter has obviously not been installed on your system. In this case, use the setup program to install the necessary features.

If *Word* displays strange characters in the converted document, then you may have chosen the wrong import filter in the *Files of type* drop-down list. Close the document without saving and try a different version number in the *Files of type* drop-down list.

Formats Word can read

Word is able to read the formats of the most common word processing programs. In addition, it can open *Lotus 1-2-3* spreadsheets, *Schedule+* business contacts, addresses from your personal address book, *Works for Windows* documents, etc., provided that the right import filters have been installed. Still, *Word* cannot always reproduce all formatting in the source file. But *Word 2000* provides some additional conversion programs. For instance, you can directly load, edit and save Internet pages in *HTML* format.

Saving converted documents

Whenever possible, save the converted documents as *Word* documents *(*.doc)*. If the document will be used later on in an application that *Word* cannot open, save the document in its original format. Select *File/Save As* and choose the export filter from the *Save as type* drop-down list.

Saving Documents for Other Applications

By default all text documents you save in *Word* are given the *Word document (*.doc)* file type and the *DOC* file extension. But in *Word 2000* you can also display and save texts of various other formats.

Usually you can save only specific file types with an application. That's why the programs use different file extensions consisting of three letters.

DOC extension

A *Word* document is usually given the file extension *DOC* for *DOCument*, while a *Paint* drawing gets the extension *BMP* for *BitMaP*. To save a document in the format specific to the application you are using, first create the document, e.g., write a letter in *Word*

Save as

Then select the *Save As* command in the *File* menu. If you did not yet save the document you can also click the *Save* button 🖫 on the *Standard* toolbar.

Save in

To save a document, *Word* needs four pieces of information: the target drive, the target folder, the file name and the file type. To select the target drive and target folder, open the *Save in* drop-down box and select the drive where you want to save the file.

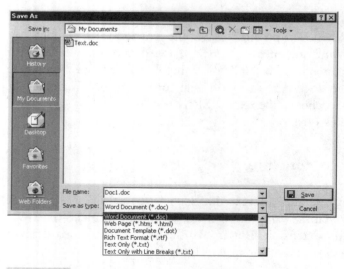

Fig. 12.2: Selecting the file type while saving

Now select the destination folder or subfolder from the list below it by double-clicking on it. With the *Up One Level* button ⬆ you can jump one level higher in the folder tree. The current folder is always displayed in the *Save in* list box.

Create New Folder

With the *Create New Folder* button 📁 you can create and name a new folder.

File name

Insert the file name of your document into the *File name* box. The file name should be clear and may consist of a maximum of 255 characters, including spaces.

Text formats

In the *Save as type* drop-down box you can now select a file type other than the *Word document* default type. Word texts can be saved in many different formats. But this only makes sense if you want to use the documents in applications that are unable to read the actual *Word document* format. Open the *Save as type* drop-down list in the *Save As* dialog box. In the list you'll find all available formats. Which one you should choose depends on the purpose for which you want to use the file.

Text only

Select *Text Only (*.txt)* if you want to use a *Word* document in an application that cannot read or convert the *Word for Windows 2000* format. The file extension *TXT* will be appended to the file name and the text will be saved without formatting.

MS-DOS text

Choose the *MS-DOS Text (*.txt)* format if you want to use a *Word* text in an *MS-DOS* program. The text will get the file extension *TXT*, all formatting will be deleted and the text will be saved in the *ASCII MS-DOS* character set. If you want to keep the line spacing for *MS-DOS*, select the *MS-DOS Text with Line Breaks (*.txt)* file type.

Rich Text Format

Select *Rich Text Format (*.rtf)* if you want to use a formatted *Word* text in a different word processing application that does not support the *Word for Windows 2000* format, but can read *RTF*.

File type selection

If you find the name of the word processing program you want to use, e.g., *WordPerfect 5.x for Windows (*.doc)*, select this file type. This is the safest way because *Word* already converts the document to the file type of the other program. The file extension can be *DOC* too.

Converting

You can also convert a *Word* document into another file type later. Open the document and save it in the desired format. The original file will keep the *Word for Windows 2000* format. But be careful, not all *Word* formatting can be saved in all file types.

Word 2000 and previous versions

Word 2000 uses a different file type than previous versions of *Word*. But you can open files created in *Word 95* or *Word 6.x* directly in *Word 2000*. All data and formatting you created in *Word 95* or *Word 6.x* is supported by *Word 2000*.

To make *Word 2000* documents readable to *Word 95,* save in the *Word 95/ Word 6.x* format, the document you created in *Word 2000*. To this purpose, select the *Word 6.0/95* option from the *Save as type* drop-down list in the *Save As* dialog box. Because not all *Word 2000* features are supported by previous versions, you may lose data or the formatting of your documents by changing the file type. In order to save a document in Word 97 format, check the radio button *Disable features not supported by Word 97* in the save options under *Tools/General Options* and do not worry about what happens later.

Exchanging Data Through the Clipboard

Use the Windows clipboard to import pictures and text from other applications into *Word* documents. In the

Paste Special

source application, select the information you want to copy and choose *Edit/Copy* to insert it into the Windows clipboard. Switch to *Word* and choose *Edit/Paste*. There are certain file types that may be difficult to import into your *Word* document and you may get error messages. This happens especially with older and exotic applications that use uncommon file formats or don't support the *OLE 2.0 (Object Linking and Embedding)* technology. In this case use the *Paste Special* command in the *Edit* menu to import information from the other program.

As

The *Paste Special* dialog box will be displayed. Depending on the file type, you can read the name of the source document of the other application in the *Source* section. In the *As* list you'll find all available ways of importing the information. Select from the *As* list the type of information that should be pasted from the clipboard into your *Word* document. In the *Result* section you get information about the selected type.

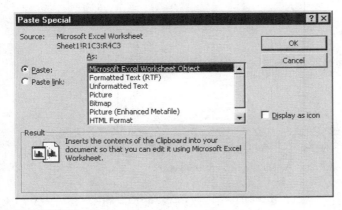

Fig12.3: Selecting the paste style

Paste

Depending on the type of information, you can choose between the *Paste* and the *Paste link* options. By selecting the *Paste* radio button, you insert the contents of the

521

clipboard at the insertion point with format chosen from the *As* list box.

Paste link

By selecting the *Paste link* radio button you insert the contents of the clipboard and create a link with the source file containing the information. This option is available only if the clipboard contents are created by an application that supports linking. Make sure to save the source file in the source application before you create a link in *Word* . Confirm with *OK* to insert the information. To edit a linked file, double-click the linked information. The source application will then start.

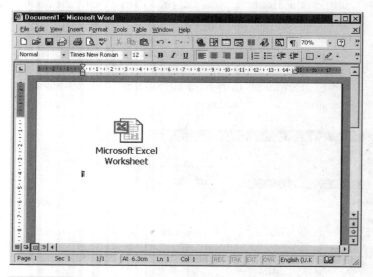

Fig. 12.4: Information of other programs inserted as icon

If you check the *Display as icon* radio button, *Word* displays the linked or embedded object as icon only. To open or edit the object, double-click the icon: the *Change icon* button will be displayed and you will be able to select another icon.

13. Search and Replace

Word has at its disposal comfortable integrated search functions to quickly find corresponding words which may be located far from one another in the text. If in addition to finding certain terms you want to replace them with others terms, you can use the *Replace* function.

Find

Word has a very convenient search function which is helpful primarily when you are searching for a certain text passage. You can also, however, use the search function of *Word* to search for symbols, formatting, formatted text, or certain objects such as graphics and tables.

Finding Text Passages in Word Documents

If in a *Word* text you want to search for certain terms, individual characters or a group of characters or words, go to the *Edit* menu and click the *Find* command. *Word* opens the *Find and Replace* dialog box. In *Word 2000*, the *Find*, *Replace* and *Go To* functions have been combined.

Find

Alternatively, you can press the shortcut Ctrl+F. In the *Find and Replace* dialog box, type the term you are looking for into the *Find what* text box.

More

Next, click the *More* button to configure the search process. If you check the *Find whole words only* check box, *Word* will look only for whole words that correspond to the term you entered into the *Find what* box. Parts of a word that match will then be ignored.

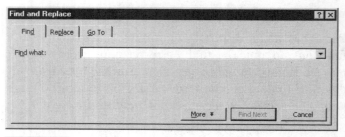

Fig. 13.1: The *Find* tab page

Match case
If you check the *Match case* check box, *Word* will look only for the corresponding words that exactly match the search word, including upper and lower cases.

Use wildcards
If you select the *Use wildcards* check box, *Word* will search for placeholders, special characters or specific search operators which you can enter into the *Find what* text box. We will introduce this special method later on in more detail. If the *Use wildcards* check box is cleared, *Word* considers all characters entered in the *Find what* text box as plain text.

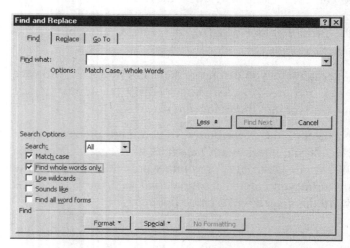

Fig. 13.2: The *Find and Replace* dialog box

Find Next

Start the search by clicking on the *Find Next* button. *Word* then selects the first match it finds. If you click on the *Find Next* button again, *Word* searches for the next corresponding item in the text.

Search repetition

After you have closed the *Find and Replace* dialog box, you can start the search again by using the *Edit/Find* command or by pressing the [Ctrl]+[F] key combination.

Search

By default, *Word* searches the entire document all in one go. If the *Down* item is selected in the *Search* drop-down list, when you come to the end of your document you will get a message asking you whether the search is to be continued from the beginning as well. If you confirm by clicking *Yes*, *Word* searches the document from its beginning down to the cursor position.

On the contrary, if you select the *Up* item, the document is searched upwards. When you come to the beginning of your document you will get a message asking you whether the search is to be continued from the end as well. If you confirm by clicking *Yes*, *Word* searches the document from its end up to the cursor position.

There is another search possibility: by selecting the *All* item in the *Search* drop-down list, the whole document will be searched.

Finish search

After the search has been completed, you receive a message which you can close by clicking *OK*. The *Find and Replace* dialog box remains open. You can close it by clicking the *Close* button [X] in the title bar or the *Cancel* button in the dialog box.

Deciding upon the Search Area

If before starting the search you selected part of the text, *Word* first of all searches only in this part. You will then be asked whether you want to continue searching the remainder of the document. If you click *Yes*, the search will go on, and if you click *No*, the search will be stopped.

Replace

In certain situations the search for specific text passages, formatting, special characters or objects might not be all that's necessary, and you might want to replace what you've found right away with something else.

Examples of such a situation could include a misspelled name or an appointment which has changed, or a formatting which you want to replace throughout the whole text with a different format.

Replacing Text Passages

Of course, *Word* also supports the finding and replacing of text passages. This procedure is very similar to the one described above. The only thing you need to do in addition to defining the search item, is to enter the item that's going to replace it and to determine at which places you want the changes to be made.

In order to change the misspelled name 'Silvia', for example, with the correct spelling – 'Sylvia' –, enter 'Silvia' into the *Find what* text box and 'Sylvia' into the *Replace with* box.

As a general procedure, choose *Edit/Replace*, and type the search text into the *Find what* text box. Then type the text which will replace it into the *Replace with* text box.

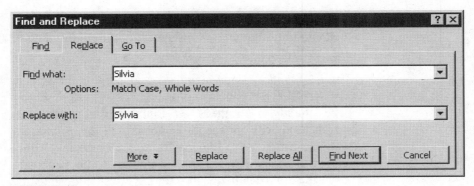

Fig. 13.3: The replacing of character chains

By clicking on the *More* button in the dialog box, you can expand the dialog box to further define the already introduced search options.

Find Next

After you have set the search options, start the search by clicking *Find Next*. A click onto *Replace* exchanges the first text passage found with the replacement. Thereafter, the search automatically continues. For each text passage you want to change, click on the *Replace* button.

Replace All

Select *Replace All* to replace all text passages with the new passage in one go. You can close the dialog box by clicking *Cancel*.

Find and Replace Special Characters or Document Elements

Normally, the *Find* function of *Word* is used to search for certain terms and replace them with other terms. With this function you can, however, also automatically replace formatting with new formats, or search for special characters and document elements and, if you wish, replace them with new ones.

Edit/Replace

If you want to search for special characters or certain elements in a *Word* document, such as dashes, for example, or footnote marks or fields, and perhaps to replace them, then choose the *Replace* command from the *Edit* menu or use the ⌈Ctrl⌉+⌈H⌉ key combination.

Replace tab page

The *Find and Replace* dialog box appears on the screen. The *Replace* tab page is automatically activated. If you have already used the *Find* function earlier, the last search term will appear automatically in the *Find what* text box. Since we're looking for items or special characters in *Word* which are not available on the keyboard, leave the *Find what* text box empty. Just click into the text box to activate it.

Special

Then configure the Find and/or Replace process for special characters or document elements. To do this, click on the *Special* button.

Select special item

In the drop-down menu, a list with all the special items available will appear. You can, for example, search for *Paragraph Mark* and replace it with *Manual Line Break* in the *Replace with* text box. Or you can enter a short dash into the *Find what* text box and exchange it with an *Em Dash* in the *Replace with* text box.

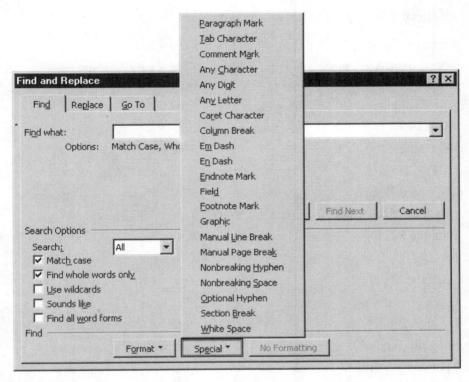

Fig. 13.4: Drop-down list of the available special characters and elements

You can search and replace the following document elements and special characters by entering the corresponding codes into the *Find what* and *Replace with* text boxes or by clicking on the respective item in the *Special* drop-down menu.

To specify	Type	In
Paragraph mark	^p	*Find What / Replace with*
Tab character	^t	*Find what / Replace with*

To specify	Type	In
Comment Mark	^a	*Find what*
ANSI- or ASCII-characters	^0nnn	*Find what / Replace with* (*nnn* is the character code)
Any Character	^?	*Find what*
Any Digit	^#	*Find what*
Any Letter	^$	*Find what*
Caret Character	^^	*Find what / Replace with*
Clipboard Contents	^c	*Replace with*
Contents of the Find what box	^&	*Replace with*
Endnote Mark	^e	*Find what*
Field	^d	*Find what*
Footnote Mark	^f	*Find what*
Graphic	^g	*Find what*
Column Break	^n	*Find what / Replace with*
Manual Line Break	^l	*Find what / Replace with*
Manual Page Break	^m	*Find what / Replace with*
Section Break	^b	*Find what*
Em Dash	^+	*Find what / Replace with*
En Dash	^=	*Find what / Replace with*
Nonbreaking Space	^s	*Find what / Replace with*
Nonbreaking Hyphen	^~	*Find what / Replace with*
Optional Hyphen	^-	*Find what / Replace with*
White Space	^w	*Find what*

Find Next
Replace

Specify the special characters or elements which you are going to search for and, if necessary, replace. Start the search by clicking the *Find Next* button. A click on the

Replace button exchanges the first item found with its replacement. The search then automatically carries on. Click on *Replace* every time *Word* finds the item you're looking for in order to replace it.

Replace all

Click onto the *Replace All* button, if you want to replace all the items with the new term straightaway.

Searching for Partially Unknown Items, Using Complex Search Criteria

The *Find* and *Replace* functions of *Word* can be configured in numerous ways. We will now look at the expanded search using search operators to exclude certain items from the search, or to find items by using complex search criteria.

More / Less

If you want to search for certain characters, words, or letter and word combinations by using placeholders, special characters, or search operators, then open the *Edit* menu and choose the *Replace* command. The shortcut key for the *Replace* command is Ctrl+H. The *Find and Replace* dialog box appears. To define the search options, you can expand the dialog box by clicking the *More* button. To reduce it again, click on the *Less* button.

If you want to replace an item with another one, then fill in the *Replace with* text box. Configure the search process first.

By selecting the *Find whole words only* check box, *Word* looks only for whole words that match the search term. Parts of words that match are thus ignored. If you check the *Match case* check box, *Word* only looks for words which correspond exactly to the search item, including the case.

If you select the *Sounds like* check box, *Word* looks for words which are written similarly to the searched term. If for example you type 'Silvia', Word will also find 'Sylvia'. This search procedure is very useful when you do not remember exactly how a word is written. The *Find all word forms* option replaces the present tense with the past tense for verbs and singular with plural forms for nouns. However, when you are using these last two options, you should never select the *Replace All* command.

By selecting the *Use Wildcards* check box, *Word* looks for the placeholders, special characters or special search operators which you entered into the *Find what* text box.

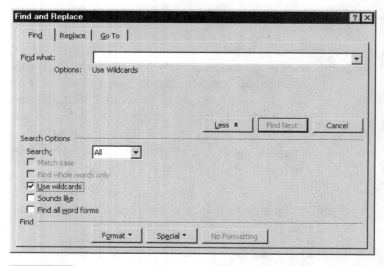

Fig. 13.5:   The *Find and Replace* dialog box with the *Use wildcards* check box selected

You can search for special characters and document elements by entering the corresponding codes into the *Find what* and *Replace with* text boxes. You can quickly enter certain wildcards into the *Find what* text box by clicking on the *Special* button and then choosing the desired element.

Search operator Now, enter one of the placeholders, special characters, or a search operator from the list on the next page into the *Find what* text box:

To find	Code	Examples
Any single character	?	s?t finds 'sat' or 'set'
Any string of characters	*	s*d finds 'sad' and started'
One of the specified characters	[ ]	w[io]n finds 'win' and 'won'
Any single character in this range	[-]	[r-t]ight finds 'right' and 'sight'. Ranges must be in ascending order
Any single character except the characters inside the brackets	[!]	m[!a]st finds 'mist' and 'most, but not 'mast'
Any single character except characters in the range inside the brackets	[!x-z]	t[!a-m]ck finds 'tock' or 'tuck', but not 'tack' or 'tick'
Exactly *n* occurrences of the previous character or expression	{n}	fe{2}d finds 'feed' but not 'fed'
At least *n* occurrences of the previous character or expression	{n,}	fe{1,}d finds 'fed' and 'feed'
From *n* to *m* occurrences of the previous character or expression	{n,m}	10{1,3} finds '10', '100' and '1000'
One or more occurrences of the previous character or expression	@	lo@t finds 'lot' and 'loot'
The beginning of a word	<	<(inter) finds 'interesting' and 'intercept', but not 'splintered'

To find	Code	Examples
The end of a word	>	(in)> finds 'in' and 'within', but not 'interesting'

You can use parentheses in order to group the wildcards as well as text, and to indicate the order of evaluation. For example, search for '<(pre)*(ed)' to find 'presorted' and 'prevented'. If you are searching for a character that is defined as a wildcard, type a backslash '\' before the character. For example, search for '\?' to find a question mark.

Find Next

Start the search by clicking *Find Next*, and replace the items found by using the *Replace* or *Replace All* buttons when necessary. Resume the search at the beginning of the document after it reaches the end, if necessary, and confirm the final message by clicking *OK*. Close the *Find and Replace* dialog box by clicking *Cancel*.

Replacing Formatting in Documents with Other Formatting

The *Replace* function in *Word* is normally used to search for certain items and replace them by others. Here, we want to show you now how you can use the *Replace* function to change certain formatting.

Replace

If you want to change the formatting of certain fonts, words, or character and word combinations, then open the *Edit* menu and choose the *Replace* command.

Search item =
Replace item

Into the *Find what* text box, enter the search item which is displayed in a certain formatting, or which you want to emphasize in a certain formatting. Into the *Replace with* text box, enter the same item, since you do not want to change the item, but only its formatting.

Configure search

Next, configure the search and replace process. We will first discuss the search options. If you select the *Find whole words only* check box, *Word* looks only for whole words, and matching word parts are ignored. By selecting the *Match case* check box, *Word* only looks for those words which correspond exactly to that word, including matching capitalization and small letters. These check boxes do not have any influence on the replacement process.

Word always replaces an item it has found with the term in the *Replace with* text box, and uses the formatting of the item found. It is precisely this feature that we want to change now.

If, for example, in a long document you want to emphasize the company's name by formatting it in bold letters in a special font every time it appears in the text, then enter the company name into both the *Find what* and *Replace with* text boxes. Then click the *Format* button. Select the *Font* item in order to open the *Replace Font* dialog box.

Select formatting

In the corresponding *Font*, *Font style* and *Size* list boxes, choose the formatting you prefer. In addition, you can select the various *Effects* check boxes, select a *Color*, or *Underline* a word.

When you have made all your changes, click *OK*.

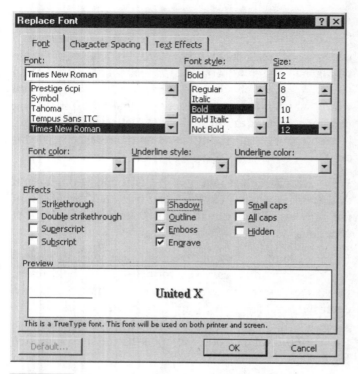

Fig. 13.6: The formatting of the replacement item

Replace

Replace all

Start the search by clicking on the *Find Next* button. A click on the *Replace* button replaces the item found with the identical item in the new formatting. The search for the next match will automatically go on. Every time *Word* has found the word in question, you have to click the *Replace* button in order to replace it. If you want to replace all items with the new formatting in one go, click the *Replace All* button.

In the same manner, you can use the *Format* button in the *Find and Replace* function in order to change the formatting of paragraphs, tabs, styles, or frames.

Replacing Formats with Other Formats

In the previous section we described how you can replace text with differently formatted text. In this way, you could give a unified format to certain passages of the text by using the *Replace* command.

Another reason to use the *Replace* command is to exchange certain formatting with other formatting, this time independent of any search text.

Find what

Format

To do this, select *Edit/Replace* and click into the *Find what* text box of the dialog box. In order to remove the formatting which may still exist in the text box from the previous search, click the *No Formatting* button. Then click the *Format* button and choose the item of the formatting category to which the formatting you are looking for belongs. Now the formatting you want to search for will appear below the *Find what* text box.

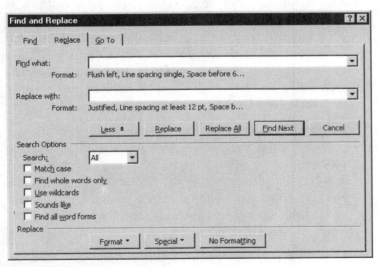

Fig. 13.7:   Replace formattings

Replace with

Format

Then click into the *Replace with* text box and, if necessary, again on the *No Formatting* button in order to clear the previous formatting. Now click the *Format* button and select the formats you want to use to replace the existing ones.

Start the search by clicking the *Find Next* button. Every time *Word* has found the sought formatting, click the *Replace* button. Or, save yourself the time it takes to make the replacements one by one and have them all done in one go by clicking the *Replace All* button.

Finish the search

You can close the dialog box by clicking the *Cancel* button.

Replacing Styles

An especially practical feature of the *Find and Replace* function is the replacement of styles, if you have formatted your document using a style in the *Style Gallery*. If your document contains certain *Font*, *Paragraph*, *Tab*, or *Style* formatting, you can specify these in the *Find what* area as well as in the *Replace with* area. Before defining the search and replace criteria, click into the corresponding text box. If you want to replace only formatting, then leave the text boxes empty.

Entries in the *Find what* and *Replace with* text boxes that may still exist from some previous search and replace process, can be deleted by selecting the contents of the text box and then pressing the Delete key Del . If there are still formatting entries shown underneath the text boxes from a previous search, delete them by clicking the *No Formatting* button.

Styles

Now click into the *Find what* text box and then click the *Format* button. In the drop-down menu, select the *Style* item. The *Find Style* dialog box opens. Select the style which you want to replace.

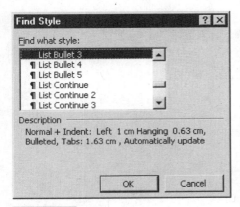

Fig. 13.8:   Find styles

Close the *Find Style* dialog box by clicking *OK*, and click into the *Replace with* text box. Again, click the *Format* button, and select the *Style* item once more. This time, the *Replace Style* dialog box appears.

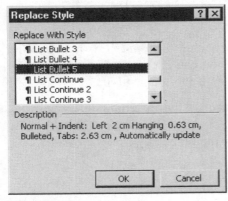

Fig. 13.9:   Replace style

In the *Replace Style* list box, select the style which is going to replace the *Find* style. Close the dialog box by clicking *OK*.

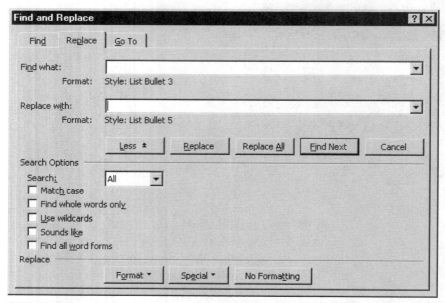

Find and Replace

Find   Replace   Go To

Find what:
    Format: Style: List Bullet 3

Replace with:
    Format: Style: List Bullet 5

    Less ▲   Replace   Replace All   Find Next   Cancel

Search Options
    Search: All
    ☐ Match case
    ☐ Find whole words only
    ☐ Use wildcards
    ☐ Sounds like
    ☐ Find all word forms
Replace

    Format ▾   Special ▾   No Formatting

Fig. 13.10:   Replace one style with another style

Start the search by clicking the *Find Next* button. With the *Replace* button, you can exchange the styles one by one each time *Word* finds the sought style.

If you want to replace all the matching styles with the new style in one go, click the *Replace All* button. Close the *Find and Replace* dialog box by clicking *Cancel*.

14. Help

The written documentation that is provided along with a word processing program is becoming more and more inadequate. Help is very important, particularly for people new to a program, as well as for people who are upgrading from a previous version and want to know what features the new version offers without having to look very hard for them.

A modern word processing program such as *Word* offers you direct on-screen help, complete with an introduction, assistance and the immediate search for a solution to your particular problem without having to browse through the pages of a manual.

This is facilitated by different Help features:

- The Office-Assistant
- Context-Sensitive Help
- An index of keywords
- A search database
- Hierarchically organised *Help* menu
- Access to Online Help on the Web

All combinations of these Help features offer a support system that can be accessed at any time, and with which you can find what you want with the help of a search word or a sentence in the form of a question.

Calling up and Using the Office Assistant

Word offers a well balanced Help system, which you should enjoy. The earlier *Help Assistant* has been replaced in *Word 97* by an animated *Office Assistant* who presents himself in his own window after *Word* starts. Click on the animated icon, enter your question into the bubble that appears, and click on *Search*.

This assistant is automatically displayed after installation and explains new features and gives you tips to improve your working efficiency. The *Office Assistant* is common to all the *Office* programs.

The *Office Assistant* that appears in the separate little window and that welcomed you after you started the program, will assist you with your daily work in *Word*.

Fig. 14.1:   The Office Assistant

The *Office Assistant* provides information about all the new functions that you'll be using for the first time. The *Office Assistant* will, in addition, display tips to help you work more efficiently and give you step-by-step instructions, as well as answer your questions.

Calling up the Office Assistant

If the *Office Assistant* is not visible, on the *Standard* toolbar click the *Office Assistant* button 🔲.

In dialog boxes that contain the *Office Assistant* button 🔲 you also have direct access to the *Office Assistant*.

Hide the Office Assistant

To hide the *Office Assistant* click with the right button on the Assistant and select the shortcut menu *Hide* or select *Hide the Office Assistant* from the *Help* menu.

Searching Help Topics

You can activate the *Office Assistant* if you have a question about a particular topic. To do so, click on the assistant and write your question or a search word into the field containing the sentence *Type your question here and then click Search.*

Searching a topic

Fig. 14.3:   A selection of Help topics

Then click the *Search* button. The Assistant searches through the Help file and displays the related Help topics. If the Assistant does not find anything relevant to your query, then a message will appear and you should reformulate your question. Click the relevant Help topic and read the Help text.

Tips

The *Office Assistant* constantly surveys everything you do and checks whether you are carrying out your tasks efficiently or tanglingly. If the Assistant is able to propose an easier or faster method for a certain operation, a yellow light bulb appears in the Assistant window.

Fig. 14.4: The Assistant has a tip

If this happens, click the Assistant to display the tip.

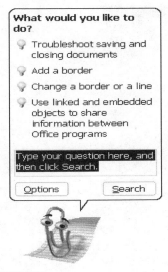

What would you like to do?

- Troubleshoot saving and closing documents
- Add a border
- Change a border or a line
- Use linked and embedded objects to share information between Office programs

Type your question here, and then click Search.

Options   Search

Fig. 14.5:   Example of a tip

Selecting a Different Office Assistant

The default Assistant called *Clippit* appears immediately after starting *Word*. You can use a different Assistant if you want a change.

To select a different Assistant, right-click the Assistant and select *Choose Assistant* to bring up the *Office Assistant* dialog box.

Click the *Next* button to display a different Assistant. The relevant animation automatically appears. If you want to go back to a previous Assistant, click *Back* again.

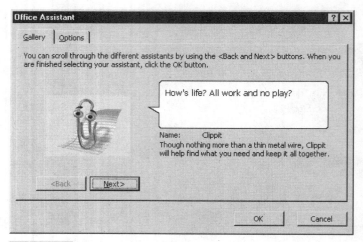

Options for an Assistant

Fig. 14.7: **The new Assistant**

Once you have selected an Assistant, click the *OK* button to display the Assistant and close the dialog box.

Assistant installation

Not all Assistants are set in the default installation. If after selecting another Assistant a message appears that the chosen Assistant could not be found, then insert the Office CD-ROM and click on *OK* so that the Assistant can be automatically installed.

Assistant Options

You can influence the way the *Office Assistant* is displayed on the *Options* tab page. To do so, right-click the Assistant and click the *Options* command.

Assistant capabilities

In the upper part of the dialog box you can determine how the *Office Assistant* operates. Check the *Respond to F1 key* check box, if you want to activate the Assistant by pressing F1, but be sure to disable this if you want to call up the *Word* Help with that key.

If you do not like the Office Assistant and you prefer working with the Help window, clear the *Use the Office Assistant* check box in the *Options* tab of the *Office Assistant* dialog box. From now on, when you press the F1 key or call up the Help function in the *Help* menu, you will immediately see the Help window with the *Contents, Answer Wizard* and *Index* tab pages where you can search for the desired topic.

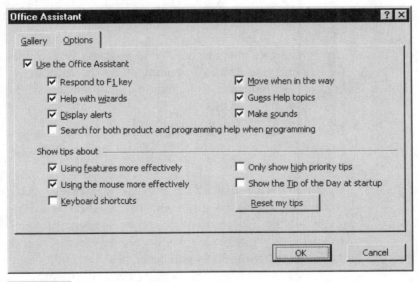

Fig. 14.8:   The *Options* tab page

Show tips about

In the *Show tips about* option group, you can set which type of tips the Assistant should display and in which way.

You can, for example, display only the tips for using the mouse or the keyboard. Click the *Reset my tips* button to restore the tips that have already been displayed if you want to view them again.

Calling Up ScreenTips for Dialog Boxes or Text Formatting

Apart from the classic *Microsoft Word Help Topics*, the word processor also disposes of additional Help features.

For instance, in almost every *Word* dialog box as well as in the various areas of the *Word* window, you can call up a special type of help – the *Context-Sensitive Help* – that gives information about screen elements in the form of *ScreenTips*.

Context-Sensitive
Help ?

The *Context-Sensitive Help* in *Word* can be tested with any screen element you like, or in a dialog box. Select, for example, the *File/Print* command. In the *Print* dialog box you will see the *Help* button ? to the left of the *Close* button on the title bar.

?

Now click the *Help* button ? once and move the mouse pointer in the dialog box. The mouse pointer also contains a question mark ?.

With the *Help* cursor ? click in the area in the dialog box for which you require Help. In case there is a Help text available for this area, Windows displays a *Screen-Tip* with an explanatory text concerning the function of the control element that you have clicked.

If there is no information available about the element you have chosen, the *Help* cursor disappears and sometimes a message will appear telling you there's no information available.

ScreenTip

In that case, click a different area in the dialog box. A *ScreenTip* can be made to disappear by clicking the mouse once.

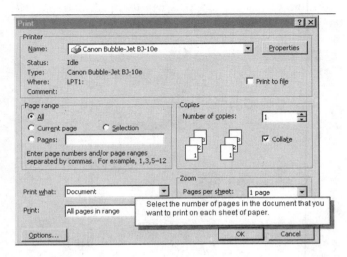

Fig. 14.9:   Calling up Context-Sensitive Help in dialog boxes

Context-Sensitive Help Beyond Dialog Boxes

The procedure for calling up the Context-Sensitive Help can also be applied to the normal *Word* screen and its elements.

To do this, first open the *Help* menu on the menu bar. In the *Help* menu click the *What's This* item. Then, using the *Help* cursor ⍰?, click on the element about which you need information. Read the information and click on the *ScreenTip* to remove it. You can also click on any text in the document with the *Help* cursor ⍰? to display information about the character and paragraph formatting of the current paragraph.

Shortcut menu

Context-Sensitive Help

Another method for calling up Help for an unknown element in a dialog box is by right-clicking in the area for which you would like to have Help. Click the *What's This?* item on the menu to display the information available for the element.

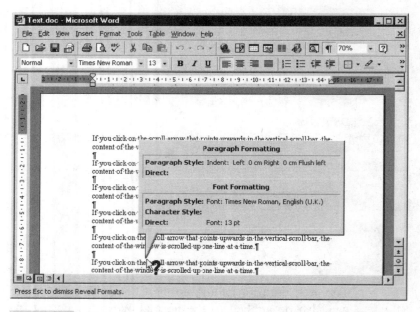

Fig. 14.10: Display formatting information with the Context-Sensitive Help

Help button

If the small *Help* button 📝 is not available in a dialog box, then click the *Help* button or press F1. Should you want to print or copy a *ScreenTip*, click on the tip with the right mouse button. Choose the *Copy* or *Print Topic* command on the shortcut menu.

The key combination for the Context-Sensitive Help for *Word* screen elements is ⇧+F1. If you press these keys the *Help* cursor ▷? will appear again.

Calling up and Using the Word Help Index

In this section we will introduce the alphabetical *Word* Help index that you can access by opening the *Microsoft Word Help* dialog box and activating the *Index* tab page. To do this, call up *Word* Help by clicking *Help* on the menu bar and then choosing *Microsoft Word Help* or simply click on the *Microsoft Word Help* on the *Standard* toolbar. Change to the *Index* tab page. If you chose the first command, this tab will be automatically displayed. If you called up the *Assistant* instead, you first have to type a question in the corresponding box. If you do not see the *Index* tab page, click the *Options* button in the *Microsoft Word Help* and choose the *Show tabs* command. Change to the *Index* tab if you want to search for a topic by entering keywords.

Type the first few letters of the word you're looking for

The *Index* tab page is divided into three parts. You can enter a word you want to look up in the text box on top, while the list box underneath displays all the index items of *Word* Help in alphabetical order. Type the first few letters of the word you want to search for in the top text box called *1. Type keywords*. It is sufficient to type the first letter of a word or just a part of it.

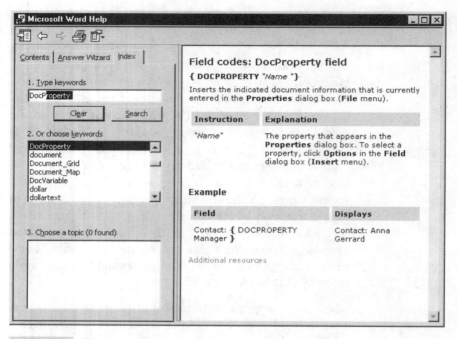

Fig. 14.11:   The *Index* tab page of Word Help

The contents of the list below will be adapted to the word for which you are looking. If you insert two letters, the list will immediately display the first item in the index that begins with those letters; for instance, if you type a 'c', then the first word to appear will be *calculations*. If you now type in additional characters, Help will compare your text with the available items and change the items in the list accordingly. If you type 'cl', Help will display *clip art*. When you see the desired topic displayed in the second list, you can either double click it or click the *Search* button. Then in the third box at the bottom you can choose from among the available topics. If you click on a topic, the corresponding text will be displayed in the right help pane. You can use the scroll bar to leaf through all available topics.

If what you need Help with is how to insert clip art, all you have to do now is to look for the topic you want under *clip art*, for example, *inserting*. You can use the scroll bar to do this.

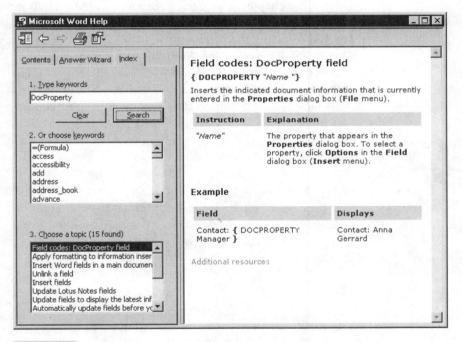

Fig. 14.12: Dialog box displaying a number of topics found

Help Content

In view of the numerous functions and features in *Word* it is not always easy, even for specialists, to maintain an overview of all the commands. According to statistics, most users require only about 10 per cent of all the possible options in a program. But this does not have to be the case, since *Word* disposes of a comprehensive Help program.

Many software developers even dispense with 'proper' manuals in this multimedia age and bundle all the program information and program functions into an online Help. This chapter will teach you how to obtain Help in *Word*. The fastest way is by choosing *Help* on the menu bar and selecting the *Microsoft Word Help* item. If in the *Options* dialog box of the Assistant you activated the *Office Assistant*, it will be now displayed. If you had cleared the *Use the Office Assistant* check box in the *Options* tab page, you immediately reach the Help screen.

If you are not yet sure whether you want to use the Assistant or instead work directly with the *Help* screen page, for instance with the *Index* tab, in the *Options* tab of the Assistant clear the *Respond to F1* option. Then if you press F1 you open the Help screen page directly, if you press the menu command or the *Microsoft Word Help* button in the *Standard* toolbar you call up the Assistant.

Use the *Contents* tab page if you are not yet sure which topic you are searching for. The *Contents* tab page is structured as a book. The items in the list box on the tab page can be expanded or displayed by double-clicking on the book icon or by clicking the plus sign in front of it. Select the page icon ? to display the relevant Help topic on the right part of the Help window. We will now explain the hierarchical organization of items in the list box of the *Contents* tab page.

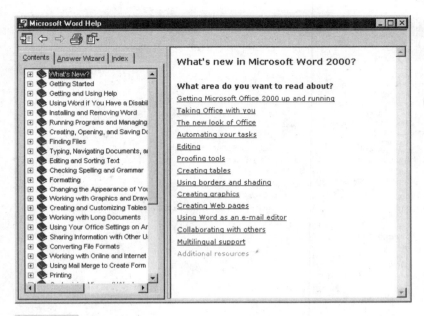

Fig. 14.13:   Word Help

Help books 📖

Word Help is organized by category, indicated by the book icon 📖. The list box represents the bookshelf containing the books. A book can be opened by double-clicking on it. Alternatively, you can click the plus sign in front of it.

After you do this, the contents of the current book will be displayed in the form of chapters that are again identified by the book icon 📖. An open book 📖 may also contain several Help items, which may be recognized by the 🔲 icon. The chapters of an open book can in turn be opened by double-clicking, and so on. Basically this resembles the idea of the folders in the structured view of the *Windows Explorer*; only instead of folder icons Help uses book icons.

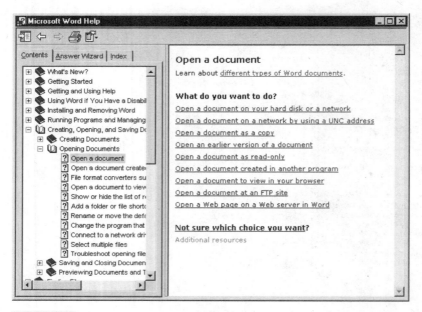

Fig. 14.14: Hierarchical view of Word Help

Opened books 📖 can be closed again by double-clicking on them or by clicking the minus sign in front of the book to reduce the amount of items in the list box. Using the scroll bar you can scroll to the undisplayed books or Help items if you have many open books.

Help Topics ? — If you click on a Help topic indicated by the ? icon on the right side of the Help screen page all content items are displayed. The text will remain on display until you select a new page or reach a new page after clicking a hyperlink. Working with hyperlinks looks like working in the Internet. Click the *Back* button to move backwards through the pages. If the Help window takes up too much room on your screen, you can reduce it by clicking the *Minimize* button.

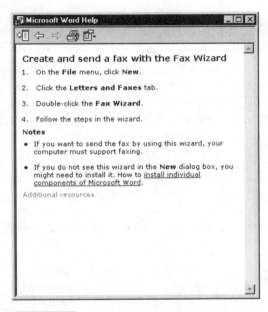

Fig. 14.15: A Help topic of Word Help

Print Topic

To print a Help topic, click on the Help screen page with the right mouse button and select the *Print* command from the shortcut menu.

Copying Topic

You can also choose to copy a Help topic. To do so choose *Select all* from the shortcut menu or select a text passage with the mouse. With the right mouse button click on the selection and choose *Copy* from the shortcut menu. The text will be copied in the clipboard and can be inserted in Office applications such as Word.

Switch off Help

You can close Help in any window at any time by clicking the *Close* button ☒.

Find and Display Help Topics Using the *Answer Wizard*

Answer Wizard
tab page

On the *Contents* tab page, Help topics are classified in books according to task in a hierarchical order, while the *Index* tab page displays Help items in alphabetical order. If you were unable to find the Help item you are looking for by either of these methods, then you are given another opportunity through the *Answer Wizard* tab page.

The *Answer Wizard* tab pretty much resembles the Office Assistant where you can type simple questions clearly. You can type in your questions as you would in the Assistant bubble, the search outcome could however be quite different.

Click the *Answer Wizard* tab page. If the tab pages are not displayed then click on the *Options* button in the *Microsoft Excel Help* dialog box and choose the *Show tabs* item. Type your question in the *What would you like to do* box and click the *Search* button. In the *Select topic to display* box the contents of the selected topic are displayed on the right of the screen page. You can scroll through the topics by using the scroll bar or the spin buttons, and you can reach new pages by selecting a hyperlink.

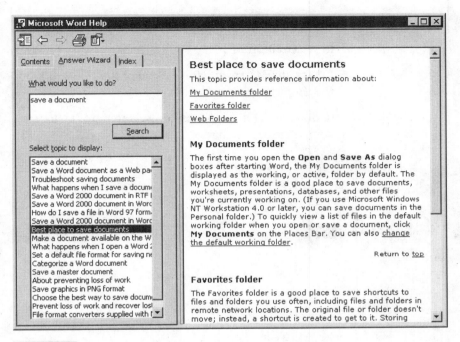

Fig. 14.16: The *Answer Wizard* tab page

Close Word Help

You can close *Word* Help at any time by clicking the *Cancel* button, by pressing the ⌐Alt⌐+⌐F4⌐ key combination or by clicking the *Close* button ⌐X⌐.

Help on the Web

You will find the *Office on the Web* item on the Help menu, accessible by selecting the *Help* command on the menu bar. By highlighting this item you activate an Internet session.

If you have access to the *Microsoft Network* or the Internet you should take advantage of these offers to access help and support directly from the Web.

This option will give you the following possibilities:

- to obtain Online support;

- to start a tutorial;

- to visit the *Microsoft Home Page* or the *Microsoft Office Home Page*;

- to download Office Accessories from the Web to your computer free of charge.

Fig. 14.17:   Help options on the Web

Selecting a command on the overlapping menu starts *Internet Explorer* and opens the dialog box requesting a connection to your service provider.

You can only take advantage of these online facilities if you have a Modem or an ISDN Card and an online service installed in the Windows *Control Panel*.

With the help of the hyperlinks that are available on each page, you can link to more pages. You can also move between the already displayed Web pages with the help of the buttons of *Internet Explorer* or the *Web* toolbar.

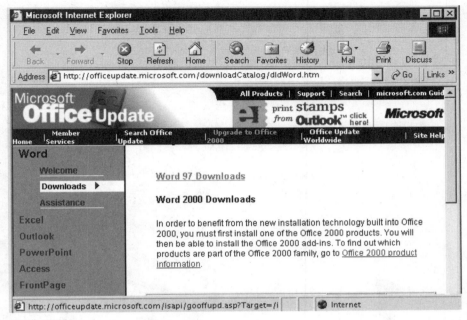

Fig. 14.19: Assistance on the Web

15. Customizing and Installation

Every software program up to the modern standard provides such a wide range of commands and options that it can cope with just about any task. But hardly anyone really needs all these features.

You will surely appreciate this great variety, because it ensures that *Word* has exactly the feature that you need for your particular purpose.

But there is also a certain disadvantage in having such a variety of features. To be compatible with the demands of as many users as possible, the program has to be equipped with a number of default settings that are useful in many working situations, such as the toolbar assignment with icons that a 'normal' *Word* user needs most frequently. To be able to use the program as efficiently as possible, you should customize it to suit your needs.

Word 2000 is compatible with both *Windows 98* and *Windows NT*. An adjustment to the respective environment may be necessary though, for example to set the default fonts, printer settings or mouse assignments.

Customizing Word

A large number of adjustments are possible in *Word* ranging from changing page settings and default fonts to setting toolbar and menu assignments.

Default Settings of Page Margins and Fonts

To customize *Word* to meet your personal requirements, start with the most important basic settings, which include the default page margins, font and size.

- You can specify the default setting of the margins for standard pages on the *Margins* tab page, accessible via *File/Page Setup*. Set the margins accordingly and click the *Default* button.

- The default setting for font and font size can be determined on the *Font* tab under *Format/Font*. Choose the desired font and size and click the *Default* button.

Another way to change default font and size, as well as other basic formatting such as line spacing and alignment, is by modifying the paragraph settings of the *Normal* style. Choose the *Style* item from the *Format* menu. In the *Style* dialog box select *Normal* from the *Styles* list box and click the *Modify* button. In the *Modify Style* dialog box check the *Add to template* check box and click the *Format* drop-down button.

Choose your option from the *Format* drop-down menu, make your adjustments and confirm with *OK*.

Automatically Setting the Space of Copied or Dragged Text

Copying and dragging text passages with the mouse is an extremely easy to handle and practical feature of *Word*, but it's an option that can cause you a headache if it has unintentionally been switched off.

The 'headache' we're referring to can happen whenever you copy or move text passages using drag-and-drop, and then at the insertion position find unnecessary spaces turning up.

Default selection of entire words

You have to manually erase these unnecessary spaces when this happens. But how do these unwanted spaces get there in the first place? There are two possible causes: either an option that we will explain later on has been unintentionally switched off, or the default selection of entire words is the source of the trouble. With this selection option *Word* extends the text passage you select up to the word which comes next and includes the space after the word in addition. If you drag or copy the text without the automatic space adjustment *Word* inserts the spaces too. This is how two spaces appear at the insertion point when only one is needed.

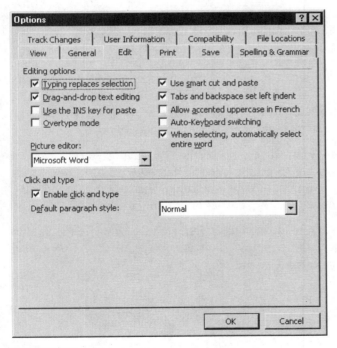

Fig. 15.1: The *Use smart cut and paste* option

Use smart cut and paste

To activate the automatic space adjustment when dragging and copying with the mouse, choose the *Options* command from the *Tools* menu. Activate the *Edit* tab page, check the *Use smart cut and paste* check box and confirm with *OK*.

Now *Word* will recognize any unnecessary spaces and erase them automatically whenever you copy or drag text using drag-and-drop.

Customizing the Recently Used File List in the *File* Menu

There are different ways to reopen saved *Word* documents for editing. If you often need to open recently saved or created files, this can be done very easily. *Word* keeps a list of the last four files you used on the *File* menu.

File list in the *File* menu

In the lower part of the *File* menu, next to the numbers '1' to '4' you will find the file names of the last four files you used, and probably their paths as well. To open one of these files just click the corresponding entry.

Tools/Options General tab

Word immediately opens the file, saving you the trouble of having to go through the *File/Open* dialog box. Once you have learned to appreciate this 'shortcut' you may discover that four entries are too few for this list.

We agree with you, so let's change that immediately. Select the *Options* command from the *Tools* menu and activate the *General* tab.

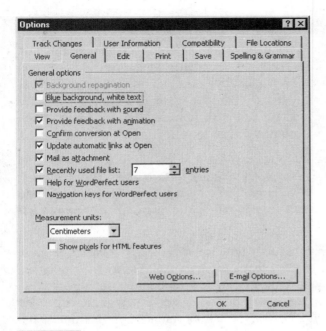

Fig. 15.2: Extending the Recently used file list

Recently used file list

Select, if necessary, the *Recently used file list* check box in the *General options* option group and increase the value in the text box with the spin buttons. A maximum of nine entries is allowed in the *Recently used file list*. Confirm with *OK*.

Before the new list in the *File* menu can be complete, the corresponding number of files have to have been saved. If you move a file to a different folder, *Word* will display an error message if you try to open the file via the *Recently used file list* because the path will no longer be valid.

567

Displaying System Information in Word

Word is able to provide important system information about your computer. No matter what type of information you need, *Word* has it – information about your printer driver, the sound card, the system, the memory or the amount and type of text converters and graphic filters. *Word* will show them all to you.

?

Microsoft System Information

Choose the *About Microsoft Word* option on the *Help* menu and click the *System Info* button. The *Microsoft System Information* window appears. The division into two panes is already familiar to us from the *Windows Explorer*.

And that's exactly how the *Microsoft System Information* can be used. Select a category and display the associated items with a click on the corresponding plus sign. All associated items will be displayed. To close the expanded view of a category, click the minus sign in front of the category name.

To get information about the system, printer or installed components, expand the view of the corresponding category and click on the entry you want.

In the right pane you'll get all the needed information. If there is no information available regarding a particular entry you'll get a message to this effect in the right pane. Close the *Microsoft System Information* dialog box with *File/Exit*, and then the *About Microsoft Word* dialog box with *OK*.

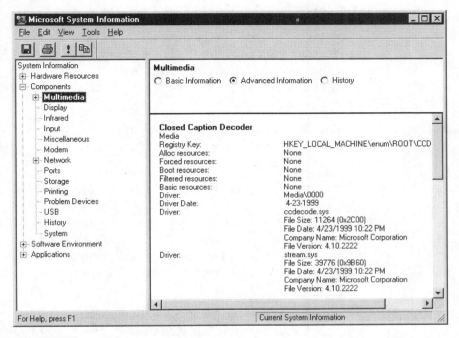

Fig. 15.3:   Gathered information about all components of the computer

File/Print

If you want to make a printout of the displayed information you can do so by choosing *File/Print*.

Customizing Toolbars to Suit your Personal Needs

Word is very flexible in its appearance. The most important commands appear as buttons on the different toolbars, ready to be used by a click of the mouse. In this
section you will learn to integrate into existing toolbars
often used commands as buttons and how to erase buttons which you rarely use from the toolbars.

Add or Remove
Buttons

The icons of a toolbar cannot all be displayed on the
screen. If you want to do so, you have to double-click on
the double arrow at the end of the toolbar. Then click on

the downward triangle and select the *Add or Remove Buttons* command. You then get a list of icons belonging to the same category. All the icons already displayed on the toolbar are marked with a tick. So, to display an icon still not shown on the toolbar, simply click on it and a tick mark will appear before its name.

Moving icons

To move an icon displayed on the toolbar to another position, keep the Alt key pressed and drag the icon to wherever you want it.

Customizing toolbars

If you want to insert icons of a different category in a toolbar, you can either display the toolbar(s) you want to customize or you can act directly on the *Standard* and *Formatting* toolbars displayed by default. Then select the *Customize* command from the *Toolbars* submenu on the *View* menu. Or activate the *Commands* tab page after selecting *Tools/Customize*.

Categories list box

Alternatively you can click the *Customize* command on the context menu of a displayed toolbar. The *Categories* list box appears on the left of the *Commands* tab page in the *Customize* dialog box. Here you find all *Word* commands sorted by category.

Description

Select the category from which you want to incorporate a command in the form of a button onto your toolbar. All available buttons in the selected category will be displayed in the right section of the dialog box. If you click on a button unfamiliar to you, you can obtain further information by clicking on the *Description* button.

Dragging a button onto the toolbar

When you have found the desired button, you can drag it, keeping the mouse button pressed, from the *Commands* tab onto any visible toolbar. Upon releasing the mouse button the new button will be inserted.

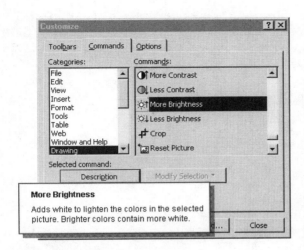

Fig. 15.4: The *Customize* dialog box

You can at any time place new buttons between already existing buttons. While you drag the button onto the toolbar, a vertical beam indicates the insertion position. Separations can be created by dragging a button slightly to the right. This way you can group buttons according to your needs.

Removing unnecessary buttons

Unnecessary buttons from default settings on the toolbars are very easy to remove. Just drag them, keeping the mouse button pressed down, from the toolbar into the *Customize* dialog box. Upon releasing the mouse button the superfluous button will be erased from the toolbar. Once you have inserted and removed all the buttons of your choosing, close the *Customize* dialog box.

The *All Commands* category contains all *Word* commands in their macro command syntax. You can also select *Fonts*, *AutoText* or *Styles* and drag them as buttons onto your toolbar.

If you want to modify the text or the glyph of a button, after inserting it into the toolbar, click the *Modify Selection* button. Choose the *Change Button Image* command and select a new icon from the palette.

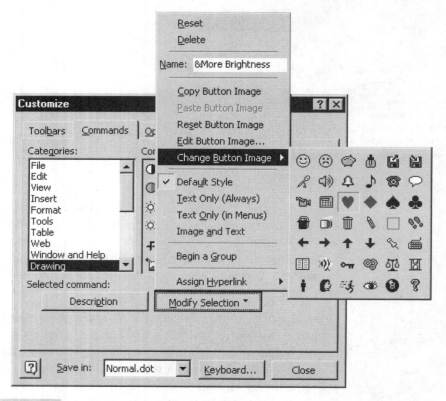

Fig. 15.5:   Modifying text or icon of a button

Button Editor   To create your own image or to change an existing one, select the *Edit Button Image* command in the *Modify Selection* menu. With the *Button Editor* you can change the design of the button.

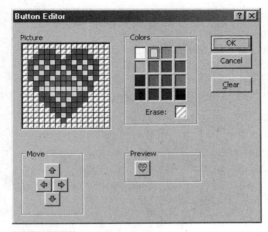

Fig. 15.6: The Button Editor

Close the *Button Editor* with *OK* and the *Customize* dialog box with *Close*.

Reset button image

To reset the modified button, select again *Tool/Customize*, click the button in question and open the *Modify Selection* drop-down menu. Choose the *Reset Button Image* command here.

If upon closing *Word* you get a message asking if you want to save the changes in the template, e.g. *Normal.dot*, confirm with *Yes*. Only then will the changes to the toolbars be saved.

Toolbars folder

Word always saves toolbars in templates. This isn't a problem as long as you create your documents on the basis of the *Word* default document that appears as soon as you start the program or every time you click on the *New* button. Any changes you make in the toolbars will be available in every document you create on the basis of this *Blank Document*.

Things are different, however, if you have customized your toolbars in another template, but want to use them in documents based on *Normal.dot* and vice versa.

The manner in which you can still use them in other documents will be explained later on in this chapter.

How to Create Your Own Toolbars and Fill Them with Buttons

Often used commands in *Word* can be incorporated as buttons into existing or new toolbars. In this section we will show you how to create your own toolbar and how to fill it with buttons of commands that you use frequently but that may not be found on the *Standard* or *Formatting* toolbars.

New toolbar

To create your own toolbars, choose the *Customize* option either from the *View/Toolbars* menu or in the context menu of a visible toolbar. On the *Toolbars* tab, click the *New* button.

Toolbar name

In the *New Toolbar* dialog box enter a name for the toolbar into the *Toolbar name* text box. Then click on *OK*.

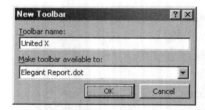

Fig. 15.7:   Entering a name for a toolbar

Make toolbar available to

From the *Make toolbar available to* drop-down list, choose the location where the new toolbar should be saved. If right now, for example, a document is open that has been created on the basis of one of the templates provided with *Word*, you can choose whether the toolbar should be available only in this document or in all documents based on the template *Blank document* (*Normal. dot*). Make your choice and confirm with *OK*.

Commands tab

Categories

Word creates a new empty toolbar with the name you have given. In the *Customize* dialog box activate the *Commands* tab. On the left side of the *Commands* tab page you find the *Categories* list box which contains a thematically sorted list of all *Word* commands.

Dragging buttons

on the new toolbar

Select a category from which you want to insert a command onto your toolbar in the form of a button. All available buttons of this category will be displayed in the right list box. If you click a button unfamiliar to you, you can get information about it by clicking on the *Description* button. A selected button can be dragged from the *Customize* dialog box to your toolbar with the mouse button held down. As soon as you release the mouse button the command button will be inserted.

Fig. 15.8:   Inserting buttons into a new toolbar

You can now choose more buttons from the same category or change categories. The size of the toolbar will be automatically adjusted, but you can also change it using the toolbar border.

If there are already buttons on your toolbar you can insert new buttons between them.

Fig. 15.9: The mouse pointer while dragging a button to the toolbar

A dashed button indicates the insertion position. Separators can be created by selecting a button from the toolbar and dragging it a bit to the right. In this way you can group the buttons according to subject.

Buttons that are unnecessary or inserted by mistake can be dragged, with the mouse button held down, from the toolbar back into the *Customize* dialog box. Upon releasing the mouse button, the unwanted button will be erased from the toolbar.

Modify Selection

By clicking the *Modify Selection* drop-down button you'll find a list with various options to change the button. You can for example change the name, choose a different image or create an image of your own. Once you have inserted all the buttons onto your toolbar, leave the *Customize* dialog box by choosing *Close*.

Making Toolbars Available to Other Documents

Frequently used *Word* commands can be inserted into existing or custom toolbars at any time. In this chapter we will deal with a peculiarity of *Word* that might cause you some trouble when you are using modified or customized toolbars.

Saving toolbars in templates

Word saves certain elements in templates. These elements include *Styles*, *AutoText* entries, macros and new or customized *Toolbars*.

Templates and Add-Ins

To make new or customized toolbars available to other templates, you have to copy the toolbars from the template in which they were created to the template in which you want to use them. Open a document based on the template in which the toolbars are saved and choose the *Templates and Add-Ins* command from the *Tools* menu.

Click the *Organizer* button in the *Templates and Add-Ins* dialog box. Switch to the *Toolbars* tab inside the dialog box that appears.

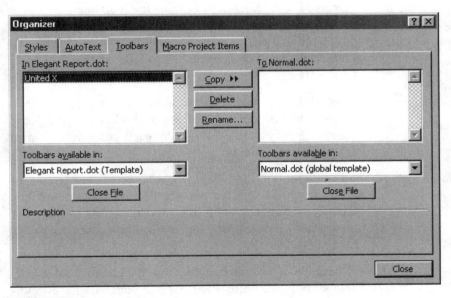

Fig. 15.10:   Organizing your own and customized toolbars

The other tabs show all elements saved in the template. On the *Toolbars* tab the current template appears in the *Toolbars available in* drop-down list. In the list box above you will see all saved toolbars.

Close File

Open File

Word assumes that these entries are not saved in the global template *Normal.dot* and offers you this template as the copy destination in the right-hand section. If you want to copy your toolbars from the current template to a template other than the *Normal.dot*, click the *Close File* button on the right and the *Open File* button that appears immediately afterwards.

Templates folder

The *Open* dialog box shows the contents of the *Word* templates folder *C:\Windows\Application Data\Microsoft\Templates*.

Opening the subfolder

Open the subfolder that contains the template into which you want to copy the toolbars. Select the corresponding template and click *Open*. The toolbars saved in this template will be shown on the right side of the *Organizer* dialog box.

Selecting toolbars

The right list box only contains customized toolbars. Now select all desired toolbars in the left list box. Keep the Ctrl key pressed and click each entry you want to copy, one after the other.

Copying toolbar entries

By moving the mouse downwards the visible section of the list will be selected and scrolled automatically. Click the *Copy* button to copy the toolbar entries to the other template. If necessary, repeat this procedure for other templates.

Leave the *Organizer* dialog box by clicking on *Close*. Now your custom toolbars and the ones you have modified will also be displayed whenever you use the other template.

Resetting Customized Toolbars

Word is very adaptable when it comes to displayed screen elements. This is true especially for toolbars that can easily be customized according to your personal needs.

Here you'll come to know how to reset the changes you have made and how to restore the default settings of the toolbar.

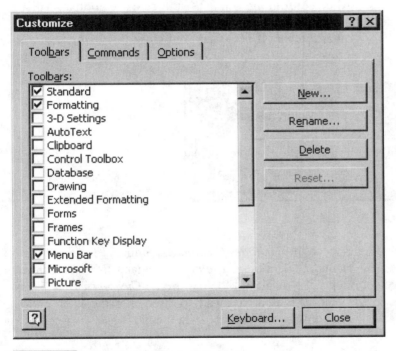

Fig. 15.11:   Resetting customized toolbars

Reset

Choose *Toolbars/Customize* from the *View* menu or, from the context menu of a visible toolbar, select the *Customize* command. Select the toolbar you want to reset from the *Toolbars* list box on the *Toolbars* tab page. Click the *Reset* button.

The *Reset Toolbar* dialog box appears. Choose the template to which you want to apply the reset operation from the *Reset changes made to [Name] toolbar for* drop-down list. Choose *Normal.dot* if the changes should affect all new documents based on the *Blank Document* type.

After confirming with *OK*, the selected toolbar will be reset to its default setting. Repeat the operation with other toolbars if necessary and close the dialog box with *Close*.

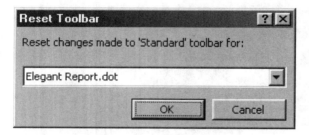

Fig. 15.12: Selecting templates to reset

Choose the *Toolbars/Customize* command from the *View* menu or select the *Customize* command from the context menu of a displayed toolbar. In the *Customize* dialog box select the toolbar you want to reset, click the *Reset* button and confirm the message with *OK*.

Customizing Menus and Menu Items

On the menu bar, the most important commands are available according to subject, listed under the menu entries. In a menu the commands are sorted by groups according to their function.

The grouping and the arrangement of the commands follows the *Word* standard and is the same in all *Microsoft Office* programs.

In the *File* menu you will always find the *Open*, *Close* and *Save* commands. But *Word* allows you to change the menus or single items on the menu.

If you want to insert additional commands or delete unnecessary ones, select the *Customize* command from the *Tools* menu. Choose the *Commands* tab.

Select an entry in the *Categories* list box. All available *Word* commands in this category will be displayed in the *Commands* list box. Further information about the selected command can be obtained by clicking on the *Description* button.

Drag a command, while keeping the mouse button pressed down, onto a menu name. The menu will open. You can then place the command at the position where you want it to appear in future.

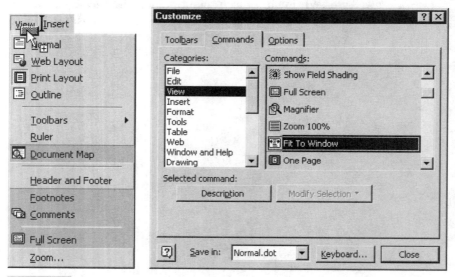

Fig. 15.13: Adding and deleting menu entries

To remove a menu entry that isn't needed, just drag it from the menu into the open *Customize* dialog box. In this way you can add all the other commands which you need to the menu and delete all those which you don't need.

Modify Selection

You can display the image of a command and its name on the menu. These and other settings can be changed as soon as you have inserted a new command onto a menu. To do this, use the items in the *Modify Selection* drop-down menu.

You can also make these changes later on by opening the *Customize* dialog box from the *Tools* menu, selecting the command in question, and then clicking the *Modify Selection* button.

New menu

To create your own menus, select the *New Menu* item at the bottom of the *Categories* list and drag the *New Menu* command onto the menu bar. After that you can change the *New Menu* default name of the menu using the *Modify Selection* button.

Deleting a menu

If you want to delete an entire menu, just drag it from the menu bar into the open *Customize* dialog box.

Resetting menus

You can reset a customized menu whenever you want. Choose the *Toolbars* tab under *Tools/Customize*. Check the *Menu Bar* check box in the *Toolbars* list box, click the *Reset* button and confirm with *OK*.

Confirm all menu changes with *Close*. If, while closing *Word*, you get a message asking you whether the changes in the template should be saved, you should by all means confirm with *Yes*.

Assigning and Changing Shortcut Keys for Commands

Many commands can be selected from the *Word* menus using the mouse. You can also select them without having to open a menu by using key combinations.

This is especially useful in a word processing program because your hands are already on the keyboard while you are typing in text.

The *shortcuts* help to avoid the constant switching back and forth between keyboard and mouse.

It is evident that you have to know the shortcut keys by heart in order to work efficiently with them. *Word* always displays the programmed key combinations next to the command in the menu.

But you can also create your own *shortcuts* or assign shortcut keys to *Word* functions that do not have a *shortcut* by default.

Keyboard

If you want to create custom or additional *shortcuts* choose the *Customize* command from the *Tools* menu and click the *Keyboard* button.

Current keys

First select an entry in the *Categories* list box. All available *Word* commands in the selected category will be displayed in the *Commands* list box. Information about the selected command can be read in the *Description* section. Available shortcut keys are displayed in the *Current keys* list box.

Press new shortcut key

If you want to assign a shortcut to a command, select the corresponding entry in the *Commands* list box, then click the *Press new shortcut key* text box.

Now type the intended key combination into the *Press new shortcut key* text box. Check whether, below the text box, a message saying *Currently assigned to: [command]* is displayed.

Assign

If so, either insert a different key combination or over-write the old one by clicking on the *Assign* button.

In this way you can assign a key combination to the desired commands in the various categories one after the other.

Select the category from the *Categories* list and choose the desired command under *Commands*. Confirm each action with *Assign*.

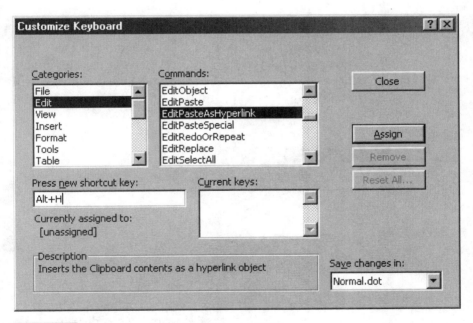

Fig. 15.14: Assigning shortcut keys to commands

Reset all

With a click on the *Reset All* button and then by confirming with *Yes*, you can reset all the changes you have made.

Save changes in

Customized or newly created shortcuts are saved by default in the *Blank Document* template. This is the document type that is automatically called up when you start *Word*. If you want to save the shortcut in a different file, choose one from the *Save changes in* drop-down list. In this case the customized or new shortcuts will be valid only in that template or file.

Confirm with Yes

A click on *Close* confirms the changes. If while closing *Word*, you get a message asking you whether the changes should be saved in the template, you should definitely click on *Yes*.

Displaying the Key Combination as a *ScreenTip*

If you don't know the name of a button on one of the toolbars displayed in *Word*, just point at the button with the mouse. After about one second a small text box will be displayed containing the name of the button. This information is called a *ScreenTip*.

Fig. 15.15: The ScreenTip of the *Save* button

ScreenTip

But *Word* is also able to provide more information on a *ScreenTip*. If you want to know which shortcut you can use to activate the corresponding command using keys rather than mouse clicks, you can have it displayed as a *ScreenTip*. Many commands that can be selected with a mouse-click on a toolbar button can also be activated with shortcut keys.

This is especially useful in a word processing program because your hands are already on the keyboard when you're typing in text.

Shortcuts in *Word* can help you to avoid the bothersome switching back and forth between the keyboard and the mouse.

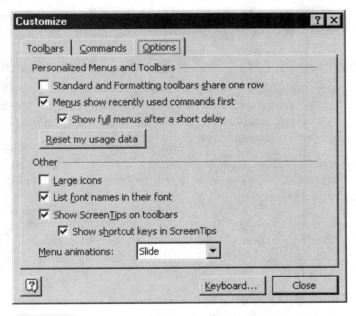

Fig. 15.16:   Displaying the key combination as ScreenTip

Show shortcut
keys in ScreenTips

To display the shortcuts in the *ScreenTips*, choose the *Customize* command from the *View/Toolbars* menu. Check the *Show shortcut keys in ScreenTips* check box on the *Options* tab page and confirm with *OK*.

Fig. 15.17: ScreenTip with shortcut key

If now you point with the mouse at a button that represents a command for which there is also a shortcut key, it will be displayed in the *ScreenTip*.

Editing User Information

For some program features, *Word* needs to know certain personal information about you. A document is, for example, saved with the name of the author to distinguish it from further editing by other authors.

Another reason is so that your address can be inserted into letters or envelopes, or when you are using initials to mark comments.

You may ask yourself how *Word* already knows certain information about you, such as your name. The answer is simple: *Word* uses the personal data you entered during installation.

But the personal data that *Word* uses for certain features may also be viewed and modified later on. To do this, select the *Options* command from the *Tools* menu.

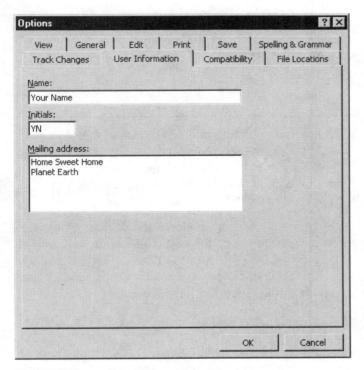

Fig. 15.18:   Editing the User Information

User Information tab

Activate the *User Information* tab. Insert your name into the *Name* text box. This entry will be used in the *Properties* dialog box of the *File* menu, on letters and envelopes, as well as to trace any changes and mark all comments in a document.

This name will be inserted automatically into the *Author* box on the *Summary* tab page in the *Properties* dialog when a new document is created.

Type the initials that you want to use for your *Comments (Insert/Comments)* as well as for various predefined letter and memo templates into the *Initials* text box.

Address

Type the default address that should be used for letters and envelopes into the *Address* text box. Confirm the changes and entries with *OK*.

Customizing Windows

Each program which runs under *Windows* is not only affected by the settings you specify in the program itself, but also by the *Windows* settings. In word processing programs such as *Word*, for example, the date format or the installed fonts of *Windows* are relevant.

Other important settings concern the devices you use to insert and edit text, i.e., the keyboard and the mouse. The display properties, the cursor's blinking rate, the repeat rate, the double-click speed, the button configuration, etc. are all under the control of *Windows*.

Keyboard Settings and Cursor Blink Rate in Windows 98

The keyboard is the most important feature of the computer when it comes to inserting text. That's why a perfect adjustment to your personal needs is so important. Unfortunately, very few users give it any thought and just go on working with the default settings of *Windows 98* for the rest of their lives.

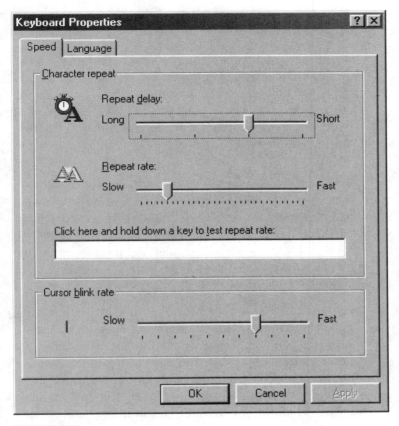

Fig. 15.19:   Setting the cursor blink rate

These default settings of *Windows 98* are also valid for *Word*. Therefore you don't need a *Word* function to customize the keyboard settings since you can do this by using the *Windows Control Panel*.

Control Panel

Click the *Start* button and choose the *Settings* item. Select *Control Panel.* from the submenu and double-click the *Keyboard* icon in the *Control Panel* folder window.

591

Speed

You can modify the settings to suit your personal needs on the *Speed* tab page.

Move the slider in the *Cursor blink rate* group box to change the rate at which the cursor blinks. You can preview the blink rate on the left of the slider. Increasing the cursor's blink rate may help you to find the position of the cursor more easily in your *Word* documents. Confirm the changes with *OK*.

Swapping the Left and Right Mouse Button

Although you type your text into *Word* using the keyboard, a suitable pointing device such as a mouse is almost indispensable for graphic interfaces. In this and the following section we will explain the procedures for the classic mouse. If you are using a different pointer such as a *Trackball*, the steps indicated also apply.

Mouse settings for left-handers

As the mouse is a very important tool in *Word* for formatting and for selecting commands, you should make sure that you feel absolutely comfortable with this electronic rodent. Experience has shown that is not easy for left-handed people to work with the mouse, through no fault of their own, of course, since the default mouse setting in *Windows 98* is meant for right-handers.

Button configuration

As you may have already guessed, it doesn't have to stay that way. Naturally the mouse can be configured to suit left-handed people. To change the button configuration, you don't need a *Word* function but rather the *Windows Control Panel*. Point to the *Settings* option on the *Start* menu and click *Control Panel* in the submenu. In the *Control Panel* folder window, double-click the *Mouse* icon shown in Figure 15.20.

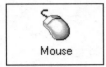

Mouse

Fig. 15.20: The *Mouse* icon in the *Control Panel* folder window

Button configuration

Now activate the *Buttons* tab of the *Mouse Properties* dialog box. To set the button configuration for left-handed people, click the *Left-handed* radio button in the *Button configuration* section.

Be careful!
This change takes immediate effect as soon as you close the dialog box. From then on you have to click the **right** mouse button instead of the left.

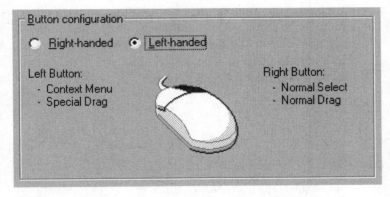

Fig. 15.21: Changing the button configuration to left-handed

Setting the Double-click Speed

Without a proper pointer you are pretty lost in the graphic interface of *Word*. But even the best mouse should be configured according to your personal preferences. Especially in the beginning many users have difficulty with the double-click speed. Double-clicking means pressing the left mouse button twice in rapid succession. This is the fastest and easiest way to select items or to open documents.

Double-click speed

If you are having difficulty with the double click in *Word* in the beginning, the reason is usually because the interval between the two mouse clicks is too long. The timing between both clicks is called the *Double-click speed*. Even this can be customized in the *Control Panel*.

To change the *Double-click speed*, point to the *Settings* option on the *Start* menu and click on *Control Panel* in the submenu. In the *Control panel* folder window, double-click the *Mouse* icon shown in Figure 15.22. The *Mouse Properties* dialog box opens.

Fig. 15.22: Double-click on this icon to open the *Mouse Properties* dialog box

Activate the *Buttons* tab and, keeping the mouse button pressed down, drag the slider in the *Double-click speed* group box in the desired direction. For beginners it is recommended to move rather in the *Slow* direction. To test the new setting, double-click in the *Test area*.

Test area

If the *Double-click speed* is correct, a Jack-in-the-box will jump out. If this funny little fellow doesn't turn up, then adjust the *Double-click speed* until he is visible in the *Test area*. When you feel comfortable with the *Double-click speed*, confirm the changes with *OK*.

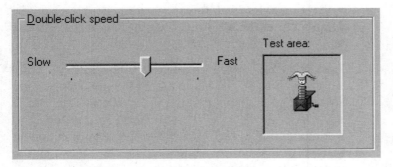

Fig. 15.23:   With the slider you can set the Double-click speed

Setting Pointer Trails for Notebook Computers

The graphic interface of *Word* makes word processing a comfortable affair even on portable PCs. To work with *Word* on notebook computers, a suitable pointing device such as a mouse is also required. If your notebook provides an integrated pointer such as a *Trackball*, *Trackpoint* or *TouchPad*, all work steps described below also apply.

The mouse pointer on notebooks

On notebook computers with a passive matrix display (LCD-Display, *DualScan*, etc.) it is often difficult to see the mouse pointer, especially to follow its fast movements. No need to blame your eyes. This disadvantage is due to the sluggishness of the passive matrix LCD display.

To solve this problem, once again we don't use a *Word* feature but the *Windows Control Panel*. If you have difficulties following the mouse pointer on your notebook screen, point at the *Settings* item in the *Start* menu and click the *Control Panel* option in the submenu.

In the *Control Panel* folder window double-click the *Mouse* icon. In the *Mouse Properties* dialog box activate the *Motion* tab page.

Show pointer trails   Check the *Show pointer trails* check box in the *Pointer trail* group box. If you move the mouse now, the pointer carries a kind of comet tail that makes it easier for you to follow its movements. If the trail is too long or too short for you, pull the slider in the respective direction to lengthen or shorten it, while keeping the mouse button pressed down. Then click *Apply* and move the mouse again to test the adjustment. Confirm the changes with *OK*.

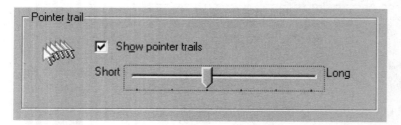

Fig. 15.24:   With the slider you can change the length of the trail

Pointer speed   In the *Pointer speed* group box you set the ratio between the mouse movement on the mouse pad and the pointer movement. With a *Slow* setting you need more space for the mouse, while *Fast* means that the pointer follows even the smallest movements of the mouse.

With the *Fast* setting it might be more difficult to place the pointer in a precise position. Confirm your adjustments with *OK* and close the *Control Panel*.

Displaying Installed Fonts in Windows 98

In *Windows 98* and in programs such as *Word*, two types of system fonts are used. These are the so-called *Bitmap* fonts and the much more efficient *TrueType* fonts.

What are
***Bitmap* fonts?**

Bitmap fonts are grid fonts. For each font size a separate file with the necessary information for each character is required. *Bitmap* fonts, like pixel graphics, consist of separate points. On printouts they appear jagged. That's why *Bitmap* fonts are generally only used as screen fonts.

What are
***TrueType* fonts?**

TrueType Fonts, on the other hand, are free scalable vector fonts. Only the mathematical function of the outline has to be saved in the font file. Using this font file *Windows 98* or *Word* can create these fonts in any size.

The biggest advantage of *TrueType Fonts* is the fact that they are displayed on the screen exactly the way they will look on the printout. This principle is called *WYSIWYG* (What you see is what you get).

Also, *TrueType* fonts are of a much higher quality than *Bitmap* fonts, regardless of their size.

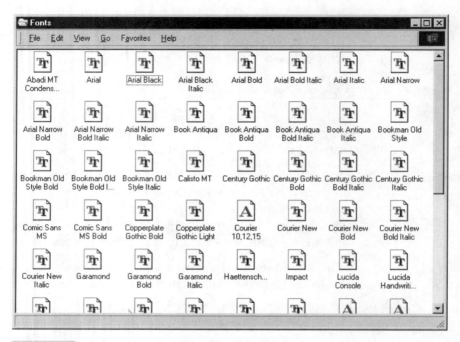

Fig. 15.25: Displaying the available Word fonts

Control Panel/
Fonts

To see a list of all the fonts available in *Word,* double-click the *Fonts* icon in the *Control Panel* folder window. In the list of the *Fonts* folder window, all installed fonts are displayed using special icons. For scalable *TrueType Fonts* the double-T icon 𝐓𝐓 is used. *Bitmap* fonts are represented by the icon: A.

You can change the way the *Fonts* list is displayed using the *View* menu. The *View* command is also available in the context menu, accessible via the right mouse button. In Figure 15.25 you see the *Large Icons* view. With the *Details* option you get further information regarding the *File name*, *Size* and the date when it was last *Modified*. If a large number of fonts are installed, the *List* view is probably the most suitable.

Printing Font Samples in Windows 98

If you are installing new fonts for *Word*, after some time there will be a large number of fonts on your computer. Handling such a large number of fonts with the *Font* drop-down list on the *Formatting* toolbar and re-membering what they all look like is difficult, even for professionals.

But you can use a *Windows 98* function to display a sample of the installed font and to make a printout if you wish.

Control Panel/
Fonts

Open the *Control Panel* folder window via *Start/Settings* and double-click the *Fonts* icon to display the *Fonts* folder. Here you get a list of all installed fonts. If necessary, change the display style in the *View* menu, choosing for example the *Large Icons* option.

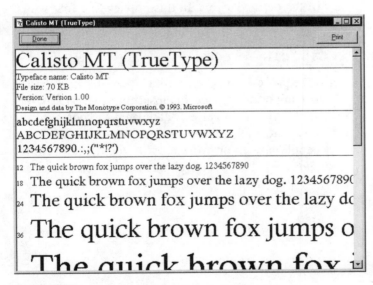

Fig. 15.26:   Getting a font preview on the screen

To get a preview of a font, just double-click the font icon or the font name in the list.

Open

Another way of doing the same thing is to select the font you're interested in and choose the *Open* command on the *File* menu or in the context menu. The font sample with the sample text, 'The quick brown fox jumps ...' will be displayed in a separate window. You can enlarge the window if necessary or use the scroll bars.

Done

By clicking the *Done* button you will find yourself back in the *Fonts* folder. Click the *Print* button instead if you want to make a printout of the font sample. The *Print* command is also available in the context menu and the *File* menu but without the display of the font sample. Print all desired fonts and close the *Control Panel*.

In the *Style* drop-down list of *Word 2000* you get a preview of the defined styles. In this preview the font which is in use and its formatting are displayed.

Customizing the Key Settings in Windows 98

In a word processing program like *Word* the keyboard is the most important device for inserting text. That's reason enough to have it perfectly adjusted to your personal needs. Unfortunately, it occurs to only very few users and most people just go on working with the default settings of *Windows 98*. These settings are also applied in *Word*.

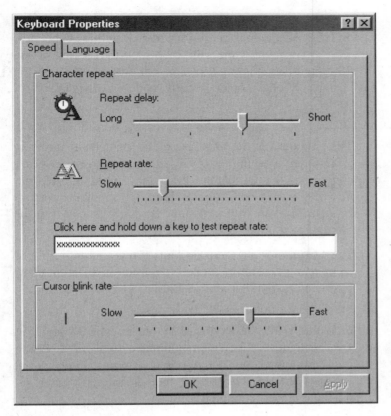

Fig. 15.27: Setting the Repeat delay and the Repeat rate of the keyboard

Control Panel

Keyboard

You don't need a *Word* command to change the keyboard configuration, just the *Windows 98 Control Panel*. To get there, point to the *Settings* option on the *Start* menu and click *Control Panel* in the submenu. In the *Control Panel* folder window, double-click the *Keyboard* icon. On the *Speed* tab page you can change the settings according to your preference.

Repeat delay

Repeat rate

Pull the slider under *Repeat delay* to fix the interval between the time a key is pressed and the time it will be repeated if you keep the key pressed down. Pull the slider under *Repeat rate* to set the speed at which the characters will be repeated while you keep the key pressed down. After clicking in the text box below you can test the changes you have made. Finally, confirm with *OK*.

Changing the Language of the Keyboard Layout

The keyboard is the most important device for inserting text while working with *Word*. But in almost every country in the world, the keyboard layout is different. The reason may be historical, but often special characters or signs are part of a particular language and have to be incorporated in the keyboard.

The Germans have their Umlauts (vowel mutations), the languages in eastern Europe have a lot of different characters and a Turkish and an English keyboard have little in common except the number of keys.

Language = Keyboard layout

In *Windows 98* the keyboard layout is called *Language*. To configure the keyboard language you don't need a *Word* command, just the *Windows Control Panel*. Point on the *Settings* option on the *Start* menu and click *Control Panel* in the submenu.

Language tab

In the *Control Panel* folder window double-click the *Keyboard* icon. On the *Language* tab, change the language according to your needs. You may, for example, need the layout of a different language on your English keyboard.

Fig. 15.28: Setting the keyboard language

The current language is displayed highlighted in the *Language* list box. If you want to change the keyboard language, click the *Add* button and choose your language from the drop-down list. Confirm with *OK*. The new language will appear in the *Language* list.

Switch languages   If you want to be able to easily switch between languages, select the desired shortcut radio button in the *Switch languages* option group and check the *Enable indicator on taskbar* check box. Then confirm with *OK*.

If you need the keyboard layout of the added language, either press the chosen key combination or click the keyboard language icon on the taskbar and choose the desired keyboard language from the menu.

Displaying Only *TrueType* Fonts in the *Font* List

Word uses two different font types: *Bitmap* fonts and the much more effective *TrueType* fonts, which are free scalable vector fonts. Only the mathematical function of the outline has to be saved in the font file. Using this font file *Word* can create fonts in any size.

TrueType Fonts

But the biggest advantage of *TrueType Fonts* is the fact that they are displayed on the screen exactly the way they will look on the printout. This principle is called *WYSIWYG* (What you see is what you get). *TrueType* fonts also have a much higher quality than *Bitmap* fonts, regardless of the size.

Bitmap Fonts

Bitmap fonts on the other hand are grid fonts. For each font size a separate file with the necessary information for each character is required. *Bitmap* fonts consist, like pixel graphics, of separate points. On printouts they can appear with somewhat jagged edges. That's why *Bitmap* fonts are used in general only as screen fonts.

We recommend to use the much more adaptable and efficient *TrueType* fonts in *Word*. To display only *TrueType* fonts in the *Font* drop-down list, you don't need a *Word* command but you have to use the *Windows Control Panel*.

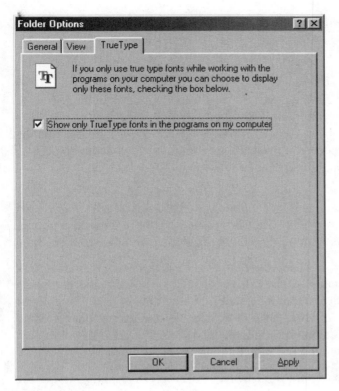

Fig. 15.29:   Show only *TrueType* fonts in Word

Show only
TrueType fonts
in the programs on
my computer

Choose *Start/Settings/Control Panel* and double-click the *Fonts* icon in the *Control Panel* folder window. In the *Fonts* folder all the available fonts are displayed. Choose the *Folder Options* command from the *View* menu, switch to the *TrueType* tab, check the *Show only TrueType fonts in the programs on my computer* check box and confirm with *OK*.

The changes will only take effect after your computer re-starts. Confirm the corresponding message with *Yes* to allow your computer to restart. Then test the changes in the *Font* list of *Word*.

Listing Fonts in Windows 98 by Similarity

The *Fonts* folder

To get a list of all available fonts on your computer use the *Windows Control Panel*. Go there via *Start/Settings/Control Panel* and double-click the *Fonts* icon in the *Control Panel* folder window. In the list of the *Fonts* folder all installed fonts are displayed in the form of special icons. For scalable *TrueType* fonts the double-T icon T is used. *Bitmap* fonts are represented by the A icon.

View

You can change the view of the *Fonts* list using the *View* menu. The *View* command is also available in the context menu which you can access with the right mouse button. You will see the *List Fonts By Similarity* item.

If you select the *List Fonts By Similarity* command, all installed fonts will be displayed in a list and compared with the font indicated in the text box of the *List fonts by similarity to* drop-down list. To change the font you want to compare, open the *List fonts by similarity to* drop-down list and select a font name.

Very similar

Next to the font names in the big list box you will see comments such as *Very similar*, *Fairly similar* and *Not similar*. Compare for example *Arial*, a font that has no serifs, with the serif font *Times New Roman*.

You will get the comment *Not similar*. This view affords typographically inexperienced users a first font comparison which is especially useful if a large number of fonts are installed on your computer. Close *Fonts* window and then the *Control Panel* with *File/Close*.

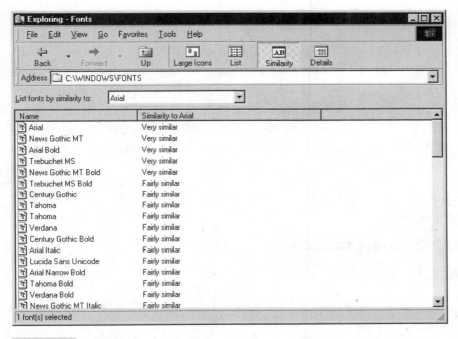

Exploring - Fonts
File   Edit   View   Go   Favorites   Tools   Help
Back   Forward   Up   Large Icons   List   Similarity   Details
Address C:\WINDOWS\FONTS
List fonts by similarity to: Arial

Fig. 15.30   Listing fonts by similarity

Adding and Deleting Fonts for Word

Windows 98 and its programs use so-called *TrueType Fonts*. *TrueType Fonts* are free scalable vector fonts of which only the mathematical formula of the outline has to be saved in the font file. This saves memory and, in addition, allows the computer to display the fonts in any size without sacrificing the quality.

TTF-Fonts

Many applications provide their own *TrueType* fonts which are installed during the setup. The *CorelDRAW!* graphics package, for example, contains 1,000 *TrueType* fonts. *Word* itself or the *Office Suite* also provide some new *TrueType* fonts.

If you want to install additional fonts from a CD or a floppy, don't just copy the font files onto your computer. To make the fonts available to *Word* and *Windows 98*, open the *Control Panel* via *Start/Settings* or via *My Computer*. In the *Control Panel* folder window, double-click the *Fonts* icon to open the *Fonts* folder.

Install New Font

Choose the *Install New Font* command from the *File* menu. In the *Add Fonts* dialog box, use the *Drives* and *Folders* list boxes to switch to the source folder of the new font. *Windows 98* then searches the folder for available fonts and displays the font names in the *List of fonts*.

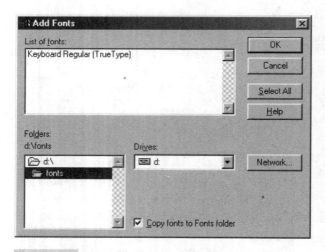

Fig. 15.31: Installing new fonts for Word

Select the desired font (to select more than one font, use the ⟨⬦⟩ or ⟨Ctrl⟩ keys). If you want to install all fonts in the list, click the *Select All* button. Once you have made your selection, confirm the installation with *OK*. Now check in the *Fonts* folder whether it contains the new fonts.

Copy fonts to
Fonts folder

Make sure that the *Copy fonts to Fonts folder* check box is selected. Only when this option is checked will the fonts be saved in the *C:\Windows\Fonts* folder.

Immediately after installation, the new fonts should be available in the *Font* drop-down list on the *Formatting* toolbar. If this isn't the case, close *Word* and restart *Windows 98*. Now the fonts will definitely be available.

If, after some time, there are hundreds of fonts on your computer, you may ask yourself how to get rid of the ones you don't need. Each font file takes up memory, adds to the time of loading when you start *Windows* and makes the *Font* list on the *Formatting* toolbar confusing.

Deleting Fonts

If you are only using specific fonts you can delete the unnecessary fonts from your hard disk. But to delete the undesired fonts, you shouldn't just delete the font files. There are two reasons for this: First, it is very difficult to make sure that you are deleting the right files because in some cases it is impossible to recognize the font name from the file name. Or did you already know that the *TT1024M_.TTF* file corresponds to the *Futura MD BT* font? Second, you also have to delete the link to the *Fonts* folder.

To make sure that *Word* does not display the unnecessary font, open the *Control Panel* via *Start/Settings* or via *My Computer*. In the *Control Panel* folder window double-click the *Fonts* icon to open the *Fonts* folder.

Delete

If there are many fonts installed on your computer it might be useful to switch to the *List* view. Select the font you want to delete (to select more than one font, use the `⇧` or `Ctrl` keys). To delete the font press `Del` or choose the *Delete* command from the *File* menu or the context menu. Confirm the *Are you sure you want to delete this font* message with *Yes*. The selected fonts will be sent to the *Recycle Bin*.

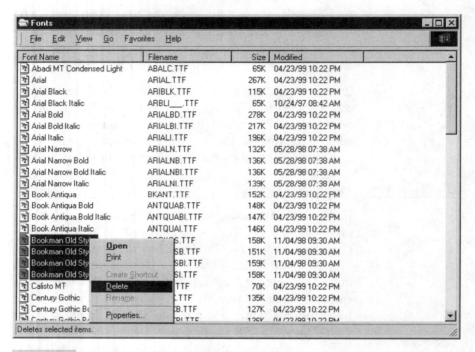

Fig. 15.32: Deleting unnecessary *TrueType* fonts

Emptying the Recycle Bin

To erase the fonts for good and thus gain more free space on your hard disk, you should empty the *Recycle Bin* once in a while. Point on the *Recycle Bin* icon, press the right mouse button and select the *Empty Recycle Bin* command.

Confirm the message with *Yes* to delete the fonts.

Installation

Before you can start to work with *Word* you have to install the program files on the hard disk of your computer. Of course you don't have to do this manually. The setup program helps you. *Windows 98* has been installed in the same way, either by you or your computer dealer. You can install the full program with all its components or customize the installation. Depending on which option you choose, the number of files copied to your computer will be larger or smaller.

In the standard installation only the most needed files, templates, tools and conversion programs are copied. However, the Word and Office package has become so extensive that Microsoft has found a new method for installation. In the Office 2000 package, components can be installed so as to be loaded only when they are called up for the first time. This means that they are displayed on your PC, but they cannot be accessed unless you put the CD-ROM in the drive to load the required files.

If, after working with *Word* for some time, you discover that a component is missing, you can be sure that it was excluded deliberately from installation, but you can load it whenever you want.

Installing Additional Word Components

Add/Remove Programs

Under *Windows 98* starting the setup program is downright easy. To install *Word* components on your computer select the *Settings* item from the *Start* menu and open the *Control Panel* folder window. Here double-click the *Add/Remove Programs* icon. In the *Add/Remove Programs Properties* dialog box, activate the *Install/Uninstall* tab.

Insert the first program disk or the setup CD-ROM in its drive. Select the *Microsoft Office 2000 Premium* entry and click the *Add/Remove* button.

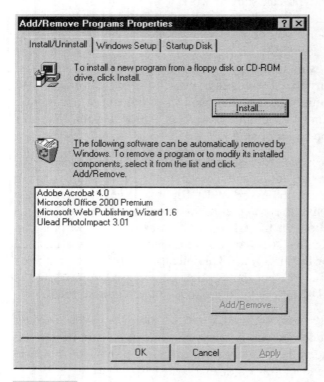

Fig. 15.33: Installation of additional Word components

Add or Remove
Features

The setup program searches for already installed components. If the *Office Shortcut Bar* is running you'll be advised to close it. After a while the Office 2000 *Maintenance mode* appears. Then click the *Add or Remove Features* button to choose the components.

First select the program to which new components have to be added. If the *Office Suite* is installed, select the

Change Option

Microsoft Word 2000 Premium entry. Then click on the plus sign before the program name to display all the components of the program. The icon appearing before the name of a component shows how that component has been installed. The hard disk icon means that all the setup files of this component have been loaded on the hard disk. If 1 is displayed on the hard disk icon, this means that the files are loaded only after calling up the corresponding component for the first time. X means that the component has not been installed. If a CD icon appears, the component is always read from the CD. The advantage of this option is that it does not take up any memory space on the hard disk, but obviously you always have to put the CD into the CD-ROM drive.

Grey background

If the hard disk icon appears on a grey background, this means that not all parts of a component are installed. Click on the plus sign before the component to display all its parts. If you want to choose another type of installation, click on the installation icon before the name of the component. You will see a menu where you can choose the type of installation you want.

Confirm your changes by clicking on *Update now*.

Now restart *Word* to check if all new components are available. If this is not the case, then restart *Windows 98*.

If you cannot find the entry for *Word* in the list box of the *Install/Uninstall* tab or if you get an error message after clicking *Add/Remove*, start the setup program with the *SETUP.EXE* from the root of the CD.

Installing Additional Conversion Programs and Graphics Filters

With the standard installation most conversion programs and graphics filters are installed so that they are loaded on the hard disk only when you call up the option for the first time. If you need a filter which has not yet been installed you will get a message asking you to insert the CD-ROM in the drive. If you do not get any message but you still cannot load the file, this means that the corresponding filter is probably not available and you have to install it manually.

Add/Remove Programs

To install *Word* components on your computer, select the *Settings* option from the *Start* menu and open the *Control Panel* folder window. Double-click the *Add/Remove Programs* icon. In the *Add/Remove Programs Properties* dialog box select the *Install/Uninstall* tab.

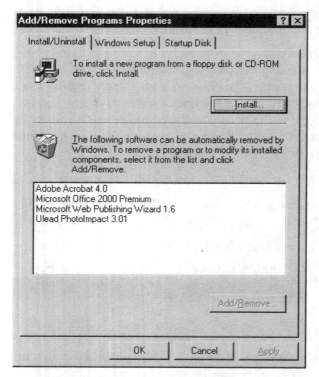

Fig. 15.34:   Installing additional conversion programs

Select the *Microsoft Office 2000 Premium* entry and click the *Add/Remove* button. Put the first program disk or the setup CD-ROM into the corresponding drive and confirm with *OK*.

The setup program searches for already installed components of *Word*. If the *Office Shortcut Bar* is running you will be advised to close it. After a while you will get the Office 2000 Maintenance mode. Then click the *Add or Remove Features* button.

Change Option

In the *Microsoft Office - Maintenance* dialog box check the *Converters and Filters* radio buttons and again click *Change Option*. In the next dialog box activate the *Text Converters* check box if you were not able to open documents of other word processing programs in *Word*. Select the *Graphics Filters* check box if *Word* was unable to open a graphic file via *Insert/Picture*.

Modify the installation setting for the desired filter by clicking on the icon before the corresponding filter name. Carry out the changes by clicking on the *Update now* button.

Check the new entries

Restart *Word* and check if the new converters are available in the *Files of type* drop-down list of the *Open* dialog box, thus enabling you to open documents of programs other than *Word*. Check also the graphics filters in the *Insert Picture* dialog box (*Insert/Picture/From File*).

If you cannot find the *Word* entry in the list box of the *Install/Uninstall* tab or if you get an error message after clicking *Add/Remove*, start the setup program with the *SETUP.EXE* from the root of the CD.

Glossary

Alignment

The horizontal alignment fixes the location at which a paragraph is placed between the left and the right column margins. The alignment is either set with the *Alignment* drop-down list in *Format/Paragraph* or with the corresponding buttons on the *Formatting* toolbar.

Animation

A formatting feature which can be activated with the *Animation* tab page via *Format/Font*. Here you find different options to apply animated highlights to selected text sections. This formatting is mainly used for Online documents.

Arrange windows

If more than one window is open, with the *Window/Arrange All* command you can arrange the windows in such a way that you can work with them simultaneously.

AutoCorrect

A *Word* function that corrects the most common typing errors automatically. By pressing the spacebar after typing a word, *AutoCorrect* automatically checks the entry and corrects it if necessary. Under *Tools/AutoCorrect* you can create entries for your most common typing errors and their correction.

AutoFit

Adjusting the column width to the size of the highest or widest entry. The fastest way to do this is to double-click on the right edge of a column. You can also use the *AutoFit* button on the *Column* tab of the *Cell Height and Width* dialog box. To get there choose the *AutoFit* command from the *Table* menu.

AutoFormat

With *Format/AutoFormat* you can format unformatted text automatically. A *Word* style will then be applied. To format tables, use the *Table AutoFormat* command on the *Table* menu.

AutoRecover

A *Word* function that automatically saves the current file at regular intervals and recovers the files after a program crash. To enable it, choose the *Save* tab under *Tools/Options*, select the *AutoRecover* option with the *Save AutoRecover info every x minutes* check box and set the interval with the spin buttons.

AutoShapes

A drawing tool of *Word 2000*. The shapes have a default order but can be changed after inserting them. *AutoShapes* include such items as hearts, arrows, flowcharts, stars and banners.

AutoSum

The fastest way to get sums in *Word* tables is to use the *Auto-Sum* button on the *Tables and Borders* toolbar. With a click on the *AutoSum* button, the cell range on the left of the current cell is added up to the next empty cell.

AutoSummarize

A *Word* function that automatically creates a summary of a document. This summary can be inserted at the beginning of the current document or in a new one. It can also be marked by highlighting.

AutoText

AutoText saves specific words or text passages together with an abbreviation by means of which these can be inserted using the [F3] key. Choose the *AutoText* tab under *Tools/AutoCorrect* to access the settings.

Background

A formatting that applies fill effects, pictures or patterns as a background for an online document. To activate this option choose *Format/Background*.

Background application

An application that is open but not active. This program cannot receive input from the user. All background applications are displayed as buttons on the taskbar.

Backup copy

Word provides the option to keep the last version of a file as a backup copy. This way, two versions of a file are always available: the current one and the backup copy. To create backup copies choose the *Tools/General Options* command in the *Save as* dialog box. Here select the *Always create backup copy* check box.

Bookmark

A name that you apply to a certain text section or a special position in the text. Bookmarks are useful to return easily or automatically to certain text positions in long documents. To create a bookmark open the *Bookmark* dialog box from the *Insert* menu.

Bullets

Symbols on the left paragraph margin that can be applied to certain paragraphs with a click on the *Bullets* button on the *Formatting* toolbar. These eye catchers mark enumerated items in texts. They can be switched off or omitted by using the context menu.

Clipboard

A protected area of the memory in which copied or cut data can be temporarily stored before pasting the data at a different position of the same document or into another document.

Closing application windows

The *Close* command in the *System* menu or the *Close* button on the title bar closes the application windows.

Columns

Usually documents are created with one column. To divide a text into more than one column choose *Format/Columns* or use the *Columns* button on the *Standard* toolbar. The column width and spacing and other settings can be fixed under *Format/ Columns*.

Command

A menu entry that can be activated with a mouse click to start an action. You can also use the keyboard to select a command from a menu. Open the menu and press the key corresponding to the underlined character in the command.

Command buttons in dialog boxes

Control in dialog boxes. A button or command button is a rectangular frame carrying a label. A mouse click starts an action, stops it or confirms certain selections and settings. The most important buttons are named *OK* and *Cancel*.

Context menu

You open a context menu by right-clicking an object. It contains commands that have particular relevance to the object or the current working situation. For instance, with a right-click on the toolbar, the context menu displays all available toolbar names.

Context-Sensitive Help (What's This?)

Help for menus and dialog boxes. You get it with a click on the *What's This* button `?` or with `Shift`+`F1`. If you activated the *Context-Sensitive Help* a question mark appears on the left of the mouse pointer. If you click on an element of a menu or dialog box a little *ScreenTip* containing an explanation appears. With a click into the Help text you can close the *Context-Sensitive Help*.

Criteria

Data you use as a comparative value for filters, conditions, *Find* operations or sorting. Criteria can consist of values or comparative operators that indicate the relation between the contents and the value so as to fulfill certain criteria. Criteria are mainly used when selecting the data sources for a mail merge.

Customize

A dialog box to set menus, toolbars and shortcut keys for *Word* commands, styles and macros or to change them according to your needs. Choose the *Tools/Customize* command.

Data Form

Dialog box in which new records for a mail merge source can be saved, edited, searched for or deleted. You open the Data Form with the *Edit Data Source* button on the *Mail Merge* toolbar.

Data Source

The file that contains the variable data of a mail merge document such as names and addresses. To create a data source click the *Get Data* button in the *Mail Merge Helper* dialog box.

Default Font

The *Default Font* is the font that is automatically chosen when you start a new document. You can set the *Default Font* in *Word* with the *Default* button on the *Font* tab of the *Font* dialog box. Open the *Font* dialog box with the *Format/Font* command.

Default Margins

The page margins are set by *Word* by default to: Top: 2.5 cm, Bottom: 2 cm, Left: 2 cm, Right: 2 cm. You can change the default margins with the *Default* button on the *Margins* tab of the *Page Setup* dialog box.

Default storage location

The folder in which *Word 97* saves your documents by default. Can be modified on the *File Locations* tab page under *Tools/Options*.

Desktop

The highest level of the *Windows* hierarchy. At the bottom of the desktop you find the taskbar with buttons for each running application. With a click on a button you can switch to the corresponding program. The desktop also stores the scrap objects containing data you want to move from one program to another by *Drag-and-Drop*.

Document area

Section of the screen in the program window of *Word* in which a document is displayed and edited.

Document map

A view that can be applied additionally. It divides the window. Parallel to the current view, it displays the heading hierarchy in the left pane of the window.

Drag-and-Drop

A very convenient way of moving text with the mouse. Selected text passages can be dragged to a new position. If you press the Ctrl key in addition, you generate a copy.

Drawing

On the *Drawing* toolbar of *Word* you find buttons to draw simple shapes such as ovals, rectangles, arrows and text boxes into your document.

Embedding

An object consisting of foreign data being inserted into a document in a special way: An embedded object is saved in the destination file but can be activated with a double-click and edited with the commands of the source application.

Export

Sending data from one application to another is called exporting data. *Word* is able to save text in the formats of different applications or in special export formats. A list of the formats supported by *Word* can be found in the *Save As* dialog box in the *Save as type* drop-down list.

Fields

Functions that insert information into a document. This information can be updated by *Word* automatically. Examples are page numbers, data fields for a mail merge, indexes or tables of content. Fields are automatically updated while opening, saving or printing a document or with the F9 key.

Fill effects

A formatting option for the background of online documents and the filling of two- or three-dimensional objects. The formatting allows you to apply fill effects such as gradients, textures, patterns and pictures.

Find and Replace

These two options are found in the *Edit* menu. Using this, you can search for text, formatting and other elements of a document and delete or replace them if necessary.

Font styles

Expression for font formatting such as *Bold*, *Italic* or *Underline*. Can be applied to selected text areas with the buttons on the *Formatting* toolbar or via *Format/Font*.

Footer

A line on the lower print margin of the document. Here *Word* prints, for example, the number of the current page and the total number of pages. To assemble footers select *View/Header and Footer*.

Grammar checker

A grammar checker works by default together with the spelling checker. You can activate, switch off or modify the grammar checker in the *Spelling and Grammar* dialog box of the *Tools* menu.

Header and Footer

With the *Header and Footer* command on the *View* menu you can insert information that should be printed outside of the page margins on each page. With the buttons on the *Header and Footer* toolbar you can insert information such as page number, date and time.

HTML

The format in which Web pages are saved. You can save normal *Word* documents to publish them on the Web if you choose the *Save as HTML* command from the *File* menu.

Hyperlink

Word 2000 provides a feature to link files the same way as Web documents. The position indicating the link is highlighted. With a click on this position you open the linked document and can then read the linked information.

Hyphenation

To hyphenate words manually, press Ctrl+- at the corresponding position. This way you create optional hyphens that will only be printed at the end of a line. To check the hyphenation in an already existing text, choose the *Language/Hyphenation* command from the *Tools* menu.

Import

The integration of data from a different application is called importing. *Word* is able to import the formats of some applications and certain special data exchange formats. A list of the formats *Word* can import can be found in the *Files of type* drop-down list of the *Open* dialog box, accessible via the *File* menu.

Indent

The distance between the paragraph and the left or right page margin. A left indent moves the text to the right, while a right indent moves the paragraph to the left. There are normal indents that move the whole paragraph and special indents such as first line indent and hanging indent. First line indent moves only the first line of a paragraph, while hanging indent moves every line except the first one.

Insert mode

The default mode for text entry. All characters on the right of the insertion point are pushed to the right with each new character or symbol inserted. To switch to the *Overtype* mode, press the ⌞Ins⌟ key.

Insertion point

The current position in a document. When inserting or modifying text in a document, the insertion point is indicated by a perpendicular, blinking 'I'-beam.

Landscape

Word supports printing in *Landscape* mode. On the *Paper Size* tab of the *Page Setup* dialog box you can switch between *Portrait* and *Landscape*.

Leader

Tab format. Fills the free space to the next tab with tab leaders. Tab leaders can consist of dots or lines. Apply the tab leaders with the *Format/Tabs* dialog box.

Line Break

To insert a line break into a document press the ⬆+↵ key combination. In this way you can move to the next line without creating a new paragraph.

Line spacing

Defines the distance between the lines of a paragraph. You find this option under *Format/Paragraph*.

Mail Merge Helper

A *Word* function that supports the creation of mail merge documents. To activate the *Mail Merge Helper* choose *Tools/ Mail Merge*.

Mail Merge Main document

A document with fixed and variable text elements that should be sent to more than one recipient. A Mail Merge Main document can be a form letter, a label, an envelope or a catalogue.

Maximize

With the system menu icon or the *Maximize* button on the title bar you can enlarge an application window to such an extent that it takes up the whole screen.

Menu bar

Horizontal bar underneath the title bar. It contains the names of all menus. To open a menu click the name. Commands in menus can also be activated with a mouse click.

Merge Field

A code used in a mail merge main document that, while printing, will be replaced with the corresponding information from the data source. A merge field is usually indicated by the «» symbols.

Minimize

With the *Minimize* command of the system menu or the corresponding button in the title bar you can minimize an application window to a button on the taskbar. With a click on this button the window opens again to its previous size.

NORMAL.DOT

The global standard template of *Word*. Each new document created automatically when *Word* starts is based on this template. If you click the *New* button on the *Standard* toolbar you also get a document based on *NORMAL.DOT*.

Numbering parapraphs

With the *Numbering* button on the *Standard* toolbar of *Word* you can automatically apply numbers to selected paragraphs. To continue the numbering for new paragraphs, press the ⏎ key. With the commands of the context menu you can skip the numbering or switch it off.

Office Assistant

A helper that works in all *Microsoft Office* applications. It provides comments and tips while working, similar to the *Tip Assistant* of previous *Word* versions. You can summon the *Office Assistant* by pressing the F1 key.

Web Layout

A view that presents a document in the way best suited for on-screen display and not for printing.

Options

A dialog box that allows the user to customize various *Word* settings. Among the options you can set are view options, edit options, print and save options, spelling and grammar options and special settings regarding compatibility. You can open the *Options* dialog box via the *Tools* menu.

Outline view

Word view showing the hierarchical structure of headings. You activate this view option with *View/Outline* or with the corresponding button next to the horizontal scroll bar.

Overtype mode

The opposite of *Insert* mode. In *Overtype* mode, the character to the right of the insertion point will be deleted as soon as you type in a new one. To activate or deactivate the *Overtype* mode press the Ins key.

Page Break

Word changes the page as soon as the lower page margin is reached. In the *Print Layout* view, *Word* indicates the *Page Break* with a simulated paper border, and in *Normal* view with a dotted line. You can change the page manually by inserting a *Page Break* at the position of the insertion point with Ctrl + ↵ or with *Insert/Break*.

Page Numbers

With the *Insert/Page Numbers* command a page number field is inserted at the selected position (header or footer), that indicates the number of the current page.

Page Setup

The *Page Setup* determines the appearance of a page. Among the possible settings are the paper size, orientation, margins, etc.

Paragraph

Word manages documents in paragraphs. It is easier and faster to format text in paragraphs. To create a paragraph press the ↵ key.

Paragraph spacing

The distance between the first and/or last line of a paragraph and the preceding/following paragraph. This is set in the *Before* and *After* text boxes in the *Spacing* option group of the *Paragraph* dialog box (via *Format* menu).

Password

Passwords are used to write and read-protect your documents. They consist of a maximum of 15 characters. You may use letters, numbers and symbols. Be aware of the capitalization.

Password to modify

A write protection. Prevents unauthorized changes of a document. When you try to open the document or the *Preview* in the *Open* dialog box you will be asked to enter the password. You can define a password from the *Save As* dialog box. To do so, choose the *Tools/General Options* command in the *Save As* dialog box.

Paste special

A command to insert objects from the clipboard, and to embed or link them.

Picture

A toolbar that is automatically displayed if you insert or select a picture. On the *Picture* toolbar you find commands to crop a picture, to set contrast and brightness and control the image type.

Print Layout View

The former *Page Layout* view is now called *Print Layout* view in *Word 2000*. It shows all elements of the document the way they will be printed out.

Print Preview

A view that simulates the printout on-screen. Switch off the *Magnifier* on the preview toolbar to make small adjustments to the text.

Read-only

A write protected (read-only) document cannot be saved under its current name. *Word* supports the *Password to modify* and *Read-only recommended* options. The commands can be activated from the *Tools/General Options* command in the *Save As* dialog box.

Restore window

Maximized windows can be set back to their previous size with the *Restore* command on the *System* menu or with the *Restore* button in the title bar. The *Restore* command is only available for maximized windows.

Ruler

A *Word* tool that you can display with *View/Ruler*. On the ruler you find special markers for the left and right indent and it also shows the position of the tabs.

ScreenTip

If you place the mouse pointer for about a second over a button on a toolbar, a Help text which displays the name of the button appears next to the mouse pointer.

Section

Connected text area with uniform formatting of paper size, orientation, headers and footers, etc. Insert a section break with the *Break* command on the *Insert* menu.

Section break

If you choose *Insert/Break* and select an option in the *Section breaks* option group, *Word* inserts a section break, separating the document into two sections. Sections can have different page setups, page numbers or headers and footers.

Shortcut key

A key combination that is linked to a command, a style or a macro. With the shortcut key you can execute the corresponding action.

Sort

In *Word*, you can sort text and tables. Choose the *Sort* command from the *Table* menu to do this. The *Sort Text* dialog box opens. Here you can fix up to three sort criteria as well as the order of the sorting process. On the *Tables and Borders* toolbar you'll find the *Sort Ascending* and *Sort Descending* buttons.

Spelling

The *Spelling and Grammar* command can be selected from the *Tools* menu or activated with the corresponding button on the *Standard* toolbar. It is a tool to manually check the spelling in documents. If the *Check spelling as you type* check box on the *Spelling & Grammar* tab page is checked, unrecognized words are underlined with red wavy lines and can be corrected from the context menu. You find the *Spelling & Grammar* tab under *Tools/Options*.

Split

With the *Window/Split* command or the split boxes on top of the vertical scroll bar you can split the window into several areas. This enables you to look at two different sections of one and the same document.

StartUp

A *Windows* folder you find under *Start/Programs*. All programs with shortcuts in this folder will be automatically started every time *Windows* is started.

Style

A style saves formatting information under a specific name. You can apply or modify the formatting saved in a style by choosing the style name from the *Styles* list in the *Style* dialog box of the *Format* menu.

Style gallery

A dialog box to view and modify styles of different templates and apply them to the current document.

Summary

A tab in the *Properties* dialog box of the *File* menu that saves title, subject, author, company, keywords and other information of the current file. These entries can be used for file management.

Symbol

Not all symbols can be inserted directly with the keyboard. To see a list of characters and symbols choose *Insert/Symbol*. The shape of the symbols displayed depends on the font.

Tab, Tab stop

Movable 'jump positions' in documents. The tab position can be set on the ruler. If you press the *Tab* key ⬚ the insertion point moves to the next tab stop. This is a comfortable way of aligning text or numbers in columns next to each other or one below the other.

Table

A grid divided into cells, rows and columns. It can be inserted at any position in the document. Table cells can contain more than one paragraph and are formatted separately. The Del key erases only the contents of selected table cells or table columns. To delete or insert rows and columns use the *Table* menu.

Tables and Borders

A toolbar in *Word* that enables you to create and edit tables with the help of buttons.

Template

Each document is based on a template. *Template* files carry the *DOT* file extension. The document generated with each *Word* start or with a click on the *New* button uses the *NORMAL.DOT* template. In a template you can save customized toolbars, styles and shortcuts.

Thesaurus

A *Word* feature that can be activated with ⌂+F7 or the *Language/Thesaurus* command on the *Tools* menu. *Thesaurus* helps you to find synonyms, i.e., words with similar meanings, for selected words.

ToolTip

Also ScreenTip. Brief information provided by *Word 97* about buttons on the toolbars, the scroll bars and other screen elements such as tabs on the ruler.

Undo

To undo your last action, click the *Undo* button on the *Standard* toolbar or press the Alt+← key combination. The drop-down list that opens with a click on the drop-down button next to the *Undo* button offers the possibility of undoing the last 100 actions.

User Information

On the *User Information* tab under *Tools/Options* you can save the address, name and initials of the user for certain *Word* functions.

Versions

A *Word* command that allows you to save different versions of a document in one file. Activate this command with *File/ Versions*.

View

Word provides various ways of displaying a document, known as views. You can change the view in the *View* menu or with the corresponding buttons to the left of the horizontal scroll bar.

Web

A *Word* toolbar providing buttons to search the Web and to move between hyperlinked Web pages. You can open the *Web* toolbar with a click on the *Web Toolbar* button on the *Standard* toolbar.

Web Page Wizard

Helps you to create new Web pages. Provides various alternatives to design Web pages. To start the *Web Page Wizard* select *File/ New/Web Pages* and double click the *Web Page Wizard* icon.

Wildcards

Wildcards can be used in *Find* or *Replace* operations in documents, or to find files in the *Open* dialog box. Use '?' as a wildcard for a single character and '*' as a wildcard for a string of characters.

Wizards

Integrated Help features that lead you through certain tasks step by step. Examples include Letter Wizard, Fax Wizard, etc.

WordArt

An additional feature of *Microsoft Office*. It allows you to insert text objects with special effects into a *Word* document. To activate *WordArt*, choose *Insert/Picture/WordArt* or click the *Insert WordArt* button on the *Drawing* toolbar.

Zoom

With the *Zoom* option you can control how large or small the current file appears on the screen. In *Word* you can choose your settings in the *Zoom* drop-down list on the *Standard* toolbar or open the *Zoom* dialog box from the *View* menu. Settings between 10% and 400% are possible.